Securing the Spectacular City

Securing the Spectacular City

The Politics of Revitalization and Homelessness in Downtown Seattle

Timothy A. Gibson

LEXINGTON BOOKS
Lanham • Boulder • New York • Toronto • Oxford

LEXINGTON BOOKS
Published in the United States of America
by Lexington Books
An imprint of The Rowman & Littlefield Publishing Group, Inc.
4501 Forbes Boulevard, Suite 200, Lanham, Maryland 20706

PO Box 317
Oxford
OX2 9RU, UK

Parts of chapters 5 and 9 were initially published by the author in "The Trope of the Organic City: Discourses of Decay and Rebirth in Downtown Seattle," *Space and Culture*, volume 6, issue 4 (November 2003). These sections are reproduced here with permission from SAGE publications and the editors of *Space and Culture*.

British Library Cataloguing in Publication Information Available

Library of Congress Cataloging-in-Publication Data

Gibson, Timothy A., 1970-
  Securing the spectacular city : the politics of revitalization and homelessness in downtown Seattle / Timothy A. Gibson.
    p. cm.
  Includes bibliographical references and index.
  ISBN 0-7391-0569-8 (alk. paper)
    1. Urban renewal—Washington (State)—Seattle. 2. Central business Districts—Washington (State)—Seattle. 3. Gentrification—Washington (State)—Seattle. 4. Inner cities—Washington (State)—Seattle. 5. Homelessness—Washington (State)—Seattle. 6. Poor—Washington (State)—Seattle. I. Title.

HT177.S24G53 2004
307.3'416'09797772—dc22
                                                                    2003060095

For Iris

Contents

Introduction   1

Part I   Economic Crisis and the Mobilization of Spectacle

  1   When Things Fall Apart (or, The Crisis in American Fordism)   15
  2   Crisis and Opportunity in the Post-Fordist City   35

Part II   Building the Spectacular City

  3   Seattle Elites and the Downtown Crisis   59
  4   Negotiating Urban Spectacle   83
  5   Public Resources, Private Power: The Struggle Over
     Seattle's Retail Core   107

Part III   Securing the Spectacular City

  6   The Project of Reassurance:
     Securing Urban Spectacle   153
  7   The Urban Reststop vs. the World-Class City:
     Hygiene Wars on Third Avenue   191
  8   Defining Revitalization in the Spectacular City   223
  9   Building A City that Truly Lives   257

Methodological Notes   287
Bibliography   293
Index   307
About the Author   313

Introduction

Securing a World-Class City:
The Seattle Story

During the 1990s, Seattle became, of all things, a media darling. Once a relatively sleepy and isolated burgh, known primarily for its misty climate and its once-abundant salmon, by 1998 national journals like *Fortune* magazine were hailing soggy Seattle as the "unofficial capital of the 1990s."[1] For a brief moment, Seattle was the "it" city in America. The city's skyline provided the backdrop for hit TV sitcoms like *Frasier*, and the city's streets and waterfront neighborhoods lent a foggy and romantic atmosphere to films like *The Fabulous Baker Boys* and *Sleepless in Seattle*. For its part, the city's vital club and music scene not only spawned the nation's brief embrace of Northwest "grunge" music, but also a series of (admittedly forgettable) "slacker" flicks like *Singles* and *Reality Bites*. And of course, thanks to Seattle-based Starbucks, today, in America, almost no one is more than five minutes away from a double-tall decaf espresso.

Of course, the national media's obsession with all things Seattle was based on more than coffee, flannel shirts, and slacker subculture. To be sure, there was Bill Gates. In American culture, immense wealth generates its own buzz, and the legendary rise of Microsoft and its subsequent battles with the U.S. Justice Department captured the imagination of a national media always looking to create, and then destroy, capitalist folk heroes. But, as boosters are quick to point out, Seattle's image as a haven for high technology extends beyond Gates and company. Amazon.com, the massive online retailer, got its start in the Emerald City, and the region is also home to other techie-giants like Real Networks, Attachmate software, Nintendo, and AT&T Wireless. With all this techie know-how concentrated in and around Seattle proper, national commentators and pundits predicted bold futures of high-tech prosperity for the region, in one case even anointing Seattle as a "digital Paris, alive with new culture and artists reacting to the dominant techniques of the age."[2] As *Fortune* magazine enthused at the pinnacle of Seattle-fueled "dot-com" mania, "no city has a better shot at replicating the potent mix of techies, dollars, and drive that made Silicon Valley great."[3] (Of course, the recent collapse of tech futures has dampened some of the techno-optimism of the era, though Alvin Toffler presumably still commands high speaking fees.)

Even so, perhaps the most often-cited emblem of Seattle's newly anointed "world-class" status (as local boosters proclaim)[4] has nothing to do with technology, coffee, or Kurt Cobain. For many in the local and national media, what separates Seattle from other American cities—especially those "back East," as Seattleites are wont to say—is its "legendary quality of life"[5] and its reputation as one of America's most livable cities.[6] Seattle is a city that works, and people are scrambling to move there, according to *Newsweek*'s Jerry Alder. "Sooner or later, it seems, everyone moves to Seattle, or thinks about it, or at least their kids do." Figuring prominently in such celebrations are the city's stunning natural inheritance and the Northwest's many opportunities for outdoor, fleece-clad adventure. With the Cascade Mountains, Puget Sound, and Olympic Peninsula just minutes away, "where else," asks one promotional pamphlet, "can you spend the morning sailing in a saltwater sound and the afternoon skiing in the mountains?"[7] What's more, Seattle's residents get to enjoy this natural inheritance along with the city's vibrant nightlife and its first-rate cultural amenities.[8] In the accounts of both local boosters and national pundits, then, Seattle's "quality of life" is really code for a particular, class-specific image of the urban good life, wherein young, vigorous, condo-dwelling twenty-somethings scamper into "the outdoors" and then return to sample liberally from the city's "high-quality shopping opportunities," its "first-rate facilities for sports," its countless gourmet restaurants, and its plethora of "innovative and first-class theaters, museums, [and] galleries."[9]

It is at this point in the recent celebrations of Seattle's livability and "quality of life" that the city's newly revamped, newly revitalized downtown core takes center stage. Once a quiet home for pensioners, itinerant sailors, office workers, and proletarian department stores, in the last fifteen years a massive building and redevelopment spree has utterly transformed the physical and social landscape of downtown Seattle. The scope and scale of this fifteen-year building spree can be difficult to grasp. During the late 1980s, for example, the city's small community of downtown property developers focused largely on the office market, thrusting one skyscraper after another into the Seattle skyline in the space of five short years. When the building frenzy subsided in 1989, a handful of downtown developers had doubled the total amount of office space in downtown Seattle, effectively transforming the financial district into a Manhattan-style office canyon. Beginning in 1993, however, an alliance of developers, civic boosters, and pro-growth city officials turned their attention away from the financial core toward an unprecedented project of retail-cultural redevelopment. The goal of this project? To create the holy grail of contemporary urban planning—the "24-hour downtown" that seamlessly weaves together upscale retail and world-class cultural activities with gleaming office towers and affluent urban residences. In this "24-hour downtown," the city becomes, in other words, not just a place of work, but a spectacular space of upscale consumption and leisure.[10]

To this end, Seattle's intertwined community of property developers and pro-development public officials have focused much of their energies (and a sizable chunk of public money) upon recentralizing high-end retail, culture, and leisure in the heart of downtown. Consider this selected list of mega-projects, built in downtown Seattle since 1991:

- Seattle Art Museum ($61 million). Completed 1991.
- Niketown theme store ($25 million). Completed 1996.
- Eagles Auditorium (ACT Theater) ($31 million). Completed 1996.
- Benaroya Music Center ($118 million). Completed 1998.
- Pacific Place Retail-Cinema Complex and Parking Garage ($248 million). Completed 1998.
- New Nordstrom Department Store ($100 million). Completed 1998.
- Safeco Field (Major League Baseball) ($517 million). Completed 1999.
- Convention Center Expansion and Museum of History and Industry co-development ($170 million). Completed 2001.
- Seahawks Stadium (Professional Football) ($430 million). Completed 2002.

Taken together, these cultural-retail projects represent over $1.4 billion in total investment downtown, with a healthy dose of over $700 million in public seed money included to sweeten the deal for the city's private real estate investors. The goal of all this investment, as one former city official put it, was to nurture "great, thriving life"[11] in the heart of downtown, primarily by building the sort of amenities that can attract tourists, conventioneers, free-spending suburban shoppers, and maybe even international investors. If it all came together, as boosters promised back in the mid-1990s, such investment in downtown would transform Seattle into a world-class city with an unparalleled quality of life.

Now, in the early years of the twenty-first century, boosters and pro-growth city officials make the claim that the spree has paid off, and paid off big. "The excitement that has come to downtown has clearly surpassed our wildest dreams," as one developer told the *Seattle Times*.[12] With the rush of investment in the late 1990s, Seattle's downtown attracted a host of nationally known retailers, including high-end brand names like Nordstrom, Eddie Bauer, Niketown, Tiffany's, and Saks Fifth Avenue. Moreover, a focus on cultural development has convinced such high culture heavyweights as the Seattle Symphony, the Seattle Art Museum, and ACT (an equity theater company) to come back downtown from their previous exile in the city's surrounding neighborhoods. In addition, the renewed concentration of upscale retail and high culture downtown has further encouraged the proliferation of posh residential condos, innumerable new cafes, and a host of new trendy nightclubs. All of this is taken to support the claim that downtown Seattle has become "the envy of any [city] in America."[13] As Gerard Schwartz, the longtime conductor of the Seattle Symphony, told the *Seattle Times*:

I believe that in years to come we will look back on the last decade of the 20th century as our region's coming of age. A new vibrancy and striving for excel-

lence courses through the region. We are no longer satisfied with merely getting by. We want the best. . . . We have truly come of age—a major city in our
country and in our world.[14]

Notice Maestro Schwartz said "we." And this gets us to the heart of the
matter. At the center of this celebration of Seattle's renaissance is a political
claim: namely, that all of this investment in spectacular urban redevelopment
has been undertaken in the *public interest*. As city officials have put it, "downtown is . . . everybody's neighborhood."[15] It is "the jewel of the region" and its
success is "vital to the health of the entire city." Therefore, if all of Seattle
benefits from a healthy and vital downtown, then "making it succeed should be
a priority" for Seattleites of all stripes, from the working class environs of
White Center to the waterfront villas on the Magnolia bluffs. If we all get the
benefits of urban revitalization, then we should all be willing to contribute to
the cause. This, of course, means that we should all support the world-class
dreams of the downtown development community—*including* the use of public
subsidies and incentives in support of such projects.

But is this indeed the case? Has downtown revitalization benefited most
Seattleites, rich and poor alike? For whom was this new downtown made? In
whose interests? And what happens if, for example, longtime residents of
downtown—including everyone from low-income single retirees and downtown's homeless community—become viewed as an obstacle, or worse, a *threat*
to the success of world-class urban revitalization? Will Seattle's leaders live up
to the claim that downtown is, after all, "everybody's neighborhood"?

This book is an attempt to answer these questions. In the end, this book
investigates the validity of the claim that building a world-class downtown in
Seattle over the past decade has truly been a *civic* endeavor—that is, an endeavor that cuts across narrow class interests and serves the community as a
whole. But to investigate such claims, we need to delve into the thick political,
economic, and discursive context of this critical juncture in Seattle's urban history. Therefore, along the way, three main questions will guide our exploration
into the politics of revitalization in Seattle:

- What is driving this rush to transform America's downtowns into spectacular centers of upscale leisure and consumption?

- How is political support for downtown revitalization cultivated both
  within City Hall and among the voting public? And how are city officials
  persuaded to invest public dollars into big-ticket revitalization projects?

- What are the social and ethical consequences of spectacular downtown
  revitalization, particularly for low-income people who have long called
  downtown home?[16]

My analysis of these questions emerged from three main bodies of qualitative data collected during 1998-1999, including: (1) twenty-five in-depth interviews of city officials, local activists, and downtown business leaders, (2) a large volume of archival research collected from the Seattle City Archives and the office files of city officials, and (3) an estimated 500 newspaper articles from the city's mainstream and alternative press (a more detailed methodological description is included as an appendix at the end of the book). Drawing on this data, the argument that follows has been divided into three sections. The first section addresses the broader economic context that has motivated urban leaders around the United States to find some way to reverse long histories of urban decline and decay. In the first chapter, I examine how the jolting economic recession of the 1970s forced many American firms to radically restructure their relationship to their employees and the federal government. The result of this thirty-year exercise in economic restructuring has been the globalization of American manufacturing to low-wage nations, a reliance on an easy-to-dismiss "contingent" and "temporary" workforce, and the federal government's long withdrawal from providing citizens with a strong social safety net. These economic transformations—and how they created conditions of intense insecurity and uncertainty in urban America—are discussed in chapter 1.

Chapter 2 then focuses on how urban public and private elites have responded to these economic transformations. How have cities across the United States, including Seattle, attempted to build a future of steady economic growth within such an unstable and uncertain global economic environment? What strategies have urban leaders employed to respond to deindustrialization and suburbanization? How can city leaders respond to secure investment from an increasingly mobile global marketplace, where multinational corporations can easily locate production and administrative facilities virtually anywhere on the globe? In this chapter, I argue that, in an attempt to compete with other urban regions for economic growth, many city leaders have seized upon the project of spectacular downtown revitalization in order to attract the attention of footloose global investors and tourists. In embracing this strategy, many city leaders have transformed their downtown retail districts and waterfronts into spectacles of upscale consumption. The hope is that, by building lavish shopping districts, concert halls, and themed entertainment attractions, America's struggling big cities will cultivate the kind of positive urban image that can attract future investment and tourism.

It is at this point that the discussion narrows down on the hopes, fears, and strategies of Seattle's tight-knit community of public and property elites. To this end, the middle section of the book begins to chart how Seattle's alliance of public officials and downtown boosters has attempted to contend with the consequences of global economic restructuring. The analysis in chapter 3 examines how, during the 1970s and 1980s, Seattle's civic elites began to diversify the city's economic base with the explicit goal of capturing for the city a disproportionate share of the global economic pie. By 1989, it seemed to many civic leaders that these strategies had largely succeed, despite evidence that many Seattleites were being left behind by the boom times of the middle 1980s.

But the national economic recession of the early 1990s threw such optimism into doubt. A series of cutbacks at the Boeing Company (still the region's largest employer) were matched by an equally dramatic slump in downtown property markets and downtown retail sales. As a number of prominent local firms downsized and moved out of downtown office space, and as longtime downtown retailers closed their doors, a palpable chill began to grip Seattle's downtown establishment. Local papers began to print dire predictions of a spiral of urban decay like that experienced by the rust belt "back East," and boosters began to demand that city officials do something about the impending decline of downtown Seattle. Chapter 3 explores the discursive dimensions of this growing concern over the future of downtown, including importantly a loud and persistent call to "take back" city streets from the downtown homeless.

Chapter 4 then turns to discuss how the city responded to this growing "downtown crisis." By 1998, the city's plan—dubbed "the Rhodes Project"—had poured over $100 million in public subsidies and $300 million in private investment into the heart of downtown, completely transforming the city's retail core in the process. For its part, chapter 4 focuses primarily on the behind-the-scenes negotiations that ultimately determined the scope of public subsidies involved in the Rhodes Project. Drawing on interviews and archival research, this chapter explores how the sense of crisis downtown weakened Mayor Rice in his negotiations with the project's developers, leading to the provision of a substantial package of subsidies and concessions. Finally, chapter 5 charts three explosive political debates generated by these public subsidies and concessions. In the end, I offer an examination of the political discourses mobilized by pro-development officials and business leaders to sell the public on both the package of subsidies and the larger redevelopment of the retail core.

In the third section, I shift the focus to the social and ethical consequences of Seattle's decade-long exercise in upscale revitalization. Just as the Rhodes Project was breaking ground, it became clear to Seattle's antipoverty activists that the city's redevelopment efforts were raising important questions about social inclusion and exclusion, for contemporary planning gurus like George Kelling were counseling Seattle's city officials that it would take more than simply building lavish downtown districts to resurrect their world-class dreams. Instead, the success of these retail and leisure projects hinged crucially on the city's ability to *convince* affluent tourists, shoppers, and investors—the "target markets" of contemporary revitalization—that downtown was once again a vibrant, attractive, and, most of all, *safe* place to be. Taking this advice to heart, many cities across the United States have embraced what I call a *project of reassurance*, wherein areas of cityspace slated for upscale consumption and leisure are cleansed of anything (and, in some cases, anyone) that might evoke in the middle-class imagination connotations of urban danger and decay.

For their part, critics argue that part and parcel of this effort to reassure potential shoppers and tourists of the sincerity of urban America's comeback has been the turn toward a more coercive approach to the homeless, including a crackdown on squatters, the strategic isolation of social services from tourist districts, and the aggressive enforcement of antiloitering and anticamping ordinances.[17] The question that occupies much of my attention in the third section of the book is whether or not Seattle's civic leaders have followed the lead of their counterparts across the United States, by embarking on their own "project of reassurance." In other words, to what extent have they worked to insulate the target markets of their own revitalization efforts from unwanted contact with the city's downtown poor and homeless?

A look at the political debates over homelessness and gentrification in the last ten years suggests that Seattle's downtown elites have indeed learned much from their counterparts around the nation. As chapter 6 documents, one of the most important struggles over downtown homelessness emerged in the early 1990s, just as city leaders began to hatch their plans to redevelop downtown into a world-class center of leisure and consumption. At this time, a series of surveys and focus groups conducted by city officials and boosters showed that potential shoppers and visitors commonly associated downtown Seattle with an elevated crime rate and the disconcerting presence of the city's homeless. In response to such negative images, city leaders—particularly Seattle's City Attorney Mark Sidran—rallied around a series of "incivility" ordinances designed to regulate what they saw as the uncivil and threatening behavior of homeless people in Seattle. Passed by acclamation in the city council, these ordinances increased the penalties levied on aggressive panhandlers and forbade individuals from lying down on city sidewalks in the city's commercial districts. Chapter 6 ends by charting the heated debates between city officials and antipoverty activists over these "incivility" ordinances and by discussing the competing notions of the public good expressed by each side.

A few years later, another debate over downtown homelessness erupted in Seattle politics, providing another opportunity to explore the social consequences of downtown revitalization. This time, the fracas began when homeless advocates proposed to locate a homeless "hygiene center," with bathrooms, showers, and laundry facilities, right across the street from the new downtown Symphony Hall. Focusing on the entangled relationships between advocates, city and federal officials, and downtown property owners, chapters 7 and 8 detail the bitter struggle waged between homeless advocates and the city's business establishment, who, in their vocal opposition, viewed the homeless hygiene center as a mortal threat to their goal of creating a vibrant cultural district around the new Symphony Hall. In this analysis, I address the political discourses deployed by both property owners and antipoverty activists, with a

particular focus on the underlying conceptions of urban vitality and urban decay woven into their arguments.

The conclusion draws together both the economic motives *for* and the political consequences *of* spectacular urban revitalization. In particular, I unpack
the ideological premises, metaphors, and images woven within elite construc-
tions of "urban vitality" and "urban decay." In other words, what do city officials and downtown boosters mean when they talk about a "healthy and vital"
downtown? What is the vision of the urban good life that is first expressed
within this discourse about urban vitality, and then built into landscape of
downtown Seattle? And, finally, who is included in and who is excluded from
this vision of the urban good life? In addressing such questions, the conclusion
attempts to weigh the costs and benefits, the gains and losses, inherent in Seattle's long road to downtown revitalization.

The gains have been overt and impressive. With the new concentration of
cultural, entertainment, and retail amenities downtown—including Benaroya
Hall, Niketown, the Eagles Auditorium (ACT Theater), a thriving club scene in
Pioneer Square, and at least three new multiscreen cinemas—Seattle has become, in the parlance of boosters, a "24-hour destination." Standing across
from Westlake Park in the retail core on a rare hot and sunny day in 2002, I
was surrounded by a lively crowd of smartly dressed shoppers shouldering bags
from Nordstrom, office workers on their lunch break chatting on park benches,
and slightly befuddled tourists heading up the street to Pike Place Market. It
was, by any standard, a vital and engaging urban scene. Additionally, this renaissance of upscale culture and leisure in the heart of the city has begun to draw
residents back downtown. Upscale condominiums now line Western Avenue
along the downtown waterfront, and Denny Regrade, the residential neighborhood directly north of downtown, has grown exponentially as developers compete with one another to throw another high-rise, upscale residential complex
into the sky. Even Pioneer Square, the nation's original skid row (originally
"skid road," named after Seattle's nineteenth-century practice of sliding enormous pine tree trunks down the middle of Yesler Road to a waterfront mill),
has seen a host of new residential, retail, and office construction spurred, in
part, by the construction of two new sports arenas just next door. Much has
indeed been gained by the redevelopment spree of the past decade.

At the same time, though they may be obscured by the glow of this downtown renaissance, the social costs of such world-class revitalization are equally
real. To appease Nordstrom department store's desire for "smooth traffic flow"
past its store, city leaders agreed to reroute auto traffic through a pedestrian
mall that formed the heart of Westlake Park. To appease an agitated business
community poised to cash in on the construction of the new downtown Symphony Hall, city leaders turned against an already approved homeless service
center that was to be located, as it turned out, uncomfortably close to this new
world-class cultural attraction. More generally, the frenzied building spree has

pushed up property values across downtown, forcing up rents and forcing out low-income and elderly tenants who have long called downtown home. Such are the costs of building the new world-class Seattle.

In the end, it seems clear that, in order to create Seattle's spectacular downtown, city leaders have embraced a very narrow and one-dimensional definition of what exactly constitutes a "healthy" or "vital" city. Again and again, during the many political struggles over the future shape of downtown waged in city hall, pro-development city officials and downtown property elites attempted to frame their pursuit of upscale, retail-cultural redevelopment as a stark choice between "urban decay" and "urban vitality." Within this binary discursive framework, Seattle's citizens and public officials could *either* embrace the political and economic priorities of the pro-development urban establishment, and thereby clear the ground for renewed "health" and "vitality" downtown, *or* they would condemn downtown to a frightening future of urban decline and decay.

To be sure, nobody wishes to see their city's retail core abandoned by retailers, office workers, and tourists, and no one benefits from the kind of economic misery that accompanied the deindustrialization of America's urban landscape. But within this *vitality/decay* dialectic the *only* alternative presented to save Seattle from this sort of spectacular urban decay was what *Seattle Times* columnist Terry Tang called "salvation by retail." In other words, for the pro-development establishment, the *only* way to stave off a disturbing future of urban decline is to embrace a vision of urban vitality organized almost wholly around the promotion and consumption of commodities—including both the luxury goods found in Nordstrom and Pacific Place as well as the cultural commodities produced and sold in downtown's sports palaces and concert halls.

The visions of "vitality" promoted by the pro-development establishment during these struggles over downtown cityspace were therefore thick with references to a "jazzy" and "eclectic" downtown shopping scene anchored by the new Nordstrom store, and to the world-class cultural district that would bloom around the new Symphony Hall, but it was a vision curiously bereft of activities unrelated to the process of upscale consumption and leisure.

In the end, this *either/or* logic had the effect of eclipsing alternative visions of downtown "health"—visions that balanced downtown's historic role as a center of upscale consumption against other priorities, including the desire to preserve space for unregulated political speech, family outings to non-commercial environments, and quiet moments away from the bustle of urban life (and the sound of the sales pitch). Instead, within the binary *vitality/decay* discourse of Seattle's pro-development community, citizens and city officials were encouraged to view their experience of downtown through the lens of the downtown business community. Activities and spaces that added to the "retail atmosphere" or the "emerging cultural district" would necessarily bring health and vitality. But if spaces, activities, or even social actors were judged to be inconsistent with (or, even worse, detrimental to) the priorities of downtown merchants, then they would promote urban blight and be subject to redevelopment or removal.

In the final pages of the argument, I discuss the prospects for promoting political values like class equity and social diversity within the contemporary U.S. urban environment. In the end, then, it is my hope that this book about Seattle's decade-long pursuit of world-class status will help provoke a conversation among scholars, activists, and citizens about the social costs and benefits of contemporary urban revitalization. Perhaps, out of this conversation, we might begin to develop notions of "urban vitality" and "urban revitalization" that express a desire for inclusion rather than exclusion, for social equity rather that social homogeneity. If nothing else, I hope this book contributes to such a dialogue.

Notes

1. Ed Brown, "Seattle," *Fortune*, 24 November 1997, 184.

2. From *Men's Journal*. Quoted in "Cyber Seattle: Software Capital," *Crossroads: Newsletter of the Trade Development Alliance of Greater Seattle* 5, no. 1 (Winter 1996).

3. Mark Fefer, "Is Seattle the next Silicon Valley?" *Fortune*, 7 July 1997, 136.

4. Harold Greene, "Chairman's Report," *1996-1997 Annual Report of the Downtown Seattle Association*.

5. Ed Brown, "Seattle," *Fortune*, 24 November 1997, 184.

6. John Wilcock, "A Livable City," in *Seattle: Insight Guides* (Boston: Houghton Mifflin, 1993), 21.

7. Trade Development Alliance of Greater Seattle pamphlet, *King County: Crossroads of the Global Economy*.

8. Trade Development Alliance of Greater Seattle, *International Promotion Plan* (internal document, December 1997).

9. Trade Development Alliance of Greater Seattle, *International Promotion Plan* (internal document, December 1997).

10. Dan Mihalopoulos, "From Skid Row to Vibrant City on the Sound: St. Louis Leaders See What a 24-hour Downtown is Really Like," *St. Louis Post-Dispatch*, 5 October 1997, 8(A).

11. Personal interview, Downtown Seattle Task Force, 24 March 1999.

12. Robert Wells, "Uptown, Downtown: The Players Get Richer and the Stakes Get Higher," *Seattle Times*, 12 September 1999.

13. Sylvia Nogaki, "Growing List of Shops, Eateries Ready to Go Downtown," *Seattle Times*, 6 May 1995. See also, Lee Moriwaki, "Boom Times: Seattle's Downtown is Evolving," *Seattle Times*, 18 January 1998; Norm Rice, "Seattle—A First-Class Downtown Community," *Downtown: The Newsletter of the Downtown Seattle Association* (Winter 1996): 1.

14. Gerard Schwarz, "Benaroya, Hallmark of City's Awakening," *Seattle Times*, 2 February 1999, 5(B).

15. Richard Buck, "F&N Plan is Called Tax Boon," *Seattle Times*, 19 August 1994.

16. To answer these questions, I have drawn on a variety of research methods and materials, ranging from detailed archival research and systematic analyses of press reports, to in-depth interviews with key individuals in government, business, and various community interest groups. A more detailed discussion of the methods used in my research, including a discussion of the rationale for using the methods chosen, can be found in a methodological appendix at the end of the book.

17. Mike Davis, *City of Quartz: Excavating the Future in Los Angeles* (London: Verso, 1992); Sharon Zukin, *The Cultures of Cities* (Cambridge, UK: Basil Blackwell, 1995); Neil Smith, *The New Urban Frontier: Gentrification and the Revanchist City* (London: Routledge, 1996).

Part I

Economic Crisis and the
Mobilization of Spectacle

Chapter 1

When Things Fall Apart
(or, The Crisis in American Fordism[1])

In a 1998 open letter to the city's business community, Seattle's newly elected mayor, the professorial Paul Schell, spoke of Seattle's growing dependence on international markets for goods, services, and capital. Now that people, capital, and technology have become increasingly mobile, he wrote, "the stakes have risen for cities" all around the world. With local economic fortunes increasingly tied to an ability to attract trade, investment, and tourists from a global market-place, Schell argued, cities must be careful to cultivate a world-class urban image among potential investors and visitors. Surveying the recent media buzz about the Pacific Northwest, Schell saw much to celebrate about Seattle's ability to compete in global markets for investment:

> I'm proud to say that to date Seattle has fared rather well in this global competition. Seattle's number one ranking by *Money Magazine* as the "best city in the U.S. West" is the most recent example. As Mayor, I want to make sure that Seattle maintains its economic, cultural, and social vitality and continues to develop its reputation as a globally competitive region.[2]

At the same time, he cautioned Seattle's business community against letting success go to their heads. "Although the Northwest is experiencing relatively good times economically," he wrote, "it is a mistake to become complacent." As one downtown developer put it, more colorfully, "sure, right now, Seattle's on a roll, [but] things change. . . . And when things change, and you haven't done it right, you're really screwed."[3] Despite Seattle's top ranking in *Money Magazine*, despite the city's much-hyped image as a "digital Paris," and despite its carefully cultivated status as a "travel destination," Seattle must watch its back and jealously guard its place in the global hierarchy.[4] As Blake Nordstrom, chair of the Downtown Seattle Association and current president of the Nordstrom department store chain, cautioned an audience of downtown business elites, "We should have a running-scared mentality, be as humble as we can. I think we've learned over the years that a city and its health and vitality are fragile."[5] Seattle's governmental and propertied elites have sounded this refrain so often in recent years that it seems like a mantra: in the best of times, we must be vigilant for the worst of times. Seattle may attract more than its share of international press and praise now, but, as the region becomes more enmeshed in a "beggar thy neighbor" competition for global investment, to-day's economic vitality can easily become tomorrow's stagnation and decay.

What explains this pervasive, and contradictory, sense of insecurity and bravado? Why do elites simultaneously celebrate Seattle's status as a world-class city and speak darkly of the fear of slipping into stagnation and decay? And how has this contradiction between boosterism and paranoia structured political debates over downtown redevelopment and gentrification in Seattle during the 1990s?

To answer such questions, we need to place these debates of revitalization and redevelopment into the wider political and economic context of contemporary North American urbanization. In short, we need to talk about global capitalism. The local economic development policies pursued by contemporary city officials and property elites are not formed in isolation from wider economic trends and transformations. Quite the opposite. Urban elites and governments must inevitably negotiate and respond to conditions imposed upon them by the disorderly, dynamic, and disruptive system of global capitalism. When transnational corporations and financial markets sneeze, localities can catch a cold (or worse). Consequently, much of what has passed for municipal policy since the early 1970s has attempted to respond to dramatic changes in a restructuring and evolving global economic system.

In the next two chapters, I want to place the actions of Seattle's elites (and their trepidation about the continuing prosperity of Seattle's retail and property economy) into the context of the disruptive history of North American urban political economy since 1970. As we will discover, when you look at the turbulent years of economic crisis and restructuring since the first major postwar recession in 1972, it is no surprise that urban policy-makers, like the good burghers of Seattle quoted above, have trouble looking into the future with confidence. Therefore, in this chapter, I want to specifically highlight some important changes in global capitalist accumulation since 1970—particularly the globalization of investment and production and the crisis of the postwar welfare state. Then, in chapter 2, I will narrow the argument and focus on how these global economic shifts have affected the citizens of major U.S. cities and how city governments have tried to respond to these disruptions in the organization of global capitalism.

The Crisis of Postwar "American Fordism"

In one respect, the fears Seattle's civic leaders express about their city's world-class status are justified. As Marshall Berman has eloquently argued, the history of capitalism has been marked by almost continuous struggle, crisis, and change. Treating Marx and Engel's *Manifesto of the Communist Party* as a classic modernist text, Berman argues that, far from merely dismissing capitalism as a failed social experiment, Marx was actually quite impressed with its inherent dynamism and its ability to survive and renew itself by restructuring its own social and economic landscape.[6] In fact, many of the most imaginative passages in the *Manifesto* celebrate this restless dynamism, including the following oft-cited section:

> Constant revolutionizing of production, uninterrupted disturbance of all social relations, everlasting uncertainty and agitation, distinguish the bourgeois epoch from all earlier times. All fixed, fast-frozen relationships, with their train of venerable ideas and opinions, are swept away, all new ones become obsolete before they can ossify. All that is solid melts into air, all that is holy is profaned.[7]

That we should feel insecure and uncertain about the future in such a social environment should not be surprising. As Berman writes, for Marx and Engels (as well as for Joseph Schumpeter and other economists more favorably disposed to capitalism) disorder and discontinuity are woven into the very fiber of life in capitalist societies.[8]

Yet, it seems that from time to time, academics and policy-makers delude themselves that the business cycle has been conquered, that their generation has resolved the inner contradictions and periodic disruptions which "distinguish the bourgeois epoch from all others." In the United States, the postwar economic expansion of the 1950s and 1960s was one such moment of self-delusion. Coming out of the massive disturbances of the Great Depression and World War II, the federal economic, labor, and social policy-makers set themselves to the task of preventing a postwar slide back into economic uncertainty and depression. The main challenge, in the view of the Roosevelt and Truman administrations of the 1940s, was to address the problem of underconsumption. In their view, what sustained the Great Depression for so many years was a vicious circle of wage cuts, layoffs, and shrinking markets. As firms competed for a share of shrinking consumer markets, their profits sagged. Firms then responded primarily by cutting wages or laying off workers, which, of course, only dampened demand and shrunk consumer markets and profits even further. By 1939, this vicious cycle had global capitalism teetering on the edge of a bloody and cataclysmic collapse.

The solution, in the view of leading policy-makers influenced by English economist John Maynard Keynes, lay in restructuring the always contradictory and perilous relations between the state, private capital, and organized labor. The old alliances of the pre-Depression years—i.e., a government-business pact to contain organized labor and to keep state regulations of production to a minimum[9]—were jettisoned in favor of a more balanced "national bargain" between labor, capital, and the state.[10] For its part, organized labor was forced, after a series of failed strikes in the mid-1940s, to accept a strict division of labor within the industrial economy. In exchange for dropping its objections to management's absolute control over the labor process, organized labor would win recognition for the right to collectively bargain for wages, benefits, and a fair grievance process.[11] A series of historic contract settlements in the late 1940s codified this bargain: management would continue to control production and would be free to further rationalize the work process in search of greater levels of productivity. In return, labor would win the right to union recognition and steadily rising wages.[12]

Standing above this new compromise between capital and labor, the state would commit itself to a new, more activist role within the economy. In addition to mediating the terms of the "national bargain" (i.e., protecting labor's right to organize while containing labor's demands to the arena of wages and benefits), the state also committed in the postwar years to what Michael Piore and Charles Sabel call a "policy of macrostabilization."[13] The state, in short, would use a variety of Keynesian economic policy tools—including social security, unemployment insurance, and the manipulation of interest rates—to help prop up consumer demand, especially during rough economic times. As Piore and Sabel argue, such interventions are inherently "counter-cyclical."[14] During downturns, as people are laid off and wages are cut, programs like unemployment insurance and social security automatically kick in, putting extra money in workers' pockets and propping up consumer demand for goods and services. Moreover, the state would step in directly and lower interest rates, flooding the economy with credit and (hopefully) stimulating investment and economic growth.[15]

All together, this "national bargain" would attempt to transform the Great Depression's vicious circle of prewar underconsumption into what Bob Jessop called the "virtuous circle" of postwar "Fordism."[16] Just as Henry Ford (hence "Fordism") opined in 1914, the virtuous circle of American Fordism tied higher wages for the "core" of unionized industrial workers to their acceptance of management's incessant demands for increased productivity.[17] As these workers began to earn higher wages (due to successful contract negotiations and overall productivity gains in the industrial economy), they began to increase their consumption of the vast array of consumer goods made available in the postwar years—including everything from the automobile to the suburban home filled with "modern" appliances. This increase in aggregate postwar consumption in turn led to expanding investment in future production capacity, and, in the end, to years of sustained economic growth. And, in a nutshell, it worked. Although many people—most notably women, minorities, and non-union employees—were left out of the unprecedented economic expansion of postwar America, the rise in real wages and the expansion of the welfare state on the whole helped support working-class incomes and even slowly reduced the inequality of wealth in America.[18]

American Fordism worked so well, in fact, that many academics, including leftists and conservatives alike, got caught up in the moment and forgot Marx's (not to mention Joseph Schumpeter's) warning that capitalism is nothing if not a radically disruptive and crisis-prone system. On the left, for example, the Frankfurt School's Herbert Marcuse looked pessimistically into the future and saw the coming of "one-dimensional society," a society in which the American industrial proletariat ultimately exchanges the dream of self-determination and social revolution for the empty pleasures of suburban prosperity and easy-to-digest mass culture.[19] And Marcuse was by no means alone in his evaluation of the total stability and ultimate triumph of monopoly capital. For his part, the French Marxist Louis Althusser was equally discouraged and, in his influential essay on "Ideological State Apparatuses," portrayed capitalism as a self-reproducing social machine, flawlessly stamping out individuals ideologically predisposed to assume their specific role within the larger capitalist social formation.[20]

On the right, what Marcuse and Althusser deplored was, of course, celebrated by Daniel Bell and other promoters of the new postwar consensus. A new wave of academic promoters of postwar capitalism argued that the compromises of American Fordism had created a perfectly balanced, well-adjusted, democratic society. To be sure, there would always be sectorial conflicts over wealth distribution and social values, but these could all be resolved within the pluralistic framework of electoral politics. In the postwar consensus between capital, labor, and the state, the larger political and ideological conflicts—the running battles between socialism, capitalism, and fascism that scarred the first half of the century—would fade into the annals of history. In short, the postwar consensus around American Fordism had brought about the "end of ideology,"[21] where, as Seymour Lipset wrote in 1963:

> The fundamental political problems of the industrial revolution have been solved: the workers have achieved industrial and political citizenship; the conservatives have accepted the welfare state; and the democratic left has recognized that an increase in overall state power carried with it more dangers to freedom than solutions for economic problems.[22]

Although this period of relative social stability and economic growth was not destined to survive the onslaught of inner-city rebellions, antiwar revolts, and global economic upheavals of the late 1960s and early 1970s, for a time, at least, American Fordism appeared invulnerable to fundamental social and economic crisis.

But, as a group of French, British, and American political economists, known collectively as "the regulation school," were to argue in the late 1970s, such periods of relative social and economic stability are merely one end of the capitalist dialectic, the other end of which is *crisis* and *instability*.[23] In direct opposition, then, to Althusser's argument that capitalism reproduces itself unproblematically, regulation school theorists asked instead how, at various times in its history, social agents within capitalism have overcome the system's internal contradictions and disruptions in order to craft provisional periods of social and economic stability.

Regulation theory, appropriately enough, answers the question of capitalism's ability to survive by pointing to the "regulatory mechanisms"—that is, the institutional forms and societal norms—which bring the contending interests and forces in capitalist accumulation (i.e., the "big players" of capital, labor, and the state) into a successful compromise and balance.[24] The key terminology of the regulation school emerges from this analysis of the paradox of crisis and stability. Two of the most important of the concepts utilized by regulation theorists are "regime of accumulation" and "mode of regulation." As Klaus Nielsen writes, the concept *regime of accumulation* refers to "a set of regularities at the level of the whole economy, enabling a more or less coherent process of capital accumulation."[25] It includes, according to Ash Amin, stable forms of industrial organization and production, common rules of industrial management, and a temporary set of norms regulating the continuing conflict over the distribution of wages, profit, and taxes.[26] In short, a specific regime of accumulation brings together and coordinates (usually via struggle, negotiation, and compromise) the behavior of capitalists, workers, state employees and financiers into a particular configuration that has the potential to sustain economic growth.[27]

The *mode of regulation* describes the "institutional ensemble (e.g., trade laws, labor laws, finance systems, wage deals, ideological apparatuses, and so on) and the complex of cultural habits and norms (e.g., the embrace of Victorian work ethic or the widespread adoption of consumerist hedonism) which secures capitalist reproduction as such."[28] The mode of regulation therefore refers to the specific constellation of institutions and practices that both regulate and sustain a particular regime of accumulation as well as reproduce consent[29] to its particular configuration of social and economic relations.[30]

The focus in regulation theory is therefore on the historically specific and contingent policies that emerge from the crucible of class struggle and which, if successful, serve to temporarily counteract the crisis tendencies and class antagonisms of capitalism. Still, as Bob Jessop argues, the stability of any such balance or compromise is "always relative, always partial, and always provisional."[31] While particular institutional forms of regulation may for a time succeed in limiting struggle and crisis in ways which do not threaten the stability of a particular regime of accumulation, they cannot succeed forever. Eventually the fragile social compromise or consensus around the specific form of social and economic regulation will unravel under the pressure of class struggle and the coercive competition between firms and nations.

Had they been writing in the late 1960s, these regulation theorists might have predicted that the society built on the foundation of postwar Fordism, while a remarkable achievement of industrial *realpolitik*, was nonetheless doomed to dissolve one day into economic instability and social upheaval. And so it did. Although the deep global recession of the early 1970s seemed to come out of nowhere at the time, in reality signs of trouble had been visible since at least the mid-1960s. In hindsight, as David Harvey argues, the sagging profit rates of U.S. firms after 1966 were the first sign that something was amiss, as wage increases (tied automatically to inflation in most unionized shops) began to outpace productivity gains.[32] By the 1970s, wildly fluctuating energy costs—the result of the first major OPEC oil embargo of 1972—sparked a dramatic inflationary spiral, increasing wages yet again while simultaneously increasing production costs. The result was the unprecedented onset of "stagflation"—an unhealthy brew of stagnant growth and an inflationary, energy-led, spiral of wages and prices, all of which cut further into the corporate bottom line.[33]

The tenuous Fordist compromises between the state, capital, and labor might have survived this bout of "stagflation," but a more fundamental tension in the global economy—the rise of cutthroat international competition for saturated consumer markets—was about to spell the end of the high-wage, high-productivity, "demand-side" American economy.[34] In the years following the war, much of America's economic expansion rested on the postwar reconstruction of Japan and Western Europe and their development into markets for excess U.S. goods. But by the late 1960s, these fully industrialized nations had saturated their domestic markets with consumer goods and were now looking to export their surplus output.[35] As Harvey writes, it was about this time that import substitution policies (especially in Latin America), combined with the first big push of multinational corporations into offshore manufacturing (especially in southeast Asia), established new regions of the world—regions with extremely low labor costs and few protections for unions or workers—as formidable industrial competitors.[36]

This dispersal of manufacturing to such low-wage environments as Latin America and Southeast Asia, combined with the increasing competition from Japan and Western Europe, had two devastating consequences for the continuance of America's particular brand of Fordism. First, the globalization of manufacturing placed unionized shops in the United States and Europe in direct competition with nonunionized and low-wage firms in the Third World, providing such firms with a competitive advantage (i.e., lower prices on worldwide markets).[37] Second, the overall intensification of international competition quickly saturated U.S. and world markets with mass-produced goods. When this fierce international competition combined with the uncertainty of stagflation, aggregate profits among U.S. manufacturing firms, which had been declining for years, began to free fall, forcing many firms to force down costs through rationalization and layoffs.[38] By 1975, the U.S. economy was floundering. The long postwar boom fueled by the compromises of American Fordism had come to, as Harvey writes, "a whimpering end."[39]

This economic crisis quickly threw many assumptions of the postwar era onto the historical ash heap. Gone was the notion shared in the most optimistic circles that the business cycle had been conquered. Gone was the idea that the steady growth of the postwar years could be sustained indefinitely, overwhelming the ruinous competition between firms and the antagonisms between workers and employers under a never-ending wave of prosperity and 1950s-style consensus politics. Instead the mid-1970s were marked by intense intercapitalist competition, uncertain and volatile financial and consumer markets, and a series of bitter labor disputes as the "Fordist bargain" between the state, capital, and labor fell apart under the pressure of declining growth and international competition.

Global capitalism, it seemed, had turned the corner from stability into crisis. And it is in the context of this crisis of the Fordist regime of accumulation that regulation theory situates its analysis of contemporary economic restructuring. As Ash Amin writes, "though not uncontroversial, there is an emerging consensus in the social sciences that the period since the mid-1970s represents a transition from one distinct phase of capitalist development to a new phase"—a phase governed by a different set of relations between the state, capital, and labor.[40]

Of course, different theorists take different positions on this notion of global economic crisis and transition. Some argue that the crisis of 1973 has led to the emergence of an entirely *new* regime of accumulation—called "flexible specialization" or "the postindustrial economy"—which promises unending horizons of innovation, prosperity, and economic growth.[41] Other scholars take issue with this optimistic view of the various efforts to restructure capitalism since the 1970s and instead argue that we are still flailing around in a profound global crisis, where any attempt to restore long-term profitability and social stability will inevitably fall apart under the pressure of global competition and shrinking worldwide standards of living.[42] The regulation theorists themselves preferred the term "neo-Fordism" to emphasize continuities in the accumulation process while recognizing new developments in the modes of regulation in different capitalist nations.

At the end of the day, however, this debate over the nature of capitalist development after the crisis of Fordism is not our main concern (though, writing after the longest period of economic expansion in American history, it seems safe to say that the crisis of Fordism eventually yielded to a period of relative economic stability, at least until the events of September 2001). This being said, whether the "after-Fordist" or "post-Fordist" regime of accumulation has solidified into a new national bargain capable of sustaining social stability and economic growth over the long term is less important than charting how firms, industries, and national, regional, and local governments have responded to the global economic crises of the 1970s and 1980s.

So how *did* firms and governments respond to this period of profound economic uncertainty? Put simply, the crisis of the mid-1970s threw most industries and governments into turmoil. Facing saturated consumer markets, competition from overseas firms, and falling corporate profits, many American corporations embarked on a number of novel organizational and technological experiments in order restore the possibility of long-term accumulation and growth. In short, corporate executives began casting about for new ways of doing business that promised to reduce costs and help their firms respond to quickly changing financial and consumer markets. According to Klaus Nielsen, the principle many CEO's and state policy-makers seized upon in their effort to restore profitability was *"flexibility."*[43] In uncertain economic times, it was argued, firms (and, as we will see shortly, government policies) must become *flexible*. In short, to remain afloat during economic crisis, the argument was that firms and governments must be willing and able to accommodate rapidly changing consumer tastes and market conditions.

But what does "flexibility" really mean? How would "flexibility" help restore profitability and economic growth? As Harvey writes, many of these experiments with organizational flexibility attempted to address the perceived *rigidities* of Fordist accumulation. First, for example, many manufacturing firms in the United States saw themselves fenced in by ostensibly "rigid" labor contracts with their mostly unionized workers. Many of these contracts locked management into automatic wage increases tied to inflation and increases in productivity. Facing increased competition from offshore firms (who had no such "Fordist" bargain with their employees) firms quickly began to view their workers' increasing wages less as a source of consumer demand than as a drag on profitability and competitiveness.[44]

As a result, one prominent move toward flexibility involved using new innovations in transportation and communication technologies to locate what Robert Reich calls routine production (i.e., low-skill manufacturing) overseas in regions of the world where labor protections are few and wages are low.[45] In addition, new transportation and communication technologies—especially digital networks, satellite communications, and reductions in overseas shipping costs—allowed large manufacturing firms to *globalize*, to locate different production and distribution facilities in different parts of the globe without a corresponding loss of coordination and control.[46]

This newfound geographical flexibility served to undermine the tenuous class compromise between labor and capital in developed nations, especially in the United States.[47] In short, manufacturing firms, under pressure from overseas competition and their own sagging profit rates, quickly sought to use their spatial mobility (or at least the threat of relocation) to craft a new bargain with labor and to restore the possibility of renewed accumulation.[48] First, spatial mobility allowed manufacturing firms to scan the globe looking for the best "business climate"—i.e., the lowest wages, the fewest taxes, and the least restrictive regulatory environment.[49] And second, this spatial mobility allowed firms to extract concessions from their workers at home. Facing the increasing viable threat of massive plant closures and relocations, union negotiators in traditional industries saw few alternatives to accepting management demands for layoffs, wage cutbacks, and other shop-floor concessions. The result was a catch-22 for American organized labor: the more unions tried to force management to increase wages and benefits, the more likely it became that the firm would take advantage of its new spatial "flexibility," simply closing down unionized shops in favor of more "business friendly" (read: antiunion) regions of the United States and beyond.[50]

Another "flexible" strategy that caught the imagination of U.S. firms concerned the downsizing of large, bureaucratic, and vertically integrated firms into what Robert Reich calls "global enterprise webs."[51] The motive for corporate "downsizing" and restructuring can also be traced back to the crisis of the mid-1970s. During this crisis, manufacturing firms faced a radically altered market landscape. Not only were consumer markets thoroughly saturated with competitors and their products, but consumer demand had become more uncertain and unstable with the successive shocks of inflation and recession.[52] Under these conditions of overall underconsumption and uncertainty in consumer demand, the traditional practice of concentrating huge numbers of full-time employees under a single, bureaucratically controlled corporate structure became viewed as too unwieldy and costly to sustain during volatile economic times.

Looking for ways to adapt more efficiently to changing market demands, many firms began to cut back on their full-time staff (with their more costly benefit packages), opting instead to either "outsource" key production inputs to smaller firms or to hire legions of temporary, part-time, or contingency workers. In short, many corporations, worried about an uncertain future, adopted a "weblike" core/periphery model of corporate organization. At the core of such firms lay an "inner web" of full-time, highly skilled "problem solvers" and "strategic brokers" who coordinate and plan the firm's future projects and who attempt to discover small niches of potentially profitable enterprise within an otherwise stagnant and overcompetitive market. As Robert Reich notes, these workers tend to be well compensated and highly sought after by these leaner, "downsized" firms.[53]

However, at the periphery of these new corporate "webs" are the less fortunate "outer webs." Populating this peripheral web are the temporary, part-time, or contract workers who are hired[54] to work on specific, short-term projects and then let go when business is slow or when market demands change.[55] For their part, these contingency workers tend to be less skilled and paid less than their full-time counterparts, and they tend to work without benefits and with little sense of job security.[56] From the firm's perspective, this "weblike" core-periphery organization has the advantage of greater flexibility and efficiency within an uncertain and competitive marketplace. So it is perhaps not surprising that the current trend in global labor markets is to reduce the number of core workers to an absolute minimum and to rely increasingly upon a workforce that can quickly be taken onboard during good times and efficiently laid off when profits sag.

All in all, this embrace of corporate flexibility—that is, the dual strategy of globalization and "downsizing"—has greatly undermined the "national bargain" of postwar Fordism and has substantially restructured the relationship between labor and capital. No longer are workers and employers linked together in a virtuous circle of rising wages, rising productivity, and mass consumption. No longer would the leading firms tacitly accept unions as partners in economic growth in exchange for relative labor peace and unfettered control over shop-floor organization. Instead, what we have seen in global capitalism since 1973 is the onset of much uncertainty, as firms cast about for organizational and technological "fixes"—anything which might improve their flexibility, and therefore profitability, in an increasingly competitive and unstable marketplace. The result has been a period of profound disruption, as firms seek to take advantage of their newfound spatial and organizational "flexibility" to forge new, more profitable, and some would say more exploitative, relationships with their workers (now as likely to live in Northern Mexico as Northern Ohio).

If the global crisis of the mid-1970s undermined the Fordist national bargain and prepared the ground for a more coercive, globalized, and downsized relationship between capital and labor, what have these transformations meant for the relationship between capital and the state? In the jargon of regulation theory, what has been the fate of the Fordist *mode of regulation*—what Bob Jessop calls "the Keynesian welfare state"? As noted above, the Keynesian welfare state emerged as the key arbiter of the postwar "national bargain." In this regard, many of the core features of the welfare state developed during the 1930s and 1940s, as the federal government cast about for ways to address two problems at the heart of the Great Depression: (1) the violent swings in the business cycle, which was threatening to undermine the legitimacy of capitalist accumulation, and (2) the continuing problem of slack consumer demand, which was widely viewed as the underlying cause of the global economic crisis.[57] Since Fordist-style mass production entails large investments in fixed machinery, manufacturing firms require stable and steadily growing consumer markets in order to be consistently profitable.[58] As a result, the welfare state (first under the direction of the Roosevelt administration), assumed the responsibility of smoothing out business cycles and propping up consumer demand through a variety of interventionist monetary and fiscal policies—including social expenditures designed to underpin the social wage and the active manipulation of interest rates to assure steady rates of growth.[59]

However, the globalization of financial and industrial capital in response to the crisis of the mid-1970s has undermined the ability of the welfare state to prop up demand and to regulate the economy through such direct interventions. For example, the rise of multinational corporations and the dispersal of routine production to the developing world have made it difficult for national states to "trap" private capital for the purpose of demand-side redistribution. Writing as early as 1987, Scott Lash and John Urry noted that between 35 and 45 percent of world trade "now takes place internally within the global corporations," making it easy to avoid taxation or tariffs on international flows of money or goods.[60] What's more, the newfound mobility of multinational corporations places a lot of pressure on national (and local) governments to present the best possible "business climate" to potential investors or producers. Freed by advanced communication and transport technology to locate production facilities virtually anywhere on the planet, corporations like Intel or Honda are able play one nation off another, offering jobs and investment in return for subsidies and special favors.[61] In such an "all against all" environment, welfare state programs (including pro-labor or redistributive policies) are increasingly viewed as liabilities in the international competition for investment than as supports for expanding domestic demand.[62]

Unable to "trap" increasingly global capital and unwilling to alienate increasingly footloose multinational corporations (who, during the hard times of the 1970s and early 1980s, held out a crucial promise of jobs and investment), the welfare state in most industrialized nations faced an acute legitimation crisis.[63] Caught in a double-bind between falling revenues and increased demand for state provision—such as unemployment insurance and welfare—many national states fell into fiscal crisis as debt piled up and interest payments began to take a larger and larger chunk of national revenues. By the early 1980s, facing a long-term recession with no guarantee of a quick turnaround—and unwilling to impose new rounds of taxation or regulation on an already agitated and now increasingly mobile business sector—many national governments were forced to withdraw from their commitments to maintain the social wage through welfare and health care provision.[64] The result was a dramatic erosion of legitimacy for the welfare state as it proved unable to deliver on the postwar promises of steady economic growth and rising standards of living.[65]

Caught between, on the one hand, public demands for equity and a renewed expansion of social benefits, and, on the other, corporate demands for deregulation and antilabor policies which might (in their view) restore the possibility of renewed accumulation, the outcome of this crisis of legitimation was almost inevitable. As David Harvey writes, "as soon as the political choices were seen as a trade-off between growth or equity, there was no question which way the wind would blow for even the most reformist of governments."[66] Claus Offe's work from the 1970s reiterates the point: since the capitalist state depends upon economic growth for revenue, it is a rare government that will choose to alienate capital instead of labor during times of economic stagnation and crisis, especially in the face of intense international competition.[67] As a result, in the rush to jump-start stagnant domestic growth rates, states across the capitalist world embarked during the 1970s and 1980s on a long process of deregulation (especially regarding labor laws and environmental regulations), privatization, and fiscal retrenchment—all in an effort to present increasingly mobile investors and producers with an enticing "business climate."[68]

The result of this round of fiscal and regulatory restructuring—in U.S. capitalism, especially—has been, in Jessop's words, a transition from the Keynesian welfare state to a post-Fordist "Schumpeterian workfare state."[69] The purpose of this Schumpeterian workfare state is not to intervene on the "demand side" (through social spending) but rather to target investment on the "supply side" in order to promote technological innovations, labor flexibility (i.e., restrictions on the closed-shop or other pro-labor laws), and international competitiveness. For example, such supply-side interventions might include tax cuts for business, a rollback of labor and environmental protections, or the active promotion of high-tech industries through tax credits or other subsidies.[70] Finally, national states intervene to help promote investment and growth by acting in international negotiations on behalf of their own "home-based" multinationals—especially by managing trade disputes, enforcing intellectual property rights, and securing access to international markets.[71]

This new Schumpeterian state has crafted a new bargain with capital. In this bargain, the state acts more as an advocate for its multinational "clients" (at least those clients who agree to invest within their boundaries), and they work diligently to secure the domestic conditions—for example, favored trading status, subsidized infrastructure, an educated workforce, a quiescent labor environment—necessary for accumulation. Under pressure to make its highly mobile and fickle corporate "clients" happy, the state becomes more and more entrepreneurial.[72] Governments at all levels of the federal system learn quickly to do what it takes to secure jobs and investment from global corporations, lest that investment flow to other (equally entrepreneurial) regions or nations. What has commenced, therefore, in this international competition for investment and trade is the oft-cited "race to the bottom," in which national and local governments leapfrog one another to lower trade barriers, cut back corporate taxes, and reduce protections for workers and the environment—all in the hope of attracting the attention of footloose multinational capital.

By the 1980s, then, policy-makers, workers, and CEOs all faced a social and economic landscape utterly changed from that of the heady days and high times of postwar Fordism. The dialectic of crisis and stability that Marx identified as an inherent feature of capitalist societies had, by the early 1970s, once again plunged the global economy into the chaos of recession and restructuring. During this economic crisis, the stakes were raised significantly for those with an inherent interest in the reproduction of capitalist relations. If profits were to be restored, if growth was to be renewed, then desperate measures—measures that would be dismissed as too disruptive or too confrontational during better times—had to be aggressively pursued. [73]

And so ended the tenuous "national bargain" of postwar Fordism. Taking advantage of the spatial mobility and flexibility offered by new communication and transportation technologies, many firms boxed their workers into a corner, using the threat (and the reality) of plant closure and relocation to force wage concessions and to smooth the acceptance of downsizing, outsourcing, and the hiring of a contingency workforce. In addition, the recession of the 1970s, along with the ensuing restructuring of multinational capital, forced a radical realignment of government priorities and policies. Faced with a choice between alienating capital by maintaining its commitment to expanding social spending and alienating labor by cutting back and deregulating the marketplace, the American state chose to woo capital.

As a result, the U.S. federal government, after the mid-1970s, began to embark on its own project of restructuring. With the globalization of investment and production a sobering reality, national governments around the capitalist world increasingly made creating the best "business climate" for mobile flows of jobs and investment their highest priority. National states became, as Harvey writes, competitive and "entrepreneurial." More and more, corporations could pick and choose among a variety of locales, from Europe to Asia to North America, to find the best possible "deal" for investment. As a result, the U.S. federal government in particular began its own long march away from its commitment to maintain postwar levels of social welfare spending.

To return to the question asked at the beginning of this chapter, why would Seattle's burghers, standing in 1998, presiding over nearly six years of uninterrupted growth and prosperity, enjoying the benefits of not only a booming high-tech sector but also a brisk trade in tourism and professional services, still express anxiety about the future? Why would they still warn civic leaders that they should still operate on "a running scared mentality"? The answer, it would seem, is that the recent trauma of global economic restructuring has given public and private leaders in major cities much to be worried about. The twenty years prior to the mid-1990s were, in short, marked by a degree of global economic uncertainty and disruption not seen since the last global crisis of the 1930s. Just how these macroshifts in the American economy have shaped and reshaped the political economy of major U.S. cities like Seattle is the topic of the next chapter. As we shall see, the collapse of American Fordism, the globalization of investment and production, and the withdrawal of the welfare state have collectively had a profound, and often devastating, effect on the urban American landscape, leaving local governments, antipoverty advocates, and even downtown business elites scrambling for ways to adjust to the emergent, post-Fordist, era of capitalist accumulation.

Notes

1. The chapter title comes with thanks to the Nigerian novelist Chinua Achebe.

2. "Letter from Seattle Mayor Paul Schell," *Crossroads* 7, no. 3 (Summer 1998).

3. Personal interview, Seattle Property Owner.

4. Personal interview, Seattle-King County Convention and Visitors Bureau.

5. Lee Moriwaki, "Downtown Urged to 'Retain Soul,'" *Seattle Times*, 30 May 1998.

6. Marshall Berman, *All That is Solid Melts into Air: The Experience of Modernity* (New York: Penguin, 1982), 99.

7. Karl Marx and Frederich Engels, "The Manifesto of the Communist Party," in *The Marx-Engels Reader*, ed. Robert Tucker (New York: Norton, 1978), 476.

8. As Schumpeter writes in *Capitalism, Socialism, and Democracy* (New York: Harper & Row, 1950), 82-3: "Capitalism, then, is by its very nature a form or method of economic change and not only never is, but never can be stationary. . . . The opening up of new markets . . . and the organizational development from the craft shop and factory to such concerns as U.S. Steel illustrate the same process of industrial mutation—if I may use that biological term—that incessantly revolutionizes the economic structure from within, incessantly destroying the old one, incessantly creating a new one."

9. Steve Lash and John Urry, *The End of Organized Capitalism* (Madison, WI: University of Wisconsin Press, 1987), 73.

10. Robert Reich, *The Work of Nations* (New York: Basic Books, 1991), 67.

11. Michael Piore and Charles Sabel, *The Second Industrial Divide* (New York: Basic Books, 1984), 101-2. According to Piore and Sabel, after World War II, the United Auto Workers tried to gain control of (or at least have a say within) the production process through a series of strikes against General Motors. In addition to demanding a 30 percent wage increase, lower auto prices, and a guarantee on collective bargaining rights, the UAW also demanded increased union control over shop-floor organization. Facing defeat at the picket lines in 1946, the UAW was forced to withdraw this last demand. As Piore and Sabel write, "defeat put an end to all vague hopes for a cooperatively managed economy. And it set the stage for the model 1948 agreement regularizing relations between the union and the company."

12. Piore and Sabel, *The Second Industrial Divide*, 102. Perhaps the most important symbol of this new "bargain" between capital and labor was the 1948 settlement between the UAW and GM. In this contract, the union acknowledged management's authority over production, and management agreed to tie wage increases automatically to inflation plus the rise in national productivity rates.

13. Piore and Sabel, *The Second Industrial Divide*, 90-91.

14. Piore and Sabel, 90-91.

15. Piore and Sabel, 90-91.

16. Bob Jessop, "Post-Fordism and the State," in *Post-Fordism: A Reader*, ed. A. Amin (Oxford: Blackwell, 1994), 253.

17. This national bargain between captial, labor, and the state has been termed "Fordism" by a number of scholars (beginning with Antonio Gramsci), in recognition that it was Henry Ford who first argued for the development of a high-wage, high-consumption, high-productivity economy. While Ford initially offered higher wages to

workers to smooth their acceptance of his new (and alienating) assembly line process, Ford soon discovered that higher wages were crucial to the future of capitalist growth. As David Harvey writes in *The Condition of Postmodernity* (Cambridge, Mass.: Blackwell, 1990), 125, Ford correctly saw that mass production necessarily required mass consumption, and, as a result, workers' wages had to rise so that firms could find markets for their goods.

18. Lawrence Grossberg, *We Gotta Get Out of This Place* (London: Routledge, 1992), 138. Grossberg reports that American personal incomes increased nearly 300 percent from 1940 to 1955. See also David Harvey, *The Condition of Postmodernity* (Cambridge, MA: Blackwell, 1989), 193.

19. Herbert Marcuse, *One-Dimensional Society* (London: Abacus, 1972).

20. Louis Althusser, *Lenin and Philosophy and Other Essays* (London: New Left Review, 1971).

21. Stuart Hall, "The Rediscovery of Ideology: Return of the Repressed in Media Studies," in *Culture, Society, and the Media*, ed. M. Gurevitch, T. Bennett, and J. Wollacott (London: Methuen, 1982), 60.

22. Quoted in Hall, "The Rediscovery of Ideology," 60.

23. Quoted in Harvey, *The Condition of Postmodernity*, 10.

24. Bob Jessop, *State Theory: Putting the Capitalist State in its Place* (Oxford: Blackwell, 1990), 308.

25. Klaus Nielsen, "Towards a Flexible Future: Theories and Politics," in *The Politics of Flexibility: Restructuring State and Industry in Britain, Germany, and Scandinavia*, ed. B. Jessop, H. Kastendiek, K. Nielsen, and O. Pedersen (Brookfield, VT: Edward Elgar, 1991), 22.

26. Ash Amin, "Post-Fordism: Models, Fantasies, and Phantoms of Transition," in *Post-Fordism: A Reader*, ed. A. Amin (Oxford: Blackwell, 1994), 8.

27. David Harvey, *The Condition of Postmodernity*, 121. For example, many regulation theorists argue that the Fordist regime of accumulation combined the economies of scale achieved through mass production techniques with the formation of mass markets to create a sustainable mode of economic growth marked by mass consumption of standardized goods.

28. Klaus Nielsen, "Towards a Flexible Future," 22.

29. The concept of *mode of regulation*, it seems to me, derives much from Antonio Gramsci's notion of hegemony—in short, the notion that reproduction of existing capitalist relations requires, especially in a liberal democratic context, the cultivation of consent-to-rule in addition to what Marx called "the dull compulsion of the economic" and the ever-present threat of state violence.

30. For example, for many regulation theorists, the Fordist mode of regulation combines the legitimation of social welfare state policies with the "high-wage/high-productivity" labor bargain in order to sustain a "demand-side" model of economic growth. Political and social stability was cultivated through the continuous rise in standards of living as well as through the mobilization of cold war (anticommunist) ideologies.

31. Bob Jessop, *State Theory* (Cambridge, MA: Blackwell, 1990), 309.

32. Harvey, *The Condition*, 143. As Bluestone and Harrison note, U.S. corporate profits rates from 15.5 percent in 1966 to a lowly 10 percent in 1974, a drop of over 50

percent in just eight short years. The free fall in profits was even more pronounced in the auto industry, with profits sagging by a massive 65 percent from 1968 to 1975. See Barry Bluestone and Bennett Harrison, *The Deindustrialization of America: Plant Closings, Community Abandonment, and the Dismantling of Basic Industry* (New York: Basic Books, 1982), 147-8.

33. Piore and Sabel, *The Second Industrial Divide*, 183.

34. Harvey, *The Condition*, 185.

35. Harvey, *The Condition*, 141.

36. Harvey, *The Condition*, 141. See also Piore and Sabel, *The Second Industrial Divide*, 183, and Robert Reich, *The Work of Nations* (New York: Basic Books, 1991), 69-70.

37. The development of container ship transport and satellite communication also reduced the "barrier of space" between far-flung Third World producers and U.S. consumer markets, allowing offshore firms to compete effectively with domestic producers. See Harvey, *The Condition*, 293-4.

38. Harvey, *The Condition*, 143.

39. David Harvey, "Flexible Accumulation Through Urbanization: Reflections on 'Post-modernism' in the American City," in *Post-Fordism: A Reader*, ed. A. Amin (Oxford: Blackwell, 1994), 361.

40. Ash Amin, "Post-Fordism: Models, Fantasies," 1.

41. See, for example, Piore and Sabel, *The Second Industrial Divide*.

42. See especially, Jamie Peck and Adam Tickell, "Searching for a New Institutional Fix: The After-Fordist Crisis and the Global-Local Disorder," in *Post-Fordism: A Reader*, ed. A. Amin (Oxford: Blackwell, 1994), 281.

43. Klaus Nielsen, "Towards a Flexible Future," 21.

44. Jamie Peck and Adam Tickell, "Searching for a New Institutional Fix," 291.

45. Reich, *The Work of Nations*, 90; see also Harvey, *The Condition*, 141.

46. Saskia Sassen, *The Global City: New York, London, Tokyo* (Princeton, NJ: Princeton University Press, 1991), 10.

47. Jamie Peck and Adam Tickell, "Searching for a New Institutional Fix," 291. As Peck and Tickell write, under the pressure of recession and international competition, manufacturing firms in the United States (especially those in the export sector) began to view wages and benefits not as a source of consumer demand—in the classic Fordist sense—but rather as a drag on economic competitiveness.

48. Harvey, *The Condition*, 145.

49. Ash Amin and Kevin Robins, "The Re-emergence of Regional Economies? The Mythical Geography of Flexible Accumulation," *Environment and Planning D: Society and Space* 8 (1990): 7-34.

50. A. Sivanandan, "All That Melts into Air is Solid: The Hokum of New Times," *Race & Class* 31 (1989): 8.

51. Robert Reich, *The Work of Nations*, 87.

52. Piore and Sabel, *The Second Industrial Divide*, 184. As Piore and Sabel argue, the recession of 1973-1975 (marked by saturated markets, high unemployment, and declining wages) caused consumer demand to stagnate. At the same time, traditional consumer markets for appliances, electronics, and automobiles were flooded with cheaply produced goods. Under these conditions, the "virtuous circle" of Fordism—i.e.,

mass production for mass markets—was no longer profitable, especially for firms located in high-wage zones of the global economy. As Robert Reich argues, this led many manufacturing firms to target the more specialized segments of consumer markets, that is, those high-end consumers who are willing to "pay a premium for goods and services that extactly meet their needs." These markets are by definition smaller and more volatile than the traditional "mass markets," and therefore can be exploited more profitably by leaner, more specialized, more highly skilled firms than by the huge corporate bureaucracies of the Fordist era. However, the fact that smaller firms can conceivably address these niche consumer markets does not mean the "end of the corporate giant," as Piore and Sable sometimes seem to imply. Instead, as Reich argues, what we are seeing is the rise of large multinational firms which coordinate specific projects designed to exploit specialized markets, but which subcontract out much of the actual production, marketing, and distribution activities involved in addressing these "niche" market demands. See Reich, *The Work of Nations*, 83-98.

53. Reich, *The Work of Nations*, 219.

54. Sometimes firms hire these workers individually, but more often they contract with smaller firms (including temporary agencies) to provide the inputs—i.e., everything from clerical work to routine production—necessary to meet the demands of specific project or enterprise.

55. Reich, *The Work of Nations*, 93.

56. Harvey, *The Condition*, 150.

57. Jessop, "Post-Fordism and the State," 255. See also Harvey, *The Condition*, 129.

58. Piore and Sabel, *The Second Industrial Divide*, 183.

59. Peck and Tickell, "Searching," 291.

60. Lash and Urry, *The End of Organized Capitalism*, 197. See also John Logan and Harvey Molotch, *Urban Fortunes: Toward a Political Economy of Place* (Berkeley, CA: University of California Press, 1987), 252.

61. To be sure, there are some practical limits on where corporations would be willing to invest. Some regions of the globe enjoy neither the legal and security apparatus, the political stability, nor the technological infrastructure to sustain large-scale commerce. Multinational corporations are unlikely to move routine production to nations where laws are changed monthly, where local authorities demand escalating bribes for routine government services, and where the legal system is unable to protect property rights—no matter how cheap the labor is. My thanks to Dr. Robert Stebbins for raising this point.

62. Jessop, "Post-Fordism and the State," 256. Jessop argues that during the 1970s, firms increasingly began to view generous welfare provision as a barrier to their desire to force lower wages on a recalcitrant workforce. As William J. Wilson writes, this was especially true in Europe where many low-paying service-sector jobs went unfilled as citizens rationally chose to collect unemployment insurance rather than accept low wages. See William J. Wilson, *When Work Disappears: The World of the New Urban Poor* (New York: Knopf, 1995), 221.

63. Jürgen Habermas, *Legitimation Crisis* (Boston: Beacon Press, 1975).

64. Harvey, *The Condition*, 167.

65. J. Hirsch, "From the Fordist to the Post-Fordist State," in *The Politics of flexi-*

bility: Restructuring State and Industry in Britain, Germany, and Scandinavia, ed. B. Jessop, H. Kastendiek, K. Nielsen, and O. Pedersen (Brookfield, VT: Edward Elgar, 1991), 70.

66. Harvey, *The Condition*, 168.

67. Bob Jessop, *State Theory*, 40.

68. Hirsch, "From the Fordist to the Post-Fordist State," 73-4.

69. Jessop, "Post-Fordism and the State," 263.

70. Hirsch, "From the Fordist to the Post-Fordist State," 73-4.

71. Jessop, "Post-Fordism and the State," 261-62.

72. David Harvey, "Flexible Accumulation Through Urbanization: Reflections on 'Post-modernism' in the American City."

73. Harvey, *The Condition*, 181.

Chapter 2

Crisis and Opportunity in the Post-Fordist City

The high times of American Fordism were good times for Seattle's community of downtown business and policy elites.[1] In fact, these years culminated a long struggle to build Seattle into a leading national city. Prior to World War II, however, this dream seemed quixotic at best. Before the war, Seattle's economy was dependent largely on a brisk trade in timber and agricultural goods, and so its early political and economic history reads much like many other resource-based port towns: an unending cycle of boom and bust tied always volatile commodity markets. During this time, Seattle remained a regional player, an important conduit for resources and a center of the timber industry, to be sure, but just one of many up and down the West Coast. So while city elites periodically dreamed big about building Seattle into the preeminent city on the last American frontier, most notably during the 1909 Alaska-Yukon-Pacific Exposition that promoted Seattle as the "gateway to Alaska," they spent as much of their time fighting local labor battles as they did building and promoting Seattle's world-class status.

It was World War II that utterly changed Seattle's urban fortunes. As Carl Abbott argues, the war in the Pacific forced the federal government to move the focus of its military-industrial capacity to the West Coast, a development that led to massive military expenditures along the Western frontier. In this Western wartime boom, the cities that benefited most were those that could build on existing industries and facilities. And, in 1940, Seattle was in an especially good position to cash in. Already home to the Boeing Company (which was founded during World War I), the Puget Sound region also hosted Bremerton's Naval Shipyard and sprawling Fort Lewis, one of the largest military reservations on the West Coast. As a result, $2.5 billion in defense contracts—and thousands of desperately needed industrial workers—poured into the region, swelling Seattle's population and the bank accounts of the area's industrialists and landowners (who now had tenants competing fiercely for housing and factory space).[2] After the war, most of the workers and families drawn to the area by the mobilization simply chose to stay, boosting King County's population by 45 percent to the delight of Seattle's civic boosters and property-owning elites.[3]

The spectacular growth in the region emboldened Seattle's city officials. No longer merely one of many regional nodes of timber and trade, Seattle had emerged, in the view of boosters, as the preeminent city in the Pacific Northwest, able to compete with its larger Californian rivals for trade, investment, and growth. Yet at the same time, even during the expansion of the 1950s, there were some unsettling clouds on the horizon, especially for business elites with connections to Seattle's central city. First, according to John Findlay, a Seattle historian, the city's dependence on Boeing presented a series of problems for downtown landowners. Although the aerospace giant was in large part responsible for city's spectacular growth, Boeing's newest factories were located in the suburban fringe. And while Seattle had not yet experienced the wholesale flight of middle-class residents suffered by its eastern and Midwestern counterparts, the expansion of Boeing into suburbia—along with the construction of suburban thruways, the construction of new shopping malls outside city limits, and the provision of federally subsidized mortgage rates for new suburban housing—fueled elite concerns over East Coast-style suburbanization and urban decline.

In 1959, with the fiftieth anniversary of the Alaska-Yukon-Pacific Exposition approaching, the city's civic and business establishment began to coalesce around an idea. What if the city were to host a new and even more spectacular World's Fair? This would present civic leaders with an opportunity to accomplish two goals at once—to *both* promote Seattle's new, postwar prominence *and* to reconcentrate economic growth downtown.[4] As Seattle historian John Findlay writes, city boosters quickly rallied around the idea, forming a Central Association Board to coordinate planning and acquiring thirty-five acres of land just north of downtown for the fairgrounds. Fueled by more than $9 million in federal grants, the Century 21 Exposition, as it came to be called, would, first and foremost, announce Seattle's arrival on the world stage. Organized around a "space-age" theme—featuring both the new Pacific Science Center, and, of course, the *Jetsons*-esque Space Needle—the Fair ostensibly celebrated the triumph of American Cold War-era science and technology, but in the main promoted Seattle as America's leading "city of the future."

Furthermore, the downtown business community was enthused about the potential for the Fair to help concentrate future urban growth where it belonged—right downtown. For city elites, the Century 21 Exposition grounds seemed to offer everything Seattle's current central city seemed to lack. Downtown Seattle needed open space to compete with the greenways of the suburbs, and, after the Fair, the grounds would remain to add much-needed park space. Seattle had few pedestrian-friendly walkways, so Fair planners closed off auto and truck traffic from the site. After the demolition of many historic theaters in the early part of the century, downtown hosted few cultural activities; as a result, planners built a series of performance halls to make the fairgrounds the cultural center of the region. Eventually, the fairgrounds (renamed "Seattle Center" after the festivities were over) would become home to the Seattle Opera, Seattle Symphony, and the Pacific Northwest Ballet. Finally, to cement the fairground's association with downtown, the Fair's planners linked the grounds to downtown with an elevated monorail system built, appropriately enough, by the same firm Walt Disney hired to ferry theme park patrons around Anaheim's Magic Kingdom. In the end, boosters were excited about the Fair's potential to contribute to a "vital, cohesive, enlarged downtown"—one that might compete effectively with the suburbs for middle-class and upscale patronage.[5]

By all accounts, the Century 21 Exposition was a remarkable success for civic boosters, ultimately drawing over 10 million visitors in 1962 and confidently proclaimed Seattle's future as a center of "space-age" prosperity. And, for civic leaders in the mid-1960s, there seemed to be much to celebrate. The Fair had cemented the central city's role as a center of arts and recreation, drawing visitors to concerts, dance performances, and sporting events. Furthermore, despite the continuing concerns about suburban growth, employment at Boeing had blossomed from 40,000 employees in the early 1950s to over 100,000 in 1969.[6] Finally, attracted by Boeing's status as a leading Cold War defense contractor, a host of smaller manufacturing and research firms began to locate in the region, supplementing Seattle's traditional role as a timber and port town. By the mid-1960s, the city's population had grown to nearly 550,000—a rise of nearly 100,000 individuals during a time in which other cities around the nation were shrinking rapidly due to middle-class outmigration.

It was a heady time to be a member of the downtown establishment. Three years after the Fair, James Ellis, a partner in the city's most prominent law firm and a longtime civic leader, sought to capitalize on the civic momentum and proposed, in a speech to the Rotary Club, a series of ambitious public works and infrastructure programs. Calling it "Forward Thrust" (in an evocative, if somewhat disturbing, turn of phrase), Ellis called upon Seattle's elite to lead the charge for a $340 million plan to build new urban parks and plazas, a world trade center, an aquarium, and a new domed stadium (the much-maligned and now imploded Kingdome) designed to finally attract major-league sports to the Emerald City. Flush with the optimism of the times, Ellis told the assembled Rotarians:

> The heart of the metropolitan area should serve as the rallying point for this forward thrust, but the welfare of the entire area should be its aim. With the tools of urban design, a regard for human values, and plenty of work we could see the beginning of a golden age for Seattle. We could build here one of the great cities of man.[7]

At the time, hardly anyone would believe the celebration would only last a few more years, but the brewing crisis of American Fordism would soon find its way even to "space-age" Seattle. By 1969, the party was over. For one thing, Pentagon budget cuts and shrinking airline orders led Boeing to cut over 60,000 jobs in the Seattle area between 1969 and 1971, paring its workforce from over 100,000 to just under 40,000.[8] As Seattle journalist Eric Lucas recalls, "the Seattle economy staggered. Thousands of families packed up and left. And Houston, where unemployed engineers sought jobs in the space program, was known as Seattle South."[9] The Boeing Bust, as it would be called in Seattle folklore, soon became fodder for gallows humor. Most famously, at one point during the bust, an anonymous jokester paid to have a roadside billboard erected that asked fleeing motorists "will the last person to leave Seattle please turn out the lights?"

Though it was probably cold comfort to unemployed Boeing machinists, Seattle's economic woes barely registered on the pain scale in comparison to the crushing fate suffered by such industrial centers as Detroit, Cleveland, New York, and Baltimore. As William Julius Wilson has shown, the loss of manufacturing jobs due to relocation and shutdown following the global recession of the early 1970s undermined the economies of most American industrial giants, sparking a wave of suburbanization and out-migration unheard of in American history.[10] Between 1970 and 1980, for example, New York lost over 10 percent of its population, while Cleveland, Detroit, and St. Louis each lost over 20 percent to the suburbs and the cities of the Sunbelt. By 1980, then, the exodus of traditional manufacturing jobs and the flight of legions of middle-class residents to the suburban fringe had left in their wake rising unemployment, intensified poverty, and a brewing social and fiscal crisis.

In short, the crisis of American Fordism discussed in the previous chapter had, in just a few short years, spawned a dramatic national *urban* crisis. Taken together, the "flexible" corporate strategies pursued by multinational corporations—including the globalization of routine production, the accelerated use of subcontracted or contingency workers, and an all-out assault on the American labor movement—have had a reverberating effect on the fortunes and fates of American central cities and their residents. Municipal governments and urban property elites were, of course, greatly distressed by these developments, and have spent the better part of three decades searching for a way to deal with the social and economic wreckage left behind by the collapse of American Fordism.

In this chapter, I discuss both the social and economic consequences of post-Fordist corporate and political restructuring as well as some of the strategies hatched by local policy and property elites to reverse their recent urban fortunes. In doing so, I argue that the downtown establishment in Seattle—as in other cities across the United States—has been much more concerned with property values than poverty and has targeted most of its interventions around elaborate and expensive downtown redevelopment and gentrification projects, all launched with the hope of attracting (at almost any cost) tourists, trade, and investment from an increasingly fickle and competitive global marketplace.

The Post-Fordist City: A Time of Crisis

As we have seen, it was during the serial recessions of the 1970s that corporate executives concluded that the fundamental bargain of American Fordism had, in fact, fallen apart. In the midst of the economic crisis, facing a market saturated with competitors and low-priced goods, the postwar practice of steadily increasing wages became viewed as an intolerable drag on profits. Beginning in the early 1970s, then, American manufacturing and service firms began to experiment with various strategies for restoring the possibility of steady growth. And, in the end, the strategies that corporate leaders seized upon, grouped loosely under the concept of "flexibility," had important, and often devastating, consequences for America's central cities.

Consider, for example, the decision to use new innovations in transportation and communication technology to locate low-skill manufacturing in low-wage regions of the nation and the world.[11] These innovations would allow manufacturing firms the "flexibility" to scan the globe, looking for localities that presented the best "business climate," defined most typically by the locality's ability to deliver cheap labor in a political environment hostile to unionism and lax in its enforcement of environmental regulations. As Bluestone and Harrison have pointed out, this strategy proved irresistible for many manufacturing firms, and, before long, those firms which managed to survive the crisis,[12] began to move en masse out of their traditional homes in or near major U.S. cities—so much so that Philadelphia lost 64 percent of its manufacturing jobs, while Chicago and New York lost 60 and 58 percent, respectively.[13] Nationwide, the United States lost nearly a third of its manufacturing plants to closure or relocation between 1969 and 1976, with many of these closures concentrated in union-friendly Northeast and Midwest.[14]

All in all, the combination of plant relocation and other industrial strategies—including an increasing corporate reliance on a "flexible," temporary and part-time workforce—undermined the economies of many American cities. Central city neighborhoods that had long depended upon a core of unionized manufacturing jobs saw them shipped off to low-wage zones of the world economy. As Wilson has written, the inner-city neighborhoods left behind were simply devastated. Those families who could find white-collar or service jobs in the suburbs simply moved out, leaving behind only the most desperately poor.[15] At the same time, those jobs that were indeed created in central cities during these years were typically concentrated in the gleaming skyscrapers of the Central Business District (CBD), and came with education and skill requirements far out of the reach of most central city residents.[16]

The results of these economic developments were sobering for city politicians. Big-city mayors across the United States faced, on the one hand, the onset of Depression-style poverty and unemployment. As Judd and Swanstrom write, between 1970 and 1980, while the population of America's fifty largest cities declined, the poverty rate in these cities increased by nearly 12 percent.[17] Overall, less than one-third of the nation's poor lived in central cities in 1959, but by 1991 cities were home to close to one-half of poor Americans.[18] In a final cruel twist, the loss of manufacturing jobs hit the nation's African-American neighborhoods especially hard, concentrating poverty in neighborhoods already struggling with spatial and social isolation. In Chicago, for instance, eight of the ten neighborhoods that make up the city's historical "black belt" had poverty rates above 45 percent in 1990. Twenty years earlier, before the onset of crisis and recession, only two of these neighborhoods had poverty rates above 40 percent.[19]

At the same time, the federal government had made it abundantly clear to urban leaders that they would face these problems on their own. For example, in 1972 the Nixon administration summarily announced that "the urban crisis was over" and froze urban aid spending at 1972 levels.[20] Ten years later, the Reagan administration gutted urban aid programs in dramatic fashion, cutting direct aid to cities by more than 60 percent (in constant dollars) from 1981 to 1989. In addition, the Reagan administration, through a combination of budget cuts and eligibility requirements, also forced 500,000 people off AFDC (Aid for Families with Dependent Children) and nearly 1 million people lost access to food stamps—all at a time when inner-city poverty levels were reaching near Depression-era levels.[21]

In short, an unhealthy brew of economic recession, suburbanization, deindustrialization, and cuts to urban aid during the 1970s and 1980s threw many U.S. cities into economic and social turmoil. Given this turmoil, the municipal fiscal crises that exploded around the United States during this time should have surprised no one. New York City, for example, virtually went bankrupt in 1975 when banks refused to market the city's securities (i.e., cities raise money by marketing "city bonds" to investors at a given rate of return).[22] The federal government eventually stepped in and offered the city government a loan guarantee, provided the city agree to an "austerity program" of city budget cuts that gutted city services and social programs. Between 1975 and 1980, New York City's public expenditures declined by 21.4 percent, resulting in a pullback of social services at the same time as the need for these services was at a forty-year high.[23]

New York was by no means alone. In 1978, Cleveland was forced to declare bankruptcy when local banks, aroused by the mayor's refusal to support tax breaks for downtown developers, declined to refinance the city's short-term notes—a practice that had been routine for previous administrations.[24] By the recession of the early 1990s, cities all over the nation—from East Coast to West Coast, from Sunbelt to Rust Belt—had dipped into a serious fiscal crisis. For instance, a survey conducted by the National League of Cities in 1991 found that nearly 70 percent of cities were running deficits, and most cities' revenues were falling even though nearly 85 percent of those surveyed had raised taxes or fees to cover their deficits.

Finally, and most alarming to downtown property elites, the uneasy convergence of deindustrialization, middle-class flight, inner-city poverty, and cuts to city services had the further effect of driving down property values in central cities. The fate of property values in New York during the 1970s provides a vivid example. As Neil Smith writes, the Christodora Building (a sixteen-story residential building next to Tompkins Square Park on the lower east side of Manhattan) sold in 1947 for $1.3 million. Run-down and dilapidated by the late 1960s, the building attracted no bids at a public auction in 1975, selling eventually to a real estate developer for $62,500.[25] The fate of the Christodora was repeated countless times across the United States, especially in cities and neighborhoods hit hardest by successive rounds of deindustrialization and economic restructuring. By way of comparison, while the value of taxable property in Phoenix rose a stunning 251 percent between 1965 and 1973, property values rose only 2 percent in industrial Newark and 14 percent in Detroit in the same period.[26] Spread out over eight years, such rates of return failed to even keep up with inflation, sparking massive waves of divestment in the central cities in favor of suburban real estate or other investments which promised greater earnings.[27]

In short, in many respects the two decades immediately following the global crisis of 1973 were the worst of times for many American cities. The rapid deindustrialization of their economies and the accelerating pace of suburban migration left many central cities reeling under Depression-era levels of unemployment and poverty. To make matters worse, the restructuring of the welfare state and the withdrawal of the federal government from direct urban aid and other Keynesian social programs undermined these cities' ability to deal with the brewing social and economic crisis, forcing cutbacks in anti-poverty and job programs when the demand for these services had exploded. Finally, by the 1980s, in many cities the decaying industrial economy and the rapid growth of ghetto-style poverty and misery in the inner city had finally begun to drag down urban property values—not just in the struggling inner city but, in some cases, even within the hallowed terrain of the Central Business District. By the early 1990s, as we will discover in later chapters, the fourth national recession since 1970 had not only deepened the fiscal and social ills of urban America, but had this time been matched by a national real estate bust. In many U.S. cities, the search for a strategy, any strategy, to reverse their sinking urban fortunes quickly took on a more desperate and competitive tone.

The Post-Fordist City: A Time of Opportunity

To be sure, the erosion of American Fordism undermined the traditional economic bases of many U.S. cities. However, at the same time, almost perversely, the collapse of American Fordism also created new opportunities. As Marshall Berman has argued, capitalism is not merely a profoundly destructive force—it also promotes, even demands, constant innovation and creativity.[28] Indeed, Marx himself knew better than most that the genius of capitalism, the source of both its most terrible crises and its most stunning achievements, lies in the system's ability to renew itself through an always painful and always disruptive process of *creative destruction*—that is, the process by which older and traditional forms of economic and social organization are undermined, corroded, destroyed, and ultimately replaced by new forms.[29] While the economic restructuring of the last three decades clearly devastated many communities, certain sectors of the urban economy have actually expanded and thrived within the emerging post-Fordist landscape.

In short, therefore, the fallout from the economic crisis of the 1970s was unevenly felt within the urban landscape. At the same time that deindustrialization was tearing at the social fabric of many working-class African-American and Latino neighborhoods, many downtown districts across the United States saw a simultaneous and often dramatic explosion of economic growth— particularly among the office towers housing the expanding legions of white-collar workers. For example, between 1969 and 1988 New York lost 460,000 manufacturing jobs (many of these dispersed to the global assembly line), but during this time the city *added* 344,000 service jobs.[30] Nationwide, the statistics were equally dramatic, with manufacturing jobs located in the nation's ten largest metropolitan areas declining by a collective 23 percent from 1977 to 1987 while service jobs—including many high-end "professional" or "producer" service jobs—increased by 88 percent during the same decade.[31]

How does this add up? How could the American urban landscape on the one hand be reeling under the pressure of globalization and deindustrialization while on the other see a dramatic influx of professional, white-collar, and often highly paid service workers into the glittering towers of the Central Business District? The work of Saskia Sassen and of Robert Reich provides a compelling answer to these questions concerning the uneven fates of many U.S. cities and neighborhoods. First, both of these authors argue that many of the newly created white-collar jobs have filled an expanding thirst among sprawling multinational corporations for what Saskia Sassen calls "producer services." The intense period of economic restructuring during the 1970s has led to the rise of what Sassen calls "the global assembly line"—that is, the increasing production of goods in locations all over the globe, depending, in part at least, on relative wage rates and labor militancy (the less the better, in most corporations' view).[32] In this way, the flight from the high-cost commitments of American

Fordism and the welfare state has transformed traditional giants like IBM, Boeing, and General Motors into sprawling corporate webs that must coordinate an increasingly complex and "worldwide production system with plants, offices, and service branches in a multiplicity of foreign and domestic locations."[33]

The challenge of coordinating and controlling such global webs of design, investment, production, and distribution can be daunting. This complexity can be illustrated nicely by borrowing an example used by Robert Reich in his seminal book *The Work of Nations*. Say, for instance, you just bought a Pontiac LeMans from the local General Motors dealer. After a round of intense tire-kicking and haggling with the sales staff at the dealership, you hand over $20,000 and drive away to show off your new ride. But what happens to your $20,000? According to Reich's calculations:

> about $6,000 goes to South Korea for routine labor and assembly operations, $3,500 to Japan for advanced components . . . $1,500 to West Germany for styling and design engineering, $800 to Taiwan, Singapore, and Japan for small components, $500 to Britain for advertising and marketing services, and about $100 to Ireland and Barbados for data processing. The rest—less than $8,000—goes to strategists in Detroit, bankers in New York, lobbyists in Washington, insurance and health care workers all over the country, and [finally] to General Motors Shareholders.[34]

So much for "Made in America." And General Motors is by no means alone in exploiting the global assembly line. Hollywood movie studios, which at one point controlled production and distribution from the first draft of the movie script to the price of popcorn at the local theater, now subcontract most of their functions and simply coordinate a series of limited-term contracts with independent producers, directors, writers, crews, and accountants who are as likely to work in Vancouver or London as in Hollywood.[35] Even the Boeing Company, long centralized in the Puget Sound region, has exploded into a global web and now buys designs from Japan, tail cones from Canada, and engines from Britain—all to be assembled back home in Seattle.[36]

The complexity of such global webs can be mind-boggling. With their functions dispersed throughout the global assembly line, multinational firms now face the challenge of organizing production in a host of different labor, regulatory, and political environments, to say nothing of the challenges in coordinating financial investment and accounting with countless subcontractors throughout the corporate web. Faced with such complexity, multinational corporations have developed an urgent need for a host of specialized "producer services"—that is, the accounting, legal, planning, management, financial, and marketing services corporations need to organize their own particular global assembly line.[37] In short, multinational corporations have found that they simply cannot go it alone. They need highly skilled help and expert advice.

Thus, as Sassen argues, the globalization of production and investment has created a booming labor market for producer services and workers with expertise in negotiating the choppy waters of international marketing, finance, and law. As a result, an enormous opportunity has opened up for freestanding[38] service firms which can assist multinational corporations with coordinating their global production, distribution, and marketing strategies.[39] Nationally, this newfound demand for specialized business services is reflected in the growing importance of producer services in the national employment picture. As Sassen notes, while total employment in the United States increased by 15 percent from 1977 to 1981, and by another 8.3 percent from 1981 to 1985, employment in producer services for those same periods boomed by 24 and 22 percent respectively.[40] And, incidentally, this growth in the share of producer services is not limited to the American context; according to Sassen, Japan and the U.K. have posted an even more dramatic contrast between the robust growth of producer services and the sluggish increase in overall employment.[41]

For Sassen, it is this demand for workers who provide "producer services" which explains the explosion in white-collar employment in many cities across the United States. Still, the importance of producer services to the new global economy tells us nothing about *where* such services will be located. But, as Sassen notes, the new employment boom in high-end corporate services is overwhelmingly concentrated in urban centers—especially within first-tier cities like New York, London, Tokyo, and Chicago. Why is this? Why have these professionals poured into the downtowns of urban giants like New York and San Francisco instead of, say, the office parks of the suburbs or even the main streets of small town America?

The answer, according to Sassen, lies in the peculiar nature of contemporary producer services.[42] Selling traditional in-person services, such as carpet cleaning and gardening, quite obviously depends upon close proximity to buyers. It's difficult to garden from a distance. On the other hand, producer services like accounting, marketing, and legal assistance can be offered from anywhere on the globe—at least anywhere with electricity and phone lines—and would not seem to be so constrained. Yet even if such professional or producer service firms do not derive clear benefits from proximity to their multinational *clients* (who may be headquartered in Europe, Asia, or North America), they do, in fact, derive substantial benefits from locating close to a cluster of *other* producer service firms who also cater to global corporations.[43] Locating close to other freestanding professional service firms allows for close collaboration on particular projects—a common feature of many corporate endeavors in these days of subcontracting and joint ventures.[44] By agglomerating in a central location, such producer service firms can quickly coordinate their activities, propose joint ventures to potential multinational clients,[45] or easily stay abreast of sudden shifts in financial or industrial markets.

Freed from the need to locate close to their multinational clients, and increasingly aware of the synergistic benefits of proximity and agglomeration, such producer service firms have tended, especially since 1970, to cluster in the skyscrapers of the world's major urban centers.[46] There are many reasons for this, some of which have less to do with hard-nosed economics than the ready availability of sushi and a good microbrew. In other words, not only do cities such as New York, London, and Los Angeles concentrate masses of skilled service firms, but they also typically offer upper-income workers cultural amenities unavailable in most suburban strip malls and office parks. While the tangible, if less sexy, benefits of "service-sector agglomeration" certainly helps explain the concentration of high-end services in a few lucky "global cities," the more intangible pull of upscale retail, gourmet restaurants, and world-class cultural amenities on the souls of white-collar professionals must be acknowledged as well.[47]

In the years since the crisis of postwar Fordism, then, the benefits of contemporary economic growth have been distributed quite unevenly within America's cities. The complex task of relocating routine production to low-wage and nonunionized zones—in short, the very process that has sparked dramatic increases in poverty, joblessness, and dislocation in many working-class communities—has presented global firms with an enormous challenge of control and coordination. This challenge has been met by the expanding legions of white-collar "producer service" workers, who often work downtown and are usually rewarded handsomely for their efforts. So while working-class residents in cities like New York, Chicago, and Los Angeles have struggled under the weight of joblessness, social assistance cuts, and increased poverty, the fortunes of highly educated and highly skilled "symbolic analysts" (i.e., accountants, marketers, graphic artists, computer programmers, and so on) have improved dramatically.[48]

The result is a new urban landscape, marked by increasing income and social polarization and an intensification of residential differentiation. In a report appropriately titled *Pulling Apart*, social researchers Kathryn Larin and Elizabeth McNichol of the Center on Budget and Policy Priorities dramatically illustrate the depth and breadth of this social polarization. From the late 1970s to the mid 1990s, for instance, while the average income for the lowest income families (the bottom fifth of the income scale) fell by more than 20 percent, adjusting for inflation, the America's wealthiest families (the top fifth) saw their incomes jump by a hearty 30 percent. To dispel any myth that it was only the poorest of the poor who have taken the brunt of economic restructuring, Larin and McNichol note that the earnings of middle-income families also dropped by 2 percent during the 1980s. All in all, they write, "the most recent census data reveal that the incomes of families in the bottom three-fifths of the population are lower now [in December 1997] than a decade ago. Only the top two-fifths of families have average incomes above the levels of the mid-1980s."[49]

At the same time, the benefits of contemporary economic growth are not just distributed unevenly *within* American cities, as demonstrated by the yawning gap between the rich and poor. These benefits are also distributed unevenly *among* or *between* American cities. In short, not every city can be a "global city." Not every city gets to be a center of trade, finance, and international investment; there simply aren't enough producer services or command functions to spread around. What is emerging is an international urban hierarchy with cities like New York and London at the top of the urban totem pole and therefore able to pull a disproportionate share of urban economic growth from the new global marketplace.[50] These "global cities," as Sassen calls them, have capitalized on their traditional roles as financial and trade centers and their concentration of world-class cultural amenities in order to command a disproportionate share of corporate headquarters and producer services. As a result, such global cities have enjoyed a healthy boom in white-collar employment, even in the midst of deindustrialization and deepening inner-city poverty.

Following global cities in the urban hierarchy are regional centers like Minneapolis and Portland which are home to a few major multinational firms (like 3M and Nike, respectively) and which also enjoy healthy producer service sectors catering to regional industries. Bringing up the rear are a whole host of cities who, due to their historical lack of professional service firms and lack of big-city cultural amenities, have little chance of becoming command and control centers of any kind. Burdened by intense poverty and massive manufacturing job losses, sporting few jobs in finance, real estate, and producer services, and with few amenities to offer footloose corporations, midsized rust belt towns like Youngstown, Ohio and Newark, New Jersey find it extraordinarily difficult to compete for emerging sectors of economic growth.[51] So, in the end, the higher a city is in this global urban hierarchy, the more pulling power it has for future jobs and investment (since producer service firms like to locate in an already thriving professional and cultural environment), and therefore "the more control it potentially has to shape its economic future.[52]

Urban Spectacle and the Race for World-Class Status

What we have seen in the past twenty-five years, according to many urban scholars, is a no-holds-barred battle among the world's cities to move up in this international urban hierarchy—that is, to grab a disproportionate share of economic growth linked to "sunrise" industries, including information technology, producer services, and international tourism. To be sure, interurban competition for economic growth is not a recent development in urban America, as the rich history of wrangling over canal and railroad connections during the nineteenth century attests. Still, the post-Fordist economic environment adds two new dimensions to this long history of competition. First, the erosion of national economic boundaries under the assault of free trade agreements and economic globalization (as multinational corporations look to exploit the "global assembly line") means that cities in America now face a *global* competition for mobile capital investment. No longer, in short, does Seattle just compete with Portland or Phoenix for, say, Intel's newest microchip plant; but now she must contend with Singapore, London, and Sydney. Second, the withdrawal of the federal welfare state and the deep cuts to urban aid programs since 1980 have also served to instruct cities that, now more than ever, they must face this global competition alone, without the assistance of an activist federal government.

In short, if, during the postwar years, local governments looked to the federal government for assistance and development resources, city leaders—increasingly burdened with intensifying poverty, cuts in federal aid, and the wreckage of deindustrialization—have been forced to deal directly with the global marketplace to secure a future of growth and investment. Even so, some political scientists, including Margit Mayer, hail this trend, pointing to the democratic potential of political devolution and arguing that local decision-making processes are much more accessible to progressive groups than are the centralized bodies of the national state.[53] Other scholars are more pessimistic. For their part, Jamie Peck and Adam Tickell dispute Mayer's optimism, arguing that she fails to address the harsh reality of an increasingly globalized interurban competition for investment and economic growth. This competition between regions and cities for production facilities, corporate headquarters, and real estate investment, as Peck and Tickell argue, is at best a zero-sum game and at worst a destructive "race to the bottom" as localities strive to present the best possible "business climate."[54] The destructive nature of such interurban competition for jobs and investment was probably captured best by former Mayor Coleman Young of Detroit who once quipped, "this suicidal out-thrust competition has got to stop but until it does, I mean to compete. It's too bad we have a system where dog eats dog and devil takes the hindmost. But I'm tired of taking the hindmost."[55]

So how have cities tried to win this competition? How have today's pro-growth coalitions of civic officials and downtown business elites mobilized to capture economic growth—and expanding real estate profits—within the new rules of this tumultuous and competitive global economy? Desperate to jump-start stagnant economic growth and flaccid property markets and with little hope of resurrecting an economy based on traditional manufacturing, this interurban competition for footloose capital investment and renewed economic growth has assumed three distinct forms in recent years: (1) competition to become a "global city," that is, to assume the role of a command and control center for multinational capital; (2) competition to become a cultural center or

tourist destination on the order of New Orleans and Orlando; and (3) competition for the remaining high-skill, high-tech, or other emerging industries—
including computer hardware/software, defense contracting, and specialty
manufacturing firms—which demand a highly educated and skilled workforce
not easily found in emerging or developing nations.[56]

In this heightened interurban competition for mobile corporate headquarters, producer services, and sunrise industries, the goal of contemporary policy
and property elites is clear: provide the best possible business climate to attract
as much outside investment as possible. For example, cities and regions looking
to land emerging high-tech industries can pull the levers of local zoning and
industrial regulations to improve the local infrastructure (roads, sewers, electricity, etc.), lower taxes, and fast-track environmental approval for projects or
production facilities. Other strategies focus more directly on the labor environment, often going so far as to market the region's quiescent labor history and
the presence of antiunion labor laws in international trade publications.[57]

Finally, and most importantly for the story of Seattle's own search for a
winning growth strategy, cities can attract investment by carefully cultivating a
coherent and attractive "urban image" through the promotion of downtown
revitalization—that is, through the redevelopment of downtown retail and waterfront districts into lavish and glitzy spectacles of upscale tourism and leisure.
David Harvey, for his part, calls this strategy *the mobilization of spectacle* and
argues that tourist-friendly downtown revitalization projects like Boston's
Quincy Market and Baltimore's Harborplace are an attempt "to forge a distinctive image and create an atmosphere of place" that will act as "a lure to both
capital and people 'of the right sort.'"[58] It is when cities attempt to "mobilize
spectacle" that the goal of attracting tourism, growth, and investment from an
increasingly globalized marketplace merges with the dicey politics of redeveloping and "revitalizing" downtown space.[59] Unable to recapture a manufactur-
ing-based economy, and similarly powerless to force a return of the federal welfare state, local politicians and business elites must, in their effort to jump-start
property values and economic growth, deal with the cards they've been dealt.
And one of those cards, as the last two decades have shown, is their control
over downtown cityspace and, through much political maneuvering, their access to public bonds and tax funds. Accordingly, city elites around the United
States have used the tools of private property and public financing to subsidize
the creation of (hopefully) world-class downtown cultural, tourist, and retail
districts.

In building these upscale festival markets, glitzy waterfront districts, and
even high culture amenities like concert halls and art museums, city officials
are betting that such developments will help the city attract wary tourists and
suburbanites back downtown (capturing much needed consumption dollars) and
create a coherent and positive "urban image" which can sell the city to global
corporate executives and investors.[60] By redeveloping their downtowns into

centers of upscale leisure and consumption, civic elites hope that a revitalized downtown will not only boost sagging downtown property values but will also enhance the region's international image as a "livable" and dynamic urban center—thereby positioning their city well in the international competition for tourism, corporate investment, and economic growth.[61]

Different cities go about this exercise in spectacular revitalization in different ways. Some cities, for example, trade on an already established "image of place" and tailor their revitalization projects accordingly. For instance, Boston's Quincy Market, one of the nation's first "festival marketplaces," imitates closely the New England granite and polished wood of nearby historic Faneuil Hall in an explicit attempt to capture the old world panache of "revolutionary Boston."[62] When such a coherent and attractive "image of place" is unavailable, as was the case in Baltimore and Cleveland, city elites may simply choose to *invent* such a positive image out of whole cloth, typically through the thematic and coordinated redevelopment of once-abandoned retail and waterfront districts into new upscale malls, markets, and tourist attractions. In Baltimore, the end result of this strategy was Harborplace, a series of translucent waterfront pavilions which offered visiting suburbanites, tourists, and downtown office workers a dazzling array of specialty shops, ethnic foods, and entertainment (in the form of dancers, musicians, and jugglers) unavailable in any suburban shopping mall. Completed in 1980 and soon joined by the National Aquarium, Harborplace stunned both investors and national observers by outpulling Disneyland in its first year, drawing nearly 18 million visitors and positioning Baltimore as a competitive player in the tourist and convention industry.[63]

Other cities pin their hopes on a "high culture" strategy, gambling that new art galleries, concert halls, and opera houses will attract upscale patrons back downtown and lend their city an air of world-class sophistication conducive to attracting international investment. During the 1980s, for example, Los Angeles's property developers joined forces with oil magnates, entertainment kingpins, and the aggressively pro-growth city government to build what critic Mike Davis has called "a cultural infrastructure for Los Angeles' emergence as a 'world city.'"[64] Beginning in 1986 with the construction of the Museum of Contemporary Art, public and private investment poured into a variety of enormous arts projects, designed by big-name architects and specifically conceived to outflank San Francisco as the cultural capital of the American West Coast. To this end, in the years since 1986 the city has built the Bella Lewitsky Dance Gallery, Frank Gehry's Disney Concert Hall, and Richard Meier's $300 million J. Paul Getty Center, "a museum, library, and research center for the largest arts endowment in history ($3 billion plus)."[65] As Mike Davis writes, city elites in Los Angeles have fully committed themselves to this cultural strategy not out of old-fashioned philanthropy but rather because of the potential of "culture" to inflate nearby property values and to provide L.A. an advantage in the interurban competition for Pacific Rim trade and investment.[66]

This list of strategies could go on—St. Louis's multimillion investment designed to lure the NFL's Los Angeles Rams provides another kind of example—but the pattern is clear. In the years since the crisis of Fordism, city elites all over the nation have used their control over downtown space and their access to the public purse to build all manner of urban spectacle—from upscale retail districts to glitzy docklands, from convention centers to aquaria, from gentrified residential "hot spots" to elaborate sports arenas. Indeed, as the case of Seattle will demonstrate, urban elites do not confine themselves to the pursuit of one strategy, but instead embark upon as many redevelopment and revitalization projects as possible, all in the hope of improving their city's international standing among the people who matter most (to policy and property elites, at least)—the wary suburbanite, the tourist and convention-goer, the white-collar professional, and the international community of investors. In the end, what ties these redevelopment schemes together is the hope that, by redeveloping downtown space, the city will climb the post-Fordist international urban hierarchy and secure a world-class future of economic growth and real estate investment.

Notes

1. At this point, we need to get a grasp on just what constitutes "the urban elite" or "the downtown establishment" in most American cities and what, if anything, unifies this coalition of urban elites into a coherent force in the tumultuous world of big-city politics. In my analysis, "the downtown establishment" refers to a particular kind of urban political alliance between, on the one hand, downtown property owners and their financial backers and, on the other, local political leaders committed to a policy of "urban growth" in which economic and population growth translates into rising property values and increased city tax revenues. According to urban scholars John Logan and Harvey Molotch, local politics derives much of its passion and heat from a fundamental cleavage between the "use" and "exchange" values built into the urban environment (2). For Logan and Molotch, the sharpest conflicts in urban politics typically pit citizens who *use* urban space to satisfy the essential needs of life (e.g., home, work, and leisure) against entrepreneurs and investors who view urban places primarily as vehicles for profit and *exchange*. On one side of this cleavage stands an elite community of "place entrepreneurs"—that is, a downtown establishment of developers, real estate bankers, landowners, and so on—who work collectively to create conditions conducive to steady increases in "exchange" or property values (29-31). This relentless search for increased property values, increased rents, and more lucrative uses of space, however, often throws such "place entrepreneurs" afoul of average citizens and residents, who are typically the first people affected by the massive urban renewal and growth plans hatched in downtown boardrooms and back rooms. As a result, when the "use values" residents derive from their neighborhoods and green spaces are threatened by the plans of developers and investors (Logan and Molotch's "place entrepreneurs"), average citizens can

mobilize around their collective interest in preserving the specific amenities built into their neighborhoods and cities (215). This view of urban politics as a struggle between *use* and *exchange* orients our attention on the process of coalition formation within the arena of local politics and the tendency for groups to organize around their shared interest in promoting some land uses over others. In this struggle between use and exchange values, the coin of the realm is urban *growth*. As Logan and Molotch argue, landowners and developers looking to generate real estate profits share with each other an inherent interest in promoting population and economic *growth* in the locality. For landowners, more people, more industry, more development and construction intensifies the use of and demand for urban space, with the desired effect of driving up property values and aggregate rents. As a result, landowners, developers, real estate investors, and local civic officials—who all stand to benefit from citywide increases in property values— typically mobilize collectively and aggressively promote policies designed to attract and retain urban population and economic growth—at whatever cost. Urban growth is therefore a fundamental principle that unifies a city's property and policy establishment. As Logan and Molotch write, "for those who count, *the city is a growth machine*, one that can increase aggregate rents and trap related wealth for those in the right position to benefit" (50). As a result, in most U.S. cities, the downtown establishment organizes itself into a semicoherent and politically formidable pro-growth coalition, built around an interlocking network of civic and business organizations and fueled primarily by the goal of extracting more value from the ownership of urban space. Well-connected and well-funded, such coalitions attempt to use the levers of private and public authority to secure the conditions necessary for population and economic growth while at the same time marginalizing alternative visions of the purpose of local government or the meaning of urban vitality beyond that of civic boosterism and a consensus around growth. See John Logan and Harvey Molotch, *Urban Fortunes: Toward a Political Economy of Place* (Berkeley, CA: University of California Press, 1987).

2. Carl Abbot, *The Metropolitan Frontier: Cities in the Modern American West* (Tucson, AZ: University of Arizona Press, 1993), 9-11.

3. Labor Market Economic Analysis Branch, "Economic History: King County," *County Profiles* (Olympia, WA: Washington State Economic Security Department), 12.

4. John Findlay, "The Off-center Seattle Center: Downtown Seattle and the 1962 World's Fair," *Pacific Northwest Quarterly* 80 (January 1989): 2-11.

5. Findaly, "The Off-center Seattle Center," 5.

6. Labor Market Economic Analysis Branch, *Washington State Labor Area Summary, November 1998* (Olympia, WA: Washington State Economic Security Department), 12.

7. "Seattle in Transition: 1965: Growth in the Air," *Seattle Post-Intelligencer,* 25 January 1976, 10(A).

8. Labor Market Economic Analysis Branch, *Washington State Labor Area Summary, November 1998*, 12.

9. Eric Lucas, "Plane Facts about Boeing," in *Insight Guides: Seattle*, ed. John Wilcock (Boston: Houghton Mifflin Company, 1993), 85.

10. See William J. Wilson, *When Work Disappears: The World of the New Urban Poor* (New York: Knopf, 1995). Dennis Judd and Todd Swanstrom, *City Politics: Private Power and Public Policy* (New York: HarperCollins, 1994).

11. Robert Reich, *The Work of Nations* (New York: Basic Books, 1991), 90. See also Judd and Swanstrom, *City Politics*, 341-2.

12. As Bluestone and Harrison note, not all the job losses experienced during the 1970s can be blamed on relocation. Sometimes firms rationalized their operations, shutting down some plants and concentrating production in other, existing facilities. Other times, firms sought to protect profits accumulated during the high times of American Fordism by pulling investment out of their manufacturing divisions and investing these profits in other financial arenas with higher rates of return. In many cases, firms simply went bankrupt and shut their doors. Taken together, Bluestone and Harrison rank relocation of manufacturing to low-wage, antiunion regions of the globe as capital's strategy-of-second-resort during the crisis of 1973, behind only the shift of investment from manufacturing to other financial investments. See Bluestone and Harrison, *The Deindustrialization of America: Plant Closings, Community Abandonment, and the Dismantling of Basic Industry* (New York: Basic Books, 1981), 164.

13. William J. Wilson, *When Work Disappears*, 29.

14. Bluestone and Harrison, 32.

15. William J. Wilson, *When Work Disappears*; Judd and Swanstrom, *City Politics*, 377.

16. As Wilson writes, the job losses in manufacturing were offset in many U.S. cities by large gains in "knowledge-intensive" services (what Saskia Sassen calls "producer services"). Between 1953 and 1984, for example, New York City lost 600,000 manufacturing jobs but added 700,000 white-collar jobs, while in Philadelphia, a loss of 280,000 manufacturing jobs was nearly matched by a gain of 178,000 white collar jobs. But, as Wilson concludes, these employment gains have occurred in occupations with education requirements beyond the reach of most working-class workers. This mismatch between new jobs and the education of inner-city workers is especially pronounced among African-American and Latino workers, Wilson argues. Whereas a plurality of central city white men have attended at least some college, the modal category among central city black men is less than high school for all regions of the nation (except the West Coast). See William J. Wilson, *The Truly Disadvantaged: The Inner City, the Underclass, and Public Policy* (Chicago: University of Chicago Press), 102.

17. Judd and Swanstrom, *City Politics*, 377.

18. Wilson, *When Work Disappears*, 11.

19. Wilson, *When Work Disappears*, 11-12.

20. David Harvey, "Flexible Accumulation through Urbanization: Reflections on 'Postmodernism' in the American City," in *Post-Fordism: A Reader*, ed. A. Amin (Oxford, UK: Blackwell, 1994), 360.

21. These cuts were most keenly felt in the cities in the "rust belt." For instance, direct federal aid to Chicago (in the form of housing and antipoverty program grants) fell from $472 million in 1981 to $151 million in 1986, while Baltimore's grant volume fell from $220 million to $124 million, and grants to Detroit fell from $456 million to $151 million. See Judd and Swanstrom, *City Politics*, 321.

22. Judd and Swanstrom, *City Politics*, 330.

23. Judd and Swanstrom, 331. As William J. Wilson explains, in the decade between 1970 and 1980 the poverty population in the five largest cities in the United States (New York, L.A., Chicago, Philadelphia, and Detroit) increased by 22 percent even when the total population in these cities *decreased* by 9 percent. In another cruel

twist, as Wilson notes, the loss of manufacturing jobs and cutbacks in urban aid programs affected African-American and Latino populations most severely, since these groups were disproportionately represented in manufacturing industries and live in disproportionate numbers in urban areas. For more details, see Wilson, *The Truly Disadvantaged* (Chicago: University of Chicago Press, 1987), 45-46.

24. Todd Swanstrom, "Urban Populism, Uneven Development, and the Space for Reform," in *Business Elites and Urban Development: Case Studies and Critical Perspectives*, ed. S. Cummings (Albany, NY: SUNY Press, 1988).

25. Neil Smith, *The New Urban Frontier: Gentrification and the Revanchist City* (London: Routledge, 1996), 84-86.

26. Judd and Swanstrom, *City Politics*, 317.

27. Neil Smith, *The New Urban Frontier*, 84-86. David Harvey, *The Urbanization of Capital* (Baltimore: Johns Hopkins University Press, 1985), 65-6.

28. Marshall Berman, *All That is Solid Melts into Air: The Experience of Modernity* (New York: Penguin, 1982), 98.

29. Berman actually terms it "innovative self-destruction," but I prefer "creative destruction," a term coined by Joseph Schumpeter and picked up by Sharon Zukin and David Harvey.

30. Judd and Swanstrom, *City Politics,* 345. The statistics William J. Wilson cites for other cities show a similar pattern. Between 1953 and 1984, for example, Baltimore lost 75,000 manufacturing jobs but added 81,000 white-collar jobs. St. Louis lost 127,000 manufacturing jobs while adding 51,000 white-collar service jobs, and Philadelphia lost 280,000 jobs in manufacturing while adding 178,000 white-collar jobs. See *The Truly Disadvantaged,,* 102.

31. Judd and Swanstrom, 343.

32. Robert Reich, *The Work of Nations*, 90.

33. Saskia Sassen, *The Global City: New York, London, Tokyo* (Princeton, NJ: Princeton University Press), 29. See also Robert Reich, *The Work of Nations,* 90.

34. Reich, *The Work of Nations*, 90.

35. Reich, 93.

36. Reich, 112.

37. Sassen, *The Global City*, 11.

38. There are a number of reasons why such "producer services" are not conducted in-house. First, these services—including accounting, legal services, planning, investment, and marketing—require a level of expertise often unavailable in-house. Also, the "outsourcing" of such specialized services also has the advantage of reducing costs during an economic downturn. As Reich argues, when a multinational firm encounters financial difficulties or when it discontinues a specific service or product, it can simply cancel its contracts with such freestanding "business service" firms, saving money on overhead, benefits, and severance pay. See Reich, *The Work of Nations*, 95.

39. Sassen, *The Global City*, 11.

40. Saskia Sassen, "Economic Restructuring and the American City," *Annual Review of Sociology* 16 (1990): 470-71.

41. Saskia Sassen, "Economic Restructuring and the American City," 470-71. Between 1977 and 1985, national employment in Japan increased by 5 percent, but employment in finance, insurance, and real estate (FIRE) grew by 27 percent. In the U.K.,

total employment increased by 5 percent between 1977 and 1985, but FIRE employment grew by a robust 44 percent.

42. Sassen, *The Global City*, 104-5.

43. Sassen, *The Global City*, 104-5.

44. Sassen, 11. For a description of how smaller service and manufacturing firms can coordinate around specific, short-term projects (under the auspices of a multinational client), see Robert Reich, *The Work of Nations*, 90.

45. Examples of such collaboration include, for instance, a partnership between accounting and law firms with expertise on international tax regulations, or a close coordination between media production companies and global marketing firms on multinational advertising campaigns.

46. Sassen, *The Global City*, 105.

47. Sassen, *The Global City*, 105.

48. Reich, *The Work of Nations*, 197. As Reich explains, the income of the richest fifth of American families—which includes in his estimation the symbolic analysts who provide important services for coordinating global production and marketing strategies—rose 15 percent between 1977 and 1990. During the same years, the poorest fifth (which for Reich includes many of those employed in routine production and low-skill services) saw their income *drop* by about 7 percent.

49. Kathryn Larin and Elizabeth McNichol, *Pulling Apart: A State-by-State Analysis of Income Trends* (Washington, DC: The Center on Budget and Policy Priorities), executive summary.

50. Judd and Swanstrom, *City Politics*, 345.

51. Judd and Swanstrom, *City Politics*, 345.

52. Judd and Swanstrom, *City Politics*, 345.

53. Margit Mayer, "Post-Fordist City Politics," in *Post-Fordism: A Reader*, ed. A. Amin (Oxford: Basil Blackwell, 1994), 331.

54. Jamie Peck and Adam Tickell, "Searching for a New Institutional Fix: The After-Fordist Crisis and the Global-Local Disorder," in *Post-Fordism: A Reader*, ed. A. Amin (Oxford: Basil Blackwell), 304.

55. Judd and Swanstrom, *City Politics*, 382.

56. For a summary of the various growth strategies pursued by urban elites, see David Harvey, *Consciousness and the Urban Experience* (Oxford: Basil Blackwell, 1985), 268, and John Logan and Harvey Molotch, *Urban Fortunes*, 258-77. See chapter three of Sharon Zukin, *The Cultures of Cities* (Oxford: Basil Blackwell, 1995) for a discussion of how cities try to refashion themselves as cultural destinations in order to compensate for an economy devastated by deindustrialization. For a discussion of how new forms of "high-tech" or specialized production have sparked economic growth in specific cities and regions around the world (e.g., Silicon Valley, the Route 128 corridor outside Boston, etc.), see Piore and Sabel's *The Second Industrial Divide*, and Robert Reich's *The Work of Nations*.

57. Logan and Molotch, *Urban Fortunes*, 59.

58. David Harvey, *The Condition of Postmodernity*, 295.

59. David Harvey, *The Condition of Postmodernity*, 295.

60. Sharon Zukin, *The Cultures of Cities*, 14.

61. Judd and Swanstrom, *City Politics*, 347. See also Sharon Zukin, *The Cultures of Cities*, 2; David Harvey, *The Condition*, 295-96.

62. Margaret Crawford, "The World in a Shopping Mall," in *Variations on a Theme Park: The New American City and the End of Public Space*, ed. M. Sorkin (New York: Noonday Press, 1992), 17.

63. David Harvey, *The Condition of Postmodernity*.

64. Mike Davis, *City of Quartz: Excavating the Future in Los Angeles* (London: Verso, 1990), 71.

65. Mike Davis, *City of Quartz*, 74-75.

66. Mike Davis, *City of Quartz*, 71.

Part II

Building the Spectacular City

Chapter 3

Seattle Elites and the Downtown Crisis

Coming out of the crisis of the 1970s, Seattle's civic leaders, like those in other cities discussed last chapter, set themselves the task of building a global city—that is, a command and control center for trade and investment in the emerging global economy. Symbolized most dramatically by the skyscrapers that seemed to sprout like weeds after 1980, Seattle's emerging status as an important node of international trade also bore less obvious fruit—including an influx of white-collar producer services and a deepening division between rich and poor. Still, as the end of the 1980s approached, with a glittering financial district, a steady rise in white-collar employment, and strong trade ties to the expanding Pacific Rim, Seattle's world-class economic future seemed assured.

But by 1990, the wild real estate speculation that greatly fueled the 1980s skyscraper boom had come to a crashing end, dragging a number of the city's most celebrated developers into bankruptcy and ruin. The torpor of a new recession, first germinated in New England and the Northeast, quickly metastasized and spread across the nation, infecting Northwest retail by 1992. This recession would quickly force two of downtown Seattle's major department stores, including the historic Frederick & Nelson store, to shut their doors and board their windows. By 1993, the downtown business community was in full panic mode. Unable to do anything about a nationwide recession, agitated business leaders cast about for someone to blame, and, not surprisingly, found a host of scapegoats—from an inactive city government to inflated parking fees to the so-called homeless problem on downtown sidewalks. During these months, the pages of Seattle's two major dailies rang with calls for city government to "do something" about the state of downtown.

For a time, then, it seemed that Seattle's burgeoning world-class future—rebuilt so laboriously in the years following the crisis of American Fordism—was slipping away. In this chapter, we begin with a discussion of how city leaders, working in the shadow of the Boeing Bust of 1970, embarked upon a long-term project to transform Seattle from a provincial, two-horse, timber and airplane town into a world-class center of Pacific Rim trade and technological innovation. The discussion will then detail how city officials and boosters began, during the recession of the early 1990s, to once again entertain fears that downtown Seattle might spiral into a future of rust belt–style urban decay. In the end, we will discover how, for a while in the early 1990s at least, it seemed like elite dreams of a world-class Seattle, nurtured through the lean years after the Boeing Bust, were slipping away amidst a slumping retail core and a spectacular real estate collapse.

After the Boeing Bust: Rebuilding Seattle's Global City Dreams

As we learned in the last chapter, the Boeing Bust of 1970 threw elite plans of building Seattle into a world-class city into disarray. When stagnant profits and cuts in defense expenditures forced Boeing to cut its Seattle workforce by nearly 60,000 jobs, the regional economy spiraled into a profound recession.[1] Seattle's central city population also took a hit during these years, partially reversing what had been almost a century of steady, and sometimes exponential growth.[2] The signs of urban decline began to proliferate as well. Violent crime, long associated with more urban centers "back East," began to grow at rates that alarmed city leaders and neighborhood residents alike. During this decade, for example, manslaughter and murder arrests doubled while sexual assaults quadrupled. Overall, serious crimes increased dramatically from 22,639 reported crimes in 1964 to 48,870 crimes in 1974.[3]

To make matters worse for civic leaders, the periodic explosion of political dissent during the heart of the Vietnam War proved that Seattle would not be spared the social unrest flaring up elsewhere around the nation. In May of 1970, for example, student demonstrators at the University of Washington staged a series of rallies in response to the killing of four antiwar protesters at Kent State University. For three days, thousands of students marched between the University district to downtown and back again. After the first day of protests, which had been remarkably nonviolent with the exception of a few smashed windows, the city police decided to force the issue. On the second day of marches, the police descended upon the protesters in what a young Norm Rice, then a KOMO-TV reporter, called an "orgy of unmitigated violence."[4] For two more days, bloody clashes between protesters and police raged on city streets, to the horror of Seattle's downtown establishment.[5]

Perhaps most disturbing to downtown property elites, however, were the stagnant retail and office markets of the early 1970s. Facing intense competition from outlying shopping malls, total retail sales in downtown Seattle dropped 14 percent from a high of $234 million in 1967 to just over $200 million five years later.[6] As the *Post-Intelligencer* (*P-I*) reported, when adjusted for inflation, the slippage in downtown retail sales amounted to a stunning 28 percent, compared to an overall *gain* of 12 percent for the metropolitan area as a whole.[7] The office market performed slightly better than did retail during this time, with the construction of a dozen major buildings in the financial core adding over 3 million square feet of office space from 1968 and 1976.[8] However, in the early 1970s, elites began to acknowledge that talk of transforming downtown Seattle into a first-tier headquarters for national firms (on the scale of San Francisco or Chicago) was quite premature, because the primary users of new office space continued to be expanding local banks, manufacturers, and traders.[9] By 1976, downtown developers conceded that big dreams of downtown redevelopment and further office construction in downtown Seattle would have to wait for the economic crisis to settle down. "For the immediate future," as one developer told the *P-I*, "the problem will be filling up the older buildings."[10]

A sense of decline and stagnation so permeated elite circles in Seattle that, during the first two months of 1976, the *Seattle Post-Intelligencer* ran a series of features which asked "What Will Seattle Be Like in 1985?" Will Seattle, as the editors wrote in the series' inaugural article, "still be one of America's most livable cities, an inviting place to play and shop and raise children?" Or, "will Seattle become, in the horrific vision of the Rev. Peter Raible, 'a stinking cesspool surrounded by delightful suburbs?' Will Seattle follow the downward course of many other major cities and become a place of decaying schools and housing, a place to work by day and flee by night?"[11] To dramatize this contrast, the *P-I* offered two opposing and fictional visions of Seattle's future. In one lovely scene, the narrator depicted a young suburban family moving to a Denny Regrade condo and sampling the joys of a vibrant urban life—the symphony, the upscale retail, and the short walk to work. The opposing futuristic narrative offered, of course, a more frightening vision of the future, where a series of fictional news briefs chronicled a stagnant economy, exploding crime, accelerating middle-class suburbanization, and an expanding urban trade in home security systems.[12]

As a result, beginning in the late 1960s, Seattle's civic and business establishment—an interlocked coalition of pro-growth public officials, civic leaders in booster organizations like the Downtown Seattle Association (DSA), and individual downtown property developers and financiers—set itself to the twin tasks of preventing a slide into full-blown urban decay and rebuilding the elite dreams of the 1962 World's Fair.[13] Coming out of the Boeing Bust, this public/private drive to recreate Seattle as a world-class node of trade, tourism, and investment has been waged on two broad fronts: (1) the drive to diversify the regional economy, and (2) the drive to re-shape downtown into a rich hosting environment for corporate headquarters and high-end professional services.

In the first instance, after the Boeing Bust, civic leaders began to focus on the goal of economic diversification. To this end, faced with the blunt consequences of a reliance on only one or two economic sectors, Seattle's city officials and civic booster organizations like the Greater Seattle Chamber of Commerce, the Economic Development Council of Seattle-King County, and the Trade Development Alliance of Greater Seattle began to promote a vision of a diversified regional economy, where strong national and international trade ties, a robust business service sector, and an emerging base in "high technol-

ogy" (as it would soon be known) would wean Seattle and its neighbors off
their dependence on Mama Boeing and Papa Timber.

First in line in this effort was the Port of Seattle and the project of strengthening national and international trade routes. Beginning in the 1960s, a new
cadre of growth-oriented port commissioners spent more than $100 million in
public money to modernize marine terminals and the waterfront land under its
control in order to compete directly with such oceanic trade giants as Oakland
and Los Angeles.[14] In particular, the Port Commission gambled on developing
long-distance container trade with Asia, in which Seattle would form the key
link between Japan and the American East Coast. The gamble paid off
beginning in 1970, when six Japanese shipping lines made Seattle their first
point of call in the United States, cementing Seattle's place as a crucial node in
Pacific Rim marine trade.[15] By the late 1980s, the State of Washington had
become the most trade-dependent state in the nation, with imports flowing
through the Port and exports nearly tripling between 1987 and 1992.[16]

Also crucial to the city's world-class dreams, as urban historian Carl Abbott writes, was the transformation of the University of Washington (UW), located just north of downtown, from a provincial teaching institution into a leading center of medical and technological research. Like many state universities,
enrollment at the UW doubled between 1956 and 1968, fueled in part by the
baby boom and the GI bill. But, more importantly, during the 1960s and 1970s
a succession of activist university presidents encouraged UW faculty members
to claim a disproportionate share of the growing pie of federal medical and defense research funds. By 1977, the UW research frenzy gobbled up so many
federal grants that Seattle, really a one-university town, placed eighth among
all American metropolitan areas in its ability to secure federal research funds
given to universities. With this kind of R&D money floating around its rainy
streets, Seattle became a magnet for high-tech institutes and firms looking to
locate in places where technological talent and federal money can come together.[17] In the end, the concentration of brain power in the region laid the
foundation for a bustling industry in biotechnology (drawing on the University
of Washington School of Medicine, the Seattle Biomedical Research Institute,
and the Fred Hutchinson Cancer Research Center) and software development
(centered around Microsoft, the 500-pound gorilla of the software industry). By
the year 2000, the Economic Development Council could boast that 1,100 high
technology companies employed over 80,000 workers in King County, with
Microsoft commanding the largest share of this industry (14,000 employees).[18]

But what of the effort to transform Seattle into more than an important port
of call or a center of high-tech innovation? In short, has Seattle indeed moved
up in the international urban hierarchy to become a crucial node of "command
and control" in the global assembly line? As Saskia Sassen notes, truly "global"
cities can secure a disproportionate share of world economic growth by becoming rich hosting environments for professional or "producer" services—that is,

those high-end services that leading corporations require to manage their trans-national empires. With this in mind, how has Seattle fared as a provider of producer services in the years following the Boeing Bust?

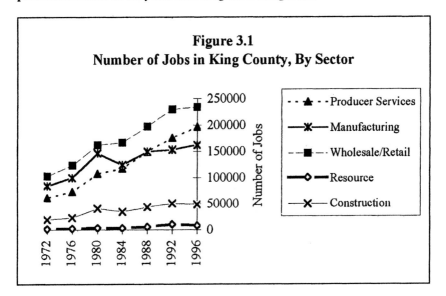

Figure 3.1
Number of Jobs in King County, By Sector

Following the procedure established by Sassen's analysis of producer services in New York, London, and Tokyo, I compiled U.S. Census data on employment in King County to discover the relative importance of producer services in Seattle's regional economy, in comparison to other economic sectors like manufacturing, retail/wholesale, and resource industries.[19] As Figure 3.1 documents above, most sectors added workers between 1972 and 1996, reflecting primarily the overall population and economic growth of King County over the years. During these years, total employment in King County more than doubled, from nearly 350,000 jobs in 1972 to nearly 900,000 in 1996. Still, some sectors experienced more robust growth than others. For example, while resource and construction jobs remained fairly flat over the years, wholesale/retail jobs more than doubled from just over 100,000 jobs in 1972 to over 230,000 in 1996. For its part, manufacturing experienced more volatility within this overall pattern of growth, losing over 20,000 jobs between 1980 and 1984 before tallying overall gain of over 75,000 jobs between 1972 and 1996. But, of all these sectors, *producer services* posted the most impressive gains, posting a threefold increase in just twenty-four years, from just over 60,000 jobs in 1972 to nearly 200,000 in 1996.

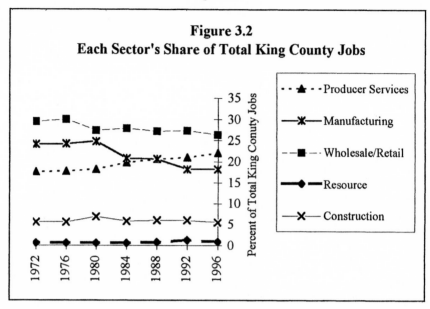

Figure 3.2

Each Sector's Share of Total King County Jobs

The growing importance of financial, real estate, insurance, and business services in the Seattle economy is perhaps best reflected by comparing the proportional share each sector commands in the total King County job picture. While most sectors held the line over the years, as figure 3.2 shows above, since the crisis of the early 1970s, there has been one highly significant changing-of-the-guard in Seattle's regional economy. Specifically, manufacturing, which in 1972 commanded a robust 24 percent of the total jobs in King County, has seen its share of the economy shrink steadily over the years to just over 18 percent in 1996. In contrast, producer services have increased their share steadily over the same period, from only 18 percent of total employment in 1972 to over 22 percent in 1996—a figure that compares favorably to Sassen's analysis of New York's robust "command and control" sector.[20]

This notable rise in producer service employment around King County cultivated a series of profound changes in Seattle's economic and social geography over the last three decades, seen most concretely in the proliferation of corporate headquarters, the unending container traffic at the Port, the rapid redevelopment of the downtown office core (the frenzied construction of which will occupy us below), and in the yawning gap between rich and poor on Seattle's streets. During the 1990s, for example, national and international giants like Boeing, Microsoft, Safeco Insurance, Weyerhaeuser (timber), Starbucks, Nordstrom, Amazon.com, AT&T Wireless, and Nintendo (North America) were all headquartered in Greater Seattle, making the region home to no less than eight Fortune 500 companies.[21] The international trade generated by these corporations, among others, has made Washington State a key node in the global flow of goods and services, with one in three jobs directly dependent on foreign commerce. As the Economic Development Council of Seattle-King County notes, while the state represents about 2 percent of the nation's population, the state's ports (chiefly Tacoma and Seattle) handle 7 percent of all U.S exports and 6 percent of the nation's imports.[22] The Herculean task of coordinating and controlling these sprawling corporate webs and the flow of goods and services through the region has therefore fallen in large part on the growing producer service sector, increasingly clustered in the office core of Seattle's downtown.

Seattle civic leaders have therefore managed to transform the regional economy into more than a port of call for timber exports and a center for aerospace manufacturing, as reflected in the growing prominence of producer services over the past three decades. But how has this transformation compared to other cities around the western United States? In short, how has this restructuring of the Seattle economy positioned the region in the national and international competition for footloose global investment? Recent comparative data is difficult to come by, but, in his book on the political economy of the U.S. West, Carl Abbott compared the "transactional" economies of fourteen major western cities between 1960 and 1990—that is, the relative importance of information industries and occupations in each city. Using an additive point system which measured each city's white-collar employment, employment in finance, insurance, real estate, and corporate administration, the proportion of all major corporate headquarters located in the region, and the region's role as a federal administrative center, Abbott found that, in 1990, Seattle ranked as the *fourth* most important "transactional economy" among western U.S. cities, just behind such giants as San Francisco, Dallas, and Los Angeles.[23]

Finally, in an effort to explore the importance of international ties and connections in the economies of western U.S. cities, Abbott devised a second additive point scale, this time measuring the number of foreign-born residents, the amount of foreign trade, the presence of foreign banks, the amount of foreign investment, the importance of foreign markets for local industries, and the city's role as a global information center. In this "global city" scale, Seattle ranked *fifth* among western U.S. cities, this time behind San Francisco, L.A., Houston, and Honolulu (with its close ties to Japan), but still ahead of larger cities like Dallas, Phoenix, and San Diego.[24] In short, the long effort to wean the regional economy off aerospace and resource industries, to transform Seattle into, as the Trade Development Alliance of Greater Seattle proclaims, "a truly global center of technology, transportation, and trade," appeared by 1990 to be largely a success. Container traffic from the Pacific Rim piled up in increasing numbers on the industrial banks of Elliot Bay. A heady combination of federal research money and UW research acumen had positioned Seattle well in the competition to attract industries and institutes dedicated to new computer and wireless technologies. Finally, slow rates of growth in resource and manufacturing industries were at least partially offset during these years by a more robust trade in white-collar producer services. And, if the economic transformations of the past thirty years had produced as many low-wage jobs in retail and wholesale as more glamorous work in new technologies or high finance, this was easy for civic boosters to ignore during the late 1980s, as white-collar workers packed themselves into a host of glittering new downtown office towers.

By 1990, then, compared to other cities around the United States, Seattle had emerged from over two decades of national and international economic crisis in relatively good shape. Unlike other cities still dealing with the wreckage of massive deindustrialization, Seattle seemed to have survived the worst of economic restructuring following the disastrous Boeing Bust of the early 1970s. With an expanding economy, a massive downtown office building spree, and a growing population, Seattle began to attract national attention as a new and refreshing contradiction: a livable American city. During the late 1980s and early 1990s, a spate of laudatory articles appeared in the pages of the national press, with upscale magazines like *Esquire* and *The Atlantic* celebrating Seattle's sophisticated cultural milieu and stunning natural setting in glowing urban profiles with titles like "The Last Livable City" and "A City that Likes Itself." For Seattle elites who remembered the dark days of the Boeing crash of the early 1970s, this was heady stuff indeed. The world-class or global dreams of city officials and boosters seemed to be within reach.[25]

From Boom to Bust in the Seattle Skyline

If the unglamorous work of developing a diversified economic foundation was arguably the most important achievement of elite Seattle's drive to re-build its world-class dreams, perhaps the most tangible symbol of the city's global city aspirations during the 1980s was the gleaming new Central Business District. Beginning in the mid-1980s, a volatile combination of excess investment capital, an expanding demand for downtown office space, and a healthy dose of competitive ego helped fuel an unprecedented office tower frenzy in Seattle's financial core. To put the construction bonanza in perspective, in the first 128 years of the city's existence, between 1851 (when the first white settlers waddled up the muddy shores of Elliot Bay) and 1979, Seattle's developers built just over 13 million square feet of office space downtown. In just one decade, the 1980s redevelopment frenzy would more than double this number, adding nearly 15 million square feet of office space to Seattle's downtown.[26]

But what fueled this office boom during the 1980s? And why did it soon collapse? On the demand side, the office boom in Seattle responded to the more fundamental changes in the regional economy noted above. As Seattle emerged as a node of international trade, the local economy, led by the increasing number of Fortune 500 corporations headquartered in the Emerald City, began to generate thousands of white-collar jobs, including the marketing, accounting, finance, real estate, and management services necessary to the smooth functioning of global capitalism. Charged with the task of administrating the flow of goods, services, and capital through the region, thousands of white-collar workers poured into downtown, fueling a spate of office construction unprecedented in Seattle's history.[27]

On the supply side, *Times* journalist Terry McDermott writes that the office boom in Seattle was also sparked by an explosive mix of Japanese capital and good old-fashioned American ego.[28] Interestingly, before the late 1970s, both ego and money were in relatively short supply in Seattle's downtown development community. While there was much talk during the late 1950s and 1960s of building the "city of tomorrow," in actuality downtown developers operated in a small market whose needs did not change quickly. In fact, as Unico president Don Covey told McDermott, before the late 1970s, Seattle was a strictly "build to suit" market, where developers would not speculate on building office space unless their already-established tenants requested it. As a result, Seattle's skyline changed at a glacial pace, expanding only to suit the evolving needs of regional players like Seafirst Bank, IBM, and the federal government.[29]

This all changed beginning with a single event in 1983—the opening of developer Martin Selig's massive, black glass-encased, seventy-six story Columbia Center. By itself, the Columbia Center added 1.4 million square feet of office space to Seattle's downtown, a figure that exceeded all of the office space built in Seattle during the decade of the 1960s.[30] As McDermott writes, the sheer scale of this project—at the time the largest building west of Chicago's loop—"so enraged the guardians of the local public weal that even before it went up they initiated an extraordinary effort to ensure nothing like it would ever happen again."[31] The culmination of these protests and efforts, led by then-Mayor Charles Royer (a one-time populist turned "pragmatist"), was the so-called 1985 Downtown Plan, a series of changes to the city's zoning codes which would make it more difficult to build such enormous buildings in the heart of downtown.

However, for a variety of reasons, the city's intervention had just the opposite effect. Instead of stopping the construction of future office behemoths, the 1985 Plan virtually assured that Seattle's developers would rush to build a series of new "trophy" skyscrapers in Seattle's once-sleepy financial district. As McDermott writes, during the early 1980s, while Selig worked to secure tenants and financing for his Columbia Center, other developers in Seattle, including Unico, Prescott, and Wright Runstad, also had big plans for building their own high-profile downtown office towers. The problem was that Selig beat them to the punch, broke ground, and built his tower while the others were still showing miniature models to potential investors. Once the Columbia Center was built, the rest of Seattle's development community could do nothing but curse

Selig's name and impatiently wait for the market to absorb the impact of his massive tower—that is, for vacancy rates to fall enough to justify the addition of more premium downtown space.[32]

But, as McDermott writes, the passage of the city's restrictive 1985 Plan, which would cut back on the allowable size and scale of their signature projects, forced the developers' hands. In real estate development, size matters. The cost of buying a specific downtown lot is a fixed, one-time-only investment. But if you can increase the density of use on that lot—in short, if you can build forty-five stories of office space instead of twenty-five—you can earn more rent and therefore more long-term profit on your investment, at least enough to make the extra costs of building a massive tower worthwhile. And there was no way, in short, that these developers were going to see their investments and high-rise dreams die on the vine just because Martin Selig's Columbia Center had aroused the antiskyscraper fury of "Joe Six Pack" and "Jane Tree Hugger." Luckily for these developers, the city's 1985 Plan contained a loophole: if you began to plan your project before the new zoning codes were passed, you could get permission to build your trophy high-rise. Therefore, in order to protect the investments they had already made in their large-scale projects, each of these developers applied for and, for some reason, received exemptions to the 1985 Plan, with the proviso that they finish construction within a short period of time. No problem, the developers told the city, and the race to match Selig's Columbia Tower with a host of new signature office towers was off and running.[33]

If a combination of ego and financial self-interest spurred developers to rush their projects from the drawing board to the construction site, it was the easy availability of finance capital—particularly foreign capital—which pushed these towers into the sky. As David Harvey writes, the rush of capital into Seattle's real estate market just prior to the recession of the early 1990s repeated a long pattern in the history of capitalist development. Immediately prior to a recession—even before anyone really knows the party is over—investors search for new opportunities to secure a healthy rate of return. With production growing more and more slowly, investors collectively begin to throw their money at real estate projects, hoping that profits unavailable in other sectors will magically appear in the latest office park or skyrise. All this money has the temporary effect of boosting property markets, which further fuels the speculative frenzy. But, in the end, the larger economic crisis almost always undermines property markets as well (as firms lay off workers and close out office space), sending investors' portfolios into a final and spectacular nosedive.[34]

In Seattle's case, the flood of capital into downtown property markets had two major sources—massive private pension funds and surplus capital from Japan. As far back as 1971, pension funds were stodgy, conservative investors, unwilling to risk their funds in volatile, if potentially lucrative, real estate markets. As Seattle developer Dick Clotfelter told the *Times'* McDermott, selling pension funds on downtown office projects at that time was tough. "Most of the people we were trying to sell knew nothing about real estate. They were stock analysts. That was their idea of investment. All they knew about real estate was buying a house. And in New York, not even that. Maybe buying a condominium."[35] This slowly began to change during the crisis of the early 1970s, as the return on other investments (particularly those in manufacturing) sank below the inflation rate. By the late 1980s, in fact, some pension funds began to invest fully a fifth of their portfolios in real estate, a significant infusion of capital given the size of these funds.[36]

Japanese investment formed the second large pool of surplus capital in American real estate at the time. The yawning trade surpluses Japan enjoyed with the United States during the 1980s poured billions of U.S. dollars into the island nation, mostly in the form of profits from exports and wages earned by Japanese workers. Furthermore, because Japanese workers were so eager to save, banks could offer very low interest rates and still attract depositors. The result was a huge surplus of capital in Japanese banks, and since interest rates in Japan were so much lower than rates of return in foreign nations, most Japanese banks sought to invest their surplus funds in overseas markets. As Jack Shaffer, managing director of the real estate investment firm which financed one of Seattle's newest high-rises, told the *Times*, the Japanese "had a lot of capital looking for a lot of places to go. There's not a lot of deals there and yields are very low."[37]

Beginning in the early 1984, Japanese capital began to pour into a great many U.S. real estate markets, completely revamping the landscape of cities like Los Angeles, where Japan's financial swashbucklers bought up nearly a third of L.A.'s new financial district. In a single stunning two-month period, for example, Tokyo's Shuwa Company Ltd. purchased nearly $1 billion of downtown L.A.'s skyline, including the twin-towered Arco Plaza, one of California's most notable properties.[38] But if California saw the lion's share of this kind of overseas investment, a good portion of Japan's surplus also found its way northward to Seattle's downtown. As Lincoln Ferris, a PR man hired by several downtown developers, told the *Times*, "institutional . . . and Japanese investors are shopping the market here quite aggressively."[39] In fact, as the *Times* noted, Washington State ranked fifth among the U.S. states most favored by Japanese real estate investors in a 1989 survey, and the Seattle metropolitan area ranked ninth out of forty-one metro areas receiving votes.[40]

This volatile mix of surplus capital and developer ego sparked an unprecedented rush of office tower construction, adding another 9.4 million square feet of office space in a market still reeling from the arrival of the Columbia Center. In fact, just two years, from 1987 to 1989, four massive projects opened for business in downtown Seattle, including Prescott's Pacific First Center (44 stories), Unico's Two Union Square (56 stories), Wright Runstad's Washington Mutual Tower (55 stories of gleaming blue glass), and, finally, Herman

Sarkowsky's Gateway Tower (62 stories). By 1990, the race to beat the new restrictions of the 1985 Plan had utterly transformed the Seattle skyline, adding the equivalent of nearly six Columbia Towers to the downtown office market.[41]

Downtown property and business elites, of course, viewed the climbing skyline with a mixture of pride and awe. As Herb Bridge, a former president of the Downtown Seattle Association told a reporter from the *Times* in 1989, the glittering new crop of downtown office towers "symbolizes vitality, progress. I look at it and see beauty."[42] In this sense, as Seattle journalist Walter Hatch notes, the building boom of the late 1980s represented for Seattle elites the culmination of the dreams they nurtured through the dark days of the Boeing Bust. Far from symbolizing the ills of urban growth gone out of control, Seattle's new and imposing skyline was for business elites the most tangible evidence of the city's arrival as a global center of trade and finance, "a world-class city with all the right ingredients—professional ballclubs, sushi bars, espresso stands, a convention center, and skyscrapers."[43] To oppose the unfettered growth of the office core would be unthinkable, as Bridge told the *Times*. It would be no less than a rejection of progress, a rejection of the spirit of 1962 (embodied, one would suppose, in the now-kitschy visage of the Space Needle). "We can't go backward," he said. "We have to keep moving forward."[44]

Of course, just as Herb Bridge was expounding on the limitless future represented by Seattle's gleaming new skyline, the bubble was about to burst. In fact, the construction of Sarkowsky's Gateway Tower was the point at which Seattle's real estate sector turned sour. Between 1989, the year the Gateway opened, and 1998, the downtown office market sunk into a long and deep recession, with only one office project of any significance breaking ground during these years. Like all property busts, the source of the crash could be located in the fickle churnings of supply and demand. By 1990, it was clear to all that Seattle's office market had been woefully overbuilt and that downtown was now flooded with acres of premium space. Downtown vacancy rates, which began the 1980s in the 5 percent range, steadily climbed as each new office monolith shot up in the air, ending the decade at nearly 20 percent with the opening of Sarkowsky's Gateway Tower.

High vacancy rates, in turn, sparked a dog-eat-dog competition for tenants across the downtown office landscape. With many of the newest buildings still half-empty by the early 1990s, developers turned on one another in a desperate free-for-all to attract tenants at virtually any price. It was the best renter's market in Seattle history, with major tenants playing landlords off each other like a superstar athlete looking for the best free agent deal. For example, Unico offered the Bogle & Gates law firm a huge "signing bonus" and fifteen years of free parking in order to lure them away from Sarkowksy's Gateway Tower and into Two Union Square.[45] In other instances, developers lured tenants away from competitors with promises of free rent for the first few months and complementary renovations to suit their particular needs and desires. When freebies and giveaways failed to beat the competition, some developers relied on another tried-and-true business tactic: the vicious rumor. As McDermott writes, perhaps the best rumor making the rounds during this time was that a certain downtown building was having serious granite problems:

> The South American stone being used wasn't breaking or anything and it wasn't going to fall on anybody. It was simply going to cause cancer. The rock was said to have been impregnated with some weird gamma ray of something. Nobody knew how, but they delighted in repeating it.[46]

Such vicious rumormongering, though, was the exception rather than the rule. More often, developers sought to attract tenants through a more traditional means and simply slashed rents across the board. Overall, by 1990, according to Tim O'Keefe of Coldwell Banker, rents were at $3 to $5 (per square foot) below what was needed to keep developers afloat in a sea of overextended debt.[47] In the end, however, the massive rush of office construction in the late 1980s had so saturated the market that there simply were not enough tenants to go around. As O'Keefe told the *Times* in 1990, "we have reached the bottom of the barrel for major tenants. There has been a steady influx of smaller companies entering the [downtown] market, but it takes a while to chip away at vacancy rates." In the interim, he said, "all landlords are having a tough time right now."[48]

Things only got worse in the early 1990s, when a national economic recession finally hit the Pacific Northwest. Facing shrinking profits, many of downtown Seattle's most notable firms began to "downsize," laying off employees and cutting back dramatically on office space. For example, in 1992, petroleum giant Chevron closed its Seattle office, leaving an entire floor of the Security Pacific Tower empty. For its part, AT&T, the high-profile tenant that helped Herman Sarkowsky build his Gateway Tower in 1989, decided in early 1992 to shrink its Seattle office space by half. Other companies, like Seattle-based Generra, simply filed for bankruptcy protection and went out of business, sacking more than 100 employees and moving out of over 60,000 square feet of downtown office space, the equivalent, according to the *Seattle Times*, of three highrise floors.[49] All in all, during the heart of the recession, more tenants were moving out of downtown than into it.[50] With downtown office vacancy rates pushed up to historic levels, and with rents dropping well below the waterline, many developers were left with empty buildings, outstanding loans, and highly agitated creditors.

For those outside this insular community of downtown Seattle developers, the scale of this downtown office bust is difficult to grasp. But for developers, even those who managed to keep their heads above water during these lean years, the memories of the "bad old days" of the early 1990s percolate just below the surface, threatening to flare up like the real estate equivalent of a bad acid flashback. As one property owner confided in an interview:

> We survived! All around us, people didn't, and we survived. . . . Fifty or sixty buildings went into foreclosure at one point or another around here. . . . All the major trophy high-rises . . . all changed hands, most of them quietly. But, I'll tell you, a lot of people lost houses and stuff like that, and vacation houses. And a lot of their network, or all their network.[51]

The stories about developers who to failed survive this crash have thus achieved mythic status within Seattle's business establishment. And the unhappy fate of Dick Clotfelter and Gary Carpenter, two of Seattle's most well-known real estate tycoons and co-developers of Pacific First Center, is perhaps the most cited example of what can happen when boom times go bust.[52]

In the early 1980s, at the same time that they were developing Pacific First Center, Clotfelter and Carpenter were also buying up most of a much-neglected stretch of downtown—Third Avenue, between Pike Street and Union Street—in order to build an ambitious thirty-five story office/theater complex, featuring two levels of retail and a brand new performance hall for Seattle's A Contemporary Theater (ACT). That Clotfelter and Carpenter would embark on such an ambitious project was not surprising: they were, according to the *Seattle Times*, well-regarded within the community of developers. After they completed their Pacific Center in 1989, for example, they soon won recognition as having built "the Office Building of the Year" in a national building-owners trade journal.[53] The partners, like most players downtown, had also devoted their time to a variety of high-profile civic and business associations, including the omnipresent Downtown Seattle Association, the Pacific Science Center, and the Bush School, an expensive private school which has spawned many of Seattle's gilded class.[54] In short, Clotfelter and Carpenter seemed well-positioned to pull off one of the larger redevelopment projects of the heady 1980s.

So what went wrong? As *Seattle Times* reporter Michelle Flores notes, bad timing was partly to blame. "Just like the stock-broker who buys before a crash," she writes, Clotfelter and Carpenter and their ACT project took on heavy debt—and therefore heavy risks—just before the Seattle real estate market imploded in the late 1980s. In 1985, Clotfelter and Carpenter borrowed $12 million from First Interstate Bank on a short-term note to secure the site and to begin planning for the project.[55] Such a gambit is pro forma among developers. In the early (and risky) stages of a large project, investors typically lend money on a short-term basis, with the intention of renegotiating the loan on longer and more favorable terms for the developer once construction starts.[56] But, to Clotfelter and Carpenter's dismay, by the time they secured the permit for the ACT project in 1988, their lender, First Interstate, gazed uneasily upon Seattle's bloated office market and summarily backed out of their promise to re-negotiate the terms of the loan. Instead, they simply called in the debt.

Desperate to find some way to refinance their debts, Clotfelter and Carpenter searched frantically for other investors willing to extend them a loan on longer and more favorable terms. Finding none, they began missing payments on the original $12 million, forcing First Interstate to foreclose on the ACT block. As Flores writes, "two years of negotiations between the developers and their lenders produced no resolution, and in 1990, Clotfelter and Carpenter put the partnership into Chapter 11 to keep the bank and other creditors [including architectural, engineering, and structural firms] at bay."[57] Once the site of such grand plans, the ACT block itself—a block which included the Glen Hotel, a deteriorating rooming house that would soon become embroiled in a bitter land-use dispute (the subject of chapter 7)—was simply splintered apart and sold off to creditors piece by piece at pennies on the dollar.

The personal financial fates suffered by Clotfelter and Carpenter were similarly grim. First Interstate, now looking to collect on $13 million in principal and interest, sold its claim for the money to a collection agent named Thomas Hazelrigg, a secretive Bellevue man "known to bankers and real estate attorneys for buying and collecting on such debts."[58] By 1992, Hazelrigg had obtained permission to seize most of Clotfelter and Carpenter's business assets from each of their nineteen partnerships (including Prescott Ltd.) and had even foreclosed on each of their sprawling waterfront homes.[59] At last report, Clotfelter and Carpenter had finally cleared themselves of liability for the ACT block and had retreated into that last refuge for developers put out to pasture—property management. All in all, the property gods had not been kind.

But, then again, the property gods were not kind to most developers in Seattle during the recession. In fact, many of the high-profile projects built in Seattle during the late 1980s quickly fell into deep financial straights. For example, Unico was forced to refinance its loan for One and Two Union Place (side-by-side high-rises) because one of its partners, Met Life Insurance, reportedly balked at Two Union Place's 45 percent vacancy rate and demanded to be bought out. Wright Runstad, facing a widening gap between rent income and debt payments, also reportedly sold off a portion its own interest in the Washington Mutual Tower in order to raise the money needed to stave off angry creditors. Finally, Martin Selig, the brash real estate tycoon who beat his competitors to the punch with his monolithic Columbia Center, fell into deep financial trouble in 1989 when New York Life sued him for $65 million in mortgage payments. After some initial wrangling, Selig was forced to sell the seventy-six story Columbia Center back to his major creditor, Seafirst Bank, for $354 million in order to pay off his debts.[60]

Seattle's downtown office core, once the most proud symbol of civic boosters' world-class dreams, was truly in a state of crisis by the early 1990s. While Seattle's high-profile developers and property managers sought to put a positive face on the situation, a hint of despair began to creep into their pronouncements to the press. As Martin Selig bravely told the *Times* in 1992, "It'll get healthy again. This is just a cycle in real estate. A bigger cycle than I ever dreamed of, but just a cycle."[61]

This office bust, however, was merely one of more dramatic woes facing the downtown establishment in the early 1990s. Of equal concern were the slumping fortunes of the retail core, located just north of the downtown's central financial district. But unlike the sudden collapse of the office market in the late 1980s, Seattle's retail sector had begun its long slide into decline way back in the mid-1970s, as downtown retailers began to lose customers to suburban malls. Beginning with the pioneering Northgate Mall, Seattle's suburbs built new shopping malls at an alarming pace, including the Southcenter Mall in Tukwila, Alderwood Mall in suburban Snohomish County, and the sprawling Bellevue Square, now home to the SUV-driving, cell-phone-gabbing set of the upscale Eastside. According to an economic analysis commissioned by the Downtown Seattle Association, by the early 1990s, the suburbanization of Seattle retail had taken its toll. Between 1978 and 1993, for example, Seattle's share of taxable retail sales in the metro area dropped from 37 percent to 28 percent.[62] This decline was most pronounced in department store retail, with Seattle's share of metropolitan department store sales falling from 40 percent in 1978 to a mere 21 percent in 1993. At street level, Seattle's downtown retail core slowly lost many of its prominent retailers, as the bigger department stores found it increasingly difficult to compete with the low property costs and free parking of the suburban fringe. As a result, such national and local chains as JCPenney, MacDougall's, Rhodes, Kress, Doces, Ernst Hardware, Klopfenstein's, I. Magnin, and Woolworth all either simply closed their doors or headed for the greener pastures of the suburbs.[63]

But the most telling blow to downtown retail came in 1992 with the jarring closure of the Frederick & Nelson department store. Ever since D. E. Frederick and Nels Nelson moved their young store from the waterfront to the more staid confines of Pine Street and Fifth Avenue in 1918, their downtown Frederick & Nelson store, ensconced in the largest retail space in the city, had anchored Seattle's retail landscape. While local arch-rival Nordstrom had developed, by the 1980s, a national reputation for customer service and upscale merchandise, Frederick & Nelson's remained the more beloved store, a long-time local favorite and home to, among other things, chocolate "Frangos" and the most popular Christmas Santa in Seattle.[64]

With its place in the hearts of Seattleites secure, the owners of Frederick & Nelson enjoyed resounding success during most of the century. Sometimes this success was simply the result of good timing. In June of 1929, for example, a scant five months before the stock market crash, the family owners of Frederick & Nelson sold out to Chicago-based Marshall Field & Co., pocketing a princely sum just before the depression set in. But by the mid-1980s, the Frederick & Nelson magic was gone. In 1985, the chain (with stores throughout the Pacific Northwest) reportedly lost $13 million. Between 1986 and 1991, the troubled downtown store changed hands three times, as various local investors sought to pump new life into the ailing giant. In 1991, Frederick & Nelson finally filed for bankruptcy protection, and, finding no investors willing to take a chance on the old store, held one last clearance sale and shut its doors for good. By the end of 1992, the handsome old store stood darkened and abandoned, leaving a long stretch of Pine Street empty and eerily quiet.[65] With Frederick & Nelson's closure and the spectacular office market bust, the downtown establishment's world-class dreams, toasted as a resounding success just a few years earlier, had come crashing down on the corner of Pine and Sixth with an echoing thud.

"Our Nightmare Was Coming True"

Set in the context of the spectacular office market bust, the closure of Frederick & Nelson sent ripples of anxiety throughout the downtown establishment. Prior to the recession of the early 1990s, the slow decline in retail sales and activity had been easy to ignore, especially with the high-profile construction of Westlake Center in 1988 (an upscale mall designed by the firm responsible for Quincy Market in Boston). But with the closure of Frederick & Nelson, however, it was impossible to escape the sense that, as one developer said, "we had a downtown that was slipping."[66] Combined with the slump in Seattle's office market (now in its third year), the accelerating decline in downtown retail sales was quite alarming to city officials and boosters. By 1994, for example, the retail vacancy rate had ballooned from under 10 percent in the late 1980s to an alarming 30 percent.[67] Even more troublesome to downtown elites were the street-level consequences of a sustained retail slump—including boarded storefronts, abandoned streets, and a general sense of decline and malaise on downtown streets. As one city councilmember said, after Frederick & Nelson's closed, followed in quick succession by the I. Magnin department store and Klopfenstein's (men's clothes):

> I mean . . . you could shoot a canon down 6th or Pine, I mean there were no people, there were no pedestrians. I've got photographs that we, kind of the "before" photographs, of the campaign. And it was filled with graffiti, the buildings were all vacant, and the crime rate had risen pretty significantly. . . . I mean, it was just a ghost town there.[68]

This councilmember was by no means alone in her pessimistic assessment of downtown. As the early 1990s progressed, the rhetoric of decline intensified with each store closure or office vacancy. In the business press, retail strategists voiced worries that the Frederick & Nelson's vacancy "could drag the rest of downtown with it."[69] Likening the empty F&N building to an all-powerful black hole, that bad boy of astro-physics, one concerned citizen worried that the Frederick's closure might spark a spiral of full-scale urban decay:

> As you know, the core area around Frederick's is seriously deteriorated. . . . There is no mystery as to what happens to decaying downtown areas once this occurs; one can look at dozens of cities throughout the country. It becomes an irreversible process. What becomes a black hole develops its own negative energy as it expands and sucks in nearby areas around it.[70]

In short, as Deputy Mayor Bob Watt put it, "our nightmare was coming true. Downtown was looking bad."[71] And, as the *Times* editorial board noted, the frightening history of postwar urban decline in America proved that if cities allow their retail core to "slip away . . . a vibrant downtown is seldom recaptured."[72] Standing in the midst of the recession, it seemed to civic boosters that a boarded up retail core and a flagging office market might be the tip of a very frightening iceberg, the top of a downhill slide into rust belt–style urban blight and decay.

Perhaps not surprisingly, it was during the height of this collective hand-wringing over the future of downtown, that many merchants began to complain bitterly to reporters and city officials about the "increasing number of vagrants" ostensibly spoiling the retail atmosphere downtown.[73] In years past, the concern about the threat panhandling and homelessness posed to the "viability" of downtown would periodically percolate in the back offices and conference tables of various civic "task forces,"[74] and over the years a number of surveys commissioned by the Downtown Seattle Association identified "homeless people" as one of the top three things shoppers, office workers, and tourists disliked about downtown.[75] But for the most part, such concerns about the perceived incivility of the city's homeless remained primarily the obsession of one segment of the merchant class and failed to attract the sustained attention of the city's agenda setters.

This changed beginning in the spring of 1993, when the issue of homelessness, largely dormant since the mid-1980s, once again found its way onto the pages of Seattle's major dailies. Often, the coverage had a "true confessions" quality to it, with merchants and shoppers telling breathless first-person stories about their disturbing encounters with Seattle's homeless. For instance, one particularly agitated letter writer told *Times* readers about his encounter with "Charlie," a "clone of Charles Manson" who aggressively shook his white styrofoam cup at pedestrians, sticking his face within inches of passersby: "he didn't say a word. He didn't have to. His menacing cold crazed eyes and body language said it all."[76]

For their part, store owners' tales of the homeless emphasized how street-level deviance undermined their bottom line. "It just seems like they're more aggressive," a downtown boutique owner told the *Seattle Times*. "It scares people who are coming downtown." To illustrate her point, the merchant described

how, in one incident, a panhandler "suddenly smacked a well-dressed 'Bellevue type lady' in the head" as she waited to cross the street to reach an adjacent department store. "I'm sure she's not coming back down here," she told the *Times*.[77] At the end of July, the *Times* editorial page weighed into the debate, calling on city government to reign the epidemic of incivility on downtown streets. Writing that "the city has a duty to maintain streets that are usable for everyone," the *Times* then called for the Rice administration to embrace policies that would "control the use of public spaces," police the behavior of "unruly drunks," and protect the investments "Seattleites have made
. . . to make downtown an economically viable, physically inviting place."[78]

Taken together, the spectacular office bust, the long decline of downtown retail, and the renewed discourse about the "incivility" of the homeless combined to place enormous pressure on the newly elected administration of Mayor Norm Rice. By 1993, the call for the mayor to "do something" about downtown began to ring with more intensity in the pages of the city's dailies and in the corridors of city hall. For example, in a speech delivered to the Seattle Rotary Club, City Attorney Mark Sidran argued forcefully that, despite the city's beauty and its function as an important port of call for Pacific Rim trade, the recent decline of downtown threatened to make claims of Seattle's world-class "quality of life" ring a bit hollow.

> we Seattleites have [developed] this anxiety, this nagging suspicion that despite the mountains and the Sound and smugness about all our advantages, maybe, just maybe we are pretty much like those other big American cities "back East," as we used to say when I was a kid . . . [79]

To be sure, Seattle had so far escaped this fate, but Sidran cautioned that "this downward spiral doesn't happen overnight and it will be more than just a bad dream if we don't wake up to the challenges we confront and act."[80] By the summer of 1993, things had deteriorated to the point where the downtown business community decided to pen an open letter to the administration, asking, "Mayor Rice, do you want to be remembered as the mayor who allowed Downtown Seattle to die?"[81]

The answer to this question, was, of course, "no." And so, while in the early days of the recession, the Rice administration had been content to offer relatively modest policy changes and hope that private investment would flow back into downtown of its own accord, by 1993, the administration was getting ready to unveil their plan to address merchants' concerns.[82] To this end, Mayor Rice announced in August of 1993 the formation of a "downtown task force" staffed by city department heads, and charged them with the task turning around downtown's slumping retail and office markets. By forming this task force, the mayor openly committed the city to a more activist pursuit of downtown revitalization, much to the delight of the downtown business and property establishment. "The health of our downtown is vital to the health of our entire community," Rice told reporters. "I don't believe this is a situation that can be fixed by rhetoric or symbolic gestures. Yes, there's a cost to some of these things I'll be proposing to keep our downtown strong, but there's a bigger cost if we allow our downtown to fall apart."[83]

And so the Rice administration embarked upon what one city official called "a multi-pronged strategy to . . . encourage great, thriving life" in downtown Seattle.[84] Norm Rice had placed downtown revitalization at the very top of his political agenda, and, as we will see, soon committed the city to an unprecedented project of publicly subsidized retail-cultural redevelopment. In short, in the years since Rice appointed his downtown task force, Seattle's public leaders have embraced the strategy that David Harvey has termed "the mobilization of spectacle." The hope was that, by finding a way to reverse downtown's fortunes, by recentralizing upscale culture, leisure, and recreation in the heart of downtown, the city might be able to create the kind of positive urban image that can attract sustained economic growth in an uncertain global environment. The hope, in other words, was that, by "mobilizing the spectacle" in downtown, civic elites might, at last, realize their long-nurtured world-class dreams.[85]

The first task, of course, would be to squarely address the retail slump by finding a suitable tenant for the empty Frederick & Nelson building. Yet, the Rice administration had other plans as well, including the expansion of the Washington State Trade and Convention Center, luring cruise ships into the Port, encouraging upscale residential development, and relocating key cultural institutions like the Seattle Art Museum and the Seattle Symphony back into the heart of downtown. When the dust cleared in the late 1990s, the urban landscape of downtown Seattle would be utterly transformed, with a totally revamped retail core and host of new cultural amenities meant to quell any fears of East Coast–style urban decay and to solidify Seattle's status as a vibrant, attractive global city.

Notes

1. Carl Abbott, *The Metropolitan Frontier: Cities in the Modern American West* (Tucson, AZ: 1993), 54.

2. Bill Sieverling, "City's Population in Major Shifts," *Seattle Post-Intelligencer*, 26 January 1976, 1(A).

3. Hilda Bryant, "Seattle in Transition: Manners and Morals," *Seattle Post-Intelligencer*, 27 January 1976, 1(A).

4. Walt Crowley, *Rites of Passage: A Memoir of the Sixties in Seattle* (Seattle, WA: University of Washington Press, 1995), 173-76.

5. Walt Crowley, *Rites of Passage*, 173-76.

6. Bill Sieverling, "Seattle in Transition: Downtown's 1,000 Acres," *Seattle Post-Intelligencer*, 1 February 1976, 6(A).

7. Bill Sieverling, "Seattle in Transition: Downtown's 1,000 Acres," 6(A).

8. Sieverling, "Downtown's 1,000 Acres," 6(A).

9. Sieverling, "Downtown's 1,000 Acres," 6(A).

10. Sieverling, "Downtown's 1,000 Acres," 6(A).

11. Bill Sieverling, "Seattle in Transition: What Will Seattle Be Like in 1985?" *Seattle Post-Intelligencer*, 25 January 1976, 1(A).

12. Bill Sieverling, "What Will Seattle Be Like in 1985?" *Seattle Post-Intelligencer*, 10(A).

13. Carl Abbott, *The Metropolitan Frontier*, 53-54.

14. Carl Abbott, "Regional City and Network City: Portland and Seattle in the Twentieth Century," *Western Historical Quarterly* (August 1992): 313.

15. Abbott, "Regional City and Network City," 313.

16. Office of Financial Management, *Washington Trends: Economy, Population, Budget Drivers, Revenues, Expenditures* (Olympia, WA: State of Washington, October 1996), 17.

17. Abbott, *The Metropolitan Frontier*, 55-56.

18. Economic Development Council. From their website: http://www.edc-sea.org.

19. Methodological Note. This data was culled from: Bureau of the Census. *County Business Patterns, 1972-1996 (Table 2: Employees, Payroll, and Establishments by Industry)*. The category of "producer services" does not appear in this data. To derive this category, I followed the procedure outlined by Saskia Sassen in *The Global City: New York, London, Tokyo* (Princeton, NJ: Princeton University Press), especially Appendix A. Following Sassen, I derived "producer services" by combining the employment numbers in Finance, Insurance, and Real Estate (SIC codes 60-67), Business Services (SIC code 73), Legal Services (SIC code 81), Membership Organizations (SIC code 86), and Engineering & Management Services (SIC code 87). From 1972 to 1984, however, Engineering & Management services were included under a different category (Miscellaneous Services, SIC code 89), so from 1972 to 1984, I substituted SIC 89 for SIC 87 in order to keep the categories consistent over the years.

20. Saskia Sassen, "Economic Restructuring and the American City," *Annual Review of Sociology*, 16 (1990): 471.

21. Economic Development Council. From their website: http://www.edc-sea.org. In 2001, Boeing Aerospace would move its corporate headquarters to Chicago, a blow that symbolically brought the manic 1990s and the latest celebrations of Seattle's world-class ambitions to a (temporary) end.

22. Economic Development Council. From their website: http://www.edc-sea.org.

23. Abbott, *The Metropolitan Frontier*, 74-75.

24. Abbott, *The Metropolitan Frontier*, 91-92.

25. Of course, not everyone in Seattle was invited to the party. For most Seattleites, the world-class or global city talk of the 1980s was merely a facade, a surface veneer of prosperity and growth masking the more fundamental pain of economic restructuring. Statewide, certain Washingtonians, particularly those with graduate or professional degrees and those working in business services (including software), health services, and high finance enjoyed a rise in incomes over the 1980s and early 1990s,

state forecasters noted that the 1980s were hard times indeed for most state residents. Indeed, the State of Washington began the 1980s as a high-wage state, with the typical resident earning 8 percent more than the national average. By 1990, however, the state had fallen 2 percent *behind* the national average, due primarily to slow job growth in traditional high-wage industries open to working-class citizens and rapid job growth in low-wage retail and service (i.e., "McJob") sectors. Even those workers who managed to keep their jobs in manufacturing and resource industries felt the squeeze during these years, with slow productivity gains and intense global competition, reducing the wages of a typical aerospace worker, for example, by about $1,000 (in 1994$) over the 1980s. The result was a widening gap between rich and poor in Washington State, a gap which mirrored trends nationwide and which belied the notion that the state had somehow escaped the corrosive effects of economic crisis and restructuring. During the 1980s, for example, only the wealthiest 10 percent of Washington's workers earned more in 1989 than they did in 1979. The other *90 percent* of workers saw their real incomes fall during the decade. And while average incomes in Washington started rising beginning in 1990, by the late 1990s, the bottom three-fifths of state income-earners *still* had not gained back all the ground they lost during the eighties. See especially Office of Financial Management, *Washington Trends: Economy, Population, Budget Drivers, Revenues, Expenditures* (Olympia, WA: State of Washington, October 1996, 12). Like their counterparts nationwide, Washington workers with only a high school education felt the brunt of the state's restructuring economy, with those who never finished high school earning, on average, 27 percent less in 1989 than they did in 1979. See Kathryn Larin and Elizabeth McNichol, *Pulling Apart: A State-by-State Analysis of Income Trends* (Washington, DC: Center on Budget and Policy Priorities, 1997). Even in Seattle proper, which fared better than the state as a whole during these years, the number of residents living in poverty rose steadily since the crisis of the early 1970s, from just over 10 percent in 1970 to 12.4 percent in 1990 (dropping an additional 8,000 people into poverty over 20 years). All in all, by the early 1990s, the hype about the "last livable city," while pleasing to local boosters and the downtown establishment, must have rung a bit hollow for residents struggling to make ends meet with less and less, particularly those without access to the kinds of skills and education most in demand in Seattle's world-class future (data from the U.S. Bureau of Census. *General Social and Economic Characteristics, Washington State [1970-1990]*, see Table 90, Table 125, Table 178).

26. Walter Hatch, "City Limits," *Seattle Times*, 30 April 1989, 1(A).

27. Personal interview, Seattle Displacement Coalition, 3 February 1999.

28. Terry McDermott, "High Rise: Making the Deal—Seattle Developer Digs into Foreign Pockets for Millions of Dollars to Get Gateway Going," *Seattle Times*, 9 July 1989, 1(A).

29. McDermott, "High Rise," *Seattle Times*, 9 July 1989, 1(A).

30. Walter Hatch, "City Limits," *Seattle Times*, 30 April 1989, 1(A).

31. McDermott, "High Rise," *Seattle Times*, 9 July 1989, 1(A).

32. McDermott, "High Rise," 1(A).

33. McDermott, "High Rise," 1(A).

34. David Harvey, *The Urbanization of Capital* (Baltimore: Johns Hopkins University Press, 1985), 6-7.

35. McDermott, "High Rise," *Seattle Times*, July 9, 1989, 1(A).

36. McDermott, "High Rise," 1(A).

37. McDermott, "High Rise," 1(A).

38. Mike Davis, *City of Quartz: Excavating the Future in Los Angeles* (New York: Vintage, 1992). 136.

39. Terry Lawhead, "Pacific Center Draws Interest," *Seattle Times*, 28 December 1989.

40. Lawhead, "Pacific Center Draws Interest."

41. Hatch, "City Limits," 1(A).

42. Hatch, "City Limits," 1(A).

43. Hatch, "City Limits," 1(A)..

44. Hatch, "City Limits," 1(A).

45. Michelle Flores, "What's Up Downtown: An Oversupply of Office Space Leaves Developers Stretching to Cover Costs," *Seattle Times*, 28 October 1990, 1(E).

46. McDermott, "High Rise," 1(A).

47. Terry Lawhead, "Downtown Vacancies, Rents Hurting Developers," *Seattle Times*, 26 April 1990, 1(E).

48. Lawhead, "Downtown Vacancies," 1(E).

49. *Seattle Times*, "Bright Lights, Empty Space," 10 July 1992, 1(A).

50. *Seattle Times*, "Bright Lights, Empty Space," 1(A).

51. Personal interview, Downtown Property Developer, 3 December 1998.

52. In the Seattle market at least. The crash of the real estate market—described here with reference to Seattle's downtown—actually took on global dimensions during this time, driving a number of the world's most notable developers to the edge of bankruptcy and beyond.

53. Michele Flores, "End of a Dream: Developers Lost Millions of Dollars, Titles to Homes," *Seattle Times*, 15 October 1992, 1(A).

54. Flores, "End of a Dream," 1(A).

55. Flores, "End of a Dream," 1(A).

56. Flores, "End of a Dream," 1(A).

57. Flores, "End of a Dream," 1(A).

58. Flores, "End of a Dream," 1(A).

59. Flores, "End of a Dream," 1(A).

60. "Bright Lights, Empty Space," *Seattle Times*, 10 July 1992.

61. "Bright Lights, Empty Space," *Seattle Times*, 10 July 1992.

62. Economics Research Associates, *An Economic Evaluation of the Rhodes–Nordstrom Project* (August 1994), 7.

63. Economics Research Associates, *An Economic Evaluation*, 7.

64. Sylvia Nogaki, "Downtown Wonderland? Retailers are Determined Not to Have a Blue Christmas without F&N," *Seattle Times*, 23 November 1992, 1(E).

65. Nogaki, "Downtown Wonderland?"

66. Monte Enbysk, "Destination: Downtown Seattle," *Washington CEO* (November 1996): S-4.

67. Larry Liebman, "Downtown's Supporters Hopeful for Good News," *Puget Sound Business Journal*, 13 May 1994.

68. Personal interview, Seattle City Council, 15 December 1998.

69. Sylvia Nogaki, "Retailing Talk of the 'Town': Uptown Mosquito Fleet is Part of Plan to Save Vitality of Downtown," *Seattle Times*, 22 June 1992, 1(D).

70. Letter to Seattle City Council, Seattle City Archives, Tom Weeks Subject Files (see methodological appendix for retrieval information).

71. Bob Watt, printed copy of speech to Seattle Rotary Club.

72. "Vote Yes to Reopen Pine for a Healthy Downtown [editorial]," *Seattle Times*, 12 March 1995.

73. Polly Lane and Sylvia Nogaki, "Downtown Merchants Want Action on Parking, Crime," *Seattle Times*, 23 April 1993, 1(A).

74. Homelessness was identified as a condition which "keeps people away from downtown" in previous surveys commissioned by the DSA in 1986 and 1988. And one councilmember I interviewed told me that the connection between public safety and homelessness had been explored by no less than three task forces at the local and state level during the 1980s.

75. Downtown Seattle Association, *Survey of Downtown Users, January 1993* (Seattle, WA: Elway Research, 1993).

76. Paul Crane, "Homeless in Seattle: Eliminate 'Charlie Show.'" *Seattle Times*, 24 August 1993, 5(B).

77. Sylvia Nogaki and Polly Lane, "Panhandlers Among Area's Problems," *Seattle Times*, 24 March 1993, 1(E). Lane and Nogaki, "Downtown Merchants," *Seattle Times*, 23 April 1993, 1(A).

78. "Looking for Better Ways to Curb Unruly Street Life [editorial]," *Seattle Times*, 26 July 1993, 4(B).

79. Mark Sidran, "This is the Best of Times to Keep this City Livable," *Seattle Times*, 10 August 1993.

80. Sidran, "This is the Best of Times."

81. Lane and Nogaki, "Downtown Merchants," 1(A).

82. Personal interview, Downtown Seattle Task Force, 24 March 1999.

83. Michael Paulson, "Rice Unveils Plan to Rev Up Downtown," *Seattle Post-Intelligencer*, 19 August 1993.

84. Personal interview, Downtown Task Force, 24 March 1999.

85. Sharon Zukin, *The Cultures of Cities*, 14.

Chapter 4

Negotiating Urban Spectacle

As it turned out, Seattle's public officials and private boosters were by no means alone in their desire to recharge visions of world-class status through the mobilization of spectacle. Facing down decades of urban decline and suburbanization, city leaders have poured millions of taxpayer funds into all manner of centrally located retail and cultural projects. Detroit's civic elites, for example, have pinned their hopes for an urban comeback on sports and gambling, building two new sports stadiums (Comerica Park and Ford Field) and an elaborate waterfront casino project in the last four years alone. For their part, under the direction of Mayor Wellington Web, the city of Denver has focused its revitalization plans around providing incentives for market-priced downtown housing and building the sorts of amenities that bring suburban crowds to city streets. Since 1991, the city has built a new library, a new performing arts complex, an aquarium, a new convention center, and two new sports arenas. According to Jennifer Moulton, Denver's planning director, the hope is that these publicly subsidized amenities will spark a virtuous circle where the spectacle of downtown streets filled with tourists, sports fans, and symphony patrons will persuade privately financed art galleries and new restaurants to locate downtown.[1] Eventually, suburbanites who once spurned the central city will—after numerous trips to sample the newly revitalized retail-cultural scene—begin to dream about *living* downtown. With more downtown residents, the city would then attract further retail and cultural investment, which would then attract more housing to the CBD, and the virtuous cycle of consumption, residence, and investment would begin anew. In the end, the new vibrant downtown scene would yield further benefits, chief among these an enhanced urban "image" that could sell Denver as a prime locale for multinational corporate investment.[2]

This is the hope at least. Although Moutlon and Webb rightly claim some important victories in Denver's revitalization effort, such as a small but noteworthy increase in downtown residents and the opening of over thirty new downtown restaurants and art galleries, it is less clear if the publicly subsidized investment in new retail-cultural amenities has paid off in enough increased tax revenue to offset the cost to taxpayers. Moutlon and Webb also concede that Denver's inner-city neighborhoods—where rates of concentrated poverty remain high—have not yet benefited from the city's "comeback." In this way at least, Denver's experience mirrors the experience of Baltimore, a city whose burghers embarked on their own consumption-based redevelopment spree a decade earlier with the construction of Harborplace and Camden Yards, the much-admired home of the Orioles (major-league baseball). Yet, despite being held up by the Urban Land Institute as a model for sparking an urban renaissance, Baltimore's city officials acknowledge openly that the revitalization of the city stops for the most part at the edge of the tourist district.[3]

For this reason, we should view the recent flurry of commentary on the "comeback of the American city"[4] and the rise of a new and more prosperous "postindustrial age"[5] in urban America with some suspicion. Although central cities across the United States have embarked on a host of high-profile and big-ticket revitalization projects, and although new aquaria, new sports arenas, and new cultural institutions now dot the urban landscape, the actual economic payoffs of these investments remain in doubt.[6] For one, many of these big-ticket investments simply fail to generate the profits and tax revenues their boosters promise. Publicly financed sports stadiums have a particularly spotty track record in this regard. After the construction, operating, and maintenance costs are factored in, the nominal increases in sports-related sales tax revenue and the meager number of jobs created by professional sports usually add up to a net loss for cities and counties.[7] The economic benefits of publicly subsidized convention centers and casinos are equally questionable, even when analysts account for the spin-off benefits for nearby restaurants and retailers.[8]

Moreover, as the experience of Baltimore and Denver demonstrates, even in the success stories of the new urban comeback the benefits of recent economic restructuring arguably only trickle down to a small segment of the community.[9] Even if spectacular downtown redevelopment pays off by bringing in new corporate headquarters and high-tech firms attracted by the city's lively cultural and retail scene, jobs in these industries come with education and skill requirements beyond the reach of most residents, particularly those who live in depressed central city neighborhoods. Furthermore, the jobs directly created by opening a new downtown shopping mall, or building a new symphony hall tend to be low-wage, part-time, service-sector jobs without benefits or opportunity for advancement.[10] For these residents, who live paycheck-to-paycheck, who may work in these spectacular consumption environments but cannot afford a sweater from J. Crew or a night at the symphony, such celebrations around the "postindustrial" renaissance of their cities likely ring a bit hollow.

Still, as Bruce Katz argues, it's not as if city leaders have a lot of options. With suburbs continuing to attract most of the metropolitan growth in jobs and residents, and with central cities home to a disproportionate share of the nation's most desperately poor, city leaders have become desperate to turn around histories of decline.[11] Unable to force the federal government to come to their aid, and facing a now-global competition for future economic growth and investment, city leaders have turned to spectacular retail-cultural development to attract suburban consumption dollars and to build the sort of world-class urban image that can impress international investors and multinational corporations. In the process, once ignored and "redlined" downtown streets and docklands across the United States have been appropriated and redeveloped into all manner of retail, cultural, and recreational amenities—often at great public expense. In short, as Zukin writes, in the scramble to present the best possible face to potential tourists, shoppers, and corporate investors, "culture" and "leisure" has become more and more the *business* of cities.[12]

Between 1993 and 1999, Seattle's downtown establishment seized upon this "culture and leisure" growth strategy with boundless enthusiasm. The result has been a flurry of retail, cultural, and recreational redevelopment that has utterly transformed the visage of the city's retail core. Beginning in 1991 with the relocation of the Seattle Art Museum from its longtime home on Capital Hill to a new $61 million building designed by postmodern architect Robert Venturi, the frenzy of retail-cultural development has since spawned the construction of a new Symphony Hall, a $25 million performing arts center, two new multimillion dollar professional sports palaces (for a combined $900 million), an expanded convention center, a new downtown Museum of History and Industry, and, as we will discuss in this chapter, massive, $400 million makeover of the city's retail core. While the projects themselves may run the cultural gamut from a new home for the Seattle Seahawks to a new home for the Seattle Symphony, from Halfback to Handel as it were, they nonetheless share a common underlying goal—keeping tourists, potential investors, and Seattle's expanding class of urban professionals titillated and satiated well into the twenty-first century.

Beginning with a discussion of how a concentration of downtown retail-cultural amenities helps civic boosters sell "Seattle" to multinational businesses and globe-trotting tourists, this chapter will then turn to how Seattle's public and private elites responded to the closure of the Frederick & Nelson site and the more general slump in downtown retail during the early 1990s. In particular, the chapter will detail how a coalition of public officials, downtown developers, and retailers coalesced around "the Rhodes Project"—a massive, $400 million retail redevelopment project that would completely revamp the downtown core. Focusing in particular on the behind-the-scenes negotiations between the project's leading developer and city officials, this chapter will discuss how, in the heat of negotiations, the Rice administration was persuaded to forward $100 million in public subsidies toward the redevelopment effort.

Selling Seattle Abroad: Exploiting Urban Cultural Capital

To be sure, Seattle's renewed commitment to big-ticket, publicly subsidized, retail-cultural redevelopment reflects a larger national trend in which "culture"—that is, the high-profile construction of artistic and recreational environments targeted toward the tastes of the international elite—is drafted in the service of "economy" and the imperative of urban economic growth. Yet, depending on their resources and history, different cities will approach this process in different ways, with different outcomes. They will, in other words, mobilize different "brands" of spectacle in order to position themselves favorably in the interurban competition for tourism and economic investment. In other words, while Orlando promotes itself as a wholesome destination for family fun, New Orleans trades on frenzied debauchery; and while Santa Fe's tourism depends upon a certain claim to cultural authenticity (as in "authentic southwest art and cuisine"), Las Vegas proudly celebrates its simulations, fantasies, and illusions.

For their part, Seattle's redevelopment plans have been explicitly crafted to project an attractive image of the "quality of life" enjoyed by residents of the Pacific Northwest. Carefully cultivated by city boosters and dutifully publicized by national and international media, the promotion of Seattle as a "livable city" with an unparalleled quality of life has become in recent years a crucial part of the city's growth and development strategy and now lies at the heart of the public-private effort to both sell the city to global tourists and investors.[13]

Not surprisingly, every recent effort to promote Seattle's quality of life has begun with evocative accounts of the region's natural surroundings—the mountains, the forests, and the sound—and the many outstanding opportunities for outdoor recreation.[14] But, as the promotional literature produced by trade and tourist organizations enthuses, in Seattle this stunning natural inheritance is just a stone's throw from the city's varied and vibrant street life, where the best in "urban culture combines with natural surroundings to make life easier, healthier, better, and fun."[15] In this way, the recentralization of elaborate retail environments, high culture, and recreation in downtown has been quite helpful in the promotion of Seattle as a so-called world-class city, home not merely to a stunning natural environment but also to "diverse and high-quality shopping opportunities," "first-class facilities for sports and the arts," and a host of "innovative and first-class theaters, museums, galleries, and film festivals."[16]

In order to pitch this image of Seattle as America's "livable city," the region's boosters have formed a number of interlocking trade and tourism organizations that scan the globe, looking to sell international investors, global traders, and travel agents on both the city's eagerness to do business and on its overall quality of life. In this regard, the Trade Development Alliance of Greater Seattle is of particular interest because since its founding in the early 1990s, it has taken on the challenge of selling Seattle as an international center of manufacturing, trade, and finance around the globe, particularly in all-important "Pacific Rim" markets like Indonesia, Malaysia, China, and Japan. Moreover, the Alliance's executive board reads like a who's who of Seattle's public and private establishment, including Mayor Paul Schell (Norm Rice's successor), King County Executive Ron Sims, executives from Boeing, Bank of

America and Attachmate Software, and even Ron Judd from the King County Labor Council.[17] While this collection of urban protagonists may squabble over a host of other political and economic issues, they have quickly united around their common interest in economic growth and the goal of promoting Seattle as a "livable" and "vibrant" center of trade, tourism, and finance.

Seattle has not always been promoted around the globe with such precision. The origins of the Trade Development Alliance can be traced back to the late 1980s when George Duff, the former president of the Greater Seattle Chamber of Commerce, realized that although a host of smaller public and private organizations were involved in international activities, none were actively promoting the region as a good place to work, trade, and invest.[18] Given the region's increasing reliance on international trade and the increasing mobility of new industries—which could locate anywhere the quality of life seemed most promising—this disorganized approach to regional promotion began to set off alarm bells in civic circles. As Duff reminded his colleagues during those formative meetings of the Trade Alliance, the competition to become a global center of trade and finance had become quite fierce. "Only a few American cities will be awarded an international franchise," he told the assembled leaders in business, government and labor. "Seattle has the opportunity to be one of them."[19]

To enter into this competition for trade and investment, the main purpose of the Trade Alliance lies in its annual outbound trade missions, led by the Alliance's top staff and their colleagues in the Chamber of Commerce. Gathering together a crowd of Seattle's most notable CEO's and public dignitaries, these outbound trade junkets give local Seattle elites a chance to press the flesh and drum up business in all manner of distant locales, including important trading partners in Europe, Latin America, and around the Pacific Rim. On such missions, delegates develop contacts with political officials and industry leaders around the globe while attempting to promote both their specific wares—from Boeing 777's to Microsoft's Office—as well as the region's more general amenities, including its transportation infrastructure, its educated citizenry, and its reputation as a livable city with a unique quality of life.[20]

But while the promotion of Seattle's quality of life can sometimes figure into the give-and-take of these outbound trade missions,[21] it is when multinational executives travel to Seattle—either to discuss joint ventures with local firms or to search for a suitable spot to expand their operations—that the city's investment into the cultural, recreational, and retail infrastructure of downtown can really pay off. As one Trade Alliance official noted, if you're looking to relocate your headquarters, setting up a partnership with a local firm, or building new branch offices and facilities, you'll certainly want to know about the environment, the schools, and cost of housing in the region. But you'll also want to know you won't be bored to tears if you move your family to the region. You'll want to know about the arts and cultural opportunities, the retail and sports scene, and the general life and atmosphere of the city's public spaces. In this way, the street life and atmosphere cultivated by the construction of new retail and cultural spaces—such as a new festival mall or a new symphony hall—can become a crucial part of the "quality of life" that sells Seattle to visiting trade and business delegations.[22]

This being said, how does downtown redevelopment help seal the deal with international businesses and investors? Because delegations tend to stay in one of the many hotels in downtown Seattle, delegates typically only experience the slice of Seattle that lies within walking distance of their hotel rooms. As a result, the street atmosphere and experience of the downtown retail core can be decisive in creating either a favorable or negative image of "the city" in the imagination of these globe-trotting financial elites. Indeed, prior to the recent rush of new investment downtown, one trade official noted that downtown Seattle was a strictly 9-to-5 experience, more like London, Ontario than London, England. "I'd walk out of my office here at 5 p.m. and it'd be completely dead," he said. But now, speaking at the end of Seattle's redevelopment spree, "the urban cultural environment" around the four-star downtown hotels frequented by visiting dignitaries has been transformed with the construction of a host of new arts venues, gourmet restaurants, and upscale boutiques—in short, the very kinds of places elite delegates love to patronize on their travels abroad.[23]

So now when delegates stay in downtown Seattle, this official noted, "there's lots of things to do." They can shop at Nordstrom or walk to the new Symphony Hall. They can catch a movie at the Pacific Place cineplex or grab a bite at a trendy downtown eatery. They can see the latest Broadway musical at the Paramount Theater, or swill a microbrew at the nearest brewpub. Not surprisingly, delegates now wax enthusiastic about Seattle's downtown scene, sometimes exclaiming, as did one Indonesian delegate, "I can shop until 9 o'clock!" Moreover, as the Alliance official explained, when the Chamber of Commerce hosts dinners, banquets, and meetings for visiting delegations, they now have a variety of world-class venues at their disposal, including the Convention Center, the Seattle Art Museum, and the newly constructed Benaroya Hall. Such environments, he said, tend to impress upon visiting delegates Seattle's world-class status, and can generate the kind of goodwill that can, in the end, help cement a deal for foreign investment and trade.[24]

In addition to impressing visiting trade delegations, the cultural and recreational makeover of downtown Seattle has also made selling the Emerald City to tourists and large national conventions a much easier task, as one tourism official noted. "The image we're trying to project is that Seattle is a busy, thriving urban experience that's close to the outdoors . . . and [that] there's a lot to do after five o'clock any time of the year," one tourism official said.[25] In this regard, the recent construction of amenities like Benaroya Hall, the Seattle Art Museum, and the new Nordstrom flagship store "has been very helpful."

Consider the job of selling Seattle to the organizers of big national conventions. As one official from the Seattle-King County Convention and Visitors Bureau explained, conventioneers hate having to catch a bus or hail a cab to get to a city's key amenities. Consequently, one thing that sells a city to convention organizers is the "compact" nature of downtown amenities and attractions. The question convention planners ask, then, is "are your attractions 'walkable'? Are they within walking distance of downtown hotels?" The lure of a "walkable" downtown thus provides city leaders with a big motive for relocating attractions and amenities like sports arenas, art museums, and shopping emporia back into the city center. This places them within reach of tourists and conventioneers, making the job of "selling Seattle" to these lucrative "target markets" that much easier. And, as this tourism official explained, now that many of Seattle's cultural amenities have found their way back into the retail core,

> that's a big advantage right there. . . . All the attractions like the Pike Place Market, Pioneer Square, [and the] waterfront are all walkable. . . . Then you add to that all the new retail coming, new restaurants coming in. What that means is that the streets are filled. There's lots to do. You don't have to worry about transportation, public or otherwise. It's cheaper. It's easier. [It's] a big selling point.[26]

So, from the perspective of those charged with attracting convention delegates to Seattle, when it comes to downtown redevelopment, the mantra at the Convention and Visitors Bureau is "the more development the better."[27]

What's more, the construction and relocation of cultural, retail, and recreational amenities downtown also helps the Bureau sell Seattle's quality of life to travel agents, travel editors, and tourists. For example, one of the main activities at the Bureau involves flying to Manhattan to pitch the city to the editors of major travel magazines like *Travel and Leisure* and *Travel Holiday*. According to officials at the Convention and Visitors Bureau, what travel editors love most is to hear about "what's new, and especially if no one's covered it. They love what's going to be new maybe a year from now." As a result, "new museums, new hotels, and certainly new downtown core development . . . make our job easier—easier certainly than another city that maybe is not seeing growth. What do you talk about if there's nothing new?"[28] New developments, then, give tourism officials something new to pitch to travel agents and editors, creating an image of a city that's "up and coming" with a "busy and thriving" cultural environment. As this Bureau staffer concluded, these are the sorts of images that spawn glowing articles in travel magazines and that can attract legions of tourists from all over the globe.

In this sense, Seattle's recent investment in culture and leisure has been crafted explicitly to promote the larger strategies of the city's public and private pro-growth elite. "Culture" in this sense becomes, to borrow a term from Pierre Bourdieu, *cultural capital*.[29] In short, just as members of the middle and upper classes can trade on their accumulation of cultural knowledge (including knowledge of fine art, opera, and the literary canon) in order to impress "the right people" and accumulate economic capital (in the form of high-status jobs and connections), so can cities and regions trade on their "image" or "cultural capital" to rise in the international urban hierarchy.[30] In this way, the accumulation of cultural amenities like opera houses, symphony halls, elaborate retail environments, and other recreational attractions within easy walking distance for downtown visitors, business travelers, and conventioneers can generate a positive international "image" for a city, creating the kind of downtown "scene" which helps boosters sell the city to investors and tourists around the world.[31]

Ultimately, boosters argue, such downtown investment and redevelopment can feed on itself, creating a "critical mass" that not only draws in future investors and firms looking to locate in regions with the ever-elusive quality of life, but which also enhances the value of investments already made in downtown space. In the end, the positive image of place created by such investment in culture and recreation becomes a crucial part of the "cultural capital" Seattle's pro-growth establishment deploys in their ongoing struggle to capture a disproportionate share of future global economic growth.

The Perils of Public-Private Partnerships

The question facing city officials in Seattle was straightforward. If a future of economic growth depended—at least in part—upon cultivating a positive urban "image" through downtown revitalization, then how exactly could the city *pay* for it? Certainly the federal government would be of little help, for after the Reagan budget cuts of the early 1980s, federal funding for urban redevelopment was hard to come by. Still, whatever urban aid Washington *did* transfer to cities began to be distributed in the form of "block grants" that gave local governments great discretion in determining how funds should be spent.[32] As a result, beginning roughly in the 1980s, city officials began to use these block grants to experiment with new ways of promoting local economic development.

One prominent experiment involved using these block grants to embark upon complex and often controversial "public-private partnerships" with downtown property developers.[33] In striking such public-private deals, city governments used federal grants and local tax funds as "bait" or seed money to attract private investment into specific redevelopment projects designed to attract tourists, shoppers, and outside investors. Typically such projects—say, building an art museum or a sports stadium, for example—have been financed by a complex brew of public bonds and private investment, built by the private sector, and then managed through some sort of quasi-public development corporation designed to distribute future profits to the private and public partners. Since the 1980s, then, as cities have found themselves with few other options for jump-starting the local tax base, such public-private partnerships have become de rigueur in urban economic strategies around the United States.

As Margit Mayer writes, both private and public actors believe they have something to gain from entering into such complex redevelopment partnerships.[34] For instance, private investors gain from such deals because they can capture public subsidies to fund projects that, as developers often say, "pencil out" and seem likely to yield profits. For their part, local governments need private partners for a simple reason: that's where the money is. To be sure, private partners can also provide city hall with much-needed real estate expertise and administrative acumen, but it is the private sector's ability to *fund* big-ticket projects—projects that would otherwise remain a mere glimmer in some mayor's eye—that fuels the public longing for a private partner.

However, this hunger for private capital has often put local governments at a decided disadvantage when it comes to negotiating the terms of such public-private deals. In many cases, city leaders have found themselves under immense pressure to "save downtown" and "turn things around," and many of these leaders have pinned their hopes for economic growth (and their own re-election) on the success of high-profile redevelopment projects.[35] Given these political and ideological pressures, private negotiators have often smelled the scent of desperation wafting off public officials, and because they have the ability to walk away from "the deal" at any time, developers have been able to pressure localities into offering lucrative concessions and subsidies. In short, while the actual outcome of any specific negotiation may be "up for grabs," the reality is that the private sector has typically come to the table with the stronger hand.[36]

The end result of these complex public-private negotiations is, of course, "the deal" itself—that is, the legal agreement which distributes the risks, the costs, and the potential profits of the redevelopment project among the many private and public participants. Every agreement in this sense is unique, mostly because each specific "deal" is negotiated under very particular historical and political circumstances. Therefore, there are no absolutes here—no single guideline that can determine what level of public involvement is universally appropriate or wise. Yet, clearly, some big-city mayors are better negotiators than others. For example, the state of Maryland paid Cleveland Browns owner Art Modell $75 million and built a new stadium entirely at taxpayer expense in order to lure professional football back to Baltimore.[37] San Francisco mayor Willie Brown, on the other hand, not only persuaded the Giants (professional baseball) to stay in San Francisco, but he eventually convinced the team to build a new stadium at their *own* expense.[38] In the final analysis, the amount of largess a city showers upon its private partners can speak volumes about both the sense of desperation gripping city hall and the extent to which public officials have been captured by the downtown property establishment.

So how would Seattle's public officials fare in their negotiations with private developers over the scope of public involvement in the redevelopment of the city's retail core? As we discussed in the previous chapter, the declining fortunes of downtown retail and the stagnant property markets in the office core during the early 1990s began to spark much debate and concern during Norm Rice's first term as Seattle's mayor.[39] The Rice administration had assumed office in 1990 with the explicit goal of keeping "the downtown core, both retail and office, safe and strong." But by 1993, "it became inescapable that downtown was in deep trouble."[40] Revenues from downtown sales taxes had fallen steadily during the recession, and when the region appeared to be recovering in late 1992, city accountants found no corresponding upswing in downtown retail sales or tax revenues. By 1993, the closure of the Frederick & Nelson building had been matched by the exodus of a host of other longtime downtown retailers, sending waves of concern through the downtown establishment.

At the same time, officials in the mayor's office and pro-growth city councilors such as Jan Drago and Sue Donaldson looked out into Seattle's retail core and saw "lots of empty spaces and graffiti."[41] As one city councilmember put it, "there were no people. There were no pedestrians [and] . . . the buildings were all vacant."[42] Furthermore, the remaining downtown merchants were "squawking loudly," as one high-up official put it, demanding that Norm Rice find a way to stave off "the deterioration of downtown."[43]

As a result, as discussed in the last chapter, the Rice administration quickly came to the conclusion that extraordinary measures were needed to turn the situation around.[44] To begin with, Rice quickly put together a high-level "downtown task force" in order to find solutions to the slumping fortunes of the retail core.[45] Ostensibly formed to redress the totality of the downtown crisis (as perceived by city elites), the task force, chaired by then-Deputy Mayor Bob Watt and filled with city department heads, focused quickly and narrowly on the empty Frederick & Nelson site. While the other cultural and residential redevelopment projects, including the new Symphony Hall and the Eagles Auditorium, certainly attracted their share of city attention during this time, the primary goal of the task force—and of the Rice administration more generally—was to "figure out some way to help the private sector fill the empty F&N building." Already considered by some boosters to be a "black hole"[46] in the retail core (presumably a force from which profits cannot escape), the empty F&N site was not only a crucial symbol of decline for downtown elites but was also blamed for the closing of "dozens of stores and restaurants" in the surrounding area and for a never-substantiated increase in downtown street crime.[47] As a result, the city's task force mobilized primarily around the goal of attracting a world-class retailer to occupy and refurbish the vacant Frederick & Nelson building.

As one member of this task force noted, the city really had only one candidate in mind for the F&N site from the very beginning—Nordstrom department store. Though the administration tried to conceal its enthusiasm for a plan, any plan, that would put the upscale retailer in the vacant site, this high-ranking official said, "our primary goal was to move Nordstrom's there." Why was Nordstrom such a priority for city officials? First, as one official put it, "they were local heroes"—a company founded in Seattle but with a strong national reputation for bringing in hordes of free-spending upscale shoppers. In fact, Nordstrom was such a sought after commodity that the Mall of America in Minneapolis was reportedly willing to pay the firm $40 million just to locate a store there.[48] Second, Nordstrom had long located its national "headquarters" operations in downtown Seattle, but with the overall deterioration of downtown retail, there was some speculation that they might soon move their administrative and financial departments to the suburbs or beyond. (This speculation was fueled in part by the Nordstrom family, who have retained familial control of the publicly-traded company since its founding.) "There was talk of moving those people to Idaho," one task force member recalled. "They could work in New Zealand, for that matter. I mean, they're very portable."[49]

From the mayor's point of view, securing Nordstrom in the heart of the retail core and preventing the exodus of their headquarters operations were two goals central to the city's future. As a result, the administration was willing to go to great lengths to move Nordstrom into the F&N site. "We wanted them *here*," a high-ranking official said. "Because part of adding to the mix downtown is the vitality of office workers. That's what makes it all work . . . and [Nordstrom] has a heck of a lot of people working in downtown Seattle." As former Deputy Mayor Bob Watt told the crowd at the Rotary Club, the city needed Nordstrom to "stay put for all the right selfish reasons having to do with downtown real estate values, and all the attendant taxes generated by those folks."[50]

So it was with high hopes and barely hidden enthusiasm that the administration approached the Nordstrom family about the possibility of relocating their headquarters and flagship store across the street to the vacant F&N site. To the chagrin of the mayor's office, however, it appeared in the early days of the task force's efforts that the Nordstrom family had little interest in moving into and refurbishing the mammoth and increasingly ancient 1918 structure. It just didn't "pencil out," the retailer reportedly told the city. As one retail analyst put it, why would Nordstrom (a public company) sink $100 million to renovate a new site downtown, when it could build two or three stores elsewhere for the money?[51] By all accounts, then, this meeting was a bust. As former Deputy Mayor Bob Watt remembered, "we left feeling chastised and with the clear sense that while they might actually want to move to the F&N space," they could see no feasible way to do it. "That was *not* a good feeling," recalled Watt.[52]

Although Nordstrom remained the city's first choice, the task force reluctantly turned its attention to other proposals for the vacant F&N site. After being initially rebuffed by Nordstrom, the task force quickly "put out the word on the streets" and let it be known that the city was open to all comers who had an idea about how to turn downtown around and "especially to do something constructive with the Frederick & Nelson building."[53] Additionally, the city announced that, as one task force member put it, "we wanted to find ways to help" any developer who had such a plan to revive the fortunes of the retail core.[54] As a result, this official recalled, "we got proposals from all over," and a "steady stream of developers, lunatics, and wild idea people" descended upon the mayor's office—each pitching their plan to occupy the revered but vacant downtown block, and each looking for the city to subsidize their visions.[55]

One early idea for the block was first floated by Elizabeth (Liz) Strauss, the city's well-respected librarian, who, as one task force member recalled, decided immediately that the vacant site would be an ideal place for a new city library. While Strauss lobbied hard for her dream of a new downtown library, many top-level officials, including the mayor, questioned the wisdom of turning over a potentially revenue-generating section of the retail core over to the tax-exempt public sector. But as one of the early naysayers to the library idea said, "we loved our city librarian . . . [so] we at least wanted to make a fair run at seeing whether [the library] could work."[56]

As a result, the city sent Anne Levinson, one of Rice's three deputy mayors, to tour the building with Steve Wood, a real estate agent representing Don Padelford and his four sisters, the heirs of D. E. Frederick and co-owners of the vacant F&N site. As one task force member put it, Wood and Levinson had "some interesting conversations about price," during which it was made abundantly clear that "there was no way the public sector could pay" the $37.5 million the Padelfords were reportedly seeking.[57] This asking price, nearly triple the building's appraised value, spooked the task force and effectively shut down Strauss's dream downtown library, killing the first and best chance that the public would own the crucial downtown block. Because every city government must justify any big-ticket purchases in the local property market, such an inflated asking price meant that there was no way that, as one task force member put it, the Rice administration could "stare the taxpayers in the eyeball and say 'we paid a fair price'" for the F&N site. So with the dream of a new city library deferred, the administration again returned to the task of "seeking private sector solutions" to the downtown retail slump.[58]

Meanwhile, unbeknownst to the city, the Nordstrom family and a newcomer to the Seattle business establishment, developer Jeff Rhodes, were hatching their own plans. That the notoriously insular Nordstrom family would be open to proposals from such a newcomer to elite Seattle is a testament to Jeff Rhodes's pedigree in the national property development scene. Now a well-connected specialist in making "megadeals to finance some of the nation's most prominent hotels, office buildings . . . and shopping centers," Rhodes slipped into the development business quite unintentionally following his first year at

Yale Law School in 1972.[59] Evidently, something about the real estate business caught Rhodes's attention, because he never returned to law and instead joined the Urban Investment and Development Company (UIDC), one of the largest property development firms in the nation.

While at UIDC, Rhodes participated in many of the firm's most ambitious and high-profile projects, including Chicago's massive Water Tower Place, a seventy-four story "vertical mall" featuring stores, restaurants, hotels, and luxury condos, and Copley Place, a $530 million public-private venture which redeveloped a huge chunk of Boston's Back Bay neighborhood into a large-scale hotel, office, and retail complex.[60] On the heels of these projects, Rhodes and fellow UIDC veteran Tom Klutznick struck out on their own, joining forces with eccentric oil billionaire and movie mogul Marvin Davis in a real estate partnership controlling between $1.6 and $4 billion in assets. In one notable deal, Rhodes, as chief operating officer of Miller-Klutznick-Davis-Gray (as the new firm was called) bought the Beverly Hills Hotel in 1986 for $40 million and quickly resold it to the Sultan of Brunei for a cool $65 million.[61]

With profit margins like that, Rhodes found himself with little need for future employment, and following his marriage, the birth of his twins, and the dissolution of his partnership with Klutznick and Davis, he decided to retire in Seattle after only two decades in the development business. Thinking he would fill his days with a Seattle life of biking, hiking, and coffee-sipping, Rhodes decided in 1993 to pop in and introduce himself to one of Tom Klutznick's old friends, Jim Nordstrom. According to the *Seattle Times*, sometime during their talk Rhodes idly asked, "by the way, how come you're not moving into the empty Frederick & Nelson's building?"[62] Nordstrom reportedly replied that he'd looked at the numbers and they didn't seem promising. At home, the *Times* reports, Rhodes mulled over the idea, expanded the project, and added more retail and more parking. "Bingo," wrote the *Times*. "It penciled out."[63] He contacted Nordstrom, whose interest in the project was renewed, and officially informed his family that he was out of retirement.

With the Nordstrom family's provisional blessing, Rhodes's next move was to approach the city with his proposal. By this time, Deputy Mayor Bob Watt and the rest of the downtown task force had spent the better part of six months sifting through a number of proposals for the F&N site, few of which managed to arouse much enthusiasm. But then, in the fall of 1993, Watt looked up to find Jeff Rhodes, whom he had never met, standing in his office with Bill Bain, a longtime establishment stalwart whom the *Seattle Weekly* called "one of the city's best-connected figures."[64] As the *Weekly* explains, Bain's position in the development community derived primarily from his experience as a leading partner in NBBJ, Seattle's largest architectural firm and designer of, among other (in)famous structures, Pacific Place, Safeco Field (baseball stadium), and the much-maligned Kingdome. As Watt recalled, "Bill was well known to me. I trusted him, and thus I was predisposed to be open to anyone he brought in."[65]

According to one task force member, Bain first introduced Rhodes and told Watt, "Jeff has recently moved to Seattle, and he's done some other downtown retail-oriented projects, and I think you'll want to listen to him."[66] While most of the ideas pitched to Watt and the task force focused narrowly on occupying or renovating the F&N building, Rhodes's proposal was exponentially more ambitious (see figure 4.1). Instead of merely rehabbing the F&N site, Jeff Rhodes instead proposed to completely redevelop three entire blocks of Seattle's most expensive real estate. First, he would move Nordstrom out of its existing home in the Seaboard building and into a refurbished Frederick & Nelson building. This would fulfill the city's dreams by putting Nordstrom into the F&N site, but it would also allow Rhodes to redevelop the Seaboard building into new shops and offices. Finally, Rhodes proposed to "add critical mass" to the downtown retail scene by developing the largely abandoned Systems Block across the street from the F&N site into an elaborate and decidedly upscale five-story retail-cinema complex, built on top of seven levels of additional parking for downtown tourists and shoppers.

The result of the "Rhodes Project," as it came to be called, would be a massive recentralization of retail activity in Seattle's downtown core, designed explicitly to compete with suburban malls for the region's upscale consumers and with other cities for tourists and conventions. "It took awhile to grasp the magnitude" of Rhodes's proposal, Watt admitted. But after checking out Rhodes's bona fides in Chicago and Boston and determining that "by god, he'd done what he said he'd done," enthusiasm for the Rhodes Project began to spread throughout city hall.[67] "Frankly," as one task force member recalled, "his vision was the best by far . . . it really anchored retail downtown in a new way, [and] it captured Nordstrom," perhaps Norm Rice's most pressing priority.[68] As Watt said, "maybe there was a chance to get the local heroes into the F&N space and keep their back office operations in downtown after all."[69]

The main challenge would be getting (and keeping) the Nordstrom family onboard—a prospect that seemed increasingly unlikely as the retailer quickly began to unveil a laundry list of demands to both Rhodes and the mayor's task force. Put simply, by 1993, the Nordstrom family had grown accustomed to being wooed. According to the *Times*, cities across the country were tripping "over themselves trying to lure the retailer to their shopping malls," in most cases offering generous tax breaks, low-interest loans, and no-cost parking garages.[70] "I mean, really," as one task force member said, "in some places in the country, Nordstrom gets the building at way below market, and their whole first year's inventory and it's paid for by the city to get them there."[71] And, by most accounts, Nordstrom was ready to play this kind of entrepreneurial hardball with its hometown officials. However, it was by no means clear at that point if the city would be politically willing or legally able to offer the kinds of subsidies demanded by one of the nation's wealthiest retailers.

Figure 4.1
The Rhodes Project

- Pine Street Development (Jeff Rhodes and his investors) would buy the Frederick & Nelson building, drawing on a low-interest HUD Section 108 loan secured by the City of Seattle.

- Pine Street Development and Nordstrom would swap buildings in a straight-up trade, giving the retailer ownership of the more expensive F&N building while Pine Street Development would assume control over the smaller Nordstrom (Seaboard) building, with a plan to redevelop it into shops and offices, at an estimated cost of $100 million.

- Nordstrom would renovate the vacant Frederick & Nelson building into its flagship store, at a reported cost of $100 million.

- In order to help defray the renovation costs, Nordstrom would, first, receive a $20 million payment from Pine Street Development. Second, the City of Seattle would also support Nordstrom's application to have the facade of the Frederick & Nelson building designated as a historical landmark, qualifying Nordstrom Inc. for a property-tax exemption which would reportedly save them close to $10 million on renovation costs.

- Pine Street Development would buy the adjacent Systems Block, redeveloping the entire block into Pacific Place, a five-story retail-cinema complex connected via skybridge to the new Nordstrom store and estimated to cost $180 million.

- The City of Seattle would fund the construction of a seven-level 1,200 stall parking garage in the basement of Pacific Place.

Moreover, as discussed above, Nordstrom had up until that time expressed little enthusiasm about the notion of moving into the Frederick & Nelson building. In these crucial early discussions with Watt and Rhodes, the retailer repeatedly grumbled about the F&N building's inflated asking price and the hefty renovation costs.[72] With relocation and renovation costs estimated at nearly $100 million, as one retail analyst said, it would be difficult for Nordstrom to justify such a move to their shareholders.[73] And, indeed, as late as 1995, long after the agreement in principle had been reached by the key players, Nordstrom floated hints in the local press that they were still less than thrilled about the prospect of assuming control of the crumbling building.[74] "Nordstrom sounds ambivalent about the F&N deal," one local retail analyst told the *Times* in early 1995. "If it doesn't happen, it will almost be a relief."[75] In short, early on it was made abundantly clear to both Rhodes and the Rice administration that substantial financial incentives would have to be forthcoming in order to convince Nordstrom to make the trip across the street into the grand old F&N site.

Finally, in a surprise move, Nordstrom also presented the city with a number of last-minute demands related to what they called the "unfriendly retail atmosphere" of downtown Seattle. First, Nordstrom wanted some assurances that the proposed expansion of the Convention Center—which was languishing in the state legislature at the time—would go forward, and that the city would eventually become a port of call for international cruise ships. Both developments would, they felt, expand the pool of potential shoppers downtown by bringing in additional crowds of upscale tourists and conventioneers.[76] But most controversial of all would be their demand, forwarded at the very end of the negotiations, that the city open a one-block section of Pine Street (between Fourth and Fifth Avenues) to auto traffic. (The debate sparked by this demand will occupy much of our attention in the next chapter.)[77]

To be sure, Nordstrom was not the only private "partner" playing hardball with the city during the Rhodes Project negotiations. Early in the process, Jeff Rhodes and his investors (called Pine Street Development) also began to balk at both the scope of their own potential investment and the size of the incentives demanded by Nordstrom to secure their tenancy in the F&N site. For example, the Rhodes Plan called for Pine Street Development and Nordstrom to swap buildings in a straight-up trade after the developers purchased the vacant F&N site from the Padelford family. In this trade, the Nordstrom family would get a $26.7 million building for a mere $14 million (the assessed value of their own downtown store in the Seaboard building), while Pine Street Development would swallow a loss of over $12 million.[78] Furthermore, the developers also had provisionally agreed to forward a one-time $20 million payment to Nordstrom in order to help the national retailer defray the F&N building's high renovation costs.[79] As the cost of Nordstrom's participation in the deal began to pile up, Rhodes and his investors began to fret about their own exposure to financial risk and increasingly pressured the mayor's task force for direct city aid.[80]

As it turned out, the city was eager to deal. Given the sense of urgency around the "downtown crisis" (as it was perceived in elite circles), Norm Rice, Bob Watt, and the rest of the task force were in no mood to see the Rhodes Project slip away.[81] As one high-up official remembered, the internal discussion in the mayor's office went something like this:

> Well, we like this development. The guy [Jeff Rhodes] checked out. He's bona fide. He can do it. He has the confidence of the Nordstrom's, [and] that meets some of our most important goals . . . So we asked ourselves the question . . . "Is there anything the city could do to help?"[82]

In the State of Washington, however, finding a way to help out private developers requires an unusual degree of creativity. In most states, simply giving developers money is quite legal and even somewhat routine. However, Washington's state constitution, penned during the high tide of Western Prairie Populism in the 1880s, explicitly forbids cities from giving or even loaning money directly to an individual or corporation except to "support . . . the poor and infirm."[83] Consequently, as Bob Watt told the *Times*, city governments "have precious few tools in the state to do economic development," and merely handing over a direct subsidy to Rhodes and Nordstrom was out of the question.[84]

As one task force member recalled, the inability of the city to merely cut a check to help the developers meet Nordstrom's demands nearly smothered the Rhodes Project in its infancy. Rhodes in particular had little patience for the legal niceties of Washington State's populist constitution and periodically exploded in disbelief when he learned that a simple city giveaway was not in the offing:

> I mean, Jeff was used to people writing him big checks. Because in most other states, when you want a Nordstrom to come to your downtown, that's what you have to do. . . . And [so] we had to help educate Mr. Rhodes. It was very painful for him. "What? You can't just write us a check?" No we can't just write you a check. "What? You can't just give me some money?" No, we can't give you any money, not a penny . . . [85]

By all accounts, Rhodes, who had cut his teeth in more subsidy-friendly terrain, took a long time to come to terms with the limits on city financing. "He wasn't even on the same page with us, in terms of how the rules work around here," the task force member recalled. "And every time we'd tell him, he'd run screaming out the door."[86]

Unwilling to let the Rhodes Project die on the vine, the Rice administration decided to get creative. The question hanging over the downtown task force during this crucial time was deceptively straightforward: how could the city help make the Rhodes Project a reality without directly violating the state's prohibition on subsidies and giveaways? Looking for answers, Bob Watt made his way to the city's Office of Economic Development to brainstorm ideas about how the city could secure this redevelopment of the downtown retail core.[87] The answers came back in short order. First of all, the city could apply for a $24 million low-interest loan from the federal Department of Housing and Urban Development (HUD). If approved, the money could be quickly turned over to Pine Street Development, allowing the developers to acquire the overpriced F&N building while saving $5.5 million in interest over the life of the loan.[88] Second, the city could participate in the development of an approximately $60 million downtown parking garage, so long as the city retained control of the garage and received "tangible and intangible" benefits from their investment.[89]

Figure 4.2
Seattle's Retail Core

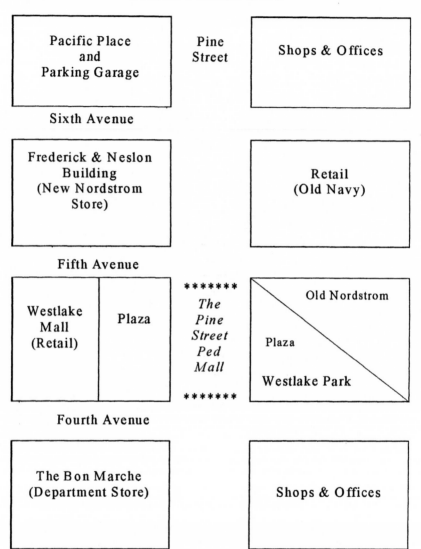

The final answer was the most simple, but also the most controversial: the city could also woo Nordstrom by agreeing to open the Pine Street pedestrian mall to traffic, an act that would route cars and trucks through the center of Westlake Park.[90]

With nearly $100 million in public subsidies and loans on the table, the complex three-way negotiations quickly picked up steam, and, after weeks of informal meetings, the *Times* reports, the key players—including Norm Rice, Bob Watt, Jim and Bruce Nordstrom, Jeff Rhodes, and Tom Klutznick—met for dinner at the Four Seasons Hotel in late 1993 to hammer out the final agreement.[91] Over coffee and dessert, these negotiators—some of the most powerful figures in the Seattle political scene—finally came to a "meeting of the minds."[92] In exchange for the $100 million in public assistance, the retail core would indeed attract $350 million in new retail investment (including the new Pacific Place Complex). But most importantly, the city would achieve its most fervent desire: a Nordstrom store at the all-important Frederick & Nelson site. In the end, the agreement hammered out at the Four Seasons Hotel would not only completely revamp the physical landscape of downtown Seattle, but would also spark some of the most heated debates in local politics in the last twenty years.

Notes

1. Jennifer Moulton, "Ten Steps to a Living Downtown," *A Discussion Paper Prepared for the Brookings Institution Center on Urban and Metropolitan Policy* (Washington, DC: Brookings Institution, 1999).
2. Though Moulton and Webb do not explicitly name an improved "urban image" as one of their goals in their Brookings Institution writings, an advertisement (circulating in airline magazines during 2001), depicted Denver as a world-class location for high-tech industries and especially highlighted the city's vibrant downtown as a main rationale for moving corporate facilities to the region.
3. Martin L. Millspaugh, "The Inner Harbor Story," *Urban Land Archives, April 2003*, retrieved from the Urban Land Institute website: http://research.uli.org. For a discussion of the limits of Baltimore's "comeback," see Judd and Swanstrom, *City Politics: Private Power and Public Policy* (New York: HarperCollins, 1994).
4. See William Hudnut, *Cities on the Rebound: A Vision for Urban America* for an example of this celebration of an urban American "comeback."
5. In some optimistic formulations, the renewed investment in downtown office space and the recentralization of upscale housing, retail, and culture in the central city has been linked by some theorists to the emergence of a "postindustrial" urban society. Liberated, in this view, from a long dependence on "dirty" smokestack manufacturing, the postindustrial city melds an economy based on professional services, cultural production, and high-tech innovation with a vibrant street life where new urban professionals and young "dot-coms" sample the best in high culture, upscale consumption, and nouveau cuisine. The contrast some self-styled futurists make between "industrial" and "postindustrial" cities was dramatized perfectly in an engraving accompanying an article by Alvin and Heidi Toffler in a recent copy of *The Futurist*. On one side of this engraving pollution pours out of factories, as a mass of huddled workers waits to start their tedious day. On the other side, white-collar workers are busy operating the new accoutrements of the "third wave" (as the Tofflers term the so-called "information society")—

they talk on cell phones, work at laptops, and send signals to a host of satellites circling the earth. Not a factory, or a blue-collar worker (or even a janitor) is to be found. See Alvin and Heidi Toffler, "Getting Set for the New Millennium," *The Futurist* (March-April 1995): 10-15. For a more restrained and defensible version of the "postindustrial" thesis, see Mike Featherstone, "City Cultures and Postmodern Lifestyles," in *Post-Fordism: A Reader*, ed. A. Amin (Oxford: Basil Blackwell), 392. David Ley, "Liberal Ideology and the Postindustrial City," *Annals of the Association of American Geographers* 70 (June 1980): 243. For a brief but incisive description of the "postindustrial city" thesis, see Andrew Mair, "The Homeless and the Postindustrial City," *Political Geography Quarterly* 5 (1986): 351-52.

6. George Lord and Albert Price, "Growth Ideology in a Period of Decline: Deindustrialization and Restructuring, Flint Style," *Social Problems* 39 (May 1992).

7. Dennis Coates and Brad Humphries, "The Growth Effects of Sports Franchises, Stadia, and Arenas," *Journal of Policy Analysis and Management* 18, no. 4: 601-24. K. L. Shropshire, *The Sports Franchise Game: Cities in Pursuit of Sports Franchises, Events, Stadiums*, (Philadelphia: University of Pennsylvania Press, 1995). See also, Sharon Zukin, "Urban Lifestyles: Diversity and Standardization in Spaces of Consumption," *Urban Studies* 35 (May 1998): 831.

8. Dennis Judd and Todd Swanstrom, *City Politics: Private Power and Public Policy* (New York: HarperCollins). See also, Amy Schwarz and Ingrid Ellen, "Cautionary Notes for Competitive Cities," a working paper available on the Brookings Institution website: www.brookings.edu.

9. Ronald Van Kempen and Peter Marcuse, "A New Spatial Order in Cities?" *The American Behavioral Scientist*, 41(November/December 1997): 285-98. See also, David Harvey, *The Condition of Postmodernity* (Oxford: Blackwell, 1990).

10. William Julius Wilson, *When Work Disappears* (New York: Basic Books, 1995). See also Saskia Sassen, *The Global City: New York, London, Tokyo* (Princeton, NJ: Princeton University Press, 1991) and Robert Reich, *The Work of Nations* (New York: Basic Books, 1991).

11. Bruce J. Katz, "Reviving Cities: Think Metropolitan," *Policy Brief #33, The Center on Urban and Metropolitan Policy, Brookings Institution*. Available from the Brookings website: www.brookings.edu.

12. Sharon Zukin, *The Culture of Cities* (Oxford: Blackwell, 1995). See also John Hannigan, *Fantasy City* (London: Routledge, 1998).

13. Trade Development Alliance of Greater Seattle, *International Promotion Plan* (December 1998): 3.

14. Trade Development Alliance of Greater Seattle, *King County: Crossroads of the Global Economy* (Promotional literature).

15. Trade Development Alliance, *International Promotion Plan*, 3.

16. Trade Development Alliance, *International Promotion Plan*, 3.

17. Trade Development Alliance, *Mission Statement*.

18. Bill Stafford and Sam Kaplan, "Greater Seattle's Secrets of the Trade," *The Regionalist* 2 (Fall 1997): 3.

19. Bill Stafford and Sam Kaplan, "Greater Seattle's Secrets of the Trade," 3.

20. Personal interview, Trade Development Alliance of Greater Seattle, 3 February 1999.

21. For example, the assurance that Seattle is indeed an interesting and vibrant place to visit can help local firms convince international companies to engage in trading relationships and partnership ventures. No one, this official explained, wants to conduct numerous and extended business trips in a place that has few amenities to offer international travelers.

22. Personal interview, Trade Development Alliance, 3 February 1999.

23. Personal interview, Trade Development Alliance, 3 February 1999.

24. Personal interview, Trade Development Alliance, 3 February 1999.

25. Personal interview, Seattle-King County Convention and Visitors Bureau, 4 February 1999.

26. Personal interview, Seattle-King County Convention and Visitors Bureau, 4 Febrary 1999.

27. Personal interview, Seattle-King County Convention and Visitors Bureau, 4 February 1999.

28. Personal interview, Seattle-King County Convention and Visitors Bureau, 4 February 1999.

29. Pierre Bourdieu, *Distinction: A Social Critique of the Judgment of Taste* (Cambridge, MA: Harvard University Press, 1984).

30. Mike Featherstone, "Postmodern City Cultures," in *Post-Fordism: A Reader*, ed. A. Amin (Cambridge, UK: Basil Blackwell, 1994).

31. Sharon Zukin, *Landscapes of Power: From Detroit to Disneyland* (Berkeley, CA: University of California Press, 1991), 261.

32. Judd and Swanstrom, *City Politics*, 294.

33. Judd and Swanstrom, *City Politics*, 337.

34. Margit Mayer, "Post-Fordist City Politics," in *Post-Fordism: A Reader*, ed. A. Amin (Cambridge, UK: Basil Blackwell, 1994).

35. David Wilson, "Metaphors, Growth Coalition Discourses, and Black Poverty in a U.S. City," *Antipode* 28 (1996): 72-96.

36. This is not to say that, over the past decade, developers *always* got what they wanted or that city officials *always* gave away the farm. The actual outcomes of these negotiations have been, and continue to be, quite variable. In fact, cities have at times won important concessions from developers, including, for example, a more equitable distribution of profits and risks or an agreement to subcontract with minority-owned firms. Still, in public-private negotiations, the pressure on the public sector to "do something" about urban decay and to compete successfully in the interurban scramble for global investment has usually played to the advantage of private developers—who, more often than not, have been in a position to take their money elsewhere. So while the actual outcome of any specific negotiation may be "up for grabs," the reality is that the private sector has typically come to the table with the stronger hand.

37. W. West, "Modell Hands Off to Glendening, But Fans Left Holding the Ball." *Insight on the News* 12 (January 1996), no. 3 48.

38. J. Soloman, "Whose Game is it Anyway?" *Washington Monthly* 31, (December 1999): 31

39. Personal interview, Greater Seattle Chamber of Commerce, 24 March 1999.

40. Bob Watt, printed copy of speech delivered to Rotary Club, date unknown. (Mr. Watt kindly printed out a copy for me to use for this project).

41. Bob Watt, printed copy of speech.

42. Personal interview, Seattle City Council Offices, 15 December 1998.

43. Personal interview, Downtown Seattle Task Force, 24 March 1999.

44. Bob Watt, printed copy of speech.

45. The importance Norm Rice attached to the project of downtown redevelopment can be seen in the makeup of this task force. The group was chaired by then-Deputy Mayor Bob Watt, a longtime Seattle business leader and future president of the Seattle Chamber of Commerce, and filled the task force with top-level administrators—mostly city department heads—along with key members of his own staff. Source: Personal interview, Downtown Seattle Task Force. See also, Sylvia Nogaki, "Task Force to Coax Retailers Downtown," *Seattle Times*, 7 August 1993.

46. Jim Erickson, "Nordstrom to Go to F&N building: Key Pieces of $400 Million Plan in Place," *Seattle Post-Intelligencer*, 27 June, 1995.

47. Rick Aramburu, Daniel Norton, Jan Drago, Kay Bullitt, and Ron Judd, "Should Pine Street be Re-Opened? Pro/Con," *Seattle Times*, 5 March 1995.

48. Draft letter in Jan Drago's Pine Street Election File, Seattle City Council Files.

49. Personal interview, Downtown Seattle Task Force, 24 March 1999.

50. Bob Watt, printed copy of speech.

51. Jeanne Sather, "No Pine Street, No deal, Rhodes says," *Puget Sound Business Journal*, 10 March, 1995.

52. Bob Watt, printed copy of speech.

53. Personal interview, Downtown Seattle Task Force, 24 March 1999.

54. Personal interview, Downtown Seattle Task Force, 24 March 1999.

55. Personal interview, Downtown Seattle Task Force, 24 March 1999.

56. Personal interview, Downtown Seattle Task Force, 24 March 1999.

57. Personal interview, Downtown Seattle Task Force, 24 March 1999. See also, Michelle Flores, "Downtown Dealmaker: Frederick & Nelson Heir Holds the Key to Revitalizing Seattle's Retail Core," *Seattle Times*, 16 January 1992, D1.

58. Personal interview, Downtown Seattle Task Force, 24 March 1999.

59. Sylvia Nogaki, "Reluctant Inhabitant of Seattle Limelight," *Seattle Times*, 20 December 1994. See also, J. Haberstroh and Polly Lane, "A 'Rookie' to the Rescue," *Seattle Times*, 28 May 1994.

60. Sylvia Nogaki, "Reluctant Inhabitant."

61. Sylvia Nogaki, "Reluctant Inhabitant."

62. Sylvia Nogaki, "Reluctant Inhabitant."

63. Sylvia Nogaki, "Reluctant Inhabitant."

64. Mark Worth, "Who Really Runs Seattle? A Who's Who of the City's Backroom Wheeler-Dealers," *Seattle Weekly*, 12 November 1998, 15.

65. Bob Watt, printed copy of speech.

66. Personal interview, Downtown Seattle Task Force, 24 March 1999.

67. Bob Watt, printed copy of speech.

68. Personal interview, Downtown Seattle Task Force, 24 March 1999.

69. Bob Watt, printed copy of speech.

70. Barbara Serrano and Deborah Nelson, "City Overpaid Pine Street Developer," *Seattle Times*, 21 December 1997, 1(A).

71. Personal interview, Downtown Seattle Task Force, 24 March 1999.

72. For details on Nordstrom's on-again-off-again enthusiasm for the Rhodes Project, see Polly Lane, "Full Steam Ahead for Flagship Downtown," *Seattle Times*, 2 No-

vember 1994; Sylvia Nogaki, "Solving the Pine Street Puzzle," *Seattle Times*, 28 November 1994; Casey O'Corr, "Pine Street Not Only Hurdle for Investors," *Seattle Times*, 15 December 1994; Jeanne Sather, "No Pine Street, No Deal, Rhodes Says," *Puget Sound Business Journal*, 10 March 1995.

73. Jeanne Sather, "No Pine Street, No Deal, Rhodes says."

74. Jeanne Sather, "No Pine Street, No Deal, Rhodes says."

75. Jeanne Sather, "No Pine Street, No Deal."

76. Personal interview, Downtown Task Force, 24 March 1999.

77. Rebecca Boren, "Pine Street Debate Opens Old Wounds," *Seattle Post-Intelligencer*, 2 December 1994, 4(A).

78. *Frederick & Nelson Redevelopment: Project Summary.* Executive report to the City Council, 14 December 1994, Seattle City Archives, Sue Donaldson Subject Files (see methodological appendix for retrieval information).

79. Barbara Serrano and Deborah Nelson, "City Overpaid Pine Street Developer," *Seattle Times*, 21 December 1997, 1(A).

80. Personal interview, Pine Street Development, 8 April 1999.

81. Barbara Serrano and Deborah Nelson, "City Overpaid Pine Street Developer."

82. Personal interview, Downtown Task Force, 24 March 1999.

83. Serrano and Nelson, "City Overpaid Pine Street Developer."

84. Serrano and Nelson, "City Overpaid Pine Street Developer."

85. Personal interview, Downtown Task Force, 24 March 1999.

86. Personal interview, Downtown Task Force, 24 March 1999. This member put Rhodes's position in these negotiations this way: "Look, he's a developer. He would love to load 100 percent of his costs on the city. The city was not willing to do that . . . and sometimes it was very difficult. He walked away from the table, and we did too."

87. Serrano and Nelson, "City Overpaid Pine Street Developer."

88. As Doug Collins reports, the HUD loan effectively reduced the interest rate paid by Pine Street Development on the purchase of the F&N site from 9 to 6 percent, representing a savings of $5,630,000 over the life of the loan. For details, see Doug Collins, "Seattle to Nordstrom: Try on Anything You'd Like," *The Washington Free Press*, June/July 1995.

89. Barbara Serrano, "City Clears Legal Review on Pine Street Garage Deal: Money to Developer Deemed Constitutional," *Seattle Times*, 23 April 1998, 1(A).

90. Personal interview, Downtown Task Force, 24 March 1999.

91. Serrano and Nelson, "City Overpaid."

92. Serrano and Nelson, "City Overpaid."

Chapter 5

Public Resources, Private Power:
The Struggle Over Seattle's Retail Core

Prohibited by state law from giving public money outright to subsidize corporations or individuals (except the "poor and infirm"), city officials in Seattle had to be creative if they wanted to funnel public support to the Rhodes Project—a project which they viewed as crucial to the survival of downtown retail and the city's tax base. In this chapter, I will focus on three debates over both the scope and scale of city involvement in the Rhodes Project, beginning with the most substantial public investment in the enterprise: the multimillion dollar parking garage built entirely at public expense. A second debate concerned the city's attempt to secure a low-interest loan from the federal Department of Housing and Urban Development (HUD)—a loan that could then be turned over to help Pine Street Development purchase the Frederick & Nelson building. Focusing their ire on the city's claim that the F&N site was a "blight" on the downtown retail core (and therefore qualified for federal anti-slum aid), activists opposed to city involvement in the Rhodes Project eventually filed a formal complaint with the national HUD office—a complaint which eventually reached the upper echelons of the Clinton administration and undermined the political ambitions of a prominent Seattle politician.

Finally, a third debate sparked by the Rhodes Project concerned a *spatial* rather than financial concession. In response to the Nordstrom family's fears that the pedestrian mall at Westlake Park (adjacent to the F&N site) would threaten the viability of a new and larger Nordstrom department store, the city decided in 1994 to allow traffic to flow once again on Pine Street, right through the heart of Westlake Park. The vocal opposition of a coalition of community activists and progressive planners to this move eventually forced an electoral showdown in early 1995, a showdown which would decide not only the future of Pine Street, but also the fate of the Rhodes Project and the future shape of downtown Seattle.

The Pacific Place Parking Garage: Let's Make a Deal

As noted earlier, during his early negotiations with the city, Jeff Rhodes began to have second thoughts about his involvement in the Rhodes Project, especially when he added up the various cash incentives Pine Street Development would have to give Nordstrom to secure their move into the F&N site. For instance, once Rhodes bought the F&N site from the Padelford family for $26.7 million, the plan called for him to immediately swap it with the Nordstrom family in a straight-up exchange for Nordstrom's current store (in the Seaboard building), valued at approximately $14 million. This exchange would force Pine Street Development to swallow a loss of nearly $13 million.[1] In addition, Rhodes and his investors had also agreed to give the Nordstrom family a one-time $20 million payment—a bribe, some might say—in order to help the retailer defray the F&N building's high rehabilitation costs.[2]

Facing nearly $33 million in direct payments to convince Nordstrom to agree to move into the F&N building, Jeff Rhodes and Pine Street Development came to the city's task force looking for financial help. Eager to keep Rhodes at the table, city officials tried to brainstorm ways to help Rhodes meet his obligations to Nordstrom without directly contravening the state's prohibition on kickbacks and giveaways. The first answer came back in short order. Because the project needed parking to succeed, the city could pay for a parking garage as part of the project, so long as the city retained control of the facility and received "tangible and intangible" benefits from the investment. Therefore, after Rice, Watt, Rhodes, and the Nordstrom family hammered out the basic outlines of the Rhodes Project in a December 1993 meeting, all the parties agreed that a city-funded parking garage would be an integral part of the deal.

The question still to be resolved was *how much* the city would pay to build the Pacific Place parking garage. Typically, cities looking to build more parking downtown would choose a suitable site and then try to get the lowest possible construction price for the project. But, during the negotiations with Pine Street Development over the price of building the parking garage, it was clear that this would not be a typical project. From the very beginning, the Rice administration made it clear to Rhodes that they were willing to substantially overpay Pine Street Development to build the garage, with the extra money earmarked to help the developers offset the losses they accumulated from giving Nordstrom such a sweet deal.[3] As Pine Street Development co-manager Matt Griffin told the *Times*, the developers themselves viewed the overpayment on the garage as a direct subsidy from the city. With the developers on the hook for nearly $33 million in direct payments to Nordstrom, Griffin recalled, "we needed all the money we could get."[4] And without a substantial profit from the construction of the garage, Rhodes and his investors would abandon the project.

By all accounts, the actual cost of building the garage would be somewhere in the $50 million range. The question then became how far *above* this figure would the city be willing to go in order to help Rhodes and his investors out. Rhodes initially wanted a cool $100 million—a figure that would cover Pine Street Development's $33 million in giveaways to Nordstrom, and then some.[5] But no one took that number seriously. As one city official put it, "[Jeff Rhodes] is a developer. He would love to load 100 percent of his costs on the city. The city was not willing to do that."[6] As a result, by the summer of 1994, Rhodes's asking price soon came down to around $70 million. Even then, city negotiators were still somewhat skeptical at this latest price tag—which would forward a $20 million overpayment to the developer—but nonetheless agreed to take a closer look.

According to the *Times*, Watt then took the $70 million price tag to the Engineering Department and "asked them to determine if the city could buy and operate a garage in that price range without losing money."[7] As Watt told the *Times*, in these discussions with city experts, he did not ask them to seek advice from parking consultants nor did he attempt to discover what other cities paid for similar parking garages. Instead, he asked the city's financial and engineering staff to determine if the parking revenues generated by such a garage would cover Rhodes's $70 million price tag.[8] "I was actually looking at, 'what can we do that pencils out for the taxpayers,'" as he told *Times* reporters Barbara Serrano and Deborah Nelson. "In my mind, the garage was one of the important points to getting the project done." In other words, the question circulating in city hall at that point was not "how could the city build a garage at the *lowest* cost" but rather "how *much* could the city pay the developers without losing money for the taxpayers?"[9]

When the city's financial advisors concluded that, yes, parking revenues would most likely cover even a $70 million investment, the negotiations over the parking garage came to a head. As the *Times* reports, in late July 1994, Mayor Rice and Jeff Rhodes signed a letter of intent laying out the basics for the city's purchase of the garage—including an estimated price range between $63 million and $68 million, pending last-minute negotiations on the final asking price.[10] A month later, Watt directed then-finance director Dwight Dively to seal the deal with Pine Street Development in the $68 million price range, and by the time the city council voted on the agreement a year later in June of 1995, the garage's final price tag had inflated to a robust $73 million.[11]

Why did the asking price suddenly rise nearly $10 million in the space of a few months? As one task force member involved in the negotiations explains, in exchange for an agreement to overpay the developers for the parking garage, the city negotiated to have a whole host of extra clauses and conditions included in the final agreement—conditions that tailored the final shape of the Rhodes Project more to the city's liking and that reduced the city's financial risk regarding their investment in the parking garage.[12] For example, in exchange for the inflated price tag on the parking garage, the city forced Rhodes to agree to a height limitation on Pacific Place, thus preserving the more human scale of the retail core (as compared to the skyscraper canyons of the financial district). In addition, the city was concerned that Rhodes's original plans for Pacific Place—which, in addition to retail and entertainment establishments, also included a large hotel—would not generate enough parking revenues to cover the cost of the city's investment. Therefore, the city forced Rhodes to nix his plans for a new downtown hotel in Pacific Place and instead got the developer to commit all of Pacific Place's space to retail and entertainment—uses which generate more downtown "visits" and therefore more parking revenues for the city.[13]

But it was the city's demand for a "no financial risk" clause in the final agreement that pushed the final asking price of the parking garage up to $73 million. The heart of this "no financial risk" clause in the Pacific Place contract was what one city official called a "put/call provision."[14] Basically this provision gave the city the right after twenty years to *require* that Pacific Place's owner—in short, Pine Street Development or whoever controlled the complex in the future—buy back the garage from the city.[15] As another city official noted, this price of this "buyback" would include any remaining outstanding debt on the city bonds used to pay the initial $73 million plus any losses incurred in the first twenty years of the garage's operation, plus interest on those losses.[16] "In other words," as one task force negotiator said, "if there's an earthquake five years from now, and downtown Seattle is destroyed and that parking garage therefore doesn't perform the way it should, the city can put the whole deal back to the developer" and force them to repay all of the city's costs that had not been covered by parking revenues collected over the past two decades.[17]

In a speech to the Rotary Club, Watt called this "no financial risk" clause an "unprecedented agreement" that forced the developer to assume all risks and which allowed that the city to "get out of the deal, have zero net costs and still benefit from the additional tax revenues, downtown parking availability, [and] new jobs created" by the redevelopment of Seattle's retail core.[18] But this "no financial risk" clause came with a hefty price tag, as Rhodes and his investors were unwilling to agree to such a provision without getting some concessions in return. First, the developers negotiated in a "call" option into the agreement. Basically, this "call" option gives Pine Street Development the ability to buy the garage back from the city after twenty years for the initial asking price of $73 million (plus any outstanding debt on the city's bonds) or 90 percent of the current appraised value of the parking garage, whichever is greater.[19] In this way, if the garage turns out to be a huge moneymaker, beginning in 2018, the developer can buy it back and assume control over the revenue stream themselves. And finally, as we have seen, the city's demand for a "no financial risk" clause motivated the developers to hold out for a meaty initial asking price, forcing the cost of the development up from $63 million to $73 million in a few short months.[20]

So, in the end, what did the city get for their $73 million investment in the Pacific Place parking garage? If the city simply spent the money to build 1,200 new spaces of downtown parking, they were clearly taken to the cleaners. As reported in the *Times*, most urban planners agree that, at $73 million, the city paid almost twice the going rate for similar downtown underground parking structures around the United States.[21] But, by all accounts, $73 million was never the price for a simple parking garage. It was the cost of doing business with Nordstrom and Pine Street Development. As one member of the Rice administration said, "the city did *not* pay $73 million dollars for a parking garage, the city paid $73 million dollars for an *agreement*" with the city's private partners—an agreement which helped the Rhodes Project become a reality and which, in his view, loaded most of the financial risk onto the developers.[22] As former councilmember Tom Weeks told the *Times* two years after the fact, it was clear to everyone in the mayor's office and on the council that the $73 million was buying the Rhodes Project, and not the BMW of urban parking structures. "It wasn't that we wanted to build a garage," Weeks said. "It was that we wanted a Nordstrom development. . . . It was presented to us as all or nothing."[23]

For their part, Pine Street Development received a check for $73 million in November of 1998, which, as co-manager Matt Griffin confirmed, allowed the developers to clear a profit of $23 million on the construction of the $50 million parking garage.[24] So where would this money go? Griffin, usually quite willing to speak to the media, was tight-lipped about the developers' plans. "Our obligations with the city are basically to provide the items of value that the city has required. It is not to tell the city how we spent the money."[25] But, as the *Times* noted, Pine Street Development owed Nordstrom a $20 million payment to offset the retailer's rehabilitation costs in the F&N site, so it was a safe bet that some of the money would be funneled directly to the upscale retailer. Moreover, as former councilmember Jim Street speculated, the profit off the garage deal would also help Pine Street Development make up the difference between what the Padelford's (the descendants of D. E. Frederick and owners of the vacant store) were asking for the vacant F&N building and what, under normal circumstances, the developers would be willing to pay.[26]

Perhaps most notably, both the city's task force and Pine Street Development had together discovered a nifty way to skirt the state constitution's prohibition on giving public money, loans, or property to any "individual, association, company or corporation, except for the necessary support of the poor and infirm."[27] Forced to demonstrate that the city government would receive "tangible benefits" from any agreement with a private party, building a parking garage at city expense presented an almost irresistible way out of this constitutional dilemma.[28] By building the garage and supporting the project, the city could argue that taxpayers would receive plenty of "benefits," including not just more downtown parking, but also more taxes from retail sales and the creation of 2,800 jobs through the redevelopment of the retail core.[29]

But by paying such a high price for the garage (and, as task force negotiators would be quick to point out, for the "no financial risk clause" and the other provisions in the agreement),[30] the city could in turn help the developers make a big profit on the garage portion of the project. This profit could then be used by the developers to offset the expensive incentives demanded by the Nordstrom family in order to secure their participation in the deal. As Roamy Valera of the International Parking Institute told the *Times* after hearing of the garage deal, "It looks like what they're saying is, 'we can't give you anything directly. But if you build it, we'll buy it for this price and that's how we'll give to the project."[31] It would seem that, in the end, in a nifty end-run around the state's constitution, Jeff Rhodes got his "big check" after all.

However, what's most remarkable in this saga about parking in Seattle is how for almost three years, it managed to utterly escape the attention of local mainstream press. When the city council finally approved the $73 million payment in June of 1995, some councilmembers, particularly Jane Noland, grumbled publicly about paying $73 million for a garage that would cost about $50 million. "The city has not negotiated. It has given a gift," she said. "I don't know what we'll say the next time somebody comes and asks for public money for a private effort."[32] When some of her colleagues on the council disputed her view of the deal, arguing that the city received fair value for the amount invested in the project as a whole, Noland reportedly held up a plastic cup and said, "Well . . . if this costs a dollar and the city pays five dollars for it, I don't know what else to say other than we overpaid."[33] In the end, however, even Noland voted to approve the city's investment in the parking garage. Citing the need to move the Rhodes Project to completion, and with some unhappy statements about feeling "pressured" to move quickly on the parking garage, the council voted 9-0 to approve the funds.

At the time, neither the *Times* nor the *Post-Intelligencer* quoted such dissenting statements extensively.[34] With the exception of then-councilmember Jim Street's statement that he was "less than delighted about the price we're paying for the garage,"[35] press accounts of the meeting merely noted in passing that there had been some dissension among councilmembers, but that, in the end, "the economic development arguments were just too persuasive to haggle over a few million dollars one way or another."[36] Absent from such accounts was any mention of the $23 million gap or the finer points of the Rhodes Project agreement (including the "no financial risk" provision). For his part, when asked why the $23 million gap and the other details of the garage deal escaped the public's attention for so long, former councilmember Jim Street argued that, when it comes to downtown redevelopment, the local media is more lapdog than watchdog.[37] "At a minimum, the press should have known it. Any serious inquiry would have revealed (the gap)," he told the *Times* years later. Sure, he conceded, "the council was probably not wildly enthusiastic about broadcasting" the gap between what the garage cost the developers and what the city paid for it. "But the press itself was so gung-ho about whatever it takes . . . [for the F&N project] to succeed, that maybe it was not being critical in its own reporting."[38]

This period of silence would end abruptly three years later, when *Seattle Times* reporters Barbara Serrano and Deborah Nelson published a series of arti-

cles spelling out the details of the garage deal, including the origins of the negotiations, the $73 million price tag, the $23 million gap between the cost of
the garage and the city's payment, and what seemed to be an attempt to skirt
the state's constitutional ban on direct subsidies to private interests.[39] Suddenly
the city's investment in downtown parking, which had largely escaped serious
attention for the better part of three years, was front-page news, and the result
was a brief but vigorous debate over the appropriateness of the city's decision to
help subsidize some of the wealthiest investors and corporations in the Pacific
Northwest. What, in fact, did the city get for the extra $23 million? Why did no
one make a concerted effort to tell the public about the $23 million gap and the
specific contract provisions (i.e., the "no financial risk clause") this extra payment ostensibly purchased? For five months in early 1998, these questions
gripped Seattle's downtown political scene.

The Rice administration's harshest critics argued that this was just the latest example of city hall's complete absorption into the downtown business and
property establishment. Citing the close to $110 million in total public invest-
ment into the Rhodes/Nordstrom Project, which included the $73 million park-
ing garage, the Seattle Displacement Coalition's John Fox exclaimed, "the gall
of the crowd . . . to tell us that all of this was good for us. Imagine what $110
million dollars could have done to help us overcome homelessness in our community. The city does not spend this kind of money in five years for construction of low-income housing."[40] In short, the notion that the city would skirt the
state constitution to funnel subsidies to developers did not shock longtime opponents of Rice and the downtown business community. As one Displacement
Coalition member said, "there is definitely a dominant class, a corporate elite in
this downtown . . . that calls the shots on public policy." This elite, the member
argued, has the resources and the political tools to "create a climate that benefits them."[41]

In a surprising move, such longtime critics of downtown redevelopment as
John Fox were briefly joined by none other than the typically pro-growth (and
always pro–Rhodes Project) *Seattle Times* editorial board. In a scathing editorial printed two days after Serrano and Nelson's initial exposé on the $23 mil-
lion gap, the *Times* weighed into the debate with a rare critique of Seattle's
development politics. The city, the editors argued, "knew they were overpaying
but were stunningly disinterested in the size of their—our—gift. Nor, it seems,
were they interested in telling the public that the deal for the garage included
money that may yet make its way to Nordstrom."[42] When it comes to public-
private partnerships, the *Times* concluded, "every deal needs thorough scrutiny,
informed questioning, arms-length relationships, and full disclosure." But instead, the city seemed to follow a policy of "don't ask, don't tell" when confronted with private demands for public subsidies.[43]

Under immense pressure to justify the parking garage deal, and particularly the stunning $23 million "overpayment," pro-growth, pro–Rhodes forces

in the mayor's office and the downtown business establishment began to rally a vigorous defense of both former Mayor Rice and the Rhodes deal as a whole. In a letter to the *Seattle Times,* Downtown Seattle Association president Kate Joncas assailed the *Times* editors for "poisoning . . . responsible, reasonable civic debate" through "the vituperative, irresponsible name-calling on your editorial page."[44] In Joncas's view, "the Mayor and the city council made tough decisions about investing in downtown projects as part of a revitalization strategy for the city, and the investment is paying off, spectacularly."

The official line, of course, was to emphasize that the $73 million was for the agreement, not the garage, and that the city also received for this payment a host of other benefits, including the taxes, jobs, and spin-off development generated by over $350 million in private investment in downtown. Arguing that *Seattle Times* reporters Serrano and Nelson printed their stories without ever reading the fine print of the agreement, including especially the put/call provisions,[45] former deputy mayor and current Chamber of Commerce President Bob Watt told the Rotary Club that "it is an awesome testimony to the power of the press that the story continues to be that the city spent $73 million dollars for a $50 million parking garage! Because the city did no such thing!"[46]

This rhetorical counterattack by the downtown business establishment seems to have had the desired effect on the mainstream media. Citing a sixteen-page opinion released by Assistant Attorney General Mary Jo Diaz, which found that the deal lived up to the letter (if not the spirit) of the state's constitution,[47] the *Seattle Times* editors effected a sudden political turnaround. Arguing that the Rhodes Project had sparked a growing renaissance in "the city's most important neighborhood—downtown," it was time to let bygones be bygones. "Last year in this space, we leveled some harsh criticism at Seattle officials for . . . investing $73 million dollars in a new downtown parking garage estimated to cost $50 million. Turns out that criticism was too harsh." While the *Times* lightly chided the city for their "skimpier-than-usual public process" and disclosure prior to the council's rushed approval of the deal, the editors nonetheless declared their concerns over the deal's finances to be ancient history. "With legal concerns over the garage put to rest" by the attorney general's findings, "it's time to celebrate the city's renewed vitality, not pick at the bones of a done deal." The hatchet, it seems, had been buried and the rift repaired. With the *Times* again onboard, the downtown establishment could walk arm in arm toward the future of a new downtown Seattle.

Norm Rice, the HUD Loan, and the Crime Wave that Wasn't

If the parking garage deal required the city to perform contortions to skirt the state constitution's restrictions on public subsidies, then the city's second answer was deceptively simple. If the prohibition on direct subsidies to for-profit firms applied only to city and state funds, why not draft the *federal* government into the service of downtown revitalization? Seattle's downtown task force was clearly onto something. Even the merest look at American history reveals federal giveaways and subsidies to private enterprise so massive that they boggle the mind.[48] As a result, during the fall of 1993, the downtown task force began to explore the variety of federal programs offered by the Department of Housing and Urban Development in their mandate to fight poverty, homelessness, and urban blight.

What they discovered in this search was HUD's Section 108 low-interest loan program. Under the Section 108 program, federal low-interest loans are made available to local governments to assist in their economic and community development projects. However, to qualify for a Section 108 loan, cities must use the funds to meet one of three broad objectives: activities that benefit low- and moderate-income families, the elimination of slums and blight, and community development activities of urgent need.[49] While most localities used the first rationale for Section 108 proposals, Seattle's application focused on the elimination of slums and blight, and they argued that the vacant F&N site was such a pernicious example of "spot blight" that it threatened to undermine the downtown core. If approved by HUD, the Section 108 loan could then be quickly turned over to Jeff Rhodes and his investors at Pine Street Development, allowing the developers to acquire the overpriced F&N building while saving them over $5.5 million in interest over the life of the loan.[50]

But before the money could be forwarded to the Rhodes Project, the task force had to overcome a number of political hurdles both in city hall and in Washington, D.C. The first challenge was to overcome internal dissension in the Rice administration over the wisdom of extending the city's credit to a private party. Under the Section 108 program, HUD's low-interest loans can indeed be forwarded to a private developer—for example, to a contractor to build low-income housing—but the city government would act as a "co-signer" and promise to repay the loan if the private partner missed their payments. As the alternative press in Seattle discovered, Venerria Knox of Seattle's Department of Housing and Human Services expressed concern over the risk of forwarding the unusually large $24 million HUD loan to Jeff Rhodes and his investors. The developers *might* default, she argued. Although Nordstrom seemed like a world-beater today, like all firms, the company could fall on hard times, dragging down Pacific Place and the rest of the redevelopment with it.[51] In short, if Pine Street Development went belly-up and defaulted on the loan, Knox argued that the city's credit rating would be bruised as well, resulting in higher interest costs for all future city projects.

As Doug Collins reports, in the rush to aid the Rhodes Project, Knox's internal concerns were quickly suppressed, and the Rice administration continued to doggedly pursue the HUD loan.[52] The next challenge, then, lay in convincing skeptical federal officials that the vacant Frederick & Nelson's building was indeed a "blight" on the surrounding neighborhood—a neighborhood which included some of the most expensive and obviously nonblighted real estate in the Pacific Northwest. In order to promote their application for HUD assistance, task force officials argued that, first, the Frederick & Nelson's building was a crumbling eyesore with few prospects for redevelopment outside of Jeff Rhodes's proposal, and, second, that the vacant building had thrown the surrounding neighborhood into a spiral of urban decay and disorder.

Demonstrating that the F&N site had become an eyesore in the center of the retail core was not a difficult task: the site's boarded-up windows and graffiti-splashed walls spoke for themselves. But demonstrating that the grand old building was a crumbling behemoth nearly beyond redemption was another matter entirely. To argue this point, the city relied heavily upon a study conducted by the Callison Partnership, a private architectural firm hired by the Nordstrom family, which concluded that the building was, to put it simply, falling apart and would undoubtedly impose large renovation costs on its eventual owner.[53] Without the HUD loan, the city argued, the cost of renovating the old structure would make it virtually impossible to find a private buyer. In fact, the city further contended that the Rhodes Project had been the only viable proposal for the building to emerge in the two years since the old retailer had shut its doors, and even Rhodes had threatened to walk from the deal if substantial public funds could not be found to help out the project.[54]

Furthermore, the city's HUD application argued, the decay of the F&N site had begun to spill out into the neighborhood surrounding the darkened and vacant structure. As one task force member put it, "you know, it's an unfortunate truism about humankind that where there are dark and dank corners, there gathers bad stuff. Well, there were dark and dank corners around the F&N building, and bad stuff was gathering."[55] Topping the list of "bad stuff," according to city officials, was a dramatic increase in street crime in the area around the vacant F&N site. Brandishing alarming Seattle Police Department statistics, the city argued that crime had exploded by 92 percent around Frederick & Nelson's since its closure (despite a 4 percent decrease in downtown overall).[56] Indeed, as one pro-development councilmember contended, the rise in street disorder around the vacant site had driven a number of other retailers out of business. The blight was spreading. Without HUD assistance, the city would have little hope of reversing the momentum of urban decline sparked by this single building's closure. As one task force member concluded, "I don't know what the definition of 'spot blight' is if it isn't that you've got an abandoned building that's attracting graffiti and drug dealing."[57]

With Norm Rice's blessing, the city submitted the loan application to HUD's Washington D.C. headquarters in the spring of 1994. To smooth its way in the federal bureaucracy, Mayor Norm Rice then asked Democratic Senator Patty Murray to lobby HUD Secretary Henry Cisneros on the city's behalf. According to the *Times*, Murray enthusiastically took up the city's cause and held many conversations with both HUD's central office and with members of the White House staff, pleading the city's case that the vacant F&N site was indeed a crucial instance of "spot blight" and in need of immediate federal assistance.[58] Despite some early rumblings at HUD's Seattle office, which, according to the *Times*, held a narrow view of what qualifies as "blight," the national headquarters indeed approved the city's Section 108 loan application in August of 1994, paving the way for the final contract between the city, Pine Street Development, and Nordstrom in the summer of 1995.

However, this use of federal money did not sit well with many of the mayor's critics in the local activist community. In particular, members of the Seattle Displacement Coalition, a local housing and antipoverty advocacy group, viewed the city's attempt to subsidize the Rhodes Project as "such a blatant example of corporate welfare that it couldn't be overlooked."[59] As one activist argued, handing a HUD loan over to some of the wealthiest investors and businesses in Seattle was "a gross misuse of limited . . . city resources . . . [I]nstead these monies should be going to serve, to meet very basic needs, housing needs, and serving communities of color and doing something substantive to overcome inequality in our community. . . . And, indeed, that was the primary purpose of [the Section 108] program."[60] Meeting with other critics of the Rhodes Project, including some local journalists looking into the nuts and bolts of the city's participation, the Displacement Coalition sat down to hammer out a way to challenge the HUD loan. What they decided during this meeting was that, in addition to challenging the constitutionality of the city's actions in state court, they could also file a formal complaint with the local HUD office and argue that the "blighted" nature of the F&N site—and the surrounding neighborhood—had been grossly exaggerated in the city's initial application.[61]

In this complaint, the Coalition first took aim at the city's contention that crime had more than doubled in the retail core. After wrestling the raw crime data away from a reluctant Police Department (by threatening a lawsuit), Coalition staffers made a startling discovery. The city cooked the books. Whole categories of crime (including 997 incidents of shoplifting) had been included in the 1993 "after closure" figures but mysteriously deleted from the 1991 "before closure" tally, leaving the mistaken impression that the crime rate around the F&N site had doubled since the building's closure.[62] When the activists compared apples to apples—in short, when they compared the same number of crime categories across the years—they discovered no appreciable rise in crime around the vacant F&N site. As Doug Collins wrote in the *Washington Free Press*, the corrected numbers show that the much-hyped "frightening crime wave"—the same crime wave which allowed the city to claim that downtown was blighted—"turned out to be no wave at all."[63]

Next, the Coalition's HUD complaint disputed the city's contention that the Rhodes Project was the only hope for redeveloping the F&N site, and, by extension, the only hope for revitalizing the downtown retail core. As Jeff Rhodes himself told the *Puget Sound Business Journal* in 1995, "there is no Plan B. There is no backup" to the Nordstrom/Rhodes deal.[64] In their many public statements on the Project, the city participated in this "all or nothing" brand of political brinkmanship, stating at one point that Pine Street Development was the only investor group "willing to go far enough to sign legal documents" regarding the redevelopment of the F&N building.[65] However, a brief look at the record indicates otherwise. According to Steve Wood, the real estate advisor representing the Padelford family (who owned the F&N site), the Rhodes Project was not the only viable offer circulating at the time. "If this one [Jeff Rhodes's proposal] doesn't happen," he told the *Puget Sound Business Journal* back in 1994, "we have lots of interest from others."[66] In fact, as Doug Collins reports, Wood had at least two other prospective buyers vying for the site, "both with the requisite qualifications and financial footing to complete a transaction."[67] As the Coalition's HUD complaint argued, the fact that other potential buyers were seeking the property casts serious doubt on the city's contention that it was Rhodes's way or the highway.

All in all, as these activists told HUD investigators, the city's argument that the vacant F&N site was "blight" on the neighborhood falls apart with the merest evaluation. As the Coalition saw it, the padded crime statistics, the concealment of two other potential buyers, and the reliance on the Nordstrom family's own evaluation of the building's condition all point to a systematic plan to deceive HUD officials in order to divert money typically earmarked for low-income projects to the city's private, for-profit development partners. As Jordan Brower told the *Washington Free Press*, "what Mayor Rice did is no laughing matter. The city purposefully misled HUD by claiming that downtown's premiere retail core was a slum."[68]

At the time, the Coalition's formal complaint seemed destined for bureaucratic obscurity. The national HUD office had quickly approved the loan back in 1994 with few questions asked[69] and, in a May 1996 visit to Seattle, HUD Secretary Henry Cisneros had publicly praised the Rice administration's aggressive promotion of downtown redevelopment, telling the assembled members of the Downtown Seattle Association that "what you're doing here is about the best of what I've seen in the country."[70] But in early December 1996, the national HUD Inspector General moved the Coalition's complaint onto the fast track when the Clinton White House tagged Seattle Mayor Norm Rice as the front-runner in the search to replace Cisneros as HUD Secretary. By December 13, the concerns raised by the inspector general's investigation threw Rice's nomination into a tailspin.[71] During the next few days, as investigators sifted through the city's Section 108 application, supporters of the other candidates, especially New York's Andrew Cuomo, mobilized inside the White House. In the end, the choice between a Seattle mayor dogged by controversy and the son of former New York governor and Democratic stalwart Mario Cuomo was a foregone conclusion. By December 20, Norm Rice's supporters conceded defeat and the mayor returned home to finish the last year of his term.[72]

Eventually, the mayor's office would be cleared of criminal wrongdoing, though the inspector general would state that some of the information included in the city's application "may have been misleading or questionable."[73] A later audit of the loan itself also concluded that while the city was less than forthcoming in its descriptions of the "blighted" F&N site, the application technically adhered to the definition of "spot blight" as spelled out in HUD regulations. But this report also noted that the HUD rules regarding what qualifies as "spot blight" were so vague that they invited the sort of administrative chicanery included in Seattle's F&N application, and, in the end, investigators recommended that the national office tighten its notion of what can constitute "blight" in its Section 108 program.[74] Although the mayor's supporters in the local press hailed these reports as vindication for the city's application and the mayor's role in promoting redevelopment downtown, local antipoverty activists, of course, held a different view. Pointing to Rice's derailed HUD nomination, one Displacement Coalition activist argued instead that the HUD investigation sent "a very strong message" to the local Seattle establishment that there would be a political price to pay "when they give away limited public resources."[75]

Nordstrom to City: Reopen Pine Street . . . Or Else

If the debates over the Rice administration's garage deal and their controversial federal loan application were largely held out of the full view of the public, the third debate over the city's concessions to the Rhodes Project would, in contrast, explode onto the public sphere and occupy the energy of Seattle's political class for close to nine months. For what was at stake in this last debate was not a few million dollars of public funds or the arcane details of a federal loan application, but rather the future of Westlake Park, a much-debated but also much-beloved civic square in the heart of the retail core. Therefore, when the Nordstrom family delivered their demand that the city reroute auto traffic through the heart of Westlake Park to "improve traffic flow" past the F&N building, they probably had some idea that their actions would spark a heated debate. They were not to be disappointed. But before we can get into the key players in this debate, their motives, and their rhetorical strategies, some background on the contentious history of Westlake Park is in order.

By all accounts, the two blocks known as Westlake Square lies at the symbolic heart of the retail core. To the west sits the historic Pike Place Market; to the east, the equally historic Paramount Theater and the Washington State Trade and Convention Center. More immediately, the Square had for years been surrounded by the three grand dames of the Seattle retail scene: the Bon

Marche, Nordstrom, and the former Frederick & Nelson store. Given its centrality, it is not surprising that Westlake Square—really just two city blocks on either side of Pine Street—has been the site of what Rebecca Boren of the *Post-Intelligencer* called "a quarter-century-old fight over who controls downtown and what kind of city Seattle will be."[76] At the heart of this debate lies a confrontation of opposing values and vision: Should the city pursue cultural or commercial objectives? Should Westlake be a tool to promote economic growth and expand the tax base, or should it be a civic gathering space in the heart of the city?[77] Such questions can arouse deeply felt emotions, and accordingly, as former mayor Charles Royer noted, when debates about Westlake periodically flare up the typical Seattle reserve is nowhere in evidence. "The problem here," Royer once said, "is we are dealing with symbols here and old scars."[78]

On one side of this divide stand architects, community activists, and urban planners who have long lobbied the city to transform the two blocks surrounding the intersection of Westlake Avenue and Pine Street into a large public park, an urban "focal point" which could function as the city's only true civic square. First emerging in earnest in the late 1960s, this movement coalesced around the vision of University of Washington architecture professor Victor Steinbrueck, whose plan called for the city to buy up the property around the intersection of Pine and Westlake, thereby piecing together a large European-style tiled plaza in the heart of the retail core.[79] The city's retailers, fearing such a plaza would clog up traffic downtown and cut into sales, unceremoniously quashed Steinbrueck's grand plan in 1968, arguing instead for a proposal that would redevelop the intersection into a large-scale hotel-retail complex.

During the 1970s and 1980s, the fate of Westlake Square remained in the balance as the city shelved plan after plan under intense pressure from both activists and retailers. Finally, in 1987, former Mayor Charles Royer crafted a compromise of sorts. Like King Solomon, Mayor Royer would cut the baby in two. Half of Steinbrueck's proposed civic plaza would be devoted to a $110 million office tower and "festival mall," designed by James Rouse of Quincy Market (Boston) fame and packed full of upscale retail and entertainment.[80] The other half of the square, really two small plazas on either side of Pine Street, would be set aside as downtown's newest civic space—now dubbed "Westlake Park." Royer's Westlake was a far cry from the grand civic plaza envisioned by activists and progressive planners for a quarter century (see figure 5.1). Instead, as reporter Rebecca Boren quips, under Royer's plan, Westlake Square became "mostly mall and office building, with two patches of park on what's left over."[81]

Not surprisingly, activists viewed Royer's plan as a colossal betrayal. Royer had, after all, been first elected partly on the basis of his well-publicized promise to oppose the commercial redevelopment of Westlake, and his sudden embrace of the shopping mall, however festive, stunned many of his onetime supporters. However, as Boren writes, the activists got an unexpected opportunity to strike back just one year later.[82] Under Royer's compromise, the city had originally planned to reopen the one-block section of Pine Street between the mall and the adjacent plaza to traffic once construction had been completed. But, as it turned out, the decorative brick tile that stretched from the base of the mall to the plaza across Pine Street buckled and broke under the relentless assault of downtown auto traffic. After a few months of dealing with hundreds of crushed tiles, the city was forced once again to shut down this one block of Pine Street to repair the problem.[83]

Sensing an opportunity, the activists who had felt betrayed by Royer and his festival mall threw their weight behind an eleventh-hour campaign to permanently close this block of Pine Street to traffic. The activists conceded that closing Pine Street would by no means give the city Steinbrueck's European-style square. The glass-encased Westlake Mall had killed that dream once and for all. But a closed Pine Street between Fourth and Fifth Avenues *would* connect the small plaza at the base of the Mall to Westlake Park across the street, linking the plazas together to form a good-sized public square—a move which would enhance the park's ability to accommodate civic gatherings.[84] As the idea of a pedestrian-only Pine Street began to gain traction among newly elected city councilmembers like Jim Street and Margaret Pageler, the retail and development community lobbied hard against the idea.[85] The retailers immediately surrounding Westlake Park were particularly incensed, as one city council staff member recalled. As they argued in angry phone calls to the council, if the *temporary* closure of Pine Street to lay the decorative bricks had cut into retail sales, a permanent closure might finish them off.[86]

Despite the merchants' objections, the city council nonetheless voted in 1989 to permanently close Pine Street to traffic, much to the dismay of the downtown business establishment.[87] After another year of intense lobbying from the business community, a reconstituted and largely pro-business city council revisited the issue, this time to vote for reopening the street to traffic. But in one of his first acts as Seattle's new mayor, Norm Rice vetoed this council measure, claiming that even limited traffic "would cut the park in half visually and aesthetically" and undermine the park's integrity.[88] While community activists hailed Rice's decision as an important, if incomplete, victory for civic space in Seattle, this time it was the downtown business community's turn to feel betrayed. "They just closed the damn thing up," as Herb Bridge, past chair of the Downtown Seattle Association, told the *Post-Intelligencer*. "It was a very traitorous thing to do. The street was never intended to be part of the park. It was never supposed to be anything but a street."[89]

Revenge, as they say, is a dish best served cold, and the downtown establishment chewed over their feelings of betrayal for five long years. During this time, the slump in retail sales in the early 1990s and the closure of Frederick & Nelson did nothing to warm the business community to the newly created pedestrian mall on Pine Street. "[The] Street's closure is simply not working," as

Figure 5.1
Seattle's Retail Core

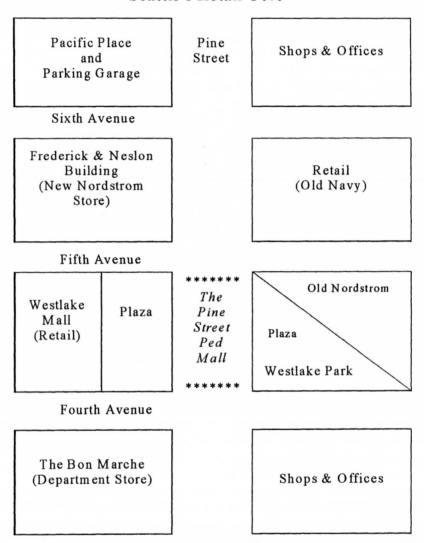

an executive of the Vance Corporation claimed in a letter to the city council. "Since its closure, we have seen the demise of Frederick & Nelson, I. Magnin, Klopfensteins, and a considerable erosion of downtown retail."[90] An executive at Bartell Drugs concurred, writing that the closure of Pine hurt their business "much more than we thought, reducing it by about ten percent."[91] While most principled business leaders admitted that the dip in sales could be attributed to many sources, including the national recession, cuts at Boeing, and the closure of Frederick & Nelson, much of the retail community's public ire focused on the closure of Pine Street and the construction of Westlake Park.[92]

So it was in their negotiations with the city over the Rhodes Project that the Nordstrom family would see a chance to reverse this defeat and place the re-opening of Pine Street squarely back on the public agenda. During the previous year, the city had amply demonstrated that they were both eager for Nordstrom's involvement in the Rhodes Project and willing to go the extra mile to make it happen—to the tune of over $100 million in public subsidies and loan guarantees. The city's enthusiasm in this way presented the retailer with an enticing political opportunity. And so it was that in November 1994, Nordstrom forwarded to deputy Mayor Bob Watt a dramatic last-minute demand: *reopen Pine Street to automobile traffic or we'll walk away from the deal.*[93]

To defend this last-minute ultimatum, Nordstrom argued that a closed Pine Street created a traffic nightmare in the heart of the city, making the trip down-town an intimidating experience for suburban drivers used to five-lane ex-pressways and the parking lot at Wal-Mart.[94] Moreover, Nordstrom executives pointed to the sagging fortunes of downtown retail in the years since the street's closure, citing in particular the complaints of merchants situated around West-lake Park.[95] Given the checkered commercial history of pedestrian malls across the nation and given the enormity of the investment the retailer was about to make in downtown Seattle, Nordstrom wanted to secure every chance for this project to pay off for its shareholders. As they claimed at the time, it was not at all clear a new flagship store with a $100 million price tag would succeed across from a closed-off Pine Street.[96]

At this late hour, Mayor Norm Rice and task force chair Bob Watt had little stomach for failure. Rather than risk seeing the Rhodes Project shatter at their feet, the administration quickly bowed to Nordstrom's last-minute demand and agreed to help push an ordinance reopening Pine Street through the city council.[97] In his official letter to the council, Rice reminded members both of the recent exodus of retailers from downtown and the city's dependence on revenue generated by downtown property and sales taxes. He then positioned the Rhodes Project as the "linchpin" to the success of the city's long effort to revitalize and redevelop the downtown core, arguing that the failure of the Rhodes Project and the continued deterioration of downtown would be an unac-ceptable price to pay for the preservation of the status quo at Westlake Park—a status quo which was, after all, just a pale version of Steinbrueck's original dream of a grand Westlake Square.[98] Coming from the very same man who *closed* Pine Street back in 1990, these arguments seemed to carry some weight with the council, and they rushed to set up a vote only two weeks after Rice's proposal hit the papers. After a single public meeting in mid-December, the assembled councilmembers voted 7-2 in favor of a resolution to re-open the street to traffic.[99]

Community activists and progressive urban planners were predictably outraged at Rice's reversal on Pine Street. Given the already substantial public subsidies involved in the Rhodes Project, activists argued the city had already done enough to support Nordstrom's move into the F&N site.[100] Organizing quickly in late 1994, opponents of Pine Street's reopening formed "the Friends of Westlake Park," a coalition of community activists, downtown residents, and architects. As Friends spokesperson Rick Aramburu later told the *Seattle Post-Intelligencer* (*P-I*), what united the group was not "anti-Nordstrom" sentiment, but rather a common desire to preserve the pedestrian mall—a public space that, as part of the larger Westlake Park, still functioned as the city's primary gathering place.[101] A scant two months after embarking on their campaign to reverse the mayor's decision and to keep Pine Street closed to traffic, the Friends succeeded in pressuring the city council to put the matter before Seattle voters in a special citywide election to be held in March 1995. The question before voters was simple: should the Pine Street pedestrian mall be opened to auto traffic?[102]

Thus began a frenzied six-week campaign over the future shape of downtown Seattle. On one side stood a pro-growth, pro-Rhodes Project coalition of city officials, property developers, downtown retailers, and even organized labor and longtime Democratic activists.[103] Organized under the name "Citizens to Restore our Retail Core" (CRORC) this coalition quickly raised $350,000[104] and promised an aggressive direct mail and phone campaign to persuade voters that, as *P-I* editor Sam Sperry put it, kissing off $300 million in private investment downtown for the sake of "a 290-foot stretch of pavement" would be the "irrational equivalent of tossing one's paycheck into a roaring fire."[105] On the other side, stood the Friends of Westlake Park—the ad hoc citizens committee, that, by early March 1995, had raised about $1,000.[106] For their part, the Friends argued that the Pine Street pedestrian mall functioned as an important part of the larger Westlake Park, and that the city should, as they put it, flatly reject Nordstrom's eleventh-hour attempt at corporate blackmail.

Having established the uneven nature of the debate, at least in terms of financial resources, a closer look at the rhetorical dimensions of this struggle is in order. After taking a moment to lay out the basic arguments advanced by both sides, the discussion will turn to an analysis of the political discourses mobilized in this debate, with a particular focus on the CRORC campaign. The chapter will then conclude with an exploration of the political consequences of CRORC's campaign to reopen Pine Street to traffic. What metaphors and narratives did CRORC deploy to persuade Seattle voters? How did this discursive environment help clear the way for the private appropriation of the Pine Street pedestrian mall? And what can CRORC's campaign teach us about similar efforts around the nation that attempt to equate a desire for urban vitality with the interests and priorities of downtown retailers and developers?

In Defense of Civic Space: Friends of Westlake Park

In their campaign, the Friends of Westlake Park presented voters with two basic arguments. First, the Friends reminded voters that Westlake Park was, after all, the city's only downtown park capable of hosting civic celebrations and gatherings. To this end, the campaign peppered references to the park's singularity throughout their comments to the press. Westlake Park was a "unique public asset," and the city's *"only* true civic square." As Rick Aramburu put it, "Seattle needs downtown open space, a gathering place, and a meeting place. There are no other such places and it is unlikely the city will create any in the future." Moreover, in the Friends' view, closing Pine Street to traffic six years before had greatly enhanced the Park's ability to host civic and political gatherings, primarily by allowing crowds to stretch from the base of the shopping mall, across the closed-off Pine Street to the small tiled square on the other side. For this reason, they argued, Nordstrom's demand must be opposed. Allowing over 1,000 cars an hour to rumble through the park would not only make the space less inviting to citizens, but it would also force gatherings to cluster on the small tiled plaza on the south side of Pine Street. Under these conditions, the ability of the park to serve its "unique" function as a "civic gathering place" would be profoundly undermined.

The Friends' second theme moved their campaign from a defense of civic space to an assault on the motives and tactics of Nordstrom and their pro–Rhodes Project allies. Accusing the retailer of "holding the city hostage," the second theme of the campaign called upon voters to reject Nordstrom's last-minute attempt at corporate extortion.[107] One agitated letter-writer put it this way:

> The more I think about Pine Street the madder I get. It begins to sound like the old playground actions of a spoiled child, "if you won't play by my rules, then I will take my ball and bat and go home." The Nordstrom family may not be children, but they are spoiled. When adults play this game, it is called "blackmail." When the Nordstrom family plays it, the Mayor and City Council jump off buildings in the name of "Civic Pride."[108]

In this way, if the first theme presented Westlake Park as a unique civic resource, the second theme positioned Nordstrom as a "big money . . . special interest" looking to capitalize on the city's fears of urban decline to advance its commercial goals. As Daniel Norton and Aramburu wrote in the *Times*, the "Friends of Westlake Park was formed because when the city was given an ultimatum by the special interests, the politicians gave in. Now they think they can scare [us] into voting yes."

Continuing the offensive, the Friends then moved to argue that Nordstrom had willfully misrepresented both the commercial risks of a closed Pine Street and the overall state of decline in the retail core. With regard to CRORC's claim that downtown was spiraling into decay, the Friends pointed to the recent arrival of Niketown and Planet Hollywood, arguing that the death of downtown retail had been greatly exaggerated. Clearly, these big-name retailers obviously "did not see the current Pine Street configuration as an obstacle to their success" and none of these companies had presented any "demands to close Westlake Park." In other words, when it comes to such talk about the deterioration of downtown Seattle, as Norton and Aramburu cautioned voters just prior to the election, try not to believe the hype.

> First they said, "we must tear down Pioneer Square or downtown will wither and die." The people said "no" and we saved a historic and vital downtown community. Then they cried, "we must destroy Pike Place Market or no one will ever want to come downtown." The people said "no" and visitors from around the world come to our market.[109]

Now the "special interests" were again claiming that "no one will ever want to spend a dime downtown again" unless Pine Street is opened to traffic. If Seattle voters say "no" to Nordstrom, they concluded, "20 years from now you will look back and be glad."[110]

As for Nordstrom's claim that a closed Pine Street would threaten the profitability of their unusually large investment in the F&N site, the Friends noted wryly that an economic report commissioned by the decidedly pro-Rhodes, pro-Nordstrom Downtown Seattle Association—a report commissioned to convince Seattle city councilmembers of the wisdom of the Rhodes Project—concluded otherwise. Taking the existing physical and economic landscape of downtown into consideration—a landscape which at that time included a *closed* Pine Street—the DSA study nonetheless concluded that the Nordstrom/Rhodes Project would be a smashing success, generating profits for investors and tax revenues for the city.[111] By refusing to offer any evidence to the contrary, it was clear to the Friends of Westlake Park that, "the thing they are counting on is that the people of Seattle will react to their ultimatum without any compelling reasons, no arguments, no statistics, that people will react by saying, 'yes, we should give in to this demand.'"[112] In the end, the Friends' campaign challenged voters to reject such self-interested and unsubstantiated demands.[113] Send a message to the downtown establishment, they pleaded. Tell them "not everything is for sale . . . certainly not the future of our downtown."[114]

Whatever the merits of these arguments, the Friends should be given some credit. With only $1,000 in donations, the ad hoc committee, seven members strong, first forced the city to put the Pine Street issue before Seattle voters, and then they mounted a spirited defense of the importance of urban civic space.[115] In doing so, they forced the debate over Pine Street and Westlake Park into the public sphere. Without their intervention, the city government, in consultation with Jeff Rhodes and the Nordstrom family, would have sealed the fate of Pine Street behind closed doors, with little opportunity for public discussion (beyond a single public hearing). The American democracy depends upon such interventions.

At the same time, with the benefit of hindsight, the Friends' campaign suffered from two important weaknesses. First, although many Seattleites were undoubtedly unhappy with Nordstrom's obvious attempt at corporate blackmail, the fact remained that, after two years, the vacant Frederick & Nelson building had become an important and tangible symbol of downtown decline. In this way, the Friends' focus on the coercive nature of Nordstrom's "ultimatum" missed the mark. Voters might reasonably choose to grit their teeth and submit to blackmail, so long as this submission resulted in the redevelopment of downtown Seattle's most important retail space. A more productive approach might have been to offer voters an *alternative* plan to redevelop the F&N site, one that did not come attached with a corporate ultimatum. With their own plan in hand, the Friends could have framed the March election as a choice between two competing plans for downtown revitalization, one of which—the Nordstrom plan—required the destruction of Westlake Park. Framed as such, the Friends' case against the reopening of Pine Street would become all the more compelling.

A second weakness lay in the Friends' attempt to defend the park as the city's only true civic square. "Seattle needs . . . a gathering place," the Friends told voters again and again.[116] Yet, the claim that civic space is important to the life of the city was never explicitly explained or defended. Why, in fact, *is* a gathering place important to a larger sense of urban vitality? The answer to that question must have seemed obvious to the Friends, but may not have been obvious to Seattle's electorate, many of whom, if Robert Putnam is correct, most likely pursue a life devoid of civic engagement and political activism.[117] For this reason, today, more than ever, the case for the political importance of public space needs to be advanced explicitly and forcefully. The task facing the Friends was therefore to *show* voters that building a truly "vital" downtown depends on more than attracting Old Navy and Pottery Barn. Instead, building a truly "vital" urban experience depends fundamentally upon preserving the kinds of civic spaces that nurture a sense of citizenship and political participation. Without such an explicit argument for the centrality of civic space in any reasonable definition of "urban vitality," the Friends were unable to counter CRORC's own equation of "urban vitality" with spectacular, upscale consumption. Once voters concluded that they were being asked to choose *either* "urban vitality" (promised by CRORC) *or* "civic space" (represented by the Pine Street pedestrian mall), the Friends' campaign was sunk.

"It's Life or Death": Citizens to Restore Our Retail Core

If the Friends' campaign faced the daunting and largely abstract challenge of defending the value of civic space in urban America, the challenge facing CRORC's pro-Nordstrom campaign was more immediate and concrete. They had to convince voters that allowing cars to rumble through Westlake Park would be a small price to pay for over $300 million in private investment and a retail "renaissance" in downtown Seattle.[118] So what political discourses did they marshal to achieve this goal? Overall, the central image of CRORC's pro-Nordstrom campaign *depicted the downtown retail core as if it were a critically ill patient in urgent need of a life-giving infusion of capital investment.* As city councilmember Jan Drago wrote, in urban America, "downtowns are fragile entities" that require "extraordinary public and private investment" in order to stay "healthy and vital."[119] But, according to a glossy CRORC pamphlet, Seattle's downtown "entity" had long been neglected by both the public and private sectors and was therefore threatening to slip into a long period of disease and decline.[120]

The first theme of CRORC's campaign therefore labored to cultivate a sense of urgency around the "downtown crisis," mostly by arguing that the health of the downtown "entity"—and even the city as a whole—hung in the balance. "There's an awful lot at stake," warned CRORC consultant Jeffrey Coopersmith. "It's the future of downtown at stake."[121] As one CRORC campaigner told the *P-I*, the retail core was "not dead yet, but it needs our attention."[122] For CRORC, then, the metaphorical patient was "slipping" and desperately needed the "shot in the arm" represented by the Rhodes Project.[123] As Kemper Freemen, a longtime real estate magnate, put it, reopening Pine Street to secure Nordstrom's investment was "a black-and-white issue as far as I'm concerned. It's life or death."[124]

Therefore, for CRORC's supporters, the consequence of a vote to keep Pine Street closed to traffic would be nothing less than the "death" of downtown. But how could they convince voters to share this almost medical sense of urgency? Drawing on opinion research that showed that Seattle residents were indeed concerned about crime downtown,[125] CRORC's second campaign theme argued that the closure of the Frederick & Nelson building marked the first step on a journey toward the kind of urban decay that has long gripped cities in the American rust belt. As CRORC argued, even a cursory look at the history of urban America proves that city governments ignore their downtown retail districts at their peril. Without the retail activity generated by the Rhodes Project, Seattle's downtown could "easily slip into wretched decay, as has happened in too many of America's cities."[126] And, as one city councilmember cautioned at a pro-Nordstrom rally, "when your downtown dies, so goes the rest of your city."[127]

In other words, CRORC's second theme argued that "it can happen here." Seattle was by no means immune from the sort of urban decline that had undermined cities "back East." To the contrary, the signs of decay were already proliferating around town. "From my office at the Paramount Theater," noted CRORC supporter Ida Cole, "all I see are abandoned buildings, empty lots with chain link fences around them, graffiti, and no people."[128] Without the Rhodes Project, and, particularly, without a successful redevelopment of the empty Frederick & Nelson site, the fate that had gripped Detroit and Buffalo would become Seattle's fate as well. As one downtown business owner argued:

> The vacant Frederick & Nelson building is a cancer in the downtown retail district. If it is not redeveloped into successful usage, there will be no question of whether downtown Seattle retailing will die, but when. . . . Just like many cancers, the effect of the Frederick & Nelson vacancy is spreading as more and more shoppers change their long-standing habits. . . . Action is required before it is too late.[129]

In this way, for CRORC, Pine Street was about more than a small stretch of downtown pavement. Instead, "Pine Street is about the future of this beautiful city. Pine Street is about making Seattle more like . . . San Francisco and less like Detroit."[130]

Finally, in their last theme, CRORC argued that a vote to *reopen* Pine Street would "breathe new life"[131] into downtown Seattle, sparking an unprecedented renaissance in the heart of the city. By approving the reopening of Pine, voters would not only "clear the way" for a new Nordstrom store, a new retail-cinema complex, and over $300 million in private investment, but this act would also "give birth to additional shops, restaurants and theaters,"[132] sparking a more general "resurgence of Downtown Seattle as a place to work, shop, and live."[133] The net result would be a more lively and exciting Pine Street, "full of people, interesting shops and spaces, with easy access to public transportation and parking."[134] As one *Times* reporter enthused, a vote to reopen Pine Street would usher in a new era in downtown Seattle, one which would transform what had been merely a place to work and shop into an vibrant and exciting urban experience.

> When . . . all the pieces are in place, a jazzy downtown could be hopping with an eclectic crowd: culture matrons wrapped in furs headed to restaurants, gawking conventioneers on generous corporate expense accounts, and teens shopping for the latest pump in their jump shoes.[135]

Having framed the debate as a matter of the life and death of downtown, CRORC then turned to their opponents' accusations. In particular, responding to their opponents' charge of "corporate blackmail" was a tricky matter for CRORC supporters. Certainly the entire struggle over Westlake Park had been sparked by Nordstrom's last-minute threat to kill the Rhodes Project unless the city reopened Pine Street. Nordstrom had also played hardball at other points in the negotiations with the city, including the time when the retailer had threatened to relocate its backroom operations—if not its downtown store—to the suburbs (or beyond) if the city could not come up with the right package of financial incentives for the Rhodes Project.[136] Whatever the merits of the Rhodes Project as a whole, it was difficult to escape the sense that the city government was being extorted by downtown's most powerful retailer.

Perhaps not surprisingly, by the end of the campaign, CRORC began to sense a swell of "anti-Nordstrom sentiment" rising among the electorate. For example, in a *Seattle Times* poll conducted just prior to the March vote, just under half the respondents said they thought Nordstrom was "being heavy-handed" in the debate over Pine Street.[137] As one voter told the *Times*, "I don't particularly care for the smoking gun that Nordstrom is holding to the city . . . to open the boulevard again."[138] In order to nip such anti-Nordstrom feelings in the bud, CRORC's politicos successfully prevailed upon the reclusive Nordstrom family to enter the political fray. In a series of public statements, including an "open letter from the Nordstrom family" sent directly to 65,000 registered voters, CRORC depicted Nordstrom as a concerned corporate citizen who, against the advice of retail experts and analysts, was ready to sink $100 million into a risky rehab of the crumbling F&N building—all in a charitable effort to help turn around a flagging downtown core.[139]

Nordstrom need not have worried about a public backlash. On March 14, Seattle voters in the end decisively approved the reopening of Pine Street, thus paving the way for traffic to be routed through Westlake Park.[140] With 61 percent of voters signaling their approval, CRORC hailed the election as a stunning endorsement of not only Pine Street's reopening but also the Rhodes Project and the city's revitalization policies more generally.[141] This may indeed be the case, but election polls and focus groups conducted by the *Seattle Times* and CRORC prior to the election suggest that many Seattle residents had mixed feelings about both the potential impact of downtown redevelopment and the move to route traffic through Westlake Park. As one resident told the *Times*, "I've certainly enjoyed having the street closed. . . . But by the same token, I can certainly understand the need for business development to continue."[142] Other residents expressed some reservations about the coming transformation of the retail core. The city "is losing its personal appeal," complained one citizen to CRORC's focus group leader. With the coming influx of multinational retail chains and restaurants, she feared that the city would become "too international" and "too impersonal."[143]

For their part, however, pro-growth city officials and downtown boosters expressed no such reservations about the Rhodes Project or the reopening of Pine Street. At an unusually celebratory meeting of the Downtown Seattle Association two months after the election, Mayor Rice promised the assembled business leaders that Seattle's downtown would soon "be a magnet for . . . economic activity" and the "envy of any in America."[144] Furthermore, the growing concentration of retail and cultural activity downtown would also position the city favorably in the competition for regional consumption dollars and international tourism and investment. "To manage to keep our major retailer in downtown when most cities would give anything for a Nordstrom store is a remarkable achievement," said deputy Mayor Anne Levinson. Not only is downtown Seattle "on tourists' radar screens," as *Washington CEO* enthused,[145] but, as Levison predicted, "for the first time, downtown Seattle will start drawing people from the suburbs instead of the other way around."[146] Two years later, as construction on the new Nordstrom store neared completion, DSA chairman Harold Greene could conclude that "downtown Seattle has begun to realize its goal of becoming a world-class city."[147]

Assessing the Struggle: The Trope of the Organic City

Such boosterism aside, it is clear that the CRORC campaign succeeded in convincing a sizable majority of Seattle voters that the sacrifice of Westlake Park was a small price to pay for over $300 million in private investment and a bold future of upscale retail in the downtown core. But *why* was the campaign so successful? This is a difficult question to answer, and some of CRORC's success surely had to do with the massive advantages they enjoyed in political and economic resources. Yet, to attribute their success merely to their superior financial backing would be a mistake, for CRORC's campaigners were skilled rhetoricians. In particular, the campaign succeeded in presenting voters with a coherent and attractive, if consumption-driven, vision of "urban vitality" that engaged both voters' desires for an urban renaissance and their fears of continued urban decline. In the remainder of the chapter, I want to take a moment to pull apart some of the symbolic threads of the pro-Nordstrom campaign and explore the discursive structures that hold it together. In the process, we will discuss both the larger vision of "urban vitality" that CRORC wove into their campaign and what this vision suggests about the future of public and civic space in downtown Seattle.

Fundamentally, CRORC's political discourse hinged on a central trope: *Downtown is a living but fragile entity.* Within this organic trope—one that imbued downtown with a "life" and (potentially) a "death"—CRORC framed the debate over Pine Street within a series of binary oppositions, with one side of each dichotomy expressing a common desire for a "vital" downtown and the other side expressing a collective fear of urban "decay."

VITALITY	DECAY
Rhodes Project	Westlake Park
Nordstrom	Pine Street Pedestrian Mall
Vibrant Downtown	Wretched Decay
Jazzy Downtown	Ghost Town[148]
Renaissance	Cancer
LIFE	DEATH

In the end, these oppositions enabled CRORC to tightly associate the Pine Street pedestrian mall with images of disease and decay, while associating Nordstrom and the Rhodes Project with images of renewal and renaissance. As a result, CRORC was able to position the reopening of Pine Street as the only rational and moral course of action. Within the discursive logic of this "city as organism" trope, rejecting Nordstrom's demands and therefore the larger Rhodes Project would seem to be an irrational, almost *unnatural*, embrace of "decay" and "death" over "vitality" and "life."

Furthermore, in the heat of the campaign, this organic trope also allowed CRORC to frame the question of Pine Street within the confines of a simple and dramatic narrative. In other words, once the organic trope imbued the city with life, this "life" could then be placed in mortal, if metaphorical, danger. To this end, CRORC's campaign narrative first presented "our downtown" as ailing from the "cancerous" Frederick & Nelson vacancy. But, as the story continued, help was on the way. The Rhodes Project would be the "shot in the arm" that would restore downtown to "great thriving life." The only thing preventing this future of "great thriving life" was, of course, the Pine Street pedestrian mall. This central conflict (i.e., the pedestrian mall versus the life of downtown) further positioned the electorate as the only potential hero(ine) in the story. If voters rejected Nordstrom's request to reopen Pine Street, the "cancer" would "spread" and downtown retailing, and, by extension, the downtown as a whole, would "die." Yet, if they ratified the decision to reopen Pine, they could assume the role of heroic urban physicians and "our downtown" could be up and "hopping" within months.[149] In the end, from within the discursive logic constructed by this trope and CRORC's campaign narrative, the choice voters faced in the Pine Street debate became, quite powerfully, a choice between "life" and "death." Presented as such, it was really no choice at all. We would never choose "death" and "decay" for ourselves, so why would we choose it for "our downtown"?

This campaign narrative became all the more powerful when CRORC tapped into the rich cultural folklore generated by urban America's postwar decline. In their remarks to the local press, for example, CRORC supporters took pains to remind voters of the experiences of other cities who let their downtowns "die" (with Detroit leading the list of cautionary examples). Furthermore, the images selected for CRORC's campaign fliers also invoked the collective cultural memory of deindustrializing cities "back East." The chain-linked fence, the abandoned lot, the boarded storefront, the graffiti-splashed wall, the much-hyped (but ultimately discredited) crime wave: together these references drew their symbolic power from the cultural storehouse of stories and images that dramatize, in the popular imagination, the consequences of postwar urban disinvestment and decline. As C. Wright Mills would put it, such invocations form a "vocabulary of precedents" concerning American urban decline. They act as cautionary tales, and they are told to shape future social action.[150] In this way, although the references to "what happened back East" certainly obscured important historical and economic differences between, say, Seattle and Detroit, they nonetheless added dramatic urgency to CRORC's larger story about the ailing downtown entity. Don't fool yourselves, fellow Seattleites. It happened in Detroit. It can happen here.

In the end, the organic city trope accomplished a lot for CRORC and Nordstrom. First, at least as strategically deployed by the CRORC campaign, it would certainly seem that the trope functioned ideologically[151]—that is to say, the trope enabled CRORC to present what was in fact a specific social interest (Nordstrom's desire for "smooth traffic flow") as a universal interest (a "vital" downtown). In this way, the notion that downtown Seattle was a (sickly) organism operated as a hegemonic *suture*, stitching together a variety of competing social and political interests under a spurious assertion of the universal "civic good."[152] In other words, in much the same way that allegiance to an abstraction like "the nation" obscures divisions of class and race, so does a decontextualized commitment to protecting the health of "our downtown."[153]

In reality, of course, "our downtown" is not alive at all. Instead, "downtown" is a symbol that derives its meaning from its position within a particular discursive formation. What "downtown" means shifts radically depending on whether you are talking to a developer surveying the city from her corner office or a pensioner whose own view of downtown remains populated with memories of people and places long since gone. These actual living human beings have a variety of overlapping and contradictory interests, some of which will be served by, for example, the reopening of Pine Street while others will not. What was required in the Pine Street debate, in short, was a discussion among competing social interests about the relative gains and losses associated with rerouting traffic through Westlake Park. But the trope of the organic city neatly supplanted this confrontation of competing and complementary interests, and instead labored to unify the public around a heroic effort to save "our downtown" from a future of urban decay. In the end, Seattle voters responded to this call to rally around the ailing downtown entity, and decisively approved the reopening of Pine.

Articulating Urban Vitality: Two Competing Visions

So what can we conclude about the organic city trope, about this way of speaking about the city? Given Seattle's experience, it may be tempting to conclude that the organic city trope is hopelessly tied to dominant commercial interests. But this would be a mistake, in my view. For example, even a cursory review of the urban planning literature reveals that organic metaphors have structured discourse about the city in ways that transcend narrow social divisions and interests. Drawing equally on the organic trope, for example, Le Corbusier announced that "we must kill the street," while Jane Jacobs rose to the urban street's defense in *The Death and Life of Great American Cities*.[154] Likewise, on his way to obliterating the South Bronx with his multilane highways, Robert Moses once quipped, "when you operate in an overbuilt metropolis, you have to hack your way with a meat ax," while his most trenchant critic, Marshall Berman, argued that Moses's expressways stabbed through "our neighborhood's heart."[155] Even the Friends of Westlake Park drew on the organic trope when, to dramatize the importance of the Pine Street pedestrian mall, they constructed a thirteen-foot sculpture depicting a human heart (labeled "Westlake Park") with a knife (labeled "corporate interests") cutting through it.[156] The list could go on, but it seems clear that the organic trope may in fact be one of the most fundamental symbolic mechanisms we have for making sense of something as complex as "the urban."

This should not surprise us. As Lakoff and Johnson have long argued, human linguistic systems are fundamentally metaphorical, and, in particular, a great many utterances are structured by *ontological* metaphors that view abstract concepts, forces, or events as *entities*. For Lakoff and Johnson, such ontological metaphors serve a crucial purpose in discourse: they allow speakers to grasp the abstract as concrete, to grasp the ineffable as if it were like our everyday experiences as living, breathing beings.[157] In this way, the organic city trope is an extremely useful tool. It allows speakers to concretely grasp the almost unbearable complexity of contemporary urbanization, wherein such abstract (but still "lived") processes as neighborhood change, economic stagnation, gentrification, and redevelopment become recast in more intimate and human terms—as urban "birth," "growth," "illness," and "death." To be sure, such tropes inevitably conceal features or urbanization that do not "fit" the organic frame (such as the role of human agency and global/local economic strategies in these processes); but it is doubtful that we could do without it for very long. It is simply too useful to toss out of the conceptual toolkit.[158]

Yet, the fact that organic metaphors may always be with us should not suggest that the public is condemned to view urban politics through the eyes of downtown developers and retailers. For, as Volosinov has shown, even commonly held linguistic signs like "vitality" and "decay" (the two poles of the organic city trope) are *multiaccentual*; that is, they are capable of taking on a variety of accents and meanings, depending upon how they are enmeshed within wider networks of associations and differences.[159] Signs like "vitality" and "decay" are therefore open to struggle, as dominant groups attempt to suppress alternative accents that might express competing, if subordinate, social perspectives. In this way, the struggle over Pine Street was, in the end, a struggle over *whose* social "accents" would be activated within the key signs of the organic city trope. What, in other words, does it mean for a city to be "alive" or "vital"? What causes urban "blight"? What policies should be pursued to nurture an urban "revitalization"? If the organic city trope provides a fundamental way of grasping issues related to urban disinvestment and redevelopment, the specific political meanings articulated by the trope nonetheless remain contingent upon contest and struggle, as urban political actors attempt to draft the language of the living city to serve their own strategic ends.[160]

The struggle over Pine Street should therefore be seen as a struggle between competing articulations of the organic city trope—that is, between competing expressions of just what urban "vitality" could mean for Seattle voters. On one hand, CRORC offered Seattle voters a vision of urban vitality built around what Guy Debord (1977) would call "the spectacle of the commodity," where the public is invited to wander through spaces of high-end consumption in order to sample a breathtaking array of goods, services, and experiences unavailable in a typical suburban shopping mall.[161] In CRORC's vision, then, a "vital" city enacts "a public realm deliberately shaped as theater."[162] Within this urban theater, the public's primary mode of interaction is one of spectatorship, as the public-as-audience is immersed in a carefully orchestrated series of thematic, and usually branded, consumption experiences and environments.[163] To be sure, the public can periodically move beyond spectatorship into full participation in the urban spectacle, but these moments usually come at a fee or involve a trip to the nearest cash register.

In the newly revitalized Seattle, for example, consumers can wander through Nordstrom's flagship store or the airy spaces of Pacific Place and peruse a range of luxury merchandise unavailable anywhere else in the Pacific Northwest. They can play out dreams of sports stardom in nearby Niketown or immerse themselves in an idealized history of "Gold Rush Seattle" in Pioneer Square, the city's restored historic district. As the city's subsequent revitalization plans clicked into place, Seattle's citizen-consumers could then end their day by sampling the world's cuisines at downtown's expanding legion of gourmet restaurants and repair to any number of cultural pursuits, from the latest performance of the Symphony to a Seattle Mariners (major-league baseball) night game at the $500 million Safeco Field.

Such was CRORC's vision. And there are real pleasures to be found in this conception of "urban vitality as urban spectacle." CRORC's vision responds, at least at some level, to popular desires for a diverse, novel, and engaging urban experience, where we are swept up in the jostling urban crowd and exposed to a stunning diversity of sights, sounds, and tastes.[164] Yet at the same time, we should not forget that this definition of urban vitality is underwritten by downtown retailers and developers with a specific set of economic interests to defend. As such, the diversity of the urban experience promoted by CRORC is, on closer evaluation, a limited and administered diversity—where the array of commodities, services, and amenities offered are carefully selected to appeal to a decidedly upscale "target market," and where private control over urban space is extended to create the best possible consumption environment for national-chain retailers.[165]

Given Nordstrom's appropriation of the Pine Street pedestrian mall, it is the immediate fate of public and civic space under CRORC's particular articulation of urban vitality that should concern us most. For their part, retailers like Nordstrom have long viewed the careful control of urban space, and the meticulous arrangement of elements with this space, as crucial to their commercial success.[166] Modern-era department stores used control over space to evoke fantasies of luxury, wealth, and exotic travel, while channeling consumption to the most profitable items. Suburban shopping malls took retailers' control over space a step further, this time enclosing the street itself and creating massive, wholly privatized "public" spaces, where every element (from the placement of benches to the temperature of the air) was arranged to provoke consumers' desires and channel them toward the act of purchase.[167]

If such total control over the spatial environment surrounding their properties eludes the grasp of downtown retailers like Nordstrom, they still seem determined to exert as much influence as possible on nearby public spaces, so that they serve, rather than detract from, the consumption imperative. In this way, the progressive *extension* of private control over urban public space for the purpose of promoting upscale retail is a crucial, if less overtly celebrated, feature of CRORC's vision of urban vitality. As the struggle over Pine Street suggests, in this vision, public spaces that are viewed by retailers as utterly incompatible with commercial priorities—such as the pedestrian mall—are candidates for outright elimination,[168] while other adjacent public spaces are subject to increased private influence and control.

In fact, the ultimate fate of public space within CRORC's vision of urban vitality may have been revealed when, just months after the vote to reopen Pine Street, a city-appointed task force floated a proposal to bring what remained of Westlake Park under the control of a nonprofit organization organized and funded by downtown retailers. In this proposal, the nonprofit organization—tentatively dubbed "Westlake Inc."—would be given the authority to "establish use guidelines and standards, to issue permits [for events], and to decorate and improve the Park." Westlake Inc. would then be charged with the task of "achieving standards of presentation throughout the park comparable to private business standards for customer spaces." To this end, Westlake Inc. would endeavor to "program" (their word) the park with activities and music all year long, with the explicit goal of ensuring that the park "complement surrounding businesses" by providing a lively environment for shoppers and pedestrians.[169] Like the demand to reopen Pine Street to auto traffic, the "Westlake Inc." proposal demonstrates the interconnectedness of spectacular consumption and private control in CRORC's vision of urban vitality.[170]

Although CRORC articulated this consumption-driven, privately controlled vision of urban vitality with great force, there indeed exist alternative visions of what makes a city "live" and "thrive." In fact, the Friends of Westlake Park, however haltingly, attempted to offer voters just such an alternative. To be sure, as discussed above, the Friends' competing conception of urban vitality never quite emerged as a full-blown and positive vision, and this was a serious weakness in their campaign.[171] Periodically, however, the Friends would hint suggestively that "there is more to downtown than shopping,"[172] and that, while a strong retail core is undoubtedly important to the commercial health of the city, a more expansive notion of the urban good life depends on preserving space for activities that transcend consumption and exchange.[173] As Friends co-chair Peter Steinbrueck told the city council, "every great city in the world has a central civic square that serves an important community purpose, not only in providing gathering space for festivals and events, but in promoting a sense of humanity and cultural spirit."[174] The only space in Seattle that served this function was Westlake Park, argued the Friends, and now voters were being asked to allow traffic to slice through the middle of this unique civic space. Focusing in particular on the *diversity of uses* hosted in the park since its creation, the Friends tried to focus attention on what would be lost if traffic were allowed to rumble through the park:

> Should 1,000 cars an hour drive through the heart of a unique public space? Should we give up the place where: Presidents speak, steel drums entertain, toddlers toddle, shoppers relax, tourists wander, demonstrators speak out, carousels whirl, horse-drawn carriages line up, sand castles are built, and more than 200 scheduled events are held every year? We say NO.[175]

What is interesting about this quotation is its focus on, for lack of a better term, the use-value of urban spaces. In other words, if CRORC's vision provides a particularly rich example of, to paraphrase Lefebvre, "the representation of space"—that is, the practice of conceiving space as something to be planned, controlled, and tethered to commercial priorities—then the Friends' vision of urban vitality focused attention on Pine Street and Westlake Park as "spaces of representation"—that is, as particularly important examples of how spaces derive meaning and significance from their appropriation and use in daily urban life.[176] What was crucial about the original Westlake Park, then, was not merely that it was a chunk of tiled open space, but rather that, through daily use, the public had claimed it as the city's premier civic square, and as such it had come to serve a crucial role in the life of the city. In other words, in the six years since its creation, through over 1,000 organized cultural events and political rallies, Seattleites had individually and collectively invested the park/pedestrian mall with social and political meaning, transforming a fairly sterile tiled square into the city's most important civic space. For the Friends, the popular creation of this civic space was an achievement that should be protected.

In this way, in the Friends' view, routing traffic through the heart of the Westlake would not merely reduce the total size of the park, *it would place material limits on the uses to which the park could be put.* With traffic rolling through the pedestrian mall, political rallies, corporate-sponsored events, musical groups, and other informal park uses would now have to compete with one another on the small tiled square left over on the south side of Pine Street. Large political rallies that once fit nicely into the park would now be forced to ask a city advisory board for permission to temporarily close Pine Street—adding another level of administration beyond the already cumbersome permitting process. The danger was that, by cutting out the heart of Westlake Park and leaving only two small tiled plazas behind, Nordstrom's proposal would leave Seattle citizens with insufficient space to collectively gather and participate jointly in important rituals of democracy and cultural celebration. For the Friends, such a move would make downtown Seattle a less hospitable environment for the enactment of civic life, and would thus drain the city of its "vitality." In other words, in the Friends' half-articulated vision, what makes the city "live" is the way in which collective performance—especially in the enactment of cultural ceremonies and joint political action—breathes life into otherwise dead urban spaces, and it is the memory of such collective action that endows urban space with life and vitality.

The debate between CRORC and the Friends of Westlake Park was, at heart, a confrontation between two competing articulations of "urban vitality," one promoting a conception of vitality built around spectacular consumption and public spectatorship and another promoting a conception of vitality as civic performance and ritual. Of course, in pragmatic political terms, the discursive debate was unequal from the start. With a war chest of nearly $350,000, CRORC was able to outspend the Friends of Westlake Park by nearly 200 to 1.[177] As a result, the public heard mostly about the exciting new consumption experiences awaiting them once they approved the reopening of the pedestrian mall. Largely unimpeded by the Friends' underfunded campaign, CRORC in the end succeeded in framing the debate as a stark choice between "life" or "death" in downtown Seattle, rather than as a contest between two competing conceptions of what it takes to nurture a living city. With the choice framed squarely within the stark poles of the *life/death* dichotomy, voters chose the most compelling vision of urban vitality available to them in this lopsided campaign, and by the end of 1995, auto traffic began to slice through Westlake Park.

Aftermath: Building the Spectacular City

Standing in 1998, as he prepared to leave office, Norm Rice would claim the redevelopment of downtown Seattle as his administration's most important achievement. It had indeed been a long road. Assuming office in the midst of a spectacular office bust, a long-term decline in downtown retail, and an accelerating global competition among regions and cities for tourism and capital investment, Rice confronted not only tight city budgets but also an agitated business community demanding that city hall commit to the revitalization of downtown property and retail markets. Rice's response to this crisis, as we have seen, was to enthusiastically embrace a policy of urban "salvation through retail."[178] Seattle would be saved by building the spectacular city. For the current generation of Seattle's public leaders, then, the Rhodes Project represented a defining moment in the history of the city and a civic achievement on a par with the 1962 World's Fair. "The signs are positive," wrote the *Times* editors after Nordstrom finally signed off on the Rhodes deal in 1995. "Years from now, Seattleites will be able to look back and say not only did the city rescue its retail core back in the 1990s, it did what was necessary to transform it into a thriving, dynamic, and interesting place."[179]

If there is a word that boosters use to describe the kind of downtown experience created by the Rhodes Project and the other retail-cultural projects built during the 1990s, it is *diversity*. The bustling crowds of daytime shoppers hosted by Nordstrom's new flagship store and Pacific Place are succeeded by the nighttime buzz generated by such diverse places as Benaroya Hall, Niketown, the Eagles Auditorium (ACT Theater), and the renovated Paramount Theater. Downtown Seattle has become for boosters a "24-hour destination," and a place to "see and be seen." Unlike the old downtown of office workers, working-class bars, and low-income pensioners, the new downtown has become home to an "eclectic crowd" of sports fans, symphony patrons, international tourists, and business travelers. As an official in the Convention and Visitors Bureau put it, "I think it's a . . . critical mass that's developed, and I think it's nice that there are elements of the arts that are new, [in addition to] retail, restaurants, and . . . the Convention Center. So, in effect, you have all those elements combining and they're thriving off of each other."[180] Taken together, the "mix" and "diversity" of office workers, upscale condominiums, new retail spaces, and new cultural and entertainment amenities have created for downtown's boosters an eclectic "critical mass" which not only assures rising property values and sales tax revenue but also has transformed Seattle into an diverse, "active" and "exciting" place to work, visit, and live.[181]

But, as the fate of Westlake Park demonstrates, by hinging downtown's future on the cause of upscale, commercially driven redevelopment—or "salvation through retail," as Terry Tang put it—Seattle's public officials have embraced a very specific definition of what constitutes urban vitality. In essence, the "vital" urban experience that is cultivated through such spectacular commercial redevelopment is one organized around the promotion of upscale consumption and the private control of urban space. The purpose of downtown Seattle's new spectacular retail core is indeed to cultivate an engaging and diverse urban experience, but it is a commodified and controlled diversity, where every element within, or even *adjacent* to, new retail-cultural developments must serve the imperative of high-end consumption and display. In this vision of urban vitality, that which contributes to the process of upscale recreation and consumption contributes to the "life" of the city, while those activities or spaces viewed as impediments to spectacular consumption are treated as potential sources of "decay" and therefore become subject to calls for private appropriation and control.[182]

To be sure, the connections between urban redevelopment, upscale consumption, and social-spatial control is by no means unique to downtown Seattle. In their drive to build spectacular new arenas of high-end consumption, and in their attempt to assure that the social and spatial environments surrounding these investments serve the interests of powerful retailers, Seattle's downtown establishment is merely following the advice of contemporary urban planners, who have long argued that the path to urban renewal lies in delivering a lively but *controlled* downtown "experience" to free-spending suburban consumers and international tourists.[183] For her part, Zukin has described the vision of urban vitality that emerges from such advice as the "Disneyfication" of the city—a term that highlights both the pleasures afforded by immersing oneself in a thematic consumption environment as well as the escalation of social surveillance and spatial control designed to ensure that visitors feel safe and welcome.

But what—or, more precisely, *who*—is left out of this *particular* vision of urban vitality and urban community? As Andrew Mair has argued, contemporary city leaders are thoroughly convinced that the material success of urban spaces like the new Nordstrom store or Pacific Place depends on an ability to convince potential consumers that "downtown" is a vibrant, diverse, and *safe* place to be.[184] Fair enough. Still, what happens if particular individuals, activities, or spaces become viewed by retailers and city officials as a *threat* to consumers' sense of comfort and well-being? We have already seen the fate of a public space that was redefined as an unacceptable barrier to the smooth flow of retail traffic in the downtown core. If city leaders responded to the *spatial* "threat" posed by the pedestrian mall so aggressively, how would they respond to concerns about the *social* environment surrounding their dramatic investments in downtown retail? How would they respond to the continuing presence of low-income housing and communities of the poor and homeless adjacent to and even within the retail spectacle now approved for construction?

It is at this point that the discussion of the city's decade-long exercise in urban revitalization begins to mesh with the heated political debates over homelessness in downtown Seattle. For, as Mair has shown, in their effort to craft a consumer-friendly image of downtown, city officials and retailers can quickly come to view the urban homeless as a mortal *threat* to the wider civic cause of urban revitalization. Put most bluntly, as Mike Davis notes, the persistence of thousands of street people near gentrifying city districts "sours the image of designer downtown living" and therefore betrays the illusion of a "downtown renaissance" so laboriously constructed by urban elites.[185]

In response to this perceived threat, city leaders across the United States have embraced a more coercive approach to homelessness on downtown streets. Los Angeles, for example, has embarked on an explicit policy of "containment," where the city's homeless are purposefully harassed into a designated skid row area and then "contained" there through a variety of police tactics and "anti-vagrant" architectural designs.[186] And, of course, Los Angeles is by no means alone in such tactics. In recent years San Francisco, Atlanta, and New York have all adopted, in one form or another, a more coercive approach to the presence of homeless citizens on city streets and in city parks—particularly in areas slated for gentrification.[187]

But what about Seattle? Would Seattle's urban leaders react any differently to the presence of homeless citizens on the streets of downtown? The initial indication from the downtown establishment seemed to be that, instead of following Los Angeles's lead, Seattle would pursue a more humanistic or progressive policy regarding the intersection of downtown revitalization and downtown homelessness. For example, in his address to the annual meeting of the Downtown Seattle Association, incoming DSA chair Blake Nordstrom first congratulated the members on their success in helping to turn downtown's fortunes around. But then he admonished the crowd ever-so-gently, arguing that downtown's business leaders should not "lose sight that what makes a great city is its people." Seattle, he concluded, is a city where "people care."[188] During interviews, other downtown property owners would also tout Seattle's innate progressive streak. As one respondent said, "there's nobody, if you're from Seattle, that is against poor people or people who are down on their luck. That's not the way Seattle operates."[189] Whether or not, in their attempt to create and promote a truly world-class downtown experience, Seattle's civic leaders would live up to these sentiments is the question that will be explored in the next three chapters.

Notes

1. *Frederick and Nelson Redevelopment: Project Summary*, Executive Report to the City Council, 14 December 1994, Seattle City Archives, Sue Donaldson Subject Files (see methodological appendix for retrieval information).

2. Barbara Serrano and Deborah Nelson, "City Overpaid Pine Street Developer," *Seattle Times*, 21 December 1997, l(A).

3. Casey, O'Corr, "Pine Street Not Only Hurdle for Investors," *Seattle Times*, 15 December 1994.

4. Serrano and Nelson, "City Overpaid Pine Street Developer," *Seattle Times*, 21 December 1997.

5. Serrano and Nelson, "City Overpaid Pine Street Developer."

6. Personal interview, Downtown Task Force, 24 March 1999.

7. Serrano and Neslon, "City Overpaid."

8. Serrano and Nelson, "City Overpaid."

9. Serrano and Nelson, "City Overpaid."

10. Barbara Serrano and Deborah Nelson, "City Spent Little Time Questioning Garage Cost: But Some on Council Were Uneasy with Deal," *Seattle Times*, 13 January 1998, 1(A). See also, personal interview, Downtown Task Force, 7 April 1999.

11. Serrano and Nelson, "City Overpaid Pine Street developer."

12. Personal interview, Downtown Task Force, 24 March 1999.

13. Personal interview, Downtown Task Force, 24 March 1999.

14. Personal interview, Downtown Task Force, 24 March 1999.

15. Personal interview, Downtown Task Force, 24 March 1999.

16. Personal interview, Downtown Task Force, 24 March 1999.

17. Personal interview, Downtown Task Force, 24 March 1999.

18. Bob Watt, printed copy of speech to Seattle Rotary Club.

19. Personal interview, Downtown Task Force, 24 March 1999.

20. Personal interview, Downtown Task Force, 24 March 1999.

21. Seranno and Nelson, "City Overpaid."

22. Personal interview, Downtown Task Force, 24 March 1999.

23. Serrano and Nelson, "City Overpaid."

24. Serrano and Nelson, "City Overpaid."

25. Serrano and Nelson, "City Overpaid."

26. Serrano and Nelson, "City Spent Little Time Questioning." As we discovered above, the Rhodes Project called for Pine Street Development to buy the F&N building from the Padelford's at the inflated asking price of nearly $27 million and then to immediately turn around and *trade* it with Nordstrom for their old store, valued at around $14 million.

27. Serrano and Nelson, "City Overpaid."

28. Barbara Serrano, "City Clears Legal Review on Pine Street Garage Deal: Money to Developer Deemed Constitutional," *Seattle Times*, 23 April 1998.

29. Barbara Serrano, "City Clears Legal Review."

30. As one task force negotiator pointed out, the agreement with Pine Street Development also included provisions which advanced some of the city's social objectives, including a clause requiring Pine Street Development to hire apprentices off the city's welfare caseload and to set aside ten percent of the construction jobs for women and minority-owned firms.

31. Serrano and Nelson, "City Overpaid."

32. Serrano and Nelson, "City Spent Little Time Questioning," *Seattle Times*, 13 January 1998. This account of the city council meeting on the parking garage was reconstructed from a videotape of the 1995 meeting and was first reported nearly *three years* after the project was approved by the council.

33. Serrano and Nelson, "City Spent Little Time Questioning."

34. This was Serrano and Nelson's conclusion. See Serrano and Nelson, "City Spent Little Time Questioning."

35. Jim Erickson, "Nordstrom to Go to F&N Building: Key Pieces of $400 Million Plan in Place," *Seattle Post-Intelligencer*, 27 June 1995.

36. "Nordstrom Project Clears Big Hurdles [editorial]," *Seattle Post-Intelligencer*, 28 June 1995.

37. I owe the "lapdog" phrase to Gina Bailey at Simon Fraser University.

38. Serrano and Nelson, "City Spent Little Time Questioning."

39. Serrano and Nelson, "City Overpaid."

40. John Fox, "A Very Big Deal: Displacement Coalition Responds to Nordstrom 'Revelation,'" *Real Change*, January 1998.

41. Personal interview, Seattle Displacement Coalition, 3 February 1999.

42. "City's Pine Street Deal Violated Public Trust [editorial]," *Seattle Times*, 23 December 1997, 4(B).

43. "City's Pine Street Deal Violated Public Trust."

44. Kate Joncas, "Pacific Place Garage: Responsible Debate Poisoned," *Seattle Times*, 4 January 1998, 5(B).

45. It should be mentioned here that this twenty-year "put" provision—where the city can force the developers to repay all losses accumulated over the previous twenty years—has a potentially important loophole. If Pine Street Development filed for bankruptcy before the twenty-year deadline, Pacific Place's mortgage holder would assume control of the building. If the value of Pacific Place did not cover the mortgage holder's initial investment in the project, the city would be unable to force the mortgage holder to pay the city's expenses in the twentieth year. However, if the mortgage holder recouped its own investment by selling off Pacific Place to another developer, the city's "put" provision would still be in force, and the city could force the new owners to pay for any and all losses accumulated in the first twenty years of the parking garage's operation. This last bit was confirmed by a personal interview with an official in the mayor's office. Personal interview, Downtown Task Force, 7 April 1999.

46. Bob Watt, printed copy of speech delivered to Seattle Rotary Club.

47. In her opinion, Assistant Attorney General Mary Jo Diaz found that because the city could plausibly contend that it received "tangible and intangible benefits" for its $73 million investment over and above the parking garage (including added jobs, tax revenues, and spin-off development), the city would most likely prevail in an argument before the state supreme court. However, the opinion only found that the benefits were not "grossly inadequate." The opinion explicitly took no position on the more broad question of whether or not the city received *fair* value for its $73 million investment. As Diaz told the *Times*, "the courts have said we're not going to question the wisdom of the transaction. That's for the electors to decide." In this way, as Brian Livingston of the Civic Foundation told the *Times*, the opinion is by no means an exoneration of the city's garage deal. "It's simply a statement that even a deal as poorly worked as the subsidy of Pacific Place garage is . . . still allowable. It doesn't even speak to the wise use of public money." For details, see Barbara Serrano, "City Clears Legal Review."

48. The list goes on and on: federal land grants to railroads, defense contract subsidies, the giveaway of the radio spectrum to private commercial interests, to name a few of the more famous examples. For details, see Howard Zinn, *A People's History of the United States* (New York: HarperPerennial edition, 1995). For a description of federal

giveaways in the communication sector see, Robert McChesney, *Rich Media, Poor Democracy* (Urbana, IL: University of Illinois Press, 1999).

49. "Probe Stalls Rice's Possible HUD Nomination: Nomination Seems on Hold as HUD Looks into Project," *Seattle Times*, 13 December 1996, 1(A).

50. As Doug Collins reports, the HUD loan effectively reduced the interest rate paid by Pine Street Associates on the purchase of the F&N site from 9 to 6 percent, representing a savings of $5,630,000 over the life of the loan. For details, see Doug Collins, "Seattle to Nordstrom: Try on Anything You'd Like," *The Washington Free Press*, June/July 1995.

51. Knox also argued that taking on the $24 million loan would force the city, in an ironic twist, to spend more than expected on low- to moderate-income projects in the future. As Knox writes, HUD requires that at least 70 percent of its aid to a particular city—Seattle, in this case—be used to aid low- and moderate-income people. If the City of Seattle takes on this large loan for Pine Street Development, they will need to apply for more federal block grants and (more likely) loans in order to meet their 70 percent quota. For details, see Doug Collins, "Seattle to Nordstrom: Try on Anything You'd Like."

52. Doug Collins, "Seattle to Nordstrom."

53. "Probe Stalls Rice's Possible HUD Nomination."

54. "Probe Stalls Rice's Possible HUD Nomination."

55. Personal interview, Downtown Seattle Task Force.

56. Citizens to Restore Our Retail Core pamphlet, *Ten Good Reasons to ReStore Pine Street*. Obtained from councilmember Jan Drago's files, Seattle City Council Offices.

57. Personal interview, Downtown Seattle Task Force, 24 March 1999.

58. "Key Loan Bolsters Downtown Project," *Seattle Times*, 15 September 1994.

59. Personal interview, Seattle Displacement Coalition, 3 February 1999.

60. Personal interview, Seattle Displacement Coalition, 3 February 1999.

61. Personal interview, Seattle Displacement Coalition, 3 February 1999.

62. Doug Collins, "Seattle to Nordstrom."

63. Doug Collins, "Seattle to Nordstrom."

64. Jeanne Sather, "No Pine Street, No Deal," *Puget Sound Business Journal*, 10 March 1995.

65. Doug Collins, "Seattle to Nordstrom."

66. Larry Liebman, "Downtown Supporters Hopeful for Good News," *Puget Sound Business Journal*, 13 May 1994.

67. Doug Collins, "Seattle to Nordstrom."

68. "Nordstrom Deal Update," *Washington Free Press*, January/February 1997.

69. HUD's local office in Seattle did at one point send a memo to the national office questioning the validity of the "spot blight" designation, arguing that the physical deterioration around the F&N site was minimal. In short, Downtown Seattle circa 1994 was not the South Bronx. However, these questions were quickly dismissed and the loan approved in a matter of months. See Susan Byrnes, "Criminal Probe Clears Rice Over HUD Loan: But Application Process Under Question," *Seattle Times*, 30 July 1997, 1(B).

70. Leyla Kokmen, "HUD Chief Lauds Creativity Downtown," *Seattle Times*, 11 May 1996.

71. "Probe Stalls Rice's Possible HUD Nomination." *Seattle Times*, 13 December 1996.

72. Robert Nelson, "Pedigree, Ambition Put Cuomo Past Rice: Campaign for HUD Job Too Late for Seattle Mayor," *Seattle Times*, 20 December 1996, 1(A).

73. Susan Byrnes, "Criminal Probe Clears Rice Over HUD Loan," *Seattle Times*, 30 July 1997, 1(B).

74. Barbara Serrano and Deborah Nelson, "City, Mayor Cleared in Loan Deal: But Report Says Public Communication about F&N Project Fell Short," *Seattle Times*, 17 November 1997, 1(B).

75. Personal Interview, Seattle Displacement Coalition, 3 February 1999.

76. Rebecca Boren, "Pine Street Debate Reopens Old Wounds Over Vision for City," *Seattle Post-Intelligencer*, 2 December 1994, 4(A).

77. I owe these questions to City Councilmember Nick Licata. See especially his op/ed piece, "Put Westlake Debate to Rest: Close Pine," *Seattle Times*, 6 December 1994.

78. Rebecca Boren, "Pine Street Debate Reopens Old Wounds Over Vision for City," 4(A).

79. Rebecca Boren, "Pine Street Debate Ropens Old Wounds."

80. Nick Licata, "Put Westlake Debate to Rest," *Seattle Times*, 6 December 1994.

81. Rebecca Boren, "Pine Street Debate Reopens."

82. Boren, "Pine Street Debate."

83. Mark Higgins, "Rice Does Pine Street U-Turn," *Seattle Post-Intelligencer*, 22 November 1994, 1(A).

84. Letter to City Council, 10 January 1995, Seattle City Archives, Tom Weeks Subject Files (see methodological appendix for retrieval information).

85. Boren, "Pine Street Debate."

86. Personal interview, Seattle City Council, 15 December 1998.

87. Personal interview, Seattle City Council, 15 December 1998.

88. Boren, "Pine Street Debate."

89. Boren, "Pine Street Debate."

90. Letter to Seattle City Council, 12 December 1994, Seattle City Archives, Tom Weeks Subject Files.

91. Letter to Seattle City Council, 6 December 1994, Seattle City Archives, Tom Weeks Subject Files.

92. Letter to Seattle City Council, 6 December 1994, Seattle City Archives, Tom Weeks Subject Files.

93. Mark Higgins, "Rice Does Pine Street U-Turn."

94. Citizens to Restore Our Retail Core, open letter from the Nordstrom family to Seattle registered voters, March 1995. See also, Alex Fryer, "Strong-Arming a Retail Rebirth," *Puget Sound Business Journal*, 14-20 July 1995, 28.

95. Personal interview, Seattle City Council, 15 December 1998.

96. Personal interview, Seattle City Council, 15 December 1998. See also Sylvia Nogaki, "Solving the Pine Street Puzzle," *Seattle Times*, 28 November 1994.

97. Mark Higgins, "Rice Does Pine Street U-Turn."

98. Letter to Seattle City Council, 28 November 1994, Seattle City Archives, Jan Drago Subject Files (see methodological appendix for retrieval information).

99. Mark Higgins, "Pine Street Project Gridlock: Group's Initiative Would Permanently Close Road to Cars," *Seattle Post-Intelligencer,* 9 January 1995.

100. J. Richard Aramburu, "Downtown Development: Obvious Public Subsidy," *Seattle Times,* 21 February 1995.

101. Mark Higgins, "Pine Street Project Gridlock," *Seattle Post-Intelligencer,* 9 January 1995.

102. Mark Higgins, "Pine Street Project Gridlock."

103. As Doug Collins notes, CRORC hired many PR consultants often associated with progressive or environmental causes, including Cathy Allen and longtime Democratic activist Jeffrey Coopersmith. In addition, CRORC recruited some of Seattle's most famous liberal heavyweights to serve on their board, including Kay Bullitt, a noted environmental activist whose Bullitt Foundation bankrolls many local progressive organizations, and Ron Judd, the chair of the King County Labor Council. Judd's support seemed especially ironic, Collins writes, because Nordstrom had recently busted its retail and office employees union, United Food and Commercial Workers 1001. For details, see Doug Collins, "Seattle to Nordstrom," *Washington Free Press,* June/July 1995.

104. Most of CRORC's funds were donated by parties with a specific financial interest in the Rhodes Project (including Jeff Rhodes, Pine Street Development, and the Padelford family, the owners of the Frederick & Nelson building).

105. Sam Sperry, "Pine Street: Council Cuts to the Chase," *Seattle Post-Intelligencer,* 22 January 1995. See also, "Pine Closure Senseless Effort [editorial]," *Seattle Post-Intelligencer,* 5 December 1994. Sperry estimates the total private investment at $300 million, a lower figure than most estimates (see Jim Erickson, "Nordstrom to Go to F&N Building.")

106. Mark Higgins, "Pine Street Vote One Week Off: The Great, and Greatly Uneven, Debate Nears End," *Seattle Post-Intelligencer,* 7 March 1995.

107. Rick Aramburu, et al., "Should Pine Street Be Re-Opened? Pro/Con."

108. Letter to Seattle City Council, 13 December 1994, Seattle City Archives, Jan Drago Subject Files.

109. Rick Aramburu, et al., "Should Pine Street Be Re-Opened? Pro/Con."

110. Rick Aramburu, et al., "Should Pine Street Be Re-Opened? Pro/Con."

111. Economic Research Associates, *An Economic Evaluation of the Rhodes-Nordstrom Project* (San Francisco, CA: ERA, August 1994). This study was commissioned by the DSA to convince the city—and perhaps skeptics in the media and the public at large—that substantial public subsidies were justified to make the Rhodes Project a reality. What neither the authors of the study nor its sponsors in the DSA could anticipate, however, was that reopening Pine Street would explode as the crucial roadblock to the project. See also J. Richard Aramburu, "Downtown Development—Obvious Public Subsidy," *Seattle Times,* 21 February 1995.

112. Mark Higgins, "Public Vote Likely on Pine Street," *Seattle Post-Intelligencer,* 21 January 1995.

113. Friends of Westlake Park, campaign flyer.

114. Friends of Westlake Park, campaign flyer.

115. Mark Higgins, "Pine Street Project Gridlock," and Mark Higgins, "Pine Street Vote One Week Off."

116. Letter to Seattle City Council, 29 November 1994, Seattle City Archives, Tom Weeks Subject Files.

117. Robert Putnam, *Bowling Alone: The Collapse and Revival of American Community* (New York: Touchstone, 2000).

118. Doug Collins, "Seattle to Nordstrom: Try on Anything You'd Like."

119. Jan Drago, draft letter to the editor, Jan Drago's Seattle City Council Office Files.

120. As one CRORC flyer put it, "What was once a thriving area—the 'jewel' of Seattle—has been abandoned. Frederick and Nelson is gone . . . Dozens of vacant storefronts line a graffiti-scarred corridor. And nothing has happened to breathe life into the area. That is . . . until now . . . [with the Rhodes Project proposal]."

121. Mark Higgins, "Last Round for Pine Street Fight: Both Sides Push Their Views on Reopening Before Voters Decide March 14," *Seattle Post-Intelligencer*, 2 March 1995.

122. Mark Higgins, "Pine Street Vote One Week Off."

123. Sylvia Nogaki, "Local Investors Back Rhodes Project: Group Provides a Big Chunk of Venture Capital," *Seattle Times*, 29 November 1994, 1(D).

124. Jeanne Sather, "No Pine Street, No Deal."

125. Downtown Seattle Association, *Survey of Downtown Users: Executive Summary* (Seattle: Elway Research Inc., January 1993). See also, CRORC Focus Group Transcript, Jan Drago's Seattle City Council Office Files.

126. Sam Sperry, "Pine Street: Council Cuts to the Chase."

127. Peyton Whitley, "'Keep Downtown Healthy,' Supporters Urge at Rally Boosting Pine Street Vote," *Seattle Times*, 5 March 1995.

128. CRORC campaign flyer.

129. Letter to City Council, 6 December 1994, Seattle City Archives, Sue Donaldson Subject Files.

130. John Alkire, "Pine Street Tied to City's Future," *Seattle Times*, 4 February 1995.

131. CRORC campaign flyer.

132. "Vote Yes to Re-open Pine Street for a Healthy Downtown [editorial]," *Seattle Times*, 12 March 1995.

133. Letter to Seattle City Council, 9 December 1994, Seattle City Archives, Sue Donaldson Subject Files.

134. CRORC campaign flyer.

135. "Coming to Life: Seattle's Retail Center Could Become a Destination Spot with More Shopping, Night Life," *Seattle Times*, 8 January 1995.

136. Personal interview, Downtown Seattle Task Force, 24 March 1999.

137. Peter Lewis, "Pine Street on Road to Redevelopment," *Seattle Times*, 15 March 1995.

138. Peter Lewis, "Pine Street on Road."

139. Nordstrom open letter, Jan Drago Office Files, Seattle City Council. "Until now," Nordstrom's letter noted, "our company would never have considered an investment of this size in any city. But Seattle has been our home for 94 years and we care about its future." Yet, despite this desire to help out, the letter continued, "our decision to proceed has to be made with care." In order to justify such a large investment, the retailer needed every assurance that the new flagship store would succeed, and that

meant reopening Pine Street to improve access and traffic flow in front of their store. However, and here Nordstrom was responding directly to the Friends accusations of "corporate blackmail," they had no intention of abandoning Seattle should the vote not go their way. "We started here and Seattle will always be our hometown," wrote Nordstrom. "Should you decide that you'd like to leave the street closed, we will stay in our current location to serve our customers . . . We'll respect your decision—whatever the outcome."

140. Peter Lewis, "Pine Street on Road."

141. Personal interview, Seattle City Council, 15 December 1998.

142. Lewis, "Pine Street on Road."

143. CRORC focus group notes. Jan Drago's Seattle City Council Office Files.

144. Sylvia Nogaki, "Growing List of Shops, Eateries Ready to Go Downtown," *Seattle Times*, 6 May 1995. Sylvia Nogaki and Peter Lewis, "Vote Energizes Downtown Deals," *Seattle Times*, 16 March 1995.

145. Monte Enbyst, "Destination: Downtown Seattle," *Washington CEO* (November 1996).

146. Jim Erickson, "Nordstrom to Go to F&N Building: Key Pieces of $400 Million Plan in Place," *Seattle Post-Intelligencer*, 27 June 1995.

147. Harold Greene, "Chairman's Report," *1996/1997 Downtown Seattle Association Annual Report*.

148. When asked to explain why she supported the decision to reroute traffic on Pine Street, one city official described what she saw as a retail core in desperate circumstances. "There were no people [downtown]. There were no pedestrians . . . the buildings were all vacant . . . It was just a ghost town there" (interview, Seattle City Council).

149. Other scholars have also noticed the use of organic metaphors in urban politics. For another discussion of how medical-organic metaphors were used in a political struggle over redevelopment see David Wilson, "Metaphors, Growth Coalitions, and Black Poverty in a U.S. City," *Antipode* 28 (1996): 72-96.

150. Clifford Shearing and Richard Erickson, "Culture as Figurative Action," *British Journal of Sociology* 42 (1991): 481-506.

151. That is, CRORC's specific articulation of the organic city trope seemed to mobilize meanings that reproduced relations of domination. See John Thompson, *Studies in the Theory of Ideology* (Berkeley, CA: University of California Press, 1984).

152. Michelle Barrett, "Ideology, Politics, Hegemony: From Gramsci to Laclau and Mouffe," in *Mapping Ideology*, ed. S. Zizek (New York: Verso, 1994). See also, Ernesto Laclau and Chantal Mouffe, *Hegemony and Socialist Strategy* (London: Verso, 2001).

153. Paul Gilroy, *There Ain't No Black in the Union Jack* (London: Hutchinson, 1987); John Tomlinson, *Cultural Imperialism: A Critical Introduction* (Baltimore, MD: Johns Hopkins University Press, 1991).

154. Le Corbusier, *Towards a New Architecture* (New York: Payson and Clarke, 1927).

155. Marshall Berman, *All That is Solid Melts into Air* (New York: Simon and Schuster, 1983).

156. Mark Higgins, "Public Vote Likely on Pine Street," *Seattle Post-Intelligencer*, 21 January 1995.

157. George Lakoff and Mark Johnson, *Metaphors We Live By* (Chicago: University of Chicago Press, 1981).

158. For other examples of how biological/organic metaphors structure ways of seeing and interpreting complex social phenomena, see A. Kraut, *Silent Travelers: Germs, Genes, and the "Immigrant Menace"* (New York: Basic Books, 1994) and Susan Sontag, *Illness as Metaphor* (New York: Farrar, Straus and Giroux, 1977).

159. V. N. Volosinov, *Marxism and the Philosophy of Language* (New York: Seminar Press, 1973).

160. Ernesto Laclau and Chantal Mouffe, *Hegemony and Socialist Strategy* (London: Verso, 2001); Stuart Hall, "The Rediscovery of Ideology: Return of the Repressed in Media Studies," in *Culture, Society, and the Media,* ed. M. Gurevitch, T. Bennett, and J. Wollacott (London: Methuen, 1982).

161. Guy Debord, *The Society of the Spectacle* (Detroit: Red and Black, 1977). See also, Sharon Zukin, "Urban Lifestyles: Diversity and Standardization in Spaces of Consumption," *Urban Studies* 35 (1998): 825-40.

162. David Crilley, "Megastructures and Urban Change: Aesthetics, Ideology, and Design," in *The Restless Urban Landscape,* ed. P. Knox (Englewood Cliffs, NJ: Prentice Hall, 1993).

163. John Hannigan, *Fantasy City: Pleasure and Profit in the Postmodern Metropolis* (London: Routledge, 1998).

164. Rob Shields, "Social Spatialization and the Built Environment: The West Edmonton Mall," *Environment and Planning D: Society and Space* 7 (1989): 147-64.

165. Susan Christopherson, "The Fortress City: Privatized Spaces, Consumer Citizenship," in *Post-Fordism: A Reader,* ed. A. Amin (Oxford: Blackwell, 1994).

166. William Leach, *Land of Desire: Merchants, Power, and the Rise of a New American Culture* (New York: Pantheon, 1993); Rosalind Williams, *Dreamworlds: Mass Consumption in Late Nineteenth Century France* (Berkeley, CA: University of California Press, 1983).

167. Margaret Crawford, "The World in a Shopping Mall," in *Variations on a Theme Park: The New American City and the End of Public Space,* ed. M. Sorkin (New York: Noonday Press, 1992).

168. Although the street remains ostensibly in public hands, the private appropriation of Pine Street goes beyond merely the reopening of the street to traffic. The city ordinance that reopened Pine Street includes a solemn promise from the city to never again close this crucial block of the street to traffic, so long as any retailer (not just Nordstrom) occupies the historic F&N building. In essence, this clause transfers control over this block of Pine to the private sector, and allows a private firm like Nordstrom to "sell" this control to the next occupant of the F&N site. Aramburu et al., "Should Pine Street Be Re-Opened? Pro/Con."

169. Westlake Management Review Task Force, *Recommendations Report* (Seattle: City of Seattle, July 1996).

170. For more on the interconnectedness of contemporary urban-based consumption spectacles and the acceleration of private control over urban space, see also Sharon Zukin, "Urban Lifestyles: Diversity and Standardization in Spaces of Consumption," *Urban Studies* 35 (1998): 825-40; and Vincent Mosco, "New York.com: A Political Economy of the 'Informational' City," *Journal of Media Economics* 12 (1999): 103-16.

171. On the defensive from the start, the Friends spent the bulk of their campaign trying to rebut the claims of their pro-Nordstrom opposition (i.e., that downtown was not "in trouble," that the city had done enough to support the Rhodes Project, and so on). As a result, the Friends never directly expressed an alternative vision of urban vitality to voters to compete with CRORC's narrow focus on shopping and retail.

172. J. R. Aramburu, "Downtown Development—Obvious Public Subsidy," *Seattle Times*, 21 February 1995.

173. For example, Peter Steinbrueck wrote the following in a letter to City Council: "To be sure, not everyone sees the need for a large civic space in the heart of downtown . . . It has been suggested that Pine Street corridor could be transformed into [a] 'great shopping street.' While this may indeed be a fine idea . . . it's no substitute for civic gathering space." Seattle City Archives, Tom Weeks Subject Files, 10 January 1995.

174. Letter to Seattle City Council, 10 January 1995, Seattle City Archives, Tom Weeks Subject Files.

175. Aramburu et al., "Should Pine Street be Reopened? Pro/Con," *Seattle Times*, 5 March 1995.

176. David Harvey, *Consciousness and Urban Experience* (Baltimore: Johns Hopkins University Press, 1985); Henri Lefebvre, *The Production of Space* (Oxford: Basil Blackwell, 1991).

177. Mark Higgins, "Pine Street Vote One Week Off."

178. Terry Tang, "Pine Street: Twisted Arms and Fractured Policies," *Seattle Times*, 25 January 1995.

179. "An Important Milestone for Downtown Seattle [editorial]," *Seattle Times*, 4 July 1995.

180. Personal interview, Seattle-King County Convention and Visitors Bureau, 4 February 1999.

181. Personal interview, Seattle-King County Convention and Visitors Bureau, 4 February 1999.

182. Susan Christopherson, "The Fortress City: Privatized Spaces, Consumer Citizenship," in *Post-Fordism: A Reader*, ed. A. Amin (Oxford: Blackwell, 1994); Terry Tang, "Pine Street: Twisted Arms and Fractured Policies," *Seattle Times*, 25 January 1995.

183. Quote from *Urban Land*, a planning trade publication, quoted in Mike Davis, *City of Quartz: Excavating the Future in Los Angeles* (New York: Vintage, 1992), 231.

184. Andrew Mair, "The Homeless and the Post-Industrial City," *Political Geography Quarterly* 5 (1986): 351-68.

185. Andrew Mair, "The Homeless and the Post-Industrial City."

186. Davis, *City of Quartz*, 233.

187. John Logan and Harvey Molotch, *Urban Fortunes: The Political Economy of Place* (Berkeley, CA: University of California Press, 1987), 289.

188. Lee Moriwaki, "Downtown Urged to 'Retain our Soul'," *Seattle Times*, 30 May 1998, 1(C).

189. Personal interview, Downtown Property Owner, 11 November 1998.

Part III

Securing the Spectacular City

Chapter 6

The Project of Reassurance: Securing Urban Spectacle

On a sunny day in mid-August 1998, an estimated 5,000 customers lined up outside the refurbished F&N building to await the grand opening of the new Nordstrom flagship store. Some customers even arrived four hours early to catch a glimpse of Seattle's newest retail centerpiece.[1] For their part, Nordstrom officials, who back in 1995 had professed much reluctance to invest in the "decrepit" F&N site, now predicted that the store would generate $100 million in sales a year and would help downtown Seattle compete directly with San Francisco for out-of-town "destination" shoppers.[2] "It's really the Nordstrom store this town has deserved for a long time," one Nordstrom official told the *Times*.[3] Two months later, and just across the street, the grand unveiling of the Pacific Place retail-cinema complex attracted its own opening-day crowd and even won praise from Seattle's architectural community for its street-friendly design and its sweeping wood-and-glass atrium. "Pacific Place has a grandeur about it," retail analyst J'Amy Owens enthused. "The interior space is almost basilica-like."[4]

Such architectural praise is all well and good, but the downtown business establishment was mostly concerned about how the now-completed Rhodes Project would contribute to the larger goal of transforming Seattle into a world-class city. And, in this regard, the enthusiastic crowds awaiting the opening of Nordstrom and Pacific Place had downtown developers and property owners feeling optimistic about the future. "We have had a long road. It's kind of hard to believe we are here, but we are here," said Matt Griffin, co-manager of Pine Street Development. "We [now] have one of the great downtowns in America."[5] In particular, downtown boosters confidently predicted that the revamped retail core would increase pedestrian traffic in the retail core and enhance the city's national and international status as a shopping, convention, and tourism destination. The concentration of brand-name retailers like Nordstrom, Niketown, Old Navy, and Banana Republic not only would attract suburban consumers from the surrounding region, but, as Steve Morris, president of the Seattle-King County Convention and Visitors Bureau told the *Times*, "all of that redevelopment is part of what we sell when we are looking to draw new (convention) business here." The result, as Morris predicted, would be a "synergy" between retail and tourism that "works in both directions," pumping dollars and jobs into the local economy.[6]

At the same time, like their counterparts in cities around the United States, Seattle's civic leaders have long known that the ultimate realization of their world-class dreams would require more than "build it and they will come."[7] It is one thing to *build* the sort of retail and cultural amenities that cater to up-scale tourists, shoppers, and business travelers, but it is quite another to convince these target markets that downtown Seattle is a place amenable to people like themselves. As a result, these target markets of Seattle's "downtown renaissance" must be lured back downtown. Above all, they must be *reassured* that downtown Seattle is once again a vibrant, clean, and safe place to be.

Given the postwar history of decay and decline across urban America (including, to a lesser extent, downtown Seattle), drawing upscale consumers, tourists, investors, and even local residents back into the central city has by no means been a simple proposition. As Neil Smith has argued incisively, the past thirty years of urban decline (and especially the representation of this decline in the mass media) has cultivated in the imagination of America's suburban middle and upper classes an *ideology of decay—that is, a commonly held sense that urban America is an amoral space of social disorder.* Although the decline of many urban neighborhoods in America since 1965 is not entirely a media-created fantasy and has very real roots in the thirty-year history of post-Fordist economic restructuring, the mere fact of economic decline need not necessarily translate into a full-scale demonization of the central city and the ideological isolation of the urban (especially nonwhite) working class. Still, as many urban commentators and scholars argue, that is exactly what we have seen in the commercial media over the last thirty years in America. In this argument, the American middle class, separated from the central city by fifty years of postwar suburbanization, has recently come to experience urban America largely through the distorted lens of local television news and gritty cop dramas, which, according to media scholars like Robert Entman, Andrew Rojecki, and George Gerbner, have typically associated urban spaces with startling (and ratings-boosting) images of violence and social disorder. As Gerbner notes wryly, "humankind may have had more bloodthirsty eras, but none as filled with images of crime and violence as the present."[8] And with the African-American and Latino urban underclass playing the villain in much of this mass-mediated violence, it should not be surprising that, as Entman and Rojecki write, many American viewers have concluded that the central city "is dominated by dangerous and irresponsible minorities."[9]

Given the prevalence of such representations of "the city" in the media, downtown elites have become convinced that the *material* success of their strategy to attract economic growth through downtown gentrification depends also upon the success of an *ideological* project—one designed to rehabilitate, not the physical, but the symbolic infrastructure of downtown space.[10] To this end, the much-celebrated revitalization efforts taking place across urban America have typically been accompanied by a much less celebrated *project of reassur-*

ance—a project wherein areas of the city slated for middle-class consumption are cleansed of anything which might evoke in the middle-class imagination images of danger, disorder, and urban decay. As the experience of cities like Los Angeles, New York, and Atlanta has shown, this effort to reassure shoppers and tourists that the bad old days of urban decline are a thing of the past often places the interests of civic and business elites squarely at odds with those of the urban poor—especially the nation's most marginalized homeless citizens—who pose the most visible threat to the image of "designer downtown living" so carefully cultivated in America's "new urban renaissance."[11]

At this point, I want to return to a question posed at the end of the previous chapter. If, as many downtown property elites across the United States have concluded, the material success of retail-cultural redevelopment depends upon the ability to convince the wary shoppers and investors that the new downtown is a safe and exciting place to be, then crowds of homeless people on the streets can quickly be viewed as an important symbolic threat. Accordingly, this elite concern over the corrosive effect of visible poverty on the "street atmosphere" of newly revitalized districts has inspired many American city governments to pursue a more coercive approach to homelessness, whereby the homeless are more aggressively policed in the name of restoring civility to key urban spaces. Beginning with a short discussion of the emergence of homelessness as a national crisis in the 1980s, this chapter will describe "broken windows theory" and how this perspective on the links between street incivility and urban decline has encouraged civic leaders to adopt a more coercive approach to homelessness on city streets. In the end, we will explore how Seattle's political leaders have embraced broken windows theory as part of their own project to assure that the target markets of the city's redevelopment plan—shoppers and tourists—would feel safe visiting (and spending) downtown.

Homelessness in America: Causes and Controversies

Homelessness, at first blush, seems straightforward. What could be simpler, and more tragic, than losing one's home? But, as any sociologist or social worker would attest, homelessness is what Andrew Sayer would call a "chaotic concept."[12] It is an inexact and an inelegant term that lumps together a contradictory and confusing set of causes and consequences, and it obscures very real differences in the actual experience of living on the streets. Even a task as seemingly simple as *counting* the number of homeless citizens in the United States has spawned widely varying estimates and an ongoing debate over the political motives behind the various head-counts. This much we do know: there is no single path to homelessness, and there was no single event or cause which sparked the sharp rise in American homelessness since 1970. However, as Jennifer Wolch and Michael Dear argue in their seminal text *Malign Neglect:*

Homelessness in an American City, although the issues are complex, it is still possible to locate the principal social and economic dynamics which, taken together, have frayed the social and economic networks of the poorest of the nation's citizens and have pushed increasing numbers of Americans onto the streets.

The key factor here is the widespread economic polarization spawned by the restructuring of the American economy since the global crisis of the 1970s.[13] As Robert Reich argues, the post-Fordist restructuring of the American economy has created a dual society, where the gap between what wealthy, well-educated Americans could earn and the wages earned by those employed in routine production and consumer services has widened dramatically.[14] For instance, during the harshest phase of restructuring (the recession of the early 1980s), national unemployment rates rose from 5.9 percent to 10.7 percent.[15] For those lucky enough to find work during this time, the job pickings were quite slim. Between 1979 and 1984, 44 percent of the new jobs created by the restructuring U.S. economy paid poverty-level wages, and over three-quarters of the total jobs created during the 1980s paid the federal minimum wage.[16] With the evaporation of high-wage jobs available to lower-skill workers and with the proliferation of service jobs paying poverty wages, it is not surprising that the bottom fifth of wage earners in America saw their incomes decline by 20 percent between the late 1970s and early 1990s.[17] Wolch and Dear conclude that the increasing economic marginality of America's poorest citizens has been a crucial contributor to the rise of homelessness. For those already struggling to make ends meet, a sharp cut in wages or the loss of a prized factory job can be the event that thrusts them out of their homes and, potentially, onto the streets.

Wolch and Dear also argue that the unwillingness of the federal government to meet the increasing demand for income and housing assistance has also created fertile ground for homelessness in America. In particular, the authors point to the dismantling of federal housing programs since 1980, noting that the wholesale retreat from a coherent housing policy has been the federal government's greatest contribution to the current homeless crisis.[18] While federal authorizations for housing were 7 percent of the total budget in 1978, by the late 1980s, such spending accounted for a mere 0.7 percent.[19] In 1977, the federal government spent $28 billion on direct housing help for low-income families. In 1988, the feds spent $12 billion. When translated into the number of low-income families helped by federal assistance, the effect of these housing cuts can be seen more clearly.[20] As Jennifer Daskal of the Center on Budget and Policy Priorities notes, between 1977 and 1981, the federal government made commitments to expand rental assistance to an average of 260,000 additional low-income households per year. From 1982 through 1997 (five years into the most recent economic expansion), new housing commitments "fell to an average of about 70,000 per year."[21] As Daskal concludes, although the slow expansion of federal commitments to subsidize low-income housing since 1977 has managed to keep pace with the loss of low-income units in the private market, the government has failed to compensate for the large increase in the number of low-income *people* over this same period.[22] As a result, there are many more poor renters chasing the same number of federally subsidized low-income apartments around the country. The result is a sort of macabre game of musical chairs. When the music stops, when all the subsidized low-income units are snatched up, there are still plenty of low-income renters left to fend for themselves.

Finally, Wolch and Dear explicitly link the explosion of homelessness in the United States to recent trends in urban housing markets, particularly the upscale residential gentrification of low-income inner-city spaces and neighborhoods. According to Peter Marcuse, one of the prime motives for such inner-city gentrification comes from the expanding ranks of affluent white-collar workers who fill the newly built skyscrapers of the central business district and who help global firms manage the complexity of their international operations.[23] As Neil Smith has argued, this expanding legion of downtown white-collar workers began, beginning in the late 1970s, to exert a new claim on central city space.[24] Celebrated as "urban pioneers" who were set to tame the "new urban frontier," many of these affluent households have been funneled by local policy-makers and developers into the once-redlined inner-city residential neighborhoods of urban America.[25]

What explains all this new interest in the long-ignored American inner city? According to Wolch and Dear, the rise of slow-growth movements at the edges of many U.S. cities (especially in the western United States) has limited the amount of new population growth allowed along the suburban fringe. As a result of this NIMBY (not-in-my-backyard) approach to new residential development, excess growth has been increasingly funneled back into the urban core of cities like Los Angeles, Seattle, and Portland.[26] In addition, the concentration of high-wage, high-skill "producer service" employment in the central city meant that developers began to focus on the residential neighborhoods closest to downtown, hoping to take advantage of their proximity to the renewed office boom. The fact that property values in the inner city were quite low (having been depressed by years of disinvestment) only encouraged developers to buy up and redevelop inner-city residential buildings, with an eye toward taking advantage of the "rent gap" between the actual value of the land and its potential value, once converted to a "higher and better use."[27]

The result has been the steady replacement of low-income inner-city units of housing with larger, more expensive units marketed to the new urban middle class. And, of course, this also results in the corresponding *displacement* of low-income tenants from their longtime apartments, neighborhoods, and social networks. As Wolch and Dear write, the pace of low-income displacement due to upscale gentrification has been fierce since the mid-1970s. Between 1973 and 1983, for example, 4.5 million units of low-income housing disappeared from the nation's stock, half of which had been occupied by low-income households.[28] The most affordable housing of all—the "single room occupancy" (SRO) units common in the traditional skid row districts of many U.S. cities—have likewise disappeared in droves due to gentrification, freeway construction, and redevelopment. As Wolch and Dear write, between 1970 and 1982, about one million SRO hotel units were lost nationally, with their marginal, pay-rent-by-the-day tenants forced to enter the fierce competition for affordable housing in urban America.[29]

Taken together, these three developments—the increasing economic marginalization of the poor, the receding welfare state, and the recent churnings of the urban housing market—have created fertile ground for the radical expansion of homelessness in the United States. As Wolch and Dear conclude, there were more poor people in America in 1995 than in 1970, and these low-income families were forced to chase a shrinking number of low-cost housing units.[30] As a result, these families have had to devote more and more of their incomes to stay off the street. In Los Angeles, for example, the demand for low-cost housing was so acute that in the mid-1990s an estimated 200,000 people were living in garages which lacked cooking facilities or even adequate sanitation.[31] And L.A. was by no means alone. Even in what former president Bill Clinton called the "best of times," many families across the United States were hanging onto their homes by the barest of threads. In the wake of post-Fordist economic restructuring, household budgets for millions of individuals and families became so tight that any setback, such as the loss of a job, a large medical bill, or a bout with substance abuse or mental illness could lead directly to missed rents, evictions, and the jolting experience of life on the streets.

Still, while economic insecurity, high housing costs, and an unresponsive government form the preconditions for homelessness, it must be acknowledged that not all people who face a personal crisis end up on the street. Indeed, as Wolch and Dear write, "the vast majority of persistently poor and precariously housed people do not become homeless."[32] Instead, they borrow money from their families; they stay with friends; or they take in a boarder or roommate—anything to stay afloat until the crisis passes. But for some individuals and families, this network of support stretches too thin to prevent a slide into homelessness. Their families might not be able to provide support. Or the recently evicted might suffer from personal vulnerabilities (including domestic violence, mental illness, or substance abuse) that either force them to flee their homes for protection or make it difficult for others to live with them. Whatever the final event that propels these people into homelessness, it is nonetheless merely the *last* step on a long road that has already been paved by structural and economic factors, including economic insecurity, rising poverty, and the disappearance of low-cost housing. These factors have created a mass of the "persistently poor and precariously housed," and, under these conditions, all it takes is a personal crisis—a crisis which wealthier people might easily withstand—to propel an individual through their frayed safety net and onto the street.[33]

In the end, the result of all these trends has been the explosion of homelessness in America over the last thirty years. Although, to a certain extent, the homeless "have always been with us," the most reliable analyses of contemporary homelessness argue that today's problem is qualitatively different from that of past eras.[34] For instance, Kim Hopper and Jill Hamberg write of the crossing of an "invisible threshold" in 1979, a year that they argue marked the beginning of the latest and most rapid escalation of homelessness.[35] As Peter Marcuse writes, the experience of New York City backs up such claims. For example, according to Marcuse, the number of homeless people in New York City tripled between 1982 and 1986, and increased by another 42 percent in the following two years. By 1998, the national situation had not improved much, even if the issue had receded from the media spotlight since the late 1980s. According to the National Low Income Housing Coalition, there were 750,000 homeless people in the United States on any given night in 1998, and over the course of the year, anywhere from 1.3 to 2 million people were homeless at one time or another.[36] At the dawn of the twenty-first century, the continuing scope of homelessness in America remains a stark reminder of the uneven nature of the 1990s economic expansion. In short, the prosperity engendered by the much-hyped "new information economy" never quite extended to help a large chunk of the national community.

Urban America's Mean Streets: The Policy Response

How has urban America responded to this homeless crisis? As Sharon Zukin argues, city officials and the voting public, faced with the daunting scope of homelessness in America, *could* have responded by approving government policies aimed toward eliminating poverty, managing ethnic competition, and integrating rich and poor alike into common public institutions. Unfortunately, this has not been the dominant response of urban leaders across the United States. Although some localities have made halting steps toward more progressive anti-poverty policies, Zukin argues that the dominant response to homelessness in urban America has been the "institutionalization of urban fear" concerning homeless people and an embrace of a coercive criminal justice approach to the presence of homeless people on city streets.[37] According to the National Law Center on Homelessness and Poverty, this move to "criminalize" the homeless—for example, enforcing restrictions on homeless people's use of public spaces (e.g., anticamping ordinances) or targeting homeless people for selective enforcement of generally applicable laws (e.g., public drinking)—has caught the imagination of big-city administrations across the United States. For example, in their survey of the nation's fifty largest cities, the Law Center found that 77 percent of the cities had existing laws restricting begging and 31 percent had recently "enacted new ordinances or amended existing ones to restrict begging."[38] In their conclusion, they argue that more and more cities across the United States have begun to pressure the homeless through restrictions placed upon their activities, and, as Gentry Lange of Seattle's *Real Change* newspaper writes, these efforts are most commonly focused on the actions "by which the homeless try to afford themselves the basic necessities of life," such as sleeping in parks and begging for meals.[39]

In many ways, New York City has taken the lead in the effort to criminalize the homeless and control their access to key public spaces. According to Neil Smith, the Lower East Side has been a particularly heated site of confrontation in New York's ongoing battles over gentrification and homelessness. Dubbed "the East Village" by developers hoping to capitalize on the yuppie panache of nearby Greenwich Village, the Lower East Side became a key locus of upscale residential redevelopment in the 1980s, a process which has resulted in the displacement of low-income tenants and squatters from the neighborhood's long-ignored and undervalued tenements.[40] Thrust unceremoniously onto the streets, many of these tenants filtered into Tompkins Square Park in the heart of the neighborhood, and by the late 1980s, they had constructed a small shantytown on the park grounds.[41]

For their part, city officials viewed this shantytown with increasing alarm. In the city's plans for the neighborhood, Tompkins Square Park was meant to be the "jewel" at the center of a gentrified, middle-class East Village—a vision that was directly threatened by the ongoing presence of the homeless encampment.[42] Therefore, for the next three years, the park became a battleground between city authorities who mounted periodic efforts—usually unsuccessful—to evict the homeless from the park, and the nearly 300 homeless squatters and advocates who viewed Tompkins Square as a "liberated space" and a symbol of the city's inability to address the needs of the poor.[43]

By the spring of 1991, however, Mayor David Dinkins had had enough. Alleging that the park had been "stolen" from the community by "the homeless," Mayor Dinkins declared that "the park is a park. It is not a place to live" and summarily evicted 200 squatters from Tompkins Square.[44] Directing more than fifty police officers to "guard" the park full-time, park officials then embarked on a $2.3 million reconstruction plan designed to limit the use of the park to a few pre-approved activities. At the end of the reconstruction, only three entrances (all guarded periodically by police) were kept open: two provided access to a fenced-off playground, and a third provided residents of the newly converted Christadora condominium access to the park's dog-run.[45] By 1992, the city had won a decisive victory in its effort to support the gentrification of the Lower East Side and its vision for a middle-class Tompkins Square Park.

This battle over Tompkins Square Park was repeated numerous times across Manhattan during the late 1980s and early 1990s, as city officials sought, in Sharon Zukin's words, to "remove the homeless from desirable commercial and residential areas."[46] To be sure, the homeless had never really been tolerated within the traditional turf of New York's glitterati (e.g., the Upper East Side). But what made the late 1980s different was that the city began to expand this "zone of exclusion" to include "those areas of Manhattan that had recently been reclaimed by gentrification," including the working-class Lower East Side and the area around Grand Central Station.[47] Within this new expanded "zone of exclusion," as Zukin writes, the desire to create attractive, socially homogenous public spaces for middle- and upper-class residents, merchants, and tourists outweighed the interests of the homeless and recently displaced evictees (who were often told to "move along").[48] As a result, public space in New York would no longer be open to the public without conditions.[49]

Such coercive approaches to homelessness may be increasing in popularity in urban America,[50] but they have not been embraced without protest. The ACLU, in particular, has mounted a series of legal challenges to the recent spate of antivagrancy and anticamping ordinances around the nation,[51] and, more to the point, the homeless themselves have actively resisted city ordinances which limit their ability to sleep in parks or move freely on city streets.[52] In addition, homeless and housing advocates have tirelessly pointed out that such coercive measures fail to address the fundamental and complex causes of homelessness, including the fact that, as the National Law Center notes, "a person working a regular work week at the minimum wage . . . still cannot afford the fair market rent for an efficiency apartment" in any of the fifty largest cities in the United States.[53] In fact, coercive approaches—such as jailing the homeless for minor infractions like camping in a public park—are clearly *more costly* than their less punitive counterparts. As the Law Center explains, "the daily cost of detaining an individual in jail . . . is roughly 25 percent higher than the daily cost of providing shelter, food, transportation, and counseling services combined."[54] Given these figures, it is difficult to see why so many cities go to such coercive (and expensive) lengths to purge the homeless from city districts slated for middle-class consumption and leisure.

Justifying the Crackdown: Broken Windows Theory

And, indeed, that is the pressing question. Why have city officials and property elites all over the United States turned so decisively toward a coercive approach to homelessness in urban America? In particular, why are so many civic boosters and officials so convinced that the homeless pose a mortal threat to the success of upscale urban revitalization? The answers to these questions are complex, but, for one, it would seem that city elites around the nation have become steeped in chapter and verse of the "broken windows" theory of urban disorder. Inspired initially by the writings of James Q. Wilson and George Kelling, broken windows theory explores the links between the minor incivilities of urban life (such as panhandling, sleeping in parks, and public drinking), perceptions of public safety, and the onset of neighborhood decline.[55] In attempting to come to grips with these tangled and complex connections, the major thesis of broken windows theory is deceptively straightforward: *city officials ignore the "small stuff," the minor incivilities of contemporary urban street life, at their peril.* Far from being merely the gritty stuff of daily urban life, even routine instances of panhandling, graffiti, and public drinking are, in fact, not "minor" at all but rather are the first harbingers of more serious crime and represent the first step on the road to urban decline.

To explain these connections, broken windows theory begins with a seemingly counterintuitive assertion: what makes people most afraid in their communities is *not* really serious or violent crime. After all, relatively few of us will ever witness, let alone be the victim of, a random attack by a stranger. Instead, as Kelling argues, citizens regularly report in surveys and focus groups that their biggest safety concerns have to do with "little crimes" like aggressive panhandling, street harassment, public drinking, and vandalism. In New York City, for example, surveys of citizens who quit using the subways during the 1980s showed that "they were fleeing not because of serious crime but because of problems commonly associated with the 'homeless': public urination and defecation, aggressive panhandling, individuals sprawling on benches and floors of trains or stations."[56] A similar survey commissioned by the city of San Francisco to study public attitudes about homelessness and panhandling found that 90 percent of residents had been approached by a beggar in a public place at least once during the year. Of those who had been approached, 39 percent had been concerned for their physical safety during at least some of these encounters. Moreover, the fear generated by such encounters led nearly a third of the San Franciscans surveyed to avoid particular places, stores, or restaurants.[57] Hardened urbanites might dismiss the fear of, say, panhandling, as mere suburban paranoia. But, according to these authors, the fears generated by street incivility are in fact quite rational, for they accurately reflect, if only on an intuitive level, the very real connections between disorderly behavior, serious crime, and urban decay.[58]

And what *are* these connections, according to Wilson and Kelling? How are serious problems like violent crime and urban decay linked to small-time offenses like panhandling? To dramatize the link, the authors ask readers to visualize an empty building with one broken window.

> Social psychologists . . . tend to agree that if a window in a building is broken and is left unrepaired, all the rest of the windows will soon be broken. . . .

[O]ne unrepaired broken window is a signal that no one cares, and so breaking more windows costs nothing.[59]

But if, as Wilson and Kelling continue, that first broken window is quickly repaired, it sends the message that "someone is watching" and "someone cares" about the building. As a result, potential vandals will be less likely to toss the next rock. Extending the analogy, Wilson and Kelling argue that small acts of social disorder and incivility—including the petty crimes of public drinking, urination, and street harassment—are a lot like that *first* metaphorical broken window. If authorities allow street incivility to escalate unchallenged, if such "small" instances of disorder are left "untended," then more "windows" will inevitably be broken. That is, through their inaction, city officials will only invite the onset of more frequent and more serious acts of incivility and crime. Over time, the escalation of disorder and incivility will inevitably push the city into a spiral of abandonment and decay.[60]

But how does the process work? How does street incivility lead to more serious crime on the streets? To begin, Wilson and Kelling argue that the first casualty of street disorder and incivility is the legitimate public's sense of security and well-being. As uncomfortable encounters with aggressive panhandlers, menacing squeegee kids, and drunken loiterers accumulate, law-abiding citizens soon regard city streets as unpleasant and even frightening. One Seattle city official put the links between incivility and public fear this way:

So if you go into a place where you have the metaphorical broken window, you have graffiti, you have people drinking in the park, you have a lot of trash, you have people acting badly. . . . When you see things on the street that tell you that "this is not a safe place, these people don't care about other people, this is not a civil society" . . . people exercise their choice to shop somewhere, to live somewhere else.[61]

If the law-abiding observe that disorderly behaviors are not held in check by social authorities, they will (correctly, in Wilson and Kelling's view) conclude that "the social order is not being maintained here" and that "this is not a safe place to be."[62]

When the law-abiding abandon the streets, the livability of city neighborhoods and public spaces can be dramatically undermined. Under normal circumstances, crowds of law-abiding people effectively deter criminal behavior because "there are people who are around who will just react. . . . They will not let something bad happen and just say, 'oh well, whatever.' They will call the police, or they'll intervene if necessary."[63] But if law-abiding citizens abandon the streets in disgust at the proliferation of street incivility, they relinquish this informal monitoring role. With no one left to chase off panhandlers, teenage vandals, and slumping inebriates, a crucial mechanism of urban social control is lost.

For this reason, Wilson and Kelling argue that "the unchecked panhandler is, in effect, the first broken window."[64] When average residents are intimidated by the rise of street incivility, and when they withdraw back into their homes (or into the suburbs), more serious criminals may conclude that they can safely negotiate city streets. Muggers and robbers are not stupid, Wilson and Kelling argue. They realize, however subconsciously, that their chances of getting caught drop dramatically if average citizens are already intimidated by crowds of panhandlers and public drunks. The thief, or worse, the drug dealer, may conclude that "if the neighborhood cannot keep a bothersome panhandler from annoying" pedestrians, then it is even less likely to call the police to confront or interfere with more serious criminals.[65] Finally, if the neighborhood is unfortunate enough to attract the drug trade, all bets are off. People can be routinely robbed as drug users prowl the area to support their habit, and innocent bystanders can be literally caught in the crossfire as dealers struggle to protect their corners from equally aggressive rivals.

At this point, even once-stable neighborhoods of families and well-kept homes can quickly spiral into "an inhospitable and frightening jungle."[66] Eventually, Wilson and Kelling write, those merchants and homeowners who can move out of the area quickly do so, and those who cannot afford to flee cower in their homes behind barred windows. As time goes on, as criminologist Wesley Skogan argues, the escalating spectacle of panhandling, public drinking, and more serious crime frightens off potential businesses and residents who wisely choose to invest elsewhere.[67] The end result, according to broken windows theory is a spiral of blight and disorder from which it can be exceedingly difficult to escape.

Perhaps the most celebrated converts to the broken windows theory of urban decline were former New York City Mayor Rudolf Guiliani and his police chief, William Bratton. Of the two, Bratton has been particularly influenced by George Kelling's ideas and began his rise to national prominence when he took over the Metropolitan Transit Authority police in 1990. Armed with a new law restricting panhandling in the subways, Bratton focused his attention on ejecting disorderly subway riders and apprehending fare-beaters—a large number of whom, as Gary Rosen notes, were carrying illegal weapons or had outstanding felony warrants.[68] By 1994, the felony rate on New York's subways had dropped by more than 75 percent, a decline hailed by Kelling and Coles as unparalleled in the annals of crime control.[69] Though it is difficult to attribute the fall of crime in New York's subways to any one factor, Bratton rode this drop in subway crime straight into the police chief's office, where he teamed up with Mayor Guiliani in a much-publicized assault on "quality of life" crimes of all kinds, including the unsolicited "squeegee-ing" of windshields, aggressive panhandling, and public drinking and urination. By the end of 1995, as Rosen reports, the robbery and murder rates had dropped to levels not seen on New York's streets since the early 1970s.[70]

New York City's much-hailed renaissance as a "livable city" can of course be attributed to a great variety of recent developments, not the least of which would be the continual drop in unemployment between 1993 and 2001. Nonetheless, the drop in New York's crime rate began to draw attention from urban policy-makers across the nation, many of whom attempted to replicate Bratton and Guiliani's crackdown on quality of life crimes. In Baltimore, for example, city officials and downtown business elites have created a 200-block "Downtown Management District" as a response to elite fears that petty street incivilities like aggressive panhandling or graffiti-tagging might spoil the festive atmosphere of the city's newly gentrified Inner Harbor. Within this management district, local businesses hired private security patrols that work closely with the police to report suspicious behavior and to move people along if they obstruct pedestrian traffic or intimidate passersby.[71] In San Francisco, former mayor Frank Jordan also assumed office after a "get tough with street disorder" campaign. Once in the mayor's office, Jordan initiated the controversial Operation Matrix, during which police were authorized to aggressively enforce anticamping bans in public parks, antipanhandling statutes, and restrictions on public drinking and urination.[72]

All over the United States, then, it would seem that city elites have warmly embraced the two central lessons of broken windows theory. First, no longer is the "small stuff" viewed lightly in urban America. Tutored at the knee of Wilson and Kelling, city officials and police departments across the country increasingly view petty street incivilities like aggressive panhandling as that first broken window, as an easy-to-overlook prelude to a future of escalating urban decay. Second, thanks to the logic of broken windows theory, city officials and downtown elites now have at their disposal a coherent theory of urban decline that justifies a singular focus on anything that might spark fear among the target markets of spectacular downtown retail-culture redevelopment. As broken windows theory cautions, if the urban and suburban middle class begins to feel threatened or even merely uncomfortable in a particular public space, they will quickly withdraw—an act that not only removes an important mechanism of informal social control, but which also inevitably undermines the economic vitality of the surrounding area. As a result, if civic leaders wish to avoid a future of urban decay, Wilson and Kelling argue that the anxieties of the law-abiding middle class must be assuaged, someway, somehow.

The Homeless in the Middle-Class Imagination

As it turns out, both of these lessons—don't ignore the small stuff, and attend carefully to the fears of the middle class—potentially frame the nation's homeless citizens as an alarming threat to urban vitality. Within this logic, the homeless have often become defined as that first broken window which, if left "unrepaired," could spark a frightening cycle of urban disorder and decay. In short, despite Kelling and Coles' protestations, it is abundantly clear that the homeless have become the primary target of new laws inspired by broken windows theory.[73]

Most fundamentally, contemporary definitions of what constitutes order and disorder in American cities almost inevitably frame the homeless as "disorderly" and "uncivil." Wesley Skogan, for instance, defines disorder as behavior inappropriate to particular public spaces.[74] But because of the chronic lack of clean and safe shelter space in most U.S. cities, the homeless must often engage in *private* activities—such as drinking, sleeping, and urinating—in *public* settings. In this way, the homeless are, by definition, disorderly. If nothing else, the simple physics of homelessness (i.e., living without a *private* sphere of one's own) positions the homeless front-and-center in the crackdown on public disorder and "quality of life" crimes.[75]

However, broken windows theory targets homelessness for another, more direct reason. With the social fears of average citizens framed as a major contributor to urban decay, Wilson and Kelling argue that city officials must do what they can to assuage the urban anxieties of the middle class.[76] In this way, whatever feelings of dread and danger that may be inspired by an encounter with homelessness are therefore, under the regime of broken windows, no longer purely a *private* matter. On the contrary, such primal aversions to homelessness become a legitimate and urgent focus of urban public policy, often fueling an impassioned call to do something about the homeless to restore order and civility in urban America.[77]

Still, it is not yet clear why encountering the homeless would provoke not merely pity, but also a volatile mix of fear and loathing among many middle-class visitors and residents. What, in fact, do the homeless signify within the contemporary middle-class imagination? To begin with, it is important to realize that the poor were not always viewed with such fear. As Andrew Mair points out, in feudal and mercantile society "the pauper" was considered to be an organic part of the close-knit agricultural community—as natural and unremarkable as the ground or the sky. The pauper, in short, had a recognized place in social order, and, as Massimo Pavarini writes, fellow villagers felt at least some "moral duty to assist him as a member of the community."[78]

However, under capitalist social relations, this began to change. As nineteenth-century sociologist Georg Simmel famously observed, everyday life in the expanding capitalist city threw citizens into a variety of associations with anonymous strangers, mediated only by the vagaries of the money economy.[79] No longer, in this sense, were communities held together by the bonds of personal or communal history. Instead, social relations under capitalism quickly became more fragmented, anonymous, and increasingly marked by a complex social division of labor.[80] If during feudalism, most folks knew the people who performed the services they did not provide for themselves, and if these intertwined relationships formed bonds of mutual dependence that stretched over generations, then, today, under the capitalist mode of production, the services citizens provide one another most often come via the impersonal and anonymous marketplace. As a consequence, our personal exchanges with others (particularly with strangers who provide us with services) are often conducted via an impersonal transaction of money rather than tendered in a tradition of mutual support and obligation.[81]

The increasingly commodified and impersonal social life of the capitalist city engenders what Simmel called a "blasé attitude" among its citizens.[82] For Simmel, the continual experience of confronting a sea of strangers connected only through the impersonal marketplace deadens our senses, forcing us to become distant and detached from virtually everyone outside of our narrow circle of family and friends.[83] The result of this atomization is the cultivation of "a matter-of-fact attitude in the treatment of persons and things, in which a formal justice is often combined with an unrelenting hardness."[84] The most typical course of action in such an anonymous and commodified society is to keep your head down and work diligently to secure for yourself and your family whatever rewards of life the society makes available.[85] Let others take care of themselves. Furthermore, any insecurities and anxieties about your place in this complex and fragmented social order can be assuaged by the self-conscious display of luxury consumer goods, signaling to others (and, most importantly, to yourself) that you, at least, have "made it" in the increasingly alienated and commodified world.[86]

In short, as Mair writes, as the scope of commodification has widened and as the division of labor has grown more complex, "the field of personal social obligations has shrunk, for many people, almost to the self."[87] And if this sense of alienation from the wider urban community is generally true, none would seem more alien to the status-seeking, luxury-goods-consuming middle class than the urban homeless. As Jennifer Wolch argues, by virtue of their distance from middle-class life, the homeless in contemporary America have become externalized and demonized as "the other." They have become, in short, a collection of strangers whose perceived differences in behavior, morality, and appearance are so profound that they seem impossibly distant from the day-to-day experience of so-called "normal" society.[88]

Still, what specifically is it about the homeless that inspires such fear, such connotations of "otherness" for many middle-class Americans? To answer this question, scholars such as Mair, Peter Marcuse, and Don Mitchell point to the ways in which the mere existence of the homeless challenges the most sacred premises of middle-class society. For instance, the widely held notion that America is a land of opportunity for all is clearly difficult to sustain in the face of the expanding legions of homeless on the streets.[89] Equally difficult to sustain is the idea that social authorities are taking adequate care of the situation, absent any personal involvement from individual members of the community.[90]

Of course, as Marcuse writes, the threat homelessness presents to these fundamental American myths can be quickly explained away, most typically by blaming the homeless for their own poverty or their perceived lack of a "work ethic."[91] But the mere fact that such ideological gymnastics are required reveals how fundamentally disturbing such encounters with visible poverty can be.

Second, the homeless are disturbing—and even frightening for some urban residents—precisely because they seem to be the ultimate social outsiders, free from both the benefits and, more importantly, the *obligations* of so-called "normal" society. Most of us, for example, lead our lives within the bounds of a social order governed by tacit rules of conduct and enforced by a system of rewards and penalties. We work even unpleasant jobs, in this sense, not because we wish to, but rather for the rewards they offer (however meager) and because the economic penalty for not working is so severe. But the homeless—almost by definition—live outside most of conventional society's systems of reward and punishment. Living in extreme poverty, they have obviously little access to the benefits of "working hard and playing by the rules," as President Clinton was fond of saying. At the same time, however, the *penalties* administered by society also carry less weight. The threat of losing one's job and home would obviously not discipline the unemployed and homeless, and even jail might seem to offer a respite from the harsh realities of the street. In this way, Bahr and Caplow write, the homeless man:

> poses a threat because he has moved out of the reward system; he is a man out of control. Being functionally, if not actually, devoid of significant others, property, and substantial responsibility, he is not subject to the usual constraints. . . . He may go along with the rules, but there is no guarantee that he will do so, and because he is not part of the system, he has no important stake in its continuity.[92]

In a cruel twist, it is the magnitude of their marginality, the profound isolation of their day-to-day existence from the lives of "the homed," that sows fear in the hearts of middle-class residents. What leverage, in short, does society have to keep the homeless in line? What is to prevent the homeless from lashing out at strangers in rage, or perhaps merely for sport? As one downtown Seattle businessman put it, "when a guy lives on the street, what does he have to lose by not being a perfect citizen? . . . What can you do to make things worse for the guy?"[93]

Finally, as Don Mitchell has argued, the spectacle of homeless citizens attending to themselves in full view of the public is disturbing in its own right. In other words, when the homeless are forced to tend to their private needs in parks, alleys, and sidewalks, public spaces begin to take on aspects of "home": they now become places to sleep, to drink, to make love, to use the toilet, and so on. In modern bourgeois societies, this is activity "out of place." This activity inverts the distinction between public and private spaces that is fundamental to middle-class notions of citizenship and propriety. Such activities can therefore signal to urban residents that the "order of things" has been unraveled—that, in *this* place at least, *things are falling apart*. As Mitchell concludes:

> the presence of homeless people in public spaces suggests in the popular mind an irrational and uncontrolled society in which the distinctions between appropriate public and private behavior are muddled.[94]

For many urban residents, the homeless have thus become something of an urban "indicator species" for social disorder, "diagnostic of the presumed ill-health" of urban life and the need to gain control and rationalize urban public space.[95]

Neutralizing the Homeless in the Revitalizing City

In this way, the homeless pose a particularly daunting problem in those elites attempting to market an urban renaissance in the heart of downtown. Evoking unsettling images of poverty, danger, and a social order gone awry, the homeless have become tightly articulated with disorder in the public imagination. Within the logic of broken windows theory, such negative cultural associations help cultivate fear and discomfort among the shoppers and visitors retailers and developers most need to attract downtown. Accordingly, as we have seen, city leaders across the United States have stepped up efforts to cleanse spaces of the city slated for revitalization of all "broken windows"—of anything, in short, that might evoke unpleasant reminders of urban danger and disorder in the middle-class imagination. Finally, as we have discovered, this project of reassurance then places the homeless directly in the crosshairs of new coercive policing strategies. For downtown boosters, the hope is that such coercive approaches to homelessness and street incivility will convince the "target markets" of contemporary revitalization—the ever-desirable crowds of tourists, shoppers, business travelers, and urban professionals—that their own particular "urban renaissance" is for real, that their downtown is once again, as *Urban Land* magazine once wrote, "the type of place that 'respectable people' like themselves tend to frequent."[96]

In this marketing effort, downtown elites across the United States would seem to know their target audiences well. As Loukaitou-Sideris and Banerjee note in their study of L.A.'s downtown revitalization efforts, planners design contemporary urban retail plazas to fulfill the specific needs and values of only that section of the public most likely to consume the private services (i.e., food courts and retail shops) tendered inside. According to Loukaitou-Sideris and Banerjee, surveys of workers show that they appreciate the "exclusionary atmosphere" of L.A.'s newest festival malls and glitzy urban plazas, citing in particular the sense of order and safety cultivated by the plazas' isolation from the streets and management's policy of banning "undesirables" from the premises.[97] Similarly, as Susan Christopherson has argued, business travelers—another key "target market"—are not typically "interested in sociability or the experience of ethnic diversity but in a predictable and secure place to purchase goods . . . and to conduct business."[98] For their part, tourists are almost legendary in their thirst for controlled, comfortable, consumer-friendly spaces. For example, as many scholars have noted, the spectacular success of Southern California's Disneyland has been based in large part on the denial of history, the abstracted presentation of a fantastical "Main Street USA," and an experience of public spaces devoid of any reference to poverty, social conflict, or racial inequality.[99] As one of Disneyland's planners told Mike Wallace, a radical historian conducting research into Disney's early days, "what we are creating is a 'Disney realism,' sort of Utopian in nature, where we carefully program out all the negative, unwanted elements, and program in the positive elements."[100]

Taking their lead from the success of "Disney Realism," contemporary urban planners across the United States take similar pains to "program out" activities, facilities, and even persons that undermine the marketable image of a lively urban renaissance so carefully woven into new downtown revitalization projects.[101] Yet, such efforts to build and market the myth of a postindustrial urban renaissance obscures the *continuation* of poverty and the social stratification and segregation of the American urban landscape. As Andrew Mair cautions, even the term *postindustrial* is at heart a misnomer, even if it is a strategic one. In the new urban renaissance enjoyed by global cities like New York, San Francisco, and Los Angeles, industry and poverty are not consigned to some distant *time* (as "postindustrial" would imply) but are instead banished to another *place*.[102] With industry already relocated to the international division of labor, the persistence of inequality and poverty in urban America stands as a potential threat to the lively and vibrant urban image promoted by downtown developers and city officials. Therefore, reminders of poverty and inequality must, in the logic of the new postindustrial city, be dispersed well outside the gentrifying downtown core or locked into designated "containment" districts.

Within these revitalizing urban spaces, then, the "target markets" of the new urban renaissance are presented with what Don Mitchell calls a "flawless fabric of middle-class work, play, and consumption . . . with minimal exposure to the horrifying level of homelessness and racialized poverty" that can characterize the street environments just blocks away.[103] But for those "undesirables" explicitly targeted for exclusion, and even those simply unable to afford the thrills of upscale consumption and leisure, this new urban renaissance portends, as Neil Smith argues, "the class conquest" of the city. "Evicted from the public and private spaces of what is fast becoming a downtown bourgeois playground," Smith concludes, "minorities, the unemployed, the poorest of the working class are destined for large-scale displacement."[104] In this drive to cleanse the new American downtown of any unsettling references to poverty or decay, the homeless are clearly the most obvious, and most vulnerable, target.

In the end, conservative columnist George Will would seem to speak for many urban policy-makers when he argued that:

> If it is illegal to litter in the street, frankly it ought to be illegal to sleep in the streets. Therefore, there is a simple matter of public order and hygiene in getting these people somewhere else. Not arrest them, but move them off somewhere so they are simply out of sight.[105]

Homelessness, Revitalization, and the Politics of Incivility in Seattle

Seattle's urban elites clearly nurtured dreams of a "downtown renaissance" as ambitious as any across the United States. But would they follow the coercive precedent set by these cities and, as George Will counseled, simply move the city's homeless "out of sight"? To put it another way, how would Seattle's downtown establishment respond to the presence of homeless citizens in the midst of their $1.4 billion effort to transform downtown Seattle into a world-class spectacle of upscale consumption and leisure? Certainly, by the mid-1990s, it was clear to almost everyone in town that Seattle had on its hands a housing and homelessness crisis of massive proportions. The origins of this crisis can be traced directly to the almost absurd competition for affordable housing in Seattle. According to city estimates, Seattle had nearly 25,000 units of low-income and subsidized housing in 1999, up respectably from a scant 10,000 in 1980. But even the city admits that this number is woefully insufficient, estimating that an *additional* 33,200 households in Seattle pay between 30 and 50 percent of their incomes on rent and desperately need to find more affordable housing.[106]

A closer look at Seattle's rapidly inflating housing market shows the dimensions of this affordability crisis. Between 1986 and 1998, for example, average rents in Seattle increased between 3 percent and 9 percent every year, reaching 9 percent increases four times in 12 years. By 1998, vacancy rates for all apartments had dipped below 2 percent. In housing circles, anything less than 5 percent is viewed as a housing emergency. By the late 1990s, the bottom line was clear: housing in Seattle was fast becoming unaffordable for many low-income residents. For example, in 1998, to afford a two-bedroom apartment in the Seattle-Bellevue area at the fair-market rate, a household would have to pay $710 a month. A renting family would have to earn $28,400 a year to afford this rent while paying 35 percent of their income on housing—a percentage which, experts say, would strain the family's ability to pay for other necessities.[107] At this price, housing advocates estimate that *38 percent* of all renters in Seattle would be unable to afford a market-rate two-bedroom apartment. Not surprisingly, the situation is much worse for those renters at the lowest reaches of the income scale. For instance, a three-person household classified as "very low income" (i.e., those households earning 30 percent of the area median income) should only pay $464 for rent on a two-bedroom apartment. But with fair-market rents going for an average of $710 a month, this leaves an "affordability gap" of $246 per month. To afford an apartment at the fair-market rate, such families would have to spend at least 53 percent of their income on rent.[108]

Compounding matters in Seattle (and nationally) has been the slow disappearance of the traditional "housing of last resort" for low-income individuals and families—the single-room apartments typically located in the skid row districts adjacent to most downtowns. As discussed above, not everyone who cannot afford housing is pushed onto the streets. Often, friends and family will step in and catch "at risk" loved ones before they are forced into homelessness.[109] Other times, government housing subsidies (which dramatically underestimate the need for housing assistance) will keep low-income families out of homeless shelters. But for individuals who, for whatever reason, do not have access to these familial "safety nets," skid row, and the ultracheap, single-room apartment "hotels" which characterize it, has traditionally been impoverished people's last chance to stay off the streets.[110] According to Susan Ruddick, skid row housing has been especially crucial for those suffering from personal problems like mental illness, drug addiction, and alcohol abuse that make it less likely that friends and family will come to the rescue.[111] But skid row has also historically served the needs of single seniors without families who, over the years, have constructed close interpersonal connections with other seniors and the low-income services provided in such districts.

Unfortunately for these folks, since the mid-1970s, such low-income districts in Seattle and nationally have become prime targets for developers looking to cash in on skid row's low property costs and its close proximity to the expanding retail and commercial core. In Seattle, the loss of skid row and other downtown low-income housing has reached crisis proportions. The city, which has little reason to inflate the loss of low-income housing, nonetheless estimates that between 1960 and 1987, Seattle *lost* over *70 percent* of its low-income units located downtown (from approximately 20,000 units in 1960 to 5,852 units in 1987), mostly due to freeway construction, fire code condemnations, and upscale redevelopment.[112] According to the city, in the years since 1987, the situation has improved slightly with the addition of 1,794 units of low-income housing, but housing advocates dispute this good news, arguing that the city inflated the latest count by adding "moderate-income" units to its count of low-income apartments in downtown Seattle. According to the Seattle Displacement Coalition, the real tally of low-income units in downtown (circa 1998) is closer to 5,700—an all-time low for the city.[113]

Put simply, Seattle's meager supply of permanent, subsidized low-income housing cannot keep up with the desperate demands of the unemployed, the impoverished, or the mentally ill. As of 1999, over 15,000 households were waiting to get into Seattle's public housing programs, including those offering housing subsidies—a figure which translates into a wait of at least three months before any help can be offered.[114] With the crush of people clamoring for the small supply of affordable and subsidized low-income housing, the result of all these trends has been, not surprisingly, the dramatic rise of homelessness in Seattle. In 1997, for instance, the city found that over 18,000 people sought homeless services in Seattle at one time or another during the course of the year.[115] Put another way, *three out of every 100 Seattleites sought homeless services at least once during 1997.*[116] Every day, according to the Seattle Displacement Coalition, anywhere between 3,000 and 5,000 people are on the streets or in shelters.[117] To make matters worse, such numbers have overwhelmed the limited shelter space available in Seattle. As the homeless newspaper *Real Change* reports, there are only approximately 2,200 shelter beds in Seattle, a woefully inadequate number by any account.[118] During November 1995, for instance, close to 7,500 individuals were turned away from Seattle's shelters, and during the entire year, the state of Washington estimates that 69,749 requests for service were turned down in King County alone.[119]

To be sure, there have been a variety of responses to the explosive crisis of homelessness in Seattle. In the years since "the homeless" first appeared on the public agenda in the late 1970s, Seattle's community of low-income and anti-poverty activists have mobilized to address the housing crisis. Along the way, they have created a whole host of new advocacy organizations, including the Low Income Housing Institute, S.H.A.R.E, the Pike Market Medical Clinic, the Seattle-King County Coalition for the Homeless, and the politically minded Seattle Displacement Coalition. State and local governments also mobilized around the issue, spawning a variety of state and city task forces investigating the causes and effects of homelessness. More concretely, the city's budget for addressing homeless services has doubled between 1987 and 1998, with $7.8 million in local funds devoted to low-income housing and emergency services. Combined with the annual federal HUD grant of approximately $14 million, the city's response, even if it has not kept pace with the problem, has indeed helped many individuals and families stay off the streets, proving that Seattle's progressive reputation is not entirely undeserved.[120]

However, during the doldrums of the early 1990s recession, a parallel response to the problem of homelessness began to emerge in Seattle's elite circles—a response that had its roots in the growing concern over downtown's declining fortunes. As it turned out, an important contributor to the sense of unease was a flurry of local news articles testifying to the "unfriendly shopping atmosphere" descending upon downtown streets, and, in many of these articles the city's homeless found themselves cast as the menacing villain.

As conservative columnist and future GOP gubernatorial candidate John Carlson argued, "the new homeless" were not the colorful and harmless "bums" of yore. "Today's crowd is different," he wrote:

> They are . . . younger and meaner. And more numerous. The older bums try to stay out of their way. They are contemptuous of authority and spit on respectability. Many are drug-addicted, others deranged. They are also professionals—they know how to play the system and they know what they can get away with. And most of the time they do.[121]

Other commentators noted a similar escalation in the incivility of the "new homeless." For instance, one downtown architect recalled that, in years past, the homeless would adhere to unwritten rules limiting their presence in key public spaces like the Pike Place Market. "The street element just stayed out," she told the *Times*. "Even the winos generally stayed on that side of the street," pointing east across First Avenue.[122] But these days, she theorized, the influence of crack cocaine and the influx of the "new," more youthful homeless now flaunt these rules and have made the Market a more threatening place. One concerned councilmember even had a theory about the "influx" of the new more menacing and "hard-core" homeless: they were really out-of-towners shipped up from California on one-way bus tickets![123]

Whether out-of-towners or homegrown, according to the flurry of anti-vagrant reports printed in the early 1990s, the homeless were nonetheless responsible for spoiling downtown's street environment, and, by extension, undermining the financial viability of the commercial core. Sometimes the accounts of homeless-inspired street deviance had a sensational, "life in the naked city" quality to them, as was the case in this *Times* columnists' encounter with an aggressive panhandler:

> He took a step closer. It both blocked my way and made his presence more threatening. . . . He was just a little taller than me and seemed in pretty good shape for someone who said he was hungry and hadn't eaten in days. His left hand was extended to receive my offering, but his right hand was raised in a semi-clenched fist . . .[124]

But more often, the daily press merely reported the loud complaints of downtown merchants and their stories of how the homeless harass their customers. "The homeless just seem more aggressive now," one boutique owner told the *Times*. "It scares people who are coming downtown to shop," she said.[125] For their part, downtown shoppers told reporters about how they "didn't like picking over people on the sidewalk," "didn't like drunks reeling toward them," or "kids in $100 shoes asking for bus fare."[126] Another merchant described to the *Times* how "a disheveled man, breath reeking from alcohol, reeled through the door." After grabbing the doorway mat and tossing it, he reportedly snatched a handbag and "staggered out the door—with one of the store's owners in hot pursuit."[127] "Sometimes," another merchant complained, "the drunks come into the store . . . they are boisterous, hostile, and a nuisance, and the customers sure leave."[128]

By the summer of 1993, local coverage of downtown street incivility had bubbled to a full-out boil. A *Seattle Times* feature summed this growing ambivalence about the street atmosphere in downtown this way: *"Ground zero: What does downtown mean to you? Drugs? Porn? Street People? Or where you can find the heart of the city?"*[129] For their part, downtown merchants began to demand that Mayor Norm Rice rein in the disorderly behavior argued to be proliferating on city streets. As one merchant told the *Post-Intelligencer*, "I don't believe [the mayor] is serious enough about the serious problems we have downtown. There is to much attention to helping the so-called homeless . . . Our government is too soft, understanding the problems of a small minority and oblivious to the needs of businesses."[130] By midsummer 1993, the editorial page of the *Seattle Times* printed a "call to arms" directed squarely at City Hall. In an unsigned editorial entitled "Looking for Better Ways to Curb Unruly Street Life," the *Times* editors argued that:

> The perception that downtown, already hit by the loss of two major department stores, is becoming run-down has to be treated seriously. Seattleites have made huge investments to make downtown an economically viable, physically inviting place. Those achievements are threatened when some streets and parks become unpoliced havens for panhandlers and unruly drunks.[131]

In short, by the summer of 1993, the internal debate within the downtown establishment about whether street incivility was a problem—and, if so, what to do about it—had been largely resolved. Downtown boosters and public officials were now unified around the demand for a more coercive approach to homelessness.

As it turned out, the man who would lead this charge for a new approach to homelessness in downtown Seattle was already ensconced in city hall. Even before he began his tenure as Seattle's city attorney in 1990, Mark Sidran was convinced that homelessness and street incivility had a corrosive effect on the urban environment, and he was more than willing to spearhead the push for broader policing powers on Seattle's streets. An early convert to Wilson and Kelling's broken windows theory, Sidran's own views on incivility and urban decay crystallized during his morning commute to City Hall. As he later described to the *Puget Sound Business Journal*, every day Sidran would drop off his wife at her downtown office. And each day, he would see a "shaggy man with a bedroll and a dog making a small bit of Pine Street his home." After a while, the *Journal* explains, "Sidran began to notice something else—lots of people crossing the street to avoid stepping over the man and his posses-

sions."[132] For Sidran, this slice of late-century urban life became symbolic of
the larger problems facing a recession-weary downtown Seattle. "It occurred to
me," he recalled, "why does everybody have to yield the right of way to him?
The net impact of that kind of behavior is that it depopulates the street. That's
not just bad for business; it's bad for public safety."[133]

With the business community again grumbling about homelessness and
downtown's street atmosphere, there would be no better political moment for
his call to crack down on urban disorder and incivility. So in early August of
1993, Sidran made the short trip from city hall to the Downtown Seattle Rotary
Club and announced his campaign to restore civility to Seattle's streets. Arguing that, despite the city's national reputation as a "livable city" and a world-
class place to do business, many Seattleites have the nagging suspicion that
"maybe, just maybe, we are pretty much like those other big American cities
'back East.'"[134] This is why, Sidran told the assembled Rotarians, visible homelessness and the spiraling incivility on Seattle's streets "touches a nerve" for so
many residents:

> If the "past is prologue" we have seen one version of the future in city after
> city, a dying retail core where there is more criminal than commercial activity,
> where the simplest rules of civility are ignored without consequence, where
> random senseless acts of violence become pervasive, culminating in the
> migration of those who can leave.[135]

This is not Seattle today, he cautioned the crowd. "But this downward spiral
doesn't happen overnight, and it will be more than just a bad dream if we don't
wake up."[136]

We must learn from the tragic history of urban America, Sidran concluded.
We must prevent Seattle from becoming just another "formerly great city."[137]
And if there is one thing this tragic history teaches us, as one official in the city
attorney's office recalled years later, it is that:

> You've got to keep the streets alive. And the difference between a dead city
> and a live city is whether or not you have enough people who feel comfortable
> going downtown.[138]

In short, if enough people abandon downtown streets due to their fears of being
harassed or panhandled, he argued, the city would begin "rotting from the inside out," with merchants and employers fleeing along with shoppers and residents to the suburban fringe.[139] This accelerating exodus of all but the very rich
("who can high-rise themselves off from the circumstances of the streets") and
the very poor would eventually corrode the city's tax base and undermine the
city government's ability to turn the situation around.[140] Such a scenario used
to be unthinkable in Seattle, as Sidran told the Rotarians back in 1993, but no
longer. We need to act now before it is too late.[141]

To this end, Sidran then proposed that the city council "strengthen our laws" in order to send the message that Seattle is a place where "people behave themselves and respect the rights of others."[142] Thus were born what came to be called the "Sidran ordinances"—a series of new laws transparently targeted at street people—each of which attempted to redress a particular form of "incivility" that, according to Sidran, had helped cultivate a sense of fear on downtown streets:

- *Sitting on the sidewalks:* As Sidran argued, "many people see those sitting or lying on the sidewalk and—either because they expect to be solicited or otherwise feel apprehensive—avoid the area." As a result, this new ordinance would directly target those citizens who lie or sit down day after day in Seattle's downtown and neighborhood commercial districts.[143]

- *Public drinking and urination:* Second and subsequent arrests for public drinking and urination would be reclassified as criminal misdemeanors, subject to up to ninety days in jail and a fine of $1,000.[144]

- *Closing alleys suspected of drug trafficking:* Under this ordinance, the police would be able to close public access to any alleys suspected of sheltering the drug trade. Unauthorized persons in such closed alleys would be subject to arrest.[145]

- *Aggressive panhandling:* Sidran's proposal would strengthen Seattle's existing laws against aggressive panhandling by making it more enforceable. To this end, the police would be given the power to stop specific behaviors, including touching, using abusive or threatening language, or repeatedly demanding money after a clear refusal.[146]

By cracking down on such misbehaviors, Sidran argued that the public could be reassured that standards of civility would be enforced on downtown streets and that city officials will do everything in their power to, as one *Seattle Times* headline proclaimed, "keep downtown alive."[147]

When Sidran's proposals became public knowledge, homeless and antipoverty advocates responded with outrage. Particularly galling to the advocacy community was Sidran's antisitting ordinance, which they saw as a direct attack on the homeless citizens' First Amendment freedoms of speech and assembly. Convinced that Sidran's antisitting law was primarily created to herd homeless people out of commercial areas, homeless advocates quickly mobilized. In fact, at the same time that Sidran announced these "incivility" proposals, 150 antipoverty advocates and homeless people staged a raucous rally in Westlake Park. Carrying an effigy of the bespectacled city attorney into the center of the park, the protesters dropped a rented port-a-potty onto the effigy's head, crushing it against the cobblestone and drawing cheers from the crowd.[148]

Arguing that the laws selectively targeted behaviors that are an unavoidable part of life on the streets, these antipoverty activists denounced the proposals as an exercise in "economic cleansing," transparently designed to give police the tools they need to clear the homeless out of downtown Seattle.[149]

For many antipoverty activists, Sidran's laws—proposed during the depths of economic recession—represented an attempt to "camouflage" the reality of poverty and homelessness "and sweep them under the rug, or, in this case . . . into overcrowded jails."[150] As John Fox and John Reese of the Seattle Displacement Coalition wrote in *Real Change*, an alternative newspaper in Seattle staffed by homeless people and homeless advocates, Sidran's laws:

> won't stem the tide of homelessness and unemployment, or stop the loss of housing that is driving increasing numbers of human beings onto our streets. Just how much further will our leaders be willing to go in the name of cleaning up downtown, in the name of accommodating business?[151]

Instead of addressing the "root causes" of homelessness and poverty, then, the proposed laws represented the "misbelief that homeless people are a problem to society and the businesses downtown, and that if we remove them, everything will be just fine."[152] By the end of the summer, a coalition of thirty-six antipoverty and civil liberties organizations, including the King County Labor Council, the National Organization for Women, the Seattle Displacement Coalition, the ACLU and several church, community, and political groups had organized around the goal of killing Sidran's ordinances before they reached the street.[153] This coalition of antipoverty groups, John Fox and John Reese warned,

> will not go "quietly into the night" and allow this law to be enforced only to be followed by even more draconian measures aimed at "cleansing our streets." We must stop the drift toward totalitarianism that we are truly seeing played out on the streets of our city. When the civil rights of the poor and homeless are at stake, the rights of all of us are threatened.[154]

To this end, the anti-Sidran coalition mounted a vigorous legal challenge to the most controversial of all the ordinances—the sitting measure—with the intention of blocking the laws before they could be enforced.[155] Other opponents of the laws promised a sustained civil disobedience campaign. In one case, because the antisitting ordinance allowed people to sit for "permitted activities" such as political protests or street parades, advocates proposed to flood the Seattle Engineering Department with thousands of applications for "sitting permits" in the hope that the new laws would become too costly to administer.[156]

In his arguments before the Seattle City Council (who, along with Mayor Rice, would have the final say on his ordinances), Sidran responded to these critics by framing the issue as a choice between the *individual's* "right" to misbehave versus the *community's* right to enforce minimum standards of civil behavior in public. As Sidran predicted when he first unveiled his ordinances, there will be those who will say that these proposals are an "attack on the homeless." On the contrary, as he told the Rotarians:

> this is not aimed at the homeless; it is aimed at the lawless. Most homeless cope with adversity without breaking the law. This is not about "getting people out of town"; it is about getting people to behave. It is reasonable to expect that all of us who live here should comply with some simple, basic rules of civil behavior.[157]

To be sure, he argued, the city should expand services for those forced onto the streets, including day shelters, public toilets, and detox centers, but regardless of how much access people have to such services, some people will still "make bad choices."[158] You can put a public toilet in the park, and some people will pee in the alley. You can build a treatment center, but some people will continue to use and abuse in public.[159] But just because people will always make their own decisions about how to live, he argued, this should not mean the city has to "accept the choices that harm the legitimate rights and interests of our community."[160] Instead, the city should act quickly to "preserve public spaces for the benefit of all."[161]

Finally, in the council hearings on the proposed laws, Sidran argued forcefully that his new laws tapped into a deep popular desire for order, a desire which was by no means confined to the city's middle- and upper-castes. In fact, the quickest way to rile up the city attorney's office is to suggest that the civility ordinances constitute an undeclared war on Seattle's poor. "I think it's rubbish," said one official.[162] Far from constituting a "war on the poor," he argued, the civility statutes *protect* the poor from having to live in an urban environment marked by crime and disorder. To illustrate his point, the official recalled "one of the most telling moments" in the city council's hearings. During one hearing, a spokesperson for the low-income tenants of Pioneer Square's Frye Building, home to much of downtown's subsidized housing, spoke out strongly in favor of Sidran's incivility statutes. And why did they support Sidran's laws?

> Because they understand on a gut level the broken windows theory. So their message was "a lot of us used to be homeless. Now we have housing. We live here. . . . We don't have anywhere else to go and we don't like being exposed to this behavior, any more than anybody else. But we know that if the behavior drives the rest of you away, we're going to be left here, not able to go out at night because it's dangerous, not able to go shopping at the neighborhood store because it's closed. We're going to be left in a vast wasteland."[163]

The thirst for order, in short, cuts across class lines. And it is this desire for order which explains the "large . . . majority consensus" backing the Sidran ordinances, at least according to the city attorney's office.[164] In this way, for Sidran, the ordinances are as much about symbolism as street crime, as much about sending messages as policing behavior. As Sidran once explained to a *Times* reporter, "symbolism matters in this war over downtown" and the message aimed at residents, tourists, shoppers and investors is simple and direct: on Seattle's streets at least, the order will be maintained.[165]

In the end, and to the surprise of few, Sidran's arguments carried the day in city hall. In early October 1993, the council passed Sidran's ordinances— including the controversial sidewalk ordinance—by overwhelming margins. In explaining their support for Sidran's statutes, most councilmembers told reporters that a "get tough" approach to street incivility promised to reverse the slumping retail core's negative image. Council veteran Margaret Pageler, fresh from a trip to Manhattan, talked about how impressed she was with clean and safe streets and, in a moment of hyperbole, argued that Seattle's streets seemed threatening by comparison.[166] Other councilmembers hoped the laws would help entice wary suburban shoppers back downtown. "Remember," one staff member explained, "it's the perception of danger, not necessarily the reality, that people go on." And the escalating sense of danger felt by suburban visitors had convinced many to stick to the shopping malls closer to home. "When you're not used to it," she said, "getting panhandled can be scary."[167] By sending a message that Seattle would not tolerate distressing behaviors like panhandling, sitting on sidewalks, or public urination, most councilmembers expressed hope that potential visitors, shoppers, and investors would once again be lured back downtown in increasingly large numbers.[168]

Although they had to wait nearly a year for all the ordinances to work their way through the courts (all were eventually upheld), Mark Sidran and Seattle's downtown establishment had won an important victory. Like their counterparts in New York and Los Angeles, Seattle's city officials had officially embarked upon their own "project of reassurance" designed to convince wary shoppers, visitors, and investors that downtown was once again a vibrant and safe place to be. Despite the city's progressive-left image, Seattle would nonetheless join New York and Los Angeles in their turn toward a more coercive approach to homelessness and street incivility.[169] Moreover, in the view of the *Seattle Times* editorial board, this embrace of a broken windows approach to disorderly behavior in downtown spaces had arrived at a crucial time for the downtown core. With the Rhodes Project negotiations heading toward completion, they wrote in the spring of 1994 that:

> the city is poised for a dramatic infusion of capital and creativity at the shuttered Frederick & Nelson corner. All over downtown, there is a realization that a turning point in the vitality of the city is at hand. Part of that vitality must come from a downtown that is pedestrian-friendly, a place where walking is unhindered and safe.[170]

While the Rhodes Project was viewed as the cornerstone of Seattle's urban renaissance, the redevelopment project would, by itself, not be enough to reverse the city's slumping urban fortunes. To this end, "the city's ordinance requiring civilized behavior by those whose home is often the streets is an important part of keeping downtown alive."[171]

For their part, however, homeless advocates expressed shock that such laws had managed to garner wide support in their hometown. As John Fox and John Reese wrote in *Real Change*:

> Our national image as a "compassionate city" has been replaced with "Seattle—leader in the crackdown on the homeless." And don't tell the homeless and those of us who are advocates that we spend great amounts on homeless services and housing. What we spend pales in relation to the need, and it pales in relation to what we spend to promote . . . downtown.[172]

As city employees began to erect signs notifying the homeless of their new obligation to stand during business hours, many in the advocacy community vowed continued opposition to city hall's new coercive stance toward the homeless. "Our society and streets are in a mean season," wrote Judith Lonquist of the Seattle Women's Commission. "As leaders in our communities, we cannot accept it, we cannot justify it, and we certainly must not honor it."[173] To this end, advocates must keep up the pressure on city hall, she argued. "We must ask the mayor and city council to use . . . the city's resources to support efforts that add to human dignity and productivity."[174] As it turned out, Seattle antipoverty activists would not have to wait long for the next battle over homeless and spectacular revitalization. Sparked in large part by the political fallout from the bitter "incivility" debates of 1993-1994, the next battle between antipoverty advocates and downtown business leaders over the social and physical landscape of downtown Seattle would soon erupt again, but this time in a most unlikely spot—a small, nondescript rooming hotel along a long-ignored stretch of Third Avenue.

Notes

1. Lee Moriwaki and Joe Heim, "High-Fives Greet New Nordstrom: 5,000 at the Door as Flagship Store Opens Today," *Seattle Times*, 21 August 1998, 1(A).
2. Lee Moriwaki and Joe Heim, "High-Fives Greet New Nordstrom."
3. Lee Moriwaki and Joe Heim, "High-Fives Greet New Nordstrom."
4. Lee Moriwaki, "Pacific Place: Will Opening of Downtown's Newest Shot in the Arm Be Clouded by Recession?" *Seattle Times*, 25 October 1998, 1(A).
5. Lee Moriwaki, "Pacific Place," 1(A).
6. Moriwaki, "High-Fives," 1(A).

7. With thanks to Canadian author W. P. Kinsella and Alex Fryer, "Strong-Arming a Retail Rebirth: The Build It and They Will Come Credo May have Some Flaws," *Puget Sound Business Journal*, 9 June 1995.

8. George Gerbner, "Foreword: Telling All the Stories," in *Consuming Environments: Television and Commercial Culture*, by M. Budd, S. Craig, and C. Steinman (New Brunswick, NJ: Rutgers University Press, 1999), p. xiv.

9. Robert Entman and Andrew Rojecki, *The Black Image in the White Mind* (Chicago: University of Chicago Press, 1999). See also, Steve Macek, "Television and the Process of Urban Decline" (Paper presented at the 1999 Conference of the Union for Democratic Communications. Eugene, Oregon).

10. See Neil Smith, *The New Urban Frontier: Gentrification and the Revanchist City* (London: Routledge, 1996); Sharon Zukin, *The Cultures of Cities* (Cambridge, UK: Basil Blackwell, 1995); Mike Davis, *Ecology of Fear: Los Angeles and the Imagination of Disaster* (New York: Vintage, 1998).

11. Mike Davis, *City of Quartz: Excavating the Future in Los Angeles* (New York: Vintage, 1992), 232.

12. Andrew Sayer, "The 'New' Regional Geography and Problems of Narrative," *Environment and Planning D: Society and Space* 7, 251-76. For an insightful discussion of the "chaotic" nature of the concept of homelessness, see also, Christopher Jencks, *The Homeless* (Cambridge, MA: Harvard University Press, 1994).

13. See David Harvey, *The Condition of Postmodernity* (Cambridge, UK: Basil Blackwell, 1990); Saskia Sassen, *The Global City: New York, London, Tokyo* (Prineton, NJ: Princeton University Press, 1991); Michael Piore and Charles Sabel, *The Second Industrial Divide* (New York: Basic Books, 1984); Scott Lash and John Urry, *The End of Organized Capitalism* (Madison, WI: University of Wisconsin Press, 1987).

14. Robert Reich, *The Work of Nations* (New York: Basic Books, 1991).

15. Jennifer Wolch and Michael Dear, *Malign Neglect: Homelessness in an American City* (San Francisco: Jossey-Boss, 1993), 7.

16. Wolch and Dear, *Malign Neglect*, 7.

17. Kathryn Larin and Elizabeth McNichol, *Pulling Apart: A State-by-State Analysis of Income Trends* (Washington, DC: Center on Budget and Policy Priorities, 1997), executive summary.

18. Wolch and Dear, 9-10. Beginning in the early 1960s, policy-makers, responding to pressure from advocates of the mentally ill, began to shut down asylums and institutions in favor of a planned switch to "community-based" mental health care. However well-intentioned, fiscal conservatives in federal and state governments (of both parties) saw this shift as an opportunity to cut costs. As a result, in most states where hospitals were shut down, little attempt was made to adequately fund the community-based services that could have made deinstitutionalization a success. As a result, many discharged patients, tossed out of hospitals but given few services and little support, drifted into inner-city neighborhoods (particularly skid row districts, where social services tend to concentrate) and some found their way to the streets, becoming a part of the "new homeless" of the 1980s.

19. Wolch and Dear, 20.

20. Wolch and Dear, 20.

21. Jennifer Daskal, *In Search of Shelter: The Growing Shortage of Affordable Rental Housing* (Washington, D. C.: Center for Budget and Policy Priorities, 1998), 4.

22. Daskal, *In Search of Shelter,* 4.

23. Peter Marcuse, "Neutralizing Homelessness," *Socialist Review* (1988): 74-75.

24. Neil Smith, *The New Urban Frontier,* 23.

25. Neil Smith, *The New Urban Frontier,* 15.

26. Wolch and Dear, 25. See also, Mike Davis, *City of Quartz,* 173-86.

27. Wolch and Dear, 25-26. See also, Neil Smith, "Gentrification, the Frontier, and the Restructuring of Urban Space," in *The Gentrification of the City,* ed. Neil Smith and Peter Williams (Boston: Allen Unwin, 1986), 23.

28. Wolch and Dear, 27.

29. Wolch and Dear, 28.

30. Although, as Jennifer Daskal notes, new federally subsidized units have kept pace with the demolition and/or redevelopment of low-income housing. The federal response to the crisis has not kept up with the expanding number of people who need low-income housing assistance. The result is a fierce competition for whatever nonsubsidized low-income housing a city has to offer. This competition has, in turn, pushed up the rents demanded for these units, in many cases putting non-subsidized, private-market housing units beyond the reach of low-income families. Therefore, if they are not lucky enough to win a federal subsidy for housing, they are forced to pay market price— a price that is unaffordable for many low-income households.

31. Robin Law and Jennifer Wolch, "Homelessness and Economic Restructuring," *Urban Geography* 12, vol. 2 (1991): 129.

32. Wolch and Dear, 34.

33. Wolch and Dear, 43.

34. Peter Marcuse, "Neutralizing Homelessness," 72.

35. Kim Hopper and Jill Hamberg, "The Making of America's Homeless, From Skid Row to New Poor, 1945-1984," in *Critical Perspectives on Housing,* eds. Rachel Bratt, Chester Hartman, and Ann Meyerson (Temple University Press: Philadelphia, PA: 1986). Quoted in Marcuse, 72.

36. National Low Income Housing Coalition, *1998 Advocates Resource Handbook* (Washington, DC: NLIHC, 1998).

37. Sharon Zukin, *The Cultures of Cities* (Cambridge, MA: Blackwell, 1995), 39.

38. Quoted in Gentry Lange, "Criminalization of Homelessness is on the Rise," *Real Change,* March 1997.

39. Gentry Lange, "Criminalization of Homelessness is on the Rise."

40. Neil Smith, "New City, New Frontier: The Lower East Side as Wild, Wild West," in V*ariations on a Theme Park,* ed. M. Sorkin (New York: Hill and Wang, 1992), 75.

41. Neil Smith, *The New Urban Frontier,* 5.

42. Neil Smith, "New City, New Frontier," 84.

43. Neil Smith, *The New Urban Frontier,* 4-5.

44. Neil Smith, *The New Urban Frontier,* 6.

45. Neil Smith, *The New Urban Frontier,* 6.

46. Sharon Zukin, *Landscapes of Power: From Detroit to Disneyland* (Berkeley, CA: University of California Press, 1991), 199-200.

47. Sharon Zukin, *Landscapes of Power,* 199-200.

48. Sharon Zukin, *The Cultures of Cities,* 29-32.

49. Zukin, *Landscapes of Power,* 200.

50. Not to be outdone, Los Angeles has also framed the issue of homelessness as largely a matter of public safety and urban social control. Responding to an increasingly vocal middle-class demand for increased insulation from "unsavory groups," L.A.'s city officials, according to Mike Davis, have pursued the twin policies of *containment* and *dispersal* in their approach to the city's homeless. As Davis writes, while some city leaders have periodically toyed with the notion of shipping indigents out of town "en masse," the more measured approach, institutionalized since the 1980s, has been to confine the homeless (and the social services targeted to the homeless) to a fifty-square block area of "skid row," L.A.'s now-official "containment district." Within this district, the homeless have access to human services unavailable elsewhere in the city and are even—in a special exemption granted to skid row—allowed to sleep in the parks and on the sidewalks. Outside of this district, however, the city pursues a strategy of *dispersal*, by which the homeless are discouraged from venturing in any sustained way out of the containment zone. Outside of skid row, the LAPD strictly enforces the city anticamping ordinance in public parks, periodically tearing down temporary shantytowns and herding the homeless back into the designated containment zone. In other L.A. parks outside skid row, the city has installed a series of outdoor sprinklers which are designed to douse "trespassing" homeless squatters in the wee hours of the morning. After a few soggy nights, the park service evidently believes the homeless will get the picture and move along back to skid row. Other public-sector tactics of dispersal are even more outrageous, including the proliferation of L.A.'s newest barrel-shaped "bum-proof" benches which offer "a minimal surface for sitting but which make sleeping virtually impossible." Taken together, as Davis concludes, these strategies of containment and dispersal have aided and abetted the ascendance of what he calls "social apartheid" on L.A.'s streets and have served to transform skid row into the "nation's largest outdoor poorhouse." For details, see Mike Davis, *City of Quartz* (New York: Vintage, 1992).

51. John Hoffman, "Court Gestures: Seattle's Sidran Ordinance has its Day(s) in Court," *Real Change*, November 1994.

52. For example, as Susan Ruddick writes, when an encampment of homeless people were hustled out of downtown to accommodate the Olympics in 1984, they quickly reestablished their camp—this time outside of city hall during the holidays—in an effort to highlight their continued marginalization during the Christmas "season of giving." See Susan Ruddick, *Young and Homeless in Hollywood: Mapping Social Idenities* (New York: Routledge, 1996), 64.

53. Gentry Lange, "Criminalization of Homelessness is on the Rise," *Real Change*, March 1997.

54. Gentry Lange, "Criminalization of Homelessness."

55. James Q. Wilson and George Kelling, "Broken Windows," *The Atlantic Monthly* (March 1982): 31.

56. George Kelling et al., "Crime Solutions: 18 things We Can Do Now to Fight Back," *The American Enterprise*, May/June 1995, 36.

57. George Kelling and Catherine Coles, *Fixing Broken Windows: Restoring Order and Reducing Crime in Our Communities* (New York: Martin Kessler, 1996), 13.

58. Wilson and Kelling, "Broken Windows," 31.

59. Wilson and Kelling, "Broken Windows," 31.

60. Wilson and Kelling, "Broken Windows," 32.

61. Personal interview, Seattle City Attorney's Office, 9 February 1999.

62. Kelling and Coles, *Fixing Broken Windows*, 20. Interestingly, Kelling and Coles argue that the fear generated by such encounters with street incivility is magnified in urban settings. In smaller rural communities, Kelling and Coles contend that such acts of incivility may not be as threatening, because the social order is maintained through continual contact with one's friends, family, and neighbors. The odd act of begging or public drunkenness may be annoying, but does not throw safety of the whole community into question. In urban life, however, such incivility can be toxic. Echoing the work of nineteenth-century sociologist Georg Simmel, Kelling and Coles argue that because urban life is characterized by the ongoing interaction with a sea of strangers, citizens need to feel that a minimum level of order and predictability is being maintained in order to feel safe. "In pluralistic cosmopolitan areas . . . we cannot be advised about those we meet by personal knowledge, history or perhaps even reputation. Instead we take our cues from activities observed on the street and shape our public behavior accordingly." Consequently, anything that threatens this delicate balance of order and civility among strangers, anything that seems threatening and unpredictable, will spark feelings of fear and will cause citizens to withdraw from public spaces and avoid particular areas. For more details, see Kelling and Coles, *Fixing Broken Windows*, 30.

63. Personal interview, Seattle City Attorney's Office, 9 February 1999.

64. Wilson and Kelling, "Broken Windows," 34.

65. Wilson and Kelling, "Broken Windows," 34.

66. Wilson and Kelling, "Broken Windows," 31-32.

67. Wesley Skogan, *Disorder and Decline: Crime and the Spiral of Decay in American Neighborhoods* (New York: The Free Press), 50.

68. Gary Rosen, "Books in Review," *Commentary* (December 1996): 64.

69. Gary Rosen, "Books in Review," 64.

70. Rosen, "Books in Review."

71. Kelling and Coles, 199.

72. Kelling and Coles, 209.

73. Kelling and Coles, 40. The same point surfaced in an interview with a high-ranking official in the Seattle City Attorney's Office.

74. Wesley Skogan, *Disorder and Decline*.

75. Don Mitchell, "The End of Public Space? People's Park, Definitions of the Public, and Democracy," *Annals of the Association of American Geographers* 85 (1995): 108-33.

76. Personal interview, Seattle City Attorney's Office, 9 February 1999.

77. Interestingly, in each of Kelling and Coles' success stories—where city officials cleaned up the streets by focusing on "quality of life" crimes—the move to a more coercive approach to street incivility was motivated at least in part by elite or public fears concerning the visibility of homelessness in downtown or gentrifying areas. For details, see Kelling and Coles, *Fixing Broken Windows*, chapter 6.

78. Andrew Mair, "The Homeless in the Post-Industrial City," *Political Geography* 5 (October 1986): 358.

79. Paul Levine, ed., *Georg Simmel: On Individuality and Social Forms* (Chicago: University of Chicago Press, 1971), 326.

80. Mair, 358.

81. Mike Budd, Steve Craig, and Clay Steinman, *Consuming environments: Television and Commercial Culture* (New Brunswick, NJ: Rutgers University Press): 10-12.

82. P. Levine, ed., *Georg Simmel,* 326-27.

83. P. Levine, ed., *Georg Simmel,* 326-27.

84. P. Levine, ed., *Georg Simmel,* 326-27.

85. For details, see Herbert Marcuse, *One-Dimensional Man* (Boston: Beacon Press, 1964).

86. For a discussion of how consumer goods are used as carriers for meanings, especially to signal status and well-being, see Bill Leiss, Steve Kline, and Sut Jhally, *Social Communication in Advertising: Persons, Products, and Images of Well-Being* (New York: Routledge, 1990), especially chapter 11; and Stuart Ewen, *All Consuming Images* (New York: Basic Books, 1988), especially chapter 5. For a classic treatment of the origins and meanings of "conspicious consumption" in American society, see Thorstein Veblen, *The Theory of the Leisure Class* (New York: New American Library, [1899] 1953).

87. Mair, 358.

88. Jennifer Wolch, "Inside/Outside: The Dialectics of Homelessness," in *Populations at Risk,* ed. G. Demko and M. Jackson (Boulder, CO: Westview Press, 1995), 81.

89. Mair, 360.

90. Mair, 361.

91. Marcuse, 87-88.

92. Quoted in Marcuse, 84.

93. Personal interview, Seattle Property Manager, 13 November 1998.

94. Mitchell, 118.

95. Mitchell, 118.

96. Quoted in Mike Davis, *City of Quartz,* 231.

97. Anatasia Loukaitou-Sideris and Tridib Banerjee, *Urban Design Downtown: Poetics and Politics of Form* (Berkeley, CA: University of California Press, 1998). As the authors conclude, "it is clear that people do not come to these plazas for a sense of togetherness, commonality, or to mix with people from different social strata."

98. Susan Christopherson, "The Fortress City: Privatized Spaces, Consumer Citizenship," in *Post-Fordism: A Reader,* ed. A. Amin (Cambridge, UK: Blackwell, 1994), 420.

99. Sharon Zukin, *Landscapes of Power,* 222.

100. Zukin, *Landscapes,* 222.

101. Sharon Zukin, *Cultures of Cities,* 64-65.

102. Mair, 363.

103. Mitchell, 120.

104. Smith, *The New Urban Frontier,* 28.

105. Quoted in Marcuse, 70.

106. City of Seattle, *1999-2000 Consolidated Plan for Housing and Community Development* (Seattle, WA: Department of Housing and Human Services, 1999), 2-35.

107. Cushing Dolbeare, *Out of Reach: The Gap Between Housing Costs and the Income of Poor People in the United States* (Washington, DC: National Low-Income Housing Coalition, September 1999).

108. City of Seattle, *1999-2000 Consolidated Plan,* 3-16. To maintain consistency between city statistics and those complied by Dolbeare in his national survey, I have adjusted city statistics to reflect a two-bedroom fair-market rate of $710 per month,

versus the $795 figure used by the city. If I used the city statistics, the affordability picture for low-income families would seem even more grim.

109. Wolch and Dear, *Malign Neglect*, 34.

110. Jennifer Wolch, "Homeless in America: A Review of Recent Books," *Journal of Urban Affairs* 12, no. 4, 450.

111. Susan Ruddick, *Young and Homeless in Hollywood: Mapping Social Identities* (New York: Routledge, 1996), 37-38.

112. Personal interview, Seattle Department of Housing and Human Services, 9 February 1999. According to city officials, most of the losses in downtown low-income housing came from the construction of Interstate 5 through the heart of the International District, the expansion of the central business district (including especially the construction of the Convention Center and the redevelopment of the Pike Place Market), and the enforcement of strict fire codes, which shut down a number of residential hotels in Pioneer Square, Seattle's traditional skid row. Finally, the most recent source of loss stems from the rush to redevelop the Denny Regrade, just north of the retail core, into a trendy condo-heavy neighborhood for Seattle's "digerati," those new young urban professionals working for software companies in and around the city. As the city notes in its *1999-2000 Consolidated Plan*, "the most dramatic change in downtown residential units is the significant increase in middle-and upper-income housing," particularly in the Regrade, 3-56.

113. Personal interview, Seattle Displacement Coalition, 3 February 1999.

114. City of Seattle, *1999-2000 Consolidated Plan for Housing and Community Development* (Seattle, WA: Department of Housing and Human Services, 1999), 2-33.

115. Of those seeking services, city surveys revealed that 31 percent gave economic reasons for needing help, including a job loss, eviction from their apartments, or a recent flurry of medical bills. Close to 20 percent gave personal reasons, including mental illness or drug addiction, and the rest gave a variety of reasons, including running away from home, fleeing abusive spouses, or simply refused to answer the question at all. The city also found that 50 percent of those seeking homeless assistance were single men, but over one-fourth were families with children. Finally, a full 64 percent of the homeless surveyed were people of color, a disproportionately high figure when compared to the citywide number (almost 25 percent nonwhite). See the *1999-2000 Consolidated Plan* for details, 2-28 to 2-29.

116. Eighteen thousand people represents approximately 3 percent of Seattle's total population in 1998 (532,000 people). This statistic presumes that all homeless individuals counted are citizens of Seattle.

117. Personal interview, Seattle Displacement Coalition, 3 February 1999.

118. Jim Massey, "No Room for the Poor: Over Half of Homeless Turned Away from Shelter," *Real Change*, February 1996.

119. Jim Massey, "No Room for the Poor."

120. The city's commitment to redressing homelessness must be placed into context, however. In 1998, when the city spent $7.8 million on homeless services, it also spent over $40 million to help build the new downtown Symphony Hall (not to mention the $23 million subsidy given to Pine Street Development via the Parking Garage agreement).

121. John Carlson, "City Needs Homeless Laws That'll Send Them Packing," *Seattle Times*, 17 August 1993, 4(B).

122. Erik Lacitis, "Ground Zero: What Does Downtown Mean to You?" *Seattle Times*, 11 July 1993, 1(L).

123. Personal interview, Seattle City Council, 15 December 1998.

124. Don Williamson, "What Toll are We Willing to Pay to Walk the Street?" *Seattle Times*, 15 August 1993.

125. Polly Lane and Sylvia Nogaki, "Panhandlers Among Area's Problems," *Seattle Times*, 29 March 1993, 1(E).

126. John Hoffman, "Court Gestures," *Real Change*, November 1994.

127. Lane and Nogaki, "Panhandlers Among Area's Problems."

128. Polly Lane and Sylvia Nogaki, "Downtown Merchants Want Action on Parking, Crime," *Seattle Times*, 23 April 1993, 1(A).

129. Eric Lacitis, "Ground Zero."

130. Michael Poulson, "Rice Unveils Plan to Rev Up Downtown," *Seattle Post-Intelligencer*, 19 August 1993.

131. "Looking for Better Ways to Curb Unruly Street Life," *Seattle Times*, 26 July 1993, 4(B).

132. Alex Fryer, "Sidran: The City Attorney as Street Cleaner," *Puget Sound Business Journal*, 21 July 1995.

133. Fryer, "Sidran," 1.

134. Mark Sidran, "This is the Best of Times to Keep This City Livable," *Seattle Times*, 10 August 1993. This op-ed piece is a reprint of the speech Sidran gave to the Downtown Seattle Rotary Club on 3 August 1993.

135. Sidran, "This is the Best of Times."

136. Sidran, "This is the Best of Times."

137. Sidran, "This is the Best of Times."

138. Personal interview, Seattle City Attorney's Office, 9 February 1999.

139. Personal interview, Seattle City Attorney's Office, 9 February 1999.

140. Personal interview, Seattle City Attorney's Office, 9 February 1999.

141. Sidran, "This is the Best of Times."

142. Large, "Seattle's Brilliant Bulldog," *Seattle Times*, 18 August 1994, 1(A).

143. Sidran, "This is the Best of Times."

144. Dick Lilly, "Sidran Details Proposals to Control Street People," *Seattle Times*, 3 August 1993, 1(B).

145. Dick Lilly, "Sidran Details," 1(B).

146. Dick Lilly, "Sidran Details," 1(B).

147. Dick Lilly, "Keeping Downtown Alive," *Seattle Times*, 19 August 1993.

148. "Homeless Protest," *Seattle Times*, 21 July 1993 1(B).

149. John Fox and John Reese, "Rude Behavior: Seattle's Harrassment of Homeless Found Intolerable," *Real Change*, October 1994.

150. Judith Lonquist, "Disorder in the Streets: City Attorney's Proposals Fail to Address Human Suffering," *Seattle Times*, 3 October 1994, 7(B).

151. John Fox and John Reese, "Whose Seattle?" *Real Change*, October 1994

152. "S.I.D.R.A.N. Strikes Back," *Real Change*, October 1994.

153. John Reese and John Fox, "Whose Seattle?" *Real Change*, October 1994.

154. Reese and Fox, "Whose Seattle?"

155. John Hoffman, "Court Gestures," *Real Change*, November 1994.

156. John Fox and John Reese, "Rude Behavior," *Real Change*, October 1994.

157. Mark Sidran, "This is the Best of Times."

158. Mark Sidran, "This is the Best of Times."

159. Mark Sidran, "This is the Best of Times."

160. Mark Sidran, "This is the Best of Times."

161. Mark Sidran, "Establishing Standards of Civil Behavior," *Seattle Times*, 10 August 1994.

162. Personal interview, Seattle City Attorney's Office, 9 February 1999.

163. Personal interview, Seattle City Attorney's Office, 9 February 1999.

164. Personal interview, Seattle City Attorney's Office, 9 February 1999.

165. Jerry Large, "Seattle's Brilliant Bulldog."

166. Dick Lilly, "Sidran Details Proposals to Control Street People." See also, C. Angelos, "Sidran Plan Recommended to City Council," *Seattle Times*, 24 September 1993.

167. Personal interview, Seattle City Council, 15 December 1998.

168. For its part, the Downtown Seattle Association wanted to cement the notion that suburbanites and shoppers were growing increasingly fearful of coming downtown. As part of their continuing lobbying effort, the Downtown Seattle Association commissioned a survey of downtown users and found that, in addition to frustrations about traffic and parking, the top reasons King County residents gave for disliking downtown included "homeless people" and "threats to personal safety." Whether this survey had an immediate impact on council member's votes is impossible to say. Still, the comments about the need to "reassure" visitors about the safety of downtown suggest that such arguments at least had carried the day in council chambers. For details of the survey, see Downtown Seattle Association, *Survey of Downtown Users, January 1993* (Seattle, WA: Elway Research, 1993).

169. Some supporters of the coercive approach in fact argued that Sidran's laws did not go far enough. Claiming that Sidran's ordinances were mostly cosmetic, conservative columnist John Carlson wrote that "changing a few laws is a mild step in the right direction, but it won't be enough. We need a policy firmly focused on running healthy, employable bums outta town. If they're bounced out of enough places, they'll eventually get the message . . . They don't belong here. Hardly any of them are from here. It's time for them to leave." Quoted in John Carlson, "City Needs Homeless Laws," *Seattle Times*, 17 August 1993, 4(B).

170. "City of Broad Sidewalks [editorial]," *Seattle Times*, 21 May 1994, 9(A).

171. "City of Broad Sidewalks [editorial]."

172. John Fox and John Reese, "Whose Seattle?" *Real Change*, October 1994.

173. Judith Lonquist, "Disorder in the Streets," 4(B).

174. Judith Lonquist, "Disorder in the Streets," 4(B).

Chapter 7

The Urban Reststop vs. the World-Class City: Hygiene Wars on Third Avenue

When you look at the Glen Hotel at 1413 Third Avenue (midway between Union and Pike Streets) it hardly seems a likely candidate for a three-year-long, knock-down-drag-out political dispute over the future shape of downtown Seattle. In its past lives, the Glen has been everything from a rooming hotel for itinerant sailors, a bar and grill beloved by downtown pensioners, and a squalid, roach-infested SRO. But in its latest incarnation, after a substantial renovation in 1994, it is an attractive but unremarkable tan building with green and terracotta trim, two upper floors of efficiency apartments, a ground level of retail space (home to Bruno's, a small "Italian-Mexican" eatery), and a large basement. Four small flower boxes adorn the windows here and there, evidence of the pride the tenants share in their newly renovated home. But the current air of calm and serenity around the Glen Hotel belies the intensity of feeling focused on this small building during the 1990s, as Seattle's business community and homeless advocates, fresh from their battles over City Attorney Mark Sidran's antivagrancy laws, collided once again over the social boundaries between homelessness and gentrification in the newly revitalized, world-class downtown Seattle. This time, however, the struggle would be waged over the basement of the Glen Hotel.

You could say it was all Mark Sidran's fault. When the city council passed his "incivility" ordinances in the fall of 1993, Seattle officially toughened penalties on public urination. Immediately, a few councilmembers and a number of homeless advocates cried foul. How could Seattle, which has virtually no public restrooms downtown, criminalize public urination? What were homeless people supposed to do? Where were they supposed to "go"? As councilmember Jane Noland argued during the final vote on Sidran's package, it is inherently unfair to punish people for a human necessity without providing access to public facilities. In the end, Noland and two other councilmembers voted against the public urination provisions of Sidran's antivagrancy laws and joined the advocates' call for more public bathrooms downtown.[1]

This put the mayor's office in an awkward position. The contradiction of criminalizing public urination in a city with virtually no public restrooms was hard to ignore. Also, there were compelling political reasons for supporting the installation of more public bathrooms downtown. By throwing his weight behind Sidran's incivility statutes, Mayor Rice had alienated many in Seattle's large advocacy and activist community, a key component of his winning coalition in the 1990 mayoral election. Facing reelection in 1994, it was time for the mayor to mend political fences. So in late 1993, the mayor's office announced that the city would not only support the advocate's demands for public toilets downtown, but would do them one better. Arguing that the downtown homeless community needed more than toilets to help them get off the streets, the mayor's office proposed a more ambitious plan. Instead of merely providing toilets, the city would build a first-of-its-kind "hygiene center" for the Seattle homeless in the heart of downtown.[2]

In the city's plan, a hygiene center would offer a full range of services for homeless men and women, including rows of hot showers, free laundry facilities, storage lockers for towels, soap, and clothes, and, of course, enough toilets to comfortably serve the clientele's most basic needs. As proponents in the city's housing and human services office argued, the mayor would, in effect, kill two birds with one stone. The toilets would address the ongoing problem of public urination, (a public health problem and a constant source of irritation for downtown businesses), and the showers and laundry facilities would provide downtown's homeless community with a way to clean the grit of the streets off their bodies and clothes. As Richard Colwell, an advocate who was once homeless himself, argued, a warm shower and clean clothes can go a long way toward helping the homeless find their way off the streets. "Fifty percent of the effort you need to get back on your feet has to do with hygiene," he told the *Times*. "If you apply for jobs wearing the same clothes you've been wearing for days and with body odor, it's hard to move up or even get started."[3]

In the view of proponents, the need for the hygiene center "speaks for itself."[4] The question facing the mayor's office at this point, however, was *where*? Where would the city place its first publicly funded, stand-alone (i.e., not connected to a shelter or soup kitchen) homeless hygiene center? From the beginning, according to homeless advocates, city officials wanted to site the hygiene center downtown, near the heart of the city.[5] A central location made the most sense, they argued. First, many of the city's homeless services have historically located near the downtown core, particularly in working-class districts like Pioneer Square, so situating the hygiene center well outside the central core—in a far-flung residential area, perhaps—would place it beyond the reach of most of Seattle's homeless community. Moreover, Metro, the region's public transit service, operated a "free ride zone" in downtown Seattle, so locating the hygiene center downtown would allow clients to travel back and forth from food banks to shelters to the hygiene center without paying bus fare. Finally, a downtown location would place the hygiene center within walking distance of much of the city's low-income housing, traditionally located in or near the central core.[6] This opened up the possibility that the hygiene center could be used by a wider swath of the Seattle community than just the city's most desperately poor. Perhaps, thought proponents, the hygiene center could serve downtown residents whose apartments lacked showers, and even bicycle commuters, tourists, and shoppers—in short, anyone stuck downtown in need of a bathroom or a warm shower.

This preference for a downtown location, was, of course, not universally shared among Seattle's political and business class. And, in fact, when city planners settled upon the basement of the quiet and nondescript Glen Hotel—located on Third Avenue near the heart of the city's tourist and retail core—as their preferred site for the city's hygiene center, all hell broke loose in City Hall.

Situating Hygiene Downtown

In the larger picture, it took a number of small miracles for the Glen Hotel to even be considered as the location for the city's first-of-a-kind hygiene center. Situated strategically between the financial district to the south, the redeveloping retail core to the north, and Pike Place Market, Washington's most popular tourist destination, to the west, this little block of Third Avenue is surrounded by some of the most expensive real estate in the Pacific Northwest. Under normal circumstances, such a location would be priced way beyond the reach of any cash-strapped low-income housing or homeless service organization. But, in the Glen Hotel's case, a series of unusual developments plopped the Hotel squarely in the lap of one of the city's best-financed and best-connected human service organizations, the Low Income Housing Institute of Seattle.

Built in the 1900s as a hotel for sailors stuck in Seattle on shore leave, the Glen Hotel had, by the mid-1980s, fallen on hard times and seemed destined for demolition. Owned during the 1970s and early 1980s by a series of absentee landlords, the Glen was, by all accounts, a dump. "It was sort of the poster child of the Tenant's Union," recalled one housing activist. "It was the building that the tenants union would take . . . city council members and the mayor's office on [a] tour and take all the reporters, saying, 'this is the type of housing landlords are getting away with. The tenants are paying rent and it's a firetrap and a health hazard.'"[7] By the mid-1980s, then, it seemed certain that the squalid Glen would be demolished and redeveloped into new office and retail space. In fact, in 1985, two of Seattle's most celebrated developers, Dick Clotfelter and Gary Carpenter, bought the Glen Hotel along with the rest of the block between Union and Pike in order to fulfill their dream of building a new home for Seattle's A Contemporary Theater (ACT) within a new sparkling thirty-four story office tower.[8] By 1987, Clotfelter and Carpenter had all of their financing settled and were about to swing the wrecking ball around Third and Pike when, as one developer put it, Seattle's office market "went all to hell."[9] By 1990, as we discussed in Chapter 3, Seattle's office bust was in full swing, and Clotfelter and Carpenter were forced to file for bankruptcy. As a result, the once-promising ACT block, as this little stretch of Third Avenue was called, fell into the hands of the U.S. bankruptcy court, destined to be sold off at bargain-basement prices.[10]

Thus, the Glen Hotel spent the early part of the 1990s mired in bankruptcy court, as Robert Steinberg, the court-appointed trustee, struggled to sell off the ACT block bit by bit, with the proceeds going to pay off Clotfelter and Carpenter's many creditors.[11] For years, the Glen found few takers, but in 1993, a series of events convinced Steinberg to kick-start his search for a new owner of the Glen Hotel. First, the Glen's tenants, tired of waiting for such bankruptcy issues to be resolved, began withholding their rent payments to protest the living conditions inside the Glen, a move that attracted the attention of both the *Times* and the *Post-Intelligencer*. The tenants' rent strike quickly forced Steinberg into negotiations over the future of the little hotel,[12] and, in the course of these negotiations, Steinberg promised both the tenants and the city's housing authority that he would try to sell the Glen to a nonprofit agency willing to take over the hotel and to make the needed repairs.[13] But easier said than done. The Glen at that time was valued at just over $1 million, a steep price for most nonprofit housing and homeless agencies in town. More realistically, the city thought that it might be able to find a nonprofit willing to lease the Glen for five years—long enough to do the needed repairs to bring the tenants' apartments up to code.[14]

So in 1993, the city sent the word out that it was looking for a housing agency willing to take on the Glen for a short-term contract and to make the necessary repairs to bring the squalid structure up to code. However, it turned out that the city had underestimated Seattle's advocacy community. One of the nonprofit groups the mayor's office called was the Low Income Housing Institute (LIHI), directed by Sharon Lee, a longtime Seattle-based antipoverty activist and wife of one of the most powerful progressive lobbyists in Washington State. According to one LIHI staffer, Lee told the mayor's office (to their delight) that LIHI was not interested in merely *leasing* the Glen. "We don't want to just do something that will help the tenants short term and then the building goes back to the . . . developer, and the project gets redeveloped," she said. "We would only be interested if we could buy it outright."[15] It seemed that the city had found its nonprofit owner for the Glen.

In late 1993, then, LIHI made the short trip uptown in late 1993 to the U.S. bankruptcy court for a hearing with Steinberg (the ACT block's court-appointed trustee) regarding their application to buy the Glen. By this time, however, other parties, including the Weiss Company, owners of the Joseph Vance Building across the street, had forwarded their own bids to Steinberg—bids that were in some cases higher than LIHI's. But, as one frustrated would-be owner of the Glen put it, Steinberg "was bound and determined that it was going to go to a nonprofit" so that he could keep his promise to the Glen's tenants.[16] In the end, Steinberg and LIHI settled on a price—just under $630,000 according to county records[17]—and forwarded their agreement to the bankruptcy judge. At this final hearing, the Weiss Company showed up to object to the sale, arguing that their offer was actually higher and that they could fix up the building for the tenants while still making a profit. The judge, however, brushed aside these objections and approved the sale of the Glen Hotel to Sharon Lee and the Low Income Housing Institute in November of 1993.[18]

As it turned out, it was exactly at this time that the mayor's office was also looking around for a nonprofit organization to build and operate the city's new centrally located hygiene center. As one LIHI staffer put it, once they had bought the Glen, it dawned on them that the hotel would be an ideal site for the city's hygiene center. "It was right in the heart of downtown," she explained. "There were no acquisition costs, because [the Glen] was already owned by a nonprofit. There would only be renovation costs." Furthermore, the Glen was "in a location that would be very hard to locate anything in because of the high cost of land and the buildings."[19] LIHI then took their proposal to the city. We have this basement that is currently not being used, they told city officials. "We could help solve the problem" of where to locate the city's first stand-alone hygiene center.[20]

According to LIHI's staff, Mayor Rice immediately expressed enthusiasm for the proposal and asked LIHI to apply for city and federal funds to construct and operate a hygiene center in the basement of the Glen Hotel.[21] By January of 1994, all the pieces were in place. Earlier that month, LIHI had received preliminary commitments from the city for over $190,000 in capital funds to build the hygiene center, and LIHI had sent off an application to the federal department of Housing and Urban Development for close to a million in operating funds over three years—an application that would eventually be approved by the HUD central office.[22] In a press conference held in the foyer of the Glen Hotel on 20 January 1994, Mayor Rice proudly announced the city's partnership with LIHI. Not only would the city help the nonprofit renovate the thirty-eight single-room apartments in the top two floors, securing them for future generations of low-income tenants, but LIHI and the city would work together to build Seattle's first-of-its-kind homeless "hygiene center" in the hotel's basement, complete with clean toilets, hot showers, and free washer/dryers.[23] This historic partnership at the Glen Hotel, the mayor told the assembled press, "demonstrates our ongoing commitment to preserve our low-income housing base" and to provide needed services to the city's homeless.[24]

Armed with capital funds from the city and with the promise of operating funds from HUD, LIHI began the long process of designing the Glen Hotel hygiene center, gaining the appropriate permits from city authorities, and notifying the immediate neighbors of their plans for the Hotel's basement—a process which would take the remainder of 1994 to complete.[25] However, while LIHI's staff busied themselves with the mundane details of planning and design, a series of events centered just one block south on Third Avenue (between Union and University) would soon throw the future of the Glen hygiene center into

serious doubt. For years, this block—just across the street from the Glen Hotel—had been home to a small office building and a large empty grassy lot. But,
during the summer of 1994, this "Marathon Block" (as it was dubbed by city
officials) suddenly became the city's preferred site for a brand new, $118 mil-
lion concert hall for the Seattle Symphony (see Figure 7.1).

As the *Times* reports, the Seattle Symphony had been looking for a new
home for nearly twenty years. Since the World's Fair of 1962, they had shared
their former home, the Opera House at Seattle Center, with both the Seattle
Opera and the Pacific Northwest Ballet. Exhausted by the fierce competition
with the Opera and Ballet for the theater's most lucrative performance times,
the Symphony began to look desperately for its own concert hall. And for years,
it seemed that the Symphony would relocate to a site just across the street from

Figure 7.1
Third Avenue in Downtown Seattle

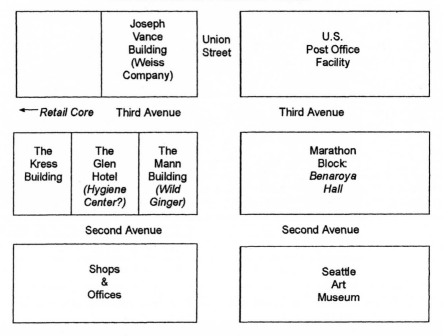

the Opera House. This site—essentially at the edge of Queen Anne, one of Seattle's most affluent residential districts—had been donated to the city in 1986 by
the Kreielsheimer Foundation to site a "major arts, cultural, or educational facility," and when the Seattle Art Museum decided to locate downtown in 1991,
it seemed certain that the Kreielsheimer property would go to the Symphony.
However, financial troubles in the Symphony's administration prevented the
orchestra from taking advantage of this gift for seven long years. Finally, in

May of 1993, Jack Benaroya, one of Seattle's most powerful property developers and a noted philanthropist, revived the Symphony's relocation dreams by giving the Symphony an unprecedented gift of $15 million to be used toward the construction of a new concert hall located at the Kreielsheimer site.[26]

With Benaroya's gift in hand, it seemed the push for a new Symphony Hall near Seattle Center was on the fast track. But not everyone was happy with the Kreielsheimer site. The Downtown Seattle Association, for one, was always on the lookout for anything that could lift downtown land values and began in the summer of 1993 to push hard for a *downtown* location for the new concert hall. "What about the Marathon Block?" outgoing DSA chair Gene Brandzel reportedly asked the Symphony's relocation committee. This block is right next to the new Seattle Art Museum, he argued, and it's located strategically close to the redeveloping retail core, Pike Place Market, and the Seattle Waterfront.[27] With the addition of a new Symphony Hall, this part of downtown could be the center of a new "cultural district" in the heart of the city, adding much-needed "oomph" (as the *Seattle Times* editorial board put it) to a downtown sorely lacking in after-hours amenities.[28]

By the summer of 1994, the *Seattle Times* editors were squarely behind a downtown location, arguing that locating the Symphony on Third Avenue would "be a huge plus for the core of the city at a critical time—just as it is making a tentative emergence from several years of stagnation and decline."[29] These arguments also found a ready convert in Mayor Norm Rice who, as we have discovered, had placed downtown revitalization at the very center of his mayoral agenda. Unhappy with the momentum toward the Kreielsheimer site, Mayor Rice intervened and opened up the site selection process in June of 1994, charging a citizen's advisory committee to reinvestigate the Kreielsheimer site and to put the Marathon Block back on the table.[30] Not surprisingly, by mid-July this advisory committee unanimously recommended that the Symphony locate downtown, a recommendation made all the more plausible by the city council's purchase of the Marathon Block earlier that month.[31] On July 15, the three prime movers behind the Symphony Hall project—Mayor Norm Rice, Jack Benaroya, and Symphony music director Gerard Schwarz—came to a meeting of minds: the Seattle Symphony would relocate to Third Avenue in the heart of downtown and build "Benaroya Hall," a $118 million concert hall named after the Symphony's most generous benefactor.[32]

As city officials would later admit, the relocation of the Seattle Symphony to the Marathon Block irrevocably changed the city's thinking about that part of Third Avenue.[33] With the arrival of the Symphony, what had been viewed as a largely abandoned and vaguely seedy stretch of downtown now began to be viewed as an "emerging cultural district," home to the Art Museum, Benaroya Hall, and, potentially, a cluster of smaller galleries and performance spaces.[34] The prospect of this "emerging cultural district" on Third Avenue, located strategically near the Pike Place Market, the Waterfront, and the redeveloping retail core had city boosters and officials waxing enthusiastic to the media.[35] As Peter Donnelly, president of the Corporate Council for the Arts in Seattle, told the *Puget Sound Business Journal*, when Benaroya Hall opens, "go downtown on any night when there's a performance going on. The streets [will be] just buzzing and people [will] feel perfectly safe walking around."[36] As Norm Rice told the *Times*, "siting the new concert hall at the Marathon block will provide a major infusion of life and energy into our downtown."[37]

For its part, the downtown business community, which had lobbied aggressively to bring the Symphony downtown, now looked to cash in on all their hard work. The property owners located on Third Avenue were particularly excited about their good luck in landing the Symphony as a neighbor. As one nearby property owner recalled, the years prior to the Symphony's announcement were tough, and during the office bust of the early 1990s he had to spend a lot of his time calming down panicky investors in his midsize high-rise. "But to have the Symphony Hall happen!" he exclaimed. "You couldn't have bribed or bought or whatever to have . . . that as a neighbor. . . . It's certainly enhanced the value of the land. It didn't decrease the value of the land." [38] In addition, smaller retailers and restaurateurs were also looking to tap into spin-off effects of the new Symphony Hall. As the *Puget Sound Business Journal* noted at the time, restaurants, pubs, and upscale boutiques were particularly well-positioned to benefit from the hordes of symphony patrons about to descend upon downtown. As a result, a number of entrepreneurs began to move into the surrounding area, opening up luxury retail stores and gourmet restaurants, including two new cafes founded by celebrity-chef Wolfgang Puck.[39]

Lost for the moment in all this celebration on Third Avenue was the Glen Hotel and LIHI's planned homeless hygiene center. All during 1994, while the mayor and the DSA worked to move the Symphony downtown, LIHI doggedly pursued their plan to build the Glen hygiene center. They hired a construction firm to renovate the SRO apartments in the upper floors.[40] They hired an architect to layout the plans for the hygiene center in the basement. They pursued additional funding from HUD and from the city to build and operate the hygiene facilities.[41] They held a number of meetings with the Downtown Seattle Association and with some of their neighbors in the immediate area regarding their plans for the hygiene center, and, by all accounts, they met with little resistance.[42] In short, at first it seemed that the Symphony's arrival would have little impact on LIHI's plans. The Glen Hotel hygiene center appeared to be right on schedule for a grand opening celebration in late 1995.

But, in hindsight, it is clear that the relocation of the Symphony to Third Avenue fundamentally changed the social and political environment around the Glen Hotel. As one city official remarked, "the whole dynamic of the block changed" after the Symphony's announcement.[43] For one, local property owners who had been indifferent to the prospect of a hygiene center in the basement before the Symphony's arrival now began to dream of owning property in the midst of an "emerging cultural district" and began to chafe openly at the idea of homeless services just down the block. As one nearby property owner recalled, the turn from indifference to active opposition occurred almost overnight:

> Well, we had heard something about [the hygiene center] early on, but it was very, it was very sketchy. . . . It was stuff you might just say, "oh, okay . . . they're doing something over there, I hope it isn't bad." But then, all of a sudden, at some point—I don't remember exactly when it was—it became like "well, wait a second . . . they're going to put this industrial-strength hygiene center there!"[44]

Newcomers to the neighborhood, especially those who wanted to buy property or start new businesses in the glow of the planned Symphony Hall, reacted in similar fashion when appraised of LIHI's plans for the Glen's basement. As it turned out, it was the arrival of one such entrepreneur to Third Avenue—an entrepreneur with grand plans to renovate the Glen Hotel's immediate neighbor, the Mann Building, into an elaborate dinner/music theater across the street from Benaroya Hall—that would thrust the Glen Hotel's basement squarely into the political spotlight.

Like most of Seattle's historic structures, the Mann Building, located just to the south of the Glen Hotel on Third Avenue and right across Union Street from Benaroya Hall, has been reinvented many times throughout its seventy-year life. Built in 1928, the Mann got its start as one of downtown's most attractive vaudeville theaters, but in more recent years tenants have used the Mann as an adult movie house, a drugstore, and a blue-collar bar.[45] Like the Glen Hotel, the Mann Building was slated for demolition in the late 1980s, as part of the ill-fated ACT block development envisioned by Dick Clotfelter and Gary Carpenter. But when the office bust swallowed up this ambitious project, the Mann reverted back to its longtime owner, David Gellatly, a small businessman and real estate entrepreneur from Wenatchee, Washington.[46]

At that time in the early 1990s, Gellatly began to play around with ideas on how to redevelop the Mann Building into a mixed-use, retail, office, and restaurant complex. For the first few years, however, he found few tenants willing to take on the expensive rehab costs associated with leasing the historic structure. In the meantime, Gellatly decided to wait out the stagnant market in Seattle and focused his attention on his Wenatchee holdings, refusing to invest in the Mann's upkeep and attracting the ire of city officials unhappy with the building's decaying and graffiti-scarred facade.[47] Finally, in 1994 when the Symphony announced that it would relocate to the Marathon Block just across Union Street from the Mann Building, Gellatly's luck changed and the offers began to pour in. One particularly interesting offer came from Rick Yoder, a prominent figure in Seattle's restaurant scene and founder of Wild Ginger, one of Seattle's most popular nightspots. According to the *P-I*, Yoder had been eyeing the Mann Building for years as the ideal spot for a new, expanded version of Wild Ginger, and the impending arrival of the Symphony across the street merely clinched it for the forty-something restaurateur.[48] In the new, post-Symphony era, the Mann seemed to be the perfect place for his longtime dream: a music/dinner theater offering gourmet meals and first-class jazz to the 3,000 symphony patrons expected to descend on downtown for every performance.[49]

So it was in late 1994 and early 1995 that Yoder and Gellatly entered into serious negotiations over the terms of Yoder's lease of the Mann Building. During this time, however, Gellatly began to have doubts about his ability to redevelop the Mann on his own—even with Yoder as his major (and high-profile) tenant. Not only would the project require him to live in Seattle for a year to oversee the development, but the rehab costs alone were estimated to reach $7 to $10 million—numbers which made Gellatly and his small company noticeably edgy.[50] Therefore, a few months into the negotiations with Yoder, Gellatly privately decided that he would abandon his plan to lease the Mann to Yoder. Instead, he would just sell the decaying structure outright to the highest bidder. Reluctantly, then, in early 1995, he called up one of Seattle's most prominent real estate firms and asked them to put the Mann on the market once and for all.[51]

But how could he tell Yoder, who had invested a lot of sweat and energy into the Mann project, that he was selling the building? As he fretted for nearly a week over how to break the news to Yoder, Cerissa Merrit of Martin Smith Real Estate called him in Wenatchee. How would he feel about selling the Mann Building to an investment team that included, among other Seattle real estate heavyweights, none other than Rick Yoder himself?[52] Instead of merely leasing the building, Yoder would become a part *owner* of the Mann, and would be free to fulfill his dream of building an expanded Wild Ginger dinner theater across the street from the new Symphony Hall. Gellatly was thrilled. Not only would he be selling the building at an opportune time—just as the Symphony announced their impending move to Third Avenue—but the Mann, which had been in his family for decades, would be sold to an owner who would lovingly restore the building to its original splendor.[53] And for downtown boosters, the prospect of a perennial eyesore in the heart of downtown being redeveloped into an upscale dinner theater proved the wisdom of moving the Symphony to Third Avenue. With the addition of Yoder's new upscale night spot, a vibrant and lively "cultural district" centered around Third and Union and anchored by the new Symphony Hall and the Seattle Art Museum, certainly seemed in the offing.[54]

But then, in the summer of 1995, Rick Yoder and his investors found out about LIHI's proposed hygiene center. Upon hearing the news, Yoder and his group were horrified. The Glen Hotel was right next door to the Mann, and here was a plan to put showers, toilets, and laundry for the city's homeless right in the basement. What if there are crowds of homeless people milling on the streets outside the Glen Hotel? Will potential dinner theater customers be willing to wade through this crowd to get to the Symphony? What about the potential for crime and drugs?[55] According to the *Times*, Yoder had heard about a recent drug bust in the shower stalls of the Compass Center, a homeless shelter just a few blocks south in Pioneer Square. Would the Glen Hotel become a nexus of the drug trade? Would violence spiral out of control in the block?[56] Questions like these, and the images of street deviance and urban decay they evoked, stopped Yoder and his investors cold. In July of 1995, they hastily called Gellatly and made their position crystal-clear: *we will not buy the Mann Building if LIHI is allowed to build their hygiene center in the Glen Hotel's basement.*[57]

Opening Salvo: The Lawsuit

According to consultants close to the negotiations, Yoder's ultimatum threw Gellatly's plans into turmoil. Not only did it look like Yoder and his investor were about to walk away, but with this new hygiene center proposed for the Glen, finding future buyers for the Mann now seemed to be an iffy proposition. With the sale to Yoder and company suddenly in jeopardy, Gellatly reviewed his options. He could hang onto the Mann and redevelop it himself, but as one consultant noted, the empty building was costing Gellatly's small firm a lot of money just in taxes and intermittent graffiti removal.[58] He could try to sell it to someone else, but Yoder was by no means the only potential buyer leery of starting a business next to a homeless hygiene center. As one source in Gellatly's company put it, "I mean, we were talking to some tenants that, you know, there isn't a chance in hell that they were going to spend good money to lease a storefront with . . . the possibility . . . that there was going to be homeless folks and what have you hanging out on the sidewalk in front."[59] The best option, it seemed, would be to salvage the deal with Yoder. This meant he had to find some way, any way, to stop LIHI from building its hygiene center in the Glen Hotel's basement.

Gellatly had to move quickly. While he was reviewing his options, LIHI applied for and received a building permit for the hygiene center, and Gellatly had been informed that they were ready to start construction immediately.[60] In August of 1995, then, Gellatly began his sustained assault on the Glen Hotel hygiene center. Along with other local property owners who opposed LIHI's plan—especially Paul and Tom Etsekson, owners of the Kress Building on the other side of the Glen—Gellatly went public for the first time with his objections in a front-page article published in the *Puget Sound Business Journal*. In this article, Gellatly and Paul Etsekson argued that, beyond killing Yoder's planned redevelopment of the Mann Building, the hygiene center would also undermine the long-awaited revitalization of Third Avenue, sparked by the impending arrival of the Symphony. "We are spending, what, $500 million to revitalize our retail core?" asked Etsekson. "I don't care how much you spend if you can't offer safety."[61] Gellatly agreed, arguing that although he understood the need for such services, placing the hygiene center in the retail core, next to the new Symphony Hall no less, simply made no sense. "We're not raising a stink about the hygiene center," he told the *Journal*, "just its location."[62]

Media coverage is nice, but to drive such objections home to city hall Gellatly needed more than one front-page story in the local business weekly. Just two weeks after going public with his opposition, then, Gellatly decided to stop LIHI's hygiene center the all-American way. He sued. Naming LIHI and the city government as co-defendants, Gellatly's suit challenged the legality of the Glen Hotel hygiene center on several procedural grounds.[63] First, Gellatly alleged that LIHI failed to comply with the city's "good neighbor" guidelines that compel human service providers to reach out to the surrounding community and inform them of any plans for expansion or for new facilities. According to Gellatly and Paul Etsekson, a co-owner of the building on the other side of the Glen, LIHI's only major effort at public outreach was to distribute a leaflet describing the hygiene center in October 1994, on the Columbus Day holiday.[64] To be sure, this is a claim vigorously denied by LIHI staffers, who note that LIHI held meetings about the hygiene center with neighbors in February 1994 and then again in the spring of 1995. During this time, LIHI also held a number of meetings with the Downtown Seattle Association concerning their plans for the Glen's basement.[65]

But perhaps the most serious allegation in Gellatly's suit was that LIHI deliberately misrepresented the size and scope of the hygiene center in their discussions with neighboring businesses and the Downtown Seattle Association. According to Gellatly's lawyer, in LIHI's initial grant application to the federal Department of Housing and Urban Development (HUD), they described a 5,000-square-foot hygiene center with showers, lockers, laundry, and toilets that would be open around the clock and would serve nearly 800 clients daily. Yet, as Gellatly's lawyer claims, LIHI's executive director Sharon Lee *later* told neighboring merchants and property owners that the hygiene center would be a small-scale, 2,000-square-foot, "limited-hours facility."[66] Why the change in size and scope? Did LIHI *truly* scale back the center? Or were they misrepresenting the size and scope in meetings with business leaders to avoid neighborhood opposition? In Gellatly's view, LIHI was simply playing a shell game— *overtly* selling neighbors on a "limited hours," "small-scale" hygiene center while *covertly* planning to build an "industrial strength," 24-hour-a-day facility.[67]

This is a claim heatedly disputed by LIHI staffers, who argued that at no point did the Institute intentionally misrepresent either the size or the scope of the facility. First of all, as LIHI's Dan Landes explained to the *Puget Sound Business Journal*, the 5,000-square-foot figure in the initial HUD application was a simple mistake, and the architectural drawings included in the same application bear this out—showing a basement with a total closer to 4,000 square feet.[68] Furthermore, LIHI staffers argued that the locker space had *always* been intended for residents only, so to include them in the figure for the hygiene center would be unfair.[69] As for the scope of the services described in the HUD application, including the "800 clients daily" and "24 hours a day" figures that so agitated nearby businesses, LIHI quickly realized that they had neither the staff nor the funding to handle that many patrons, so in the weeks following their submission to HUD, they began to scale back the hours of operation and the number of clients to be served. By the time they met with neighbors in February 1994, LIHI staffers claimed, the new "limited hours" plans accurately reflected their intentions for the Glen's basement.[70]

With a hearing scheduled for October of 1995, Gellatly, LIHI, and the city attorney's office (representing the City of Seattle, also named as a defendant in the suit) entered into a series of heated settlement negotiations. Gellatly's goal was clear. He wanted to kill the Glen hygiene center so he could sell the Mann Building to Rick Yoder. If he couldn't kill the hygiene center, maybe he could at least slow it down and sell the building before LIHI started construction.[71] LIHI's position in these negotiations, however, was more complex. As a consultant close to the negotiations explained, it was clear to LIHI from the outset that Gellatly's lawsuit had little merit and would be unceremoniously tossed out of court. "We felt our litigation position was strong," he said. "We were certain to win."[72] At the same time, however, it was equally clear that the mayor's office wanted to compromise with Gellatly and the agitated neighbors on Third Avenue. Almost Clintonesque in his aversion to conflict, Mayor Norm Rice—or "Mayor Nice" as he was (sometimes derisively) known—was a notorious conciliator, always preferring consensus to conflict, compromise to debate. In short, when it came to Gellatly's lawsuit, "Mayor Nice" wanted a deal, and, as a result, LIHI was willing to entertain a compromise, if only to preserve their relationship with the hand that feeds. As one consultant said, "we wanted the city to feel that we were on their side, and if the city wants this [compromise] bad enough, then it's worth doing the deal."[73]

From the outset, then, LIHI's position was that "we were always willing to make any kind of deal" with the Glen's opponents and the city that would still provide hygiene services for the downtown homeless community.[74] There was even the possibility that, as one LIHI supporter mused, "maybe we can end up with a better arrangement" than the proposed Glen Hotel project—a compromise, perhaps, that might yield multiple "hygiene centers" or that might extract more funding for services from public and private sources.[75] In their negotiations with Gellatly's attorney, LIHI pressed for the best deal possible. Accordingly, their first proposal to settle the dispute was, in a word, blunt. If you and the rest of the opponents give us enough money, LIHI reportedly told Gellatly, we will kill the Glen Hotel project cold. As one consultant recalled, LIHI quietly forwarded this proposal during a break in the first settlement meeting:

> We were all kind of going out and going to the bathroom and refilling coffee cups and this and that, and she [LIHI's Sharon Lee], you know, as much as said . . . well . . . she didn't say it in these exact words, but effectively said, "you know, for a million bucks, we'll go away. We'll take this thing and head down the road."[76]

When Gellatly flatly refused to pay the million dollars, LIHI switched to a second, more modest proposal. If the city government and LIHI's opponents in the business community could find an alternative site that seemed promising, then LIHI would agree to kill the Glen Hotel hygiene center. But although they *were* willing to entertain the notion of a new site for the hygiene center, LIHI insisted that any alternative would have to meet some fairly strict criteria. First, LIHI argued that an acceptable alternative must be located downtown, preferably in Metro's Free Ride Zone, so that homeless clients could easily travel to and from the facility.[77] Second, because families and children made up a growing segment of the homeless community, LIHI demanded that any alternative facility would, like the Glen, have to serve both men and women.[78] To do otherwise, they argued, would split up families and make it difficult for, say, a mother and her male children to gain easy access to hygiene services.[79] Finally, if alternative sites were indeed discovered, the city or some private party would have to cover the architectural and construction expenses already paid out by LIHI at the Glen site. A lot of time and money had already been poured into the Glen Hotel's basement. Should an alternative be discovered, they argued, it would only be fair for the city or the Downtown Seattle Association to compensate the Institute for resources already devoted to the Glen site. Still, if the city indeed found an alternative that met all of these conditions, then LIHI was willing to play nice and relocate the project.[80]

LIHI's proposal for this "search for alternatives" broke the deadlock in the negotiations, and by November of 1995, the parties had drafted the outlines of a settlement agreement. First, LIHI proposed that in order to find an alternative site, the stakeholders now embroiled in this hygiene war (including the Glen's neighbors, the Downtown Seattle Association, the city, and LIHI) should form a new "Hygiene Services Committee" (later dubbed the HSC). Once formed, this committee would scour the downtown Seattle "metro free ride zone" for any and all sites that might be suitable for a new homeless hygiene center. If the committee succeeded in finding a new site for the hygiene center—a location acceptable not only to LIHI but also to the Downtown Seattle Association and neighboring businesses and property owners—then the Glen Hotel site could be quashed once and for all.[81]

Internally, however, LIHI knew that getting all the parties to agree on a new site would be an almost Herculean task. Who is to say if any new site will be any less controversial than the Glen Hotel? What if the *new* site's neighbors rise up in protest? This new committee might get mired in negotiations for years, as members repeatedly proposed, debated, and then ultimately rejected each and every site, for one reason or another. Left to its own devices, LIHI staffers worried that such a committee might never find a consensus alternative, and the hygiene center might never get constructed.[82] Unwilling to let this happen, LIHI demanded that a strict deadline be put on the committee's search. If a suitable alternative—complete with a service provider and secured operating funds—could not be found by 30 September 1996, then LIHI would be free to move forward on the Glen Hotel site.[83]

In December of 1995, LIHI, the city, and Dave Gellatly all signed the settlement agreement. From the city's perspective, the negotiations could not have gone better. "Mayor Nice" had his compromise, and business leaders would now be working with service providers to find a consensus alternative to the Glen. For his part, Gellatly was also reportedly upbeat. As one consultant close to Gellatly noted, the owner of the Mann Building had succeeded in stopping the Glen Hotel hygiene center—at least for the immediate future. In all likelihood, Gellatly and his attorney thought, the new Hygiene Services Committee would find an alternative site, and the hygiene center would become someone else's problem. Best of all, he would be able to sell the Mann Building—if not to Wild Ginger's Rick Yoder then perhaps to someone else—and leave Seattle politics and real estate behind for good.[84]

On their end of the table, however, LIHI's mood was less festive. On the one hand, the settlement agreement meant that hygiene services would eventually be located somewhere in downtown Seattle after September of 1996—if not at some alternative site, then back at the Glen. If the new search committee indeed found a new downtown site, or even multiple sites, for hygiene services, then at least homeless families and individuals would have an accessible place to shower, shave, and wash their clothes. Finally, if the committee got bogged down and missed their September 1996 deadline, then LIHI now had an iron-clad guarantee that they could build their hygiene center in Glen Hotel's basement.[85] At the same time, there was some grumbling within LIHI. Although most of LIHI's staff agreed that it would be acceptable to find an alternative site—or perhaps even multiple sites—for the hygiene center, a vocal minority argued that "there's nothing wrong with the Glen" and that it was being "opposed for all the wrong reasons."[86] For these staffers, to search for an alternative to the Glen would mean giving in to an opposition that seemed "fueled by hysteria" and routinely expressed the "worst stereotypes about poor people."[87] Although sympathetic to this argument, Sharon Lee still wanted to give Norm Rice his compromise, so by January 1996, the search for an alternative to the Glen Hotel was off and running.

The Search for Alternatives

Sitting in their offices in Pioneer Square two years later, city staffers assigned to mediate the Hygiene Services Committee could be philosophical. The HSC was "doomed from the start," as one city official put it. For one, he said, "the process stunk."[88] The settlement agreement had placed what he considered to be ridiculous deadlines on the complex task of locating and securing an alternative site. For example, he noted that the HSC was given one short month to develop a list of viable alternatives. Such a timetable would be difficult under the best of circumstances, but this was a committee made up of bitterly divided combatants fresh from a rancorous legal dispute. "We're talking about a diametrically opposed group of people here," noted the city official, and predictably the first meeting of HSC degenerated into "yelling and screaming" as LIHI staff and the representatives of the Downtown Seattle Association (which had supported Gellatly's battle against the Glen Hotel) wrangled over how to proceed. Looking back, could the HSC have overcome such divisions and obstacles? "No chance in hell," concluded the official.[89]

Still, in early 1996, during the heady early days of the committee's mandate, the HSC eventually stopped quarreling and began to draw up a list of proposed alternative sites for homeless hygiene services. As one LIHI staffer remembers, city officials proposed nearly ten sites, and LIHI came up with "a list of between twenty and thirty sites" sprinkled all over downtown and into the inner-city neighborhoods immediately adjacent to central core. For their part, however, the Downtown Seattle Association offered six sites, and "all of them were outside the downtown core."[90] By the end of January, the HSC winnowed this list down to about twenty potential alternatives, approximately fourteen of which were concentrated in the Denny Regrade neighborhood just to the north of the retail district.

Predictably, the folks on the HSC from the Denny Regrade objected strenuously to this development. As one LIHI staffer remembers, when it became clear that most of the viable alternatives were all located north of downtown, "the Regrade folks got upset" because with the Noelle House (a homeless shelter) and the Millionair Club (which finds day jobs for homeless folks) already located in the neighborhood, "they thought they had really gotten their share."[91] So, when they got wind of the possibility that the new hygiene center might be headed north to the Regrade, "some of their big guns started showing up at the Hygiene Committee saying, 'uh, I think not!'"[92]

The objections of Denny Regrade residents forced another search for alternative sites, and by the middle of February, the committee had narrowed the list down to five finalists. LIHI immediately nixed one site, because it was located well outside the Metro Free Ride Zone. A second site fell off the table when its owner withdrew his property from consideration. This left three potential sites—all of which were located in, of all places, the Denny Regrade, cheek-by-jowl with a number of other human services already situated in the neighborhood.[93] The Denny Regrade representatives again rose in protest, and, by the end of May, it was abundantly clear that the Hygiene Services Committee was hopelessly stuck.[94]

In short, as site after site was proposed, debated, and rejected, it began to look like LIHI's initial suspicions would be realized. Perhaps no acceptable alternative would emerge from the Hygiene Services Committee after all. Slowly, haltingly, then, a plurality of the committee began to refocus their attention on the Glen Hotel.[95] Perhaps, as LIHI's staffers began to argue in later HSC meetings, a retooled Glen Hotel hygiene center, more limited in scope and built in combination with other hygiene facilities located elsewhere in the city, might indeed be consistent with the committee's goal of spreading the "burden" of hosting human services across the whole of downtown, rather than merely concentrating such services in areas like the Regrade or Pioneer Square.[96] Perhaps a revised Glen hygiene center could go forward after all.

In the meantime, just as the HSC began to refocus their attention on the Glen Hotel, next door at the Mann Building, David Gellatly and Rick Yoder were reaching an agreement of their own. After the settlement agreement put a temporary hold on the Glen Hotel hygiene center, Rick Yoder once again warmed up to the idea of buying the Mann and building his new Wild Ginger dinner theater across from the new Symphony Hall. In the first part of 1996, then, Yoder put some earnest money down on the Mann Building, and entered into a final series of negotiations with Gellatly over the asking price.[97] Still, Yoder reportedly had some lingering reservations about the Glen Hotel. After all, there were no guarantees that the HSC would find an alternative site by the September 30 deadline, in which case Yoder would be saddled with the hygiene center as an immediate and unwelcome neighbor.[98]

Chewing over this uncertainty, Yoder wrote a letter to Norm Rice to remind him of a promise the mayor had reportedly made during the settlement negotiations. Although they were eager to move Wild Ginger to the Mann Building, he wrote, "we cannot conceive of a successful Wild Ginger in that location with a hygiene center next door."[99] As a result, he concluded, "we are still counting on the assurances you have given both of us that the hygiene center would not be located in the Glen Hotel."[100] Then, in an apparent reference to the mayor's recent announcement that he would seek the Democratic nomination to be Washington State's next governor, Yoder requested an audience with the mayor to talk over the city's hygiene plans, offering an enticing political carrot in the process. "Norm," he wrote, "we would like a short meeting with you to discuss the above [plans for the Glen Hotel], hopefully arrive at a conclusion with your help, and to discuss how we can be of help to our favorite Governor."[101]

To be fair, there is no record of whether this meeting took place, and Norm Rice's campaign disclosure forms show no contributions from either Rick

Yoder or his main investor.[102] At the same time, this letter clearly shows that Yoder believed the mayor had promised him, point-blank, that a hygiene center would *never* be allowed at the Glen Hotel. With these assurances—and with a purchase agreement deadline rapidly approaching—Yoder finally decided to take the plunge in mid-April and bought the Mann for nearly $2 million.[103] Gellatly was thrilled. While sources within Gellatly's company were mystified as to why Yoder agreed to buy the Mann despite the still-unresolved status of the Glen hygiene center, they were not about to second-guess the sale. "I'm just glad to get rid of it," Gellatly told the *Post-Intelligencer*.[104] And for his part, Yoder focused his attention on renovating the decayed dinner theater, assured that the mayor's promise to nix the Glen site would be kept. "I think it's [the new Wild Ginger] going to be a real boon to the neighborhood," he predicted confidently.[105]

Less than a month later, however, a series of events in May 1996 would throw Yoder's plans for the Mann into utter confusion. By this time, as we have noted already, the HSC's "search for alternatives" to the Glen had ground to a creaking halt, raising concerns that the city might never find an alternative acceptable to all the competing interests.[106] Even worse, they feared that the city might simply shelve the whole notion of locating hygiene services downtown, concluding that offering showers and toilets to homeless people simply was not worth the political hassle.[107] While the settlement agreement required that the city release the Glen Hotel hygiene center's grant if an alternative site was not found by the end of September, there was really no guarantee the city would live up to their end of the bargain—especially if the mayor's office was facing intense pressure from the politically powerful downtown business community.[108] In LIHI's view, then, they could not simply wait for the September deadline and then rely on the city to "do the right thing." They would have to apply some political pressure of their own to make sure the city either funded the Glen Hotel site or found a viable downtown alternative as quickly as possible.[109]

But how could they pressure the city to come to a decision about finally choosing a site for a hygiene center? LIHI's only leverage at this point was their ownership of the Glen Hotel itself, and after a series of internal discussions in early May, LIHI hatched a strategy to force the city's hand.[110] What if we retool the Glen Hotel hygiene center to address some of the neighbors' concerns? What if we reduce the size a bit and cut down the number of hours and clients served? What if we declare that the search for alternatives is dead and announce that we are going forward with the Glen Hotel location? Such a declaration, LIHI reasoned, would "hold the city's feet to the fire."[111] The mayor's office would then either line up behind the retooled Glen—which, by most accounts, was really the best location for hygiene services anyway[112]—or they would accelerate their search for an alternative location. In either case, by announcing that they were starting construction on the Glen, LIHI would force the city to take hygiene services seriously and finally find a location acceptable to everyone.[113]

The Neighbors Fight Back

In May 1996, LIHI therefore began to prepare for the triumphant return of the Glen Hotel hygiene center. First, LIHI began to modify their earlier proposal in the hope that a new-and-improved design might diffuse some of their opponents' objections. They reduced the proposed hours of operation from "all day, every day," to a more manageable 5 a.m. to 9 p.m. schedule. This drop in operating hours reduced the expected number of clients from the 800 figure in the HUD application to an estimated 250 clients per day. In an effort to enhance security, they increased the number of staff in the facility from four to seven, an almost ridiculously large number by nonprofit standards.[114] LIHI also began to look closely at the interior design of the proposed hygiene facility, following the advice of police department experts and architects to improve the "sightlines" in the facility and to enhance the ability of staff to oversee its operation.[115] Taken together, LIHI felt these changes addressed both the security concerns of the neighbors and the emerging policy of "smaller, dispersed sites" established by the Hygiene Services Committee and embraced by city officials.[116]

Finally, as part of the hygiene center's makeover, LIHI also gave the Glen center a new name: *the Urban Reststop*.[117] In the view of LIHI's staff and supporters, this name change was more than cosmetic. Instead, it expressed their belief that the centrally located hygiene center should be more than simply a drab human service facility catering only to homeless people. Instead, LIHI felt that, by virtue of its presence in the heart of the retail core, the Glen could become an "Urban Reststop," a true public space open to anyone stuck downtown and in need of a place to use the bathroom, take a shower, or wash their clothes.[118] In this way, their new goal, as LIHI saw it, was to build a facility that "anyone would use," including "shoppers, tourists, cyclists, people who are homeless, our senior citizens, and families with young children."[119] Furthermore, by opening the facility to users from all walks of life, some LIHI staffers speculated that the Urban Reststop might even begin to break down some of the wider public's fear of the homeless. If all kinds of Seattleites used the facility, they argued, it may become a diverse mixing place, where people are exposed to class differences and learn to see a common, underlying humanity.[120] Finally, the name change had its political uses as well—a point not lost on one of LIHI's opponents, who noted that an "Urban Reststop just sounds better" to policy-makers than does a "homeless hygiene center."[121]

On May 29, then, LIHI unexpectedly called a public meeting downtown. At this meeting, which was attended in almost equal numbers by the Institute's supporters and by longtime foes of the Glen Hotel site, LIHI announced for the first time that, because the Hygiene Services Committee had failed to find an alternative site, they were going ahead with the Urban Reststop, a reworked hygiene center in the basement of the Glen Hotel.[122] As part of their plan to revive the Glen Hotel site, LIHI announced the formation of an advisory committee, which would be staffed by business leaders, advocates, and community members and charged with the task of formulating "operating conditions" for the proposed Urban Reststop. After inviting the assembled audience to join this advisory committee, LIHI passed around a sign-up sheet.[123]

The opponents of the Glen site, including longtime combatants like the DSA's Kate Joncas, Paul Etsekson, and Fred Weiss (owner of the Joseph Vance Building across the street from the Glen), were stunned and outraged. What happened to the court-mandated "search for alternatives"? As they would later argue in angry memos to city officials, there were still four months left until the settlement agreement's September 30 deadline. Why was the city allowing LIHI to abandon the Hygiene Services Committee and unilaterally declare the triumphant return of the Glen Hotel site?[124] By all accounts, LIHI's opponents were incensed, and according to the meeting minutes and firsthand accounts published in *Real Change*, they repeatedly shouted down Sharon Lee and LIHI staffers during their presentation.[125] As the meeting degenerated into an angry free-for-all, the Glen's opponents angrily stormed out.[126] Feeling betrayed by the city and furious at LIHI for cutting short the "search for alternatives," the opponents of the Glen began to organize and review their options.

For their part, however, the mayor's office seemed increasingly resigned to the Glen Hotel site. It was true, after all, that the HSC's "search for alternatives" had been a miserable failure, and the Glen site still had all its funding and planning in order.[127] Furthermore, LIHI's retooled Glen Hotel project seemed to respond to some of the concerns expressed by opponents during settlement negotiations. And while the Glen site still attracted a lot of opposition from the surrounding business community, LIHI's proposal to create an advisory committee looked like a promising step toward addressing community fears.[128] As a result, in a sternly worded letter to LIHI's Sharon Lee, Ven Knox of the city's Department of Housing and Human Services notified the Institute that the city was indeed willing to work toward the eventual opening of the Urban Reststop at the Glen Hotel. However, as a condition for city support, Knox demanded that LIHI include opponents and neighbors in their discussions about how to run and operate the Urban Reststop. Invite your neighbors and opponents to join your new advisory committee, as Knox advised LIHI's Sharon Lee, and make sure they have a hand in assuring that the Reststop will be a clean, safe, and well-run facility. If the city saw LIHI making a good faith effort to address the opponents' concerns, the mayor's office would release the Glen's funding.[129]

As it turned out, LIHI's neighbors were not exactly in a mood to compromise. After a brief period away from the debate, they returned to fight against the Glen Hotel hygiene center tooth and nail for the rest of the summer. One neighbor began to organize field trips down to city hall to lobby the mayor's office and the city council to withdraw their support from the Glen site. "There were lots of meetings," as one opponent recalled:

> I put together seven or eight of my tenants here, Bruno [of Bruno's Restaurant] from across the street, the Etseksons. I don't know, we'd have eight or ten people and went down one by one and each saw them [the city councilmembers]. And we just said, "you know, it's a great concern. It's just a mistake." I don't want to come across as an elitist . . . But, it's like putting a garbage dump next to the Highlands.[130]

Other opponents, including Paul Etsekson, supplemented this lobbying campaign by publishing a series of letters and op-ed pieces in the *Times* and *Post-Intelligencer*, arguing passionately that the Glen would undermine the "fragile recovery" of Third Avenue and become a locus of crime and drugs in the neighborhood.[131] While this letter-writing campaign was matched in part by LIHI's supporters, the opponents managed to gain the support of the *Times* and *P-I* editorial boards, who both eventually weighed into the debate against the Glen Hotel.[132]

But perhaps the most committed opponent to the reemergence of the Glen Hotel site was Rick Yoder, the new owner of the neighboring Mann Building. In early June, after a year of staying largely on the sidelines in the debate, Rick Yoder suddenly positioned himself as the lead opponent to LIHI's newly reworked Urban Reststop. Fueling his opposition was, of course, his fear that a hygiene center would undermine the new Wild Ginger dinner theater he had planned for the Mann Building. Actually, it would be more precise to say that it was his *investors'* fears that concerned Yoder the most. As one pro-business city councilmember noted, it is usually difficult to secure outside investment in *any* kind of restaurant or theater. Most often, the risk of failure is simply too high to attract much enthusiasm.[133] But Yoder had a track record, having built the first incarnation of Wild Ginger into one of the most popular spots in town, and in the end he succeeding in attracting a series of private investors into his new dinner theater project.

Still, track record or no, Yoder's investors were skittish about the Mann Building. At first, according to Yoder, his investors objected to the Mann's proximity to the low-income housing located in the Glen Hotel, but after much discussion Yoder convinced them the Glen's low-income residents would have little impact on the new restaurant.[134] However, when Yoder's investors learned that the Glen Hotel had again become the preferred location for a homeless hygiene center, they threatened to bolt. As Yoder wrote in the *Times*, such a move would leave him in tatters:

The city's off-again, on-again approach to this project has brought me to the brink of financial ruin. If our financial backers walk away there will be no renovation of the Mann Building, and I'll spend the rest of my life paying off the debts I've incurred to purchase what will become a useless downtown storefront.[135]

By all accounts, Yoder was determined not to let this happen. As he told two of LIHI's supporters during a lunch meeting in May 1996, his financial future depended upon stopping LIHI's Urban Reststop, and he would do whatever he could to kill the project. "There's only one way that this project could be acceptable," he reportedly told the supporters, "and that would be if it did not go forward."[136]

To this end, after LIHI's unveiling of the re-tooled Urban Reststop, Yoder got to work. First, he hired Hillis, Clark, Martin and Peterson, one of Seattle's best-connected law firms,[137] to represent his interests in negotiations with both LIHI and the city government. Together with his attorney, Yoder then hatched a three-part plan to stop the Urban Reststop from going into the Glen. Most publicly, Yoder and his allies kept up the pressure in the media by organizing a series of aggressive responses to LIHI's arguments in press reports, editorials, and op/ed pieces printed in the *P-I* and *Times*.[138]

At the same time, Yoder also strategically engaged LIHI in a series of negotiations regarding the "operating conditions" for the Reststop, just in case the city decided to actually follow through and fund the Glen site. At first, LIHI's supporters viewed Yoder's desire to discuss the Urban Reststop's operating rules as an encouraging sign.[139] Perhaps Yoder had begun to resign himself to the Reststop, they thought. He still might not like the idea, but at least he was at the table. At least then he could see that LIHI was serious about addressing opponents' concerns. Plus, Deputy Mayor Bruce Brooks and other city officials had sternly demanded that LIHI involve opponents in the discussions over how to operate the Urban Reststop.[140] Having Yoder—the Reststop's most visible opponent—involved in these discussions would show the city that LIHI was living up to its end of the bargain. Therefore, Yoder was invited to join LIHI's Urban Reststop Advisory Committee (URAC), which had been formed to provide community oversight of the proposed facility.[141]

But Yoder wanted no part of LIHI's Advisory Committee, which many opponents felt had been stacked with LIHI's supporters in the advocacy community.[142] Instead, Yoder's attorney wanted to negotiate directly with Sharon Lee, DSA president Kate Joncas, and Deputy Mayor Bruce Brooks, Norm Rice's representative in the debate. Fine, LIHI said, but as the negotiations started, any hopes that LIHI entertained regarding Yoder's participation quickly evaporated. As one staffer recalled, every time LIHI would make some headway on Yoder's concerns or objections, new objections would immediately arise to take their place.

We would go [to the negotiations], and every time we would meet, we would have addressed their concerns. And they would come back with more concerns like "you need more staff. Seven isn't enough" [laughs]. Hello? You want us to walk in there and actually pull their pants down? I mean, it's just crazy. . . . And it was almost like he [Yoder] needed that much control over the clientele.[143]

Later on, instead of merely responding to LIHI's proposals, Yoder and his attorney began to present their own, more aggressive demands. For instance, Yoder wanted strict time restrictions on the Reststop's operation. Under no circumstances should the facility be allowed to operate after 4 p.m., he argued (just before the dinner rush at Wild Ginger, incidentally). Moreover, to prevent the specter of crowds of homeless men waiting outside to use the services, Yoder proposed that LIHI establish strict time limits on using the facilities—ten minutes for using the toilet, thirty minutes for using the shower, and ninety minutes for a wash/dry spin cycle. In addition, to prevent the facility from becoming a locus of crime and drug activity, Yoder wanted LIHI to adopt a "one strike and you're out" security policy. In short, if it could be shown that the Reststop had been the site of a single criminal incident—of unspecified severity—then LIHI would have to shut down the facility permanently. Finally, to minimize the "impacts on adjacent businesses," Yoder's attorney proposed that the entrance to the Urban Reststop be moved from the sidewalk out front to the *alley* behind the Glen Hotel. Such an alleyway entrance, Yoder argued, would "allow for better separation between the users of the hygiene center" and the users of the retail storefronts on Third Avenue.[144]

From LIHI's perspective, Yoder's last few demands reached the truly sublime. The "alley entrance" proposal in particular was the last straw for LIHI's supporters. It was transparently designed to "keep people out of sight," as one staffer put it, and it would obviously do little to enhance the security of the building or the safety of the clients.[145] The other proposals—particularly the "one strike and you're out" demand—were similarly not designed to make the Reststop a better neighbor, as one staffer concluded. "There were designed to shut it down."[146] From LIHI's perspective, the extreme nature of his demands demonstrated that Yoder "hadn't resigned [himself] to the Glen at all" and that "no set of operating conditions" would ultimately satisfy the Glen's opponents. "It was not a good faith effort," as one LIHI supporter claimed.[147] Finally, when some of the meetings got so heated that Yoder and Joncas stormed out, LIHI's supporters concluded that Yoder was still committed to killing the Glen—even while he was ostensibly meeting with LIHI's supporters to make the Urban Reststop site "work" for everyone.[148]

Stopping the Reststop: The Mayor's Reversal

As it turned out, LIHI's suspicions were correct. As gleaned from archived phone messages in the city council files, at the same time that Yoder was sitting in negotiations with LIHI over the Reststop's "operating conditions," his attorney was desperately hunting down an alternative site for hygiene services.[149] An important turning point seems to have come on August 13, just six weeks before the September 30 deadline mandated by LIHI's settlement agreement. On this day, Yoder's attorney called city councilmember Jan Drago and announced that Yoder had signed a thirty-day lease option on a building in the Denny Regrade, right next to the Noelle House, a shelter for homeless women.[150] Moreover, Yoder had even convinced the Archdiocesan Housing Authority to agree to run the proposed hygiene facility. It was all coming together. If the city could be convinced to move the hygiene center to Yoder's handpicked building in the Regrade, then the Urban Reststop at the Glen Hotel would be dead-on-arrival.

But would Yoder's last-minute gambit be enough to kill the city's support of the Glen site? Early on, it did not seem likely. For one, Mayor Rice had just sent LIHI a letter that commended its staff for their community outreach efforts and expressed his belief that "the Urban Reststop will be an asset to the downtown area and will help meet the need we have in Seattle for such services."[151] In addition, DSA president Kate Joncas told city councilmember Jan Drago that while she backed Yoder's search for an alternative to the Glen Hotel, she could not support locating a mixed-gender hygiene center in Yoder's Regrade site. At the most, she would agree to a smaller "women's only" facility in the Regrade.[152] Joncas's "women's only" demand threw Yoder's plans for the Regrade site into doubt. After all, the settlement agreement mandated that any alternative to the Glen Hotel must serve both men and women. As a result, in order to gain the city's support and stop the Urban Reststop, Yoder and Joncas had to quickly find *another* location for hygiene services—this time a "men's only" facility somewhere within the Metro Free Ride Zone.

It was at this point that Yoder, Kate Joncas, city councilmember Jan Drago, and Deputy Mayor Bruce Brooks entered into a hurried series of negotiations over how to find that all-important "men's only" site to supplement Yoder's "women's only" Regrade proposal.[153] Bruce Brooks's position in this negotiation was crystal clear. Although the mayor was open to the idea of killing the Glen site and the political headaches it had sparked, moving the hygiene center out of the Glen Hotel would cost LIHI and the city dearly in lost time, now-pointless planning fees, and future relocation expenses. As a result, if the opponents wanted an alternative to the Glen Hotel, they would have to come up with some money. Yoder and the DSA would have to, as one city official said, "put your money where your mouth is" and pay for the new hygiene center themselves.[154] For their part, Yoder and Joncas were willing to pass the hat around among the city's business community, but the question was how much money would the city demand? A high figure—the $500,000 to $1 million range—might present a problem, since many opponents were dead set against giving into what they viewed as an exercise in public extortion (i.e., pay up or we'll move the hygiene center next to the Symphony Hall).[155] But a low figure, below $150,000 for example, would not even begin to cover the city's new expenses.

During the remainder of August and the early part of September, then, Joncas, Yoder, and Bruce Brooks batted figures back and forth. At one point, Brooks apparently received a promise from DSA chairman Tom Harville (the CEO of the Bon Marche) for a $500,000 grant, but by the end of September the size of the private grant had dropped to $350,000.[156] On September 24—just one week ahead of the September 30 deadline, a deadline that would automatically revert city funds back to the Glen Hotel—Bruce Brooks, Rick Yoder, and Kate Joncas came to a meeting of minds. In exchange for killing the Urban Reststop at the Glen, the city would support the opening of two new hygiene facilities: (1) a "women's only" facility funded by the city (using the grant initially awarded to LIHI at the Glen site) and located north of downtown in the Denny Regrade, and (2) a "men's only" site funded by the Downtown Seattle Association grant and located in a city-owned parking garage near Pioneer Square.[157]

After informing a stunned group of LIHI staff and supporters on September 26, the mayor's office publicly announced their decision on October 1: *the Glen Hotel will not be the site of the city's first full-service hygiene center.*[158] As Brooks told LIHI in a meeting following his announcement, the mayor's decision met all of the requirements set out by the original settlement agreement. Both sites were in the free ride zone, and, taken together, they would serve the entire homeless community, both men and women. What's more, he told LIHI, the decision is final.[159] There will be no more committees, no more reviews, and no more negotiations. The hygiene wars on Third were over.

The opponents of the Glen Hotel were, in a word, relieved. After months of bitter wrangling, Rick Yoder had seemingly succeeded in protecting his planned Wild Ginger dinner theater from the specter of the Urban Reststop next door. His investors would now be mollified, and he could go ahead with his renovation plans for the Mann Building. Perhaps stung by months of press exposure, and surely happy with his victory, Yoder quickly withdrew from the public eye.[160] Other opponents, especially DSA president Kate Joncas, had no qualms about publicly celebrating the city's decision—a decision she had carefully negotiated over the last month. "We think it'll be a better solution," she told the *Times*. "Smaller dispersed sites will be more manageable and have less impact on the neighborhood."[161] For their part, the *Times* editorial board took a larger view, hailing the decision as a key turning point in the cultural revitalization of Third Avenue.

A large hygiene center is ill-suited to Third and Pike, an area of great potential as a cultural district. The new performance hall for [the] Seattle Symphony is going up just across Pike. The Seattle Art Museum is nearby. A new dinner theater is proposed for the Mann Building adjacent to the Glen. And, with the renovation of the old Woolworth by Ross Dress for Less at Second and Pike, the city's pedestrian retail traffic is moving south to meet the emerging cultural district. That part of town is changing but still fragile, with a history of drugs and crime and loitering.[162]

As a result, the *Times* concluded, locating a homeless hygiene center in the midst of this emerging but fragile cultural district would be a fateful step in the wrong direction.[163] With the Glen Reststop now seemingly dead, it looked to the *Times* that Third Avenue had decisively turned the corner and was headed toward a spectacular revitalization.

But, as it turned out, the hygiene wars on Third were far from over. In the following months, LIHI would refuse to surrender and would instead embark on what one *Times* columnist called a "battle royal" to *return* the proposed hygiene center to the basement of the Glen Hotel.[164]

Notes

1. Constantine Angelos, "Sidran Plan Recommended to City Council," *Seattle Times*, 24 September 1993, 1(B).
2. Personal interview, Low Income Housing Institute, 9 February 1999. See also 29 May 1996 Minutes of the Public Meeting on the Urban Reststop at the Glen Hotel, Seattle City Archives, Jane Noland Subject Files (see methodological appendix for retrieval information).
3. David Fahrenthold, "Hygiene Center for Homeless—New Facility to Open in April," *Seattle Times*, 3 August 1998, 1(B).
4. Lewis Kamb, "A Place to Rest," *The Stranger*, 12 July 1996.
5. James Bush, "Hotel Rag," *Seattle Weekly*, 23 April 1997.
6. Personal interview, Low Income Housing Institute, 20 November 1998.
7. Personal interview, Low Income Housing Institute, 20 November 1998.
8. Michele Flores, "End of a Dream: Developers Lose Millions of Dollars, Titles to Homes," *Seattle Times*, 15 October 1992, 1(A).
9. Personal interview, Downtown Property Owner, 3 December 1998.
10. Michele Flores, "Downtown ACT Plans Dashed by Sale: Buyers Have Hope for Downtown Retail," *Seattle Times*, 26 March 1994, 1(D).
11. Flores, "Downtown ACT."
12. Eric Houston, "Alice Worries about Eviction: Low-Income Housing Vanishing," *Seattle Post-Intelligencer*, 19 July 1993.
13. Houston, "Alice Worries."
14. Personal interview, Low Income Housing Institute, 9 February 1999.
15. Personal interview, Low Income Housing Institute, 9 February 1999.
16. Personal interview, Downtown Property Owner, 3 December 1998.

17. King County Assessor's Office, Account Number 197570-0511-0.

18. Personal interview, Downtown Property Owner, 3 December 1998.

19. Personal interview, Low Income Housing Institute, 9 February 1999.

20. Personal interview, Low Income Housing Institute, 9 February 1999.

21. Personal interviews, Low Income Housing Institute, 20 November 1998, 11 November 1998, 9 February 1999.

22. Low Income Housing Institute, *Urban Reststop at the Glen Hotel: Annual Report*, 14 October 1996.

23. Steve Miletich, "Old Glen Hotel to be Spruced Up: Face-Lift Will Be Part of Low-Income Housing Plan," *Seattle Post-Intelligencer*, 21 January 1994.

24. Steve Miletich, "Old Glen Hotel to be Spruced Up."

25. Low Income Housing Institute, *Urban Reststop at the Glen Hotel: Annual Report*, 14 October 1996.

26. Melinda Bargreen, "The Making of a Great Place for Music," *Seattle Times*, 1 September 1998.

27. Melinda Bargreen, "Will Seattle Take the Ball and Go the Distance?" *Seattle Times*, 16 May 1993, 1(F).

28. "Build the Concert Hall in Downtown Seattle [editorial]," *Seattle Times*, 17 June 1994, 6(B).

29. "Build the Concert Hall [editorial]."

30. Melinda Bargreen, "Symphony Site: Getting Close," *Seattle Times*, 15 June 1994, 2(E). See also, "Rice Backs Downtown Site for Symphony Hall," *Seattle Times*, 14 July 1994, 4(B).

31. Melinda Bargreen, "Symphony Could Bring Oomph to Downtown: Marathon Property Hits Right Chord with Panel, not Center Site," *Seattle Times*, 8 July 1994, 1(B).

32. Melinda Bargreen and Peter Lewis, "Rice Wants New Concert Hall Downtown," *Seattle Times*, 15 July 1994, 3(B).

33. Personal interview, City of Seattle: Department of Housing and Human Services, 15 December 1998.

34. Personal interview, Seattle Symphony, 8 January 1999.

35. The term "emerging cultural district" first appeared in print, according to my records, in Mindy Cameron's op-ed piece entitled "Hygiene Center Won't Wash in Climate of Fear, Mistrust," *Seattle Times*, 23 June 1996.

36. Nancy Kim, "New Hall is Stage for Downtown Expansion," *Puget Sound Business Journal*, 4-10 September 1998, 22.

37. "Rice Backs Downtown Site for Symphony Hall," *Seattle Times*, 14 July 1994, 2(B).

38. Personal interview, Downtown Property Owner, 3 December 1998.

39. Nancy Kim, "New Hall is Stage for Downtown Expansion."

40. Dee Norton, "Hotel Becomes Home to Needy," *Seattle Times*, 22 November 1996, 3(B).

41. Personal interviews, Low Income Housing Institute, 20 November 1998, 11 November 1998, 9 February 1999.

42. Personal interviews, Low Income Housing Institute, 20 November 1998, 11 November 1998, 9 February 1999. See also James Epes, "Hygiene Center Riles Downtown Landlords," *Puget Sound Business Journal*, 11-17 August 1995, 1.

43. Personal interview, City of Seattle: Department of Housing and Human Services, 15 December 1998.

44. Personal interview, Downtown Property Owner, 11 November 1998.

45. Personal interview, Department of Housing and Urban Development, 3 February 1999. See also, Ellis Conklin, "Cheering at Third and Union: Mann Building Sold, Will be Revitalized into Theater, Shops," *Seattle Post-Intelligencer,* 10 April 1996.

46. Personal interview, Downtown Property Owner, 9 December 1998. See also James Epes, "Mann Building Rehab Plan Includes Nightclub," *Puget Sound Business Journal,* 17 March 1995, 1.

47. Ellis Conklin, "Cheering at Third and Union," *Seattle Post-Intelligencer,* 10 April 1996.

48. Conklin, "Cheering at Third and Union."

49. February 21, 1997 letter from Rick Yoder to Jane Noland, Seattle City Archives, Jane Noland Subject Files. The "3,000 a night" figure comes from an interview with a public relations officer at the Seattle Symphony.

50. Personal interview, Downtown Property Owner, 9 December 1998.

51. Personal interview, Downtown Property Owner, 9 December 1998.

52. Personal interview, Downtown Property Owner, 9 December 1998.

53. James Epes, "Mann Building Rehab Plan Includes Nightclub, Shops," *Puget Sound Business Journal,* 17 March 1995, 1.

54. "Finding the Best Spot for Public Restrooms [editorial]," *Seattle Times,* 8 October 1996.

55. Linda Keene, "Hygiene Center for Homeless Has Retailers Hot, and Suing," *Seattle Times,* 4 November 1995, 1(A).

56. Linda Keene, "Hygiene Center for Homeless." See also, James Epes, "'Hygiene Center' Riles Downtown Landlords," *Puget Sound Business Journal,* 11-17 August 1995, 1.

57. Personal interview, Downtown Property Owner, 9 December 1998.

58. Personal interview, Downtown Property Owner, 9 December 1998.

59. Personal interview, Downtown Property Owner, 9 December 1998.

60. Personal interview, Downtown Property Owner, 9 December 1998.

61. James Epes, "'Hygiene Center' Riles Downtown Landlords," *Puget Sound Business Journal,* 11 August 1995, 1.

62. James Epes, "'Hygiene Center' Riles Downtown Landlords."

63. James Epes, "'Hygiene Center' for Homeless Faces Legal Challenge," *Puget Sound Business Journal,* 25 August 1995, 3.

64. James Epes, "Hygiene Center Riles."

65. James Epes, "Hygiene Center Riles." This is not to say that Gellatly and Etsekson were not genuinely surprised by LIHI's plans for the Glen's basement. Most of LIHI's early meetings with neighbors took place before Paul and Don Etsekson bought the Kress Building on Third, and since Gellatly lives out of town, it's more than likely that he simply did not hear of LIHI's community meetings. Even neighbors who did attend these meetings were surprised to discover that the hygiene center was on the fast track to construction. In the first community meeting, as one property owner said, many neighbors reacted strongly against the idea of the hygiene center. After this heated meeting, he said, "nothing happened for a year . . . and we thought 'okay, because so many people protested, they weren't going to do it.'" Then, out of the blue, according to this

neighbor, came Norm Rice's announcement that the city had already funded and permitted the project. Source: Personal interviews, Downtown Property Owners.

66. James Epes, "'Hygiene Center' for Homeless Faces Legal Challenge."

67. For example, after looking over the HUD application and LIHI's later designs, Gellatly's lawyer found the reason for the sudden shrink in size: the Institute had relabeled the locker portion of the hygiene center as "for residents only." This effectively "removed" 2,000 square feet from the "hygiene center," bringing the total square feet of the project under 4,000. This was a crucial move, according to Gellatly's attorney, for it allowed LIHI to avoid a lengthy environment review process which is mandated by the city for any new facility over 4,000 square feet in size. And by avoiding an environmental review, LIHI also escaped the review's more stringent "public notification" process—allowing the Institute to construct its hygiene center in relative secrecy.

68. Epes, "'Hygiene Center' for Homeless Faces Legal Challenge."

69. Personal interview, LIHI Supporter, 13 January 1999.

70. As it turned out, this scaling back of the size and scope of the hygiene center was a tactical mistake. In hindsight, it seems clear that LIHI inflated its estimated operating capacity (i.e., a 24-hour facility serving 800 clients daily) to improve their chances of receiving HUD operating funds. At least this is the opinion of some in the city's Department of Housing and Human Services, who noted that serving 800 clients a day would be "physically impossible" at the Glen. So although LIHI eventually received funding from HUD, they were later forced to admit that their initial estimates were wildly out of whack, an admission which undermined their credibility with their neighbors and, more importantly, within the Rice administration. Source: Personal interview, Seattle City Official, 15 December 1998.

71. Personal interview, Downtown Property Owner, 9 December 1998.

72. Personal interview, LIHI Supporter, 13 January 1999.

73. Personal interview, LIHI Supporter, 13 January 1999.

74. Personal interview, Low Income Housing Institute, 9 February 1999.

75. Personal interview, Low Income Housing Institute, 9 February 1999.

76. Personal interview, Downtown Property Owner, 9 December 1998.

77. July 19, 1996 memo from Seattle DHHS staff to Seattle city council, Seattle City Archives, Jane Noland Subject Files.

78. Personal interviews, Low Income Housing Institute, 11 November 1998, 20 November 1998, 9 February 1999.

79. Personal interview, Low Income Housing Institute, 20 November 1998.

80. December 20, 1995 memo from mayor's office to city council, Seattle City Archives, Jane Noland Subject Files.

81. December 20, 1995 memo from mayor's office to city council, Seattle City Archives, Jane Noland Subject Files.

82. Personal interview, Low Income Housing Institute, 9 February 1999.

83. Personal interview, Low Income Housing Institute, 9 February 1999.

84. Personal interview, Downtown Property Owner, 9 December 1998.

85. Personal interview, Low Income Housing Institute, 9 February 1999.

86. Personal interview, Low Income Housing Institute, 20 November 1998.

87. Personal interview, Low Income Housing Institute, 11 November 1999.

88. Personal interview, Department of Housing and Human Services, 15 December 1998.

89. Personal interview. Department of Housing and Human Services, 15 December 1998.

90. Personal interview, Low Income Housing Institute, 20 November 1998.

91. Personal interview, Low Income Housing Institute, 20 November 1998.

92. Personal interview, Low Income Housing Institute, 20 November 1998.

93. July 19, 1996 memo from DHHS staff to Seattle City Council, Seattle City Archives, Jane Noland Subject Files.

94. Personal interview, Seattle City Councilmember, 7 January 1999.

95. July 19, 1996 letter from Larry Taylor to Cheryl Chow, Seattle City Archives, Jane Noland Subject Files.

96. March 15, 1996 memo from mayor's office to Hygiene Services Committee, Seattle City Archives, Jane Noland Subject Files.

97. March 21, 1996 Letter from Rick Yoder and John Skilling to Norm Rice, Seattle City Council, Jan Drago Office Files.

98. Personal interview, Downtown Property Owner, 3 December 1999.

99. March 21, 1996 letter from Rick Yoder and John Skilling to Norm Rice.

100. March 21, 1996 letter from Rick Yoder and John Skilling to Norm Rice.

101. March 21, 1996 letter from Rick Yoder and John Skilling to Norm Rice.

102. *1996 Gubernatorial Campaign Contributions: Norman Rice.* Olympia, WA: Washington State Public Disclosure Commission.

103. Ellis Conklin, "Cheering at Third and Union: Mann Building Sold, Will be Revitalized into Theater, Shops," *Seattle Post-Intelligencer,* 10 April, 1996.

104. Ellis Conklin, "Cheering at Third."

105. Ellis Conklin, "Cheering at Third."

106. Personal interview, Low Income Housing Institute, 9 February 1999.

107. Personal interview, LIHI Supporter, 13 January 1999.

108. Personal interview, Low Income Housing Institute, 9 February 1999.

109. Personal interview, Low Income Housing Institute, 9 Febuary 1999.

110. Personal interview, LIHI Supporter, 13 January 1999.

111. Personal interview, LIHI Supporter, 13 January 1999.

112. Personal interview, Seattle City Councilmember, 7 January 1999.

113. Personal interview, LIHI Supporter, 13 January 1999.

114. Personal interview, Low Income Housing Institute, 20 November 1998.

115. Personal interview, Urban Reststop Advisory Committee, 11 November 1998.

116. Linda Keene and Charles E. Brown, "New Name, Same Old Fight," *Seattle Times,* 18 June 1996.

117. Minutes of the first public meeting on the Urban Reststop at the Glen Hotel, 29 May 1996, Seattle City Archives, Jane Noland Subject Files.

118. Personal interviews, Low Income Housing Institute, 11 November 1998, 20 November 1998, 9 February 1999; Urban Reststop Advisory Committee, 11 November 1998.

119. Ishbel Dickens, "Urban Reststop: City Should Embrace Plans for Downtown Hygiene Center," *Seattle Times,* 23 June 1996.

120. Personal interviews, Low Income Housing Insitute, 11 November 1998, 20 November 1998. Urban Reststop Advisory Committee, 11 November 1998.

121. Personal interview, Downtown Property Manager, 13 November 1998.

122. "Groups Debate Plan for Hygiene Center," *Seattle Times,* 30 May 1996, 2(B).

123. Minutes of the first public meeting on the Urban Reststop at the Glen Hotel, 29 May 1996, Seattle City Archives, Jane Noland Subject Files.

124. July 23, 1996 letter from Sally Clarke to Cheryl Chow, Seattle City Archives, Jane Noland Subject Files.

125. "Howl: Sidranesque 'civility' rhetoric misdirects debate [editorial]" *Real Change*, August 1996.

126. "Groups Debate Plan for Hygiene Center."

127. July 19, 1996 Memo from DHHS to City Seattle Councilmember Cheryl Chow, Seattle City Archives, Jane Noland Subject Files. Also, Personal interview, Seattle City Councilmember, 7 January 1999.

128. July 16, 1996 letter from DHHS to Sharon Lee, Seattle City Archives, Jane Noland Subject Files.

129. July 16, 1996 letter from DHHS to Sharon Lee, Seattle City Archives, Jane Noland Subject Files.

130. Personal interview, Downtown Property Owner, 3 December 1998.

131. See, for example, Paul Etsekson, "Campaign for Hygiene Center Misleads," *Seattle Times*, 12 July 1996.

132. Mindy Cameron, "Hygiene Center Won't Wash in Climate of Fear, Mistrust," *Seattle Times*, 23 June 1996; "City Hygiene Plan Deserves Support [editorial]," *Seattle Post-Intelligencer*, 29 March 1997.

133. Personal interview, Seattle City Councilmember, 15 December 1998.

134. Rick Yoder, "Hygiene-Center Backers Muddy the Facts," *Seattle Times*, 12 February 1997.

135. Rick Yoder, "Hygiene-Center Backers Muddy the Facts."

136. Personal interview, Urban Reststop Advisory Committee, 11 November 1998.

137. For more on Hillis Clark Peterson, see Mark Worth, "Who Really Runs Seattle? A Who's Who of the City's Backroom Wheeler-Dealers," *Seattle Weekly*, 12 November 1998, 26.

138. Linda Keene and Charles E. Brown, "New Name, But Same Old Fight," *Seattle Times*, 18 June 1996.

139. Personal interview, Low Income Housing Institute, 20 November 1998.

140. July 16, 1996 Letter from DHHS to Sharon Lee, Seattle City Archives, Jane Noland Subject Files.

141. Personal interview, LIHI Supporter, 13 January 1999.

142. Personal interview, Downtown Property Manager, 13 November 1998.

143. Personal interview, Low Income Housing Institute, 20 November 1998.

144. July 23, 1996 letter from Sally Clarke to Bruce Brooks, Seattle City Archives, Jane Noland Subject Files.

145. Personal interview, Low Income Housing Institute, 20 November 1998.

146. Personal interview, Low Income Housing Institute, 20 November 1998.

147. Personal interview, LIHI Supporter, 13 January 1999.

148. Personal interview, LIHI Supporter, 13 January 1999.

149. Seattle City Council Files, Jan Drago's Office.

150. Rick Yoder's lease option on 2311 2nd Avenue, Seattle City Council Files. Jan Drago's Office.

151. August 1, 1996 letter from Norm Rice to Robert Siegel, Seattle City Archives, Jane Noland Subject Files.

152. Phone messages, Seattle City Council Files, Jan Drago's Office.

153. Phone messages, Seattle City Council Files, Jan Drago's Office.

154. Personal interview, Seattle City Official, 15 December 1998.

155. Personal interview, Downtown Property Owner, 3 December 1998.

156. Phone messages, Seattle City Council Files, Jan Drago's Office.

157. Seattle City Council Files, Jan Drago's Office.

158. Florangela Davila, "Hygiene Center Won't Go in Hotel," *Seattle Times*, 2 October 1996, 1(B).

159. October 2, 1996 letter from Daniel Merkle to Bruce Brooks, Seattle City Archives, Jane Noland Subject Files.

160. Linda Keene, "Hygiene Center Debate Unabated," *Seattle Times*, 3 October 1996.

161. Linda Keene, "Hygiene Center Debate Unabated."

162. "Finding the Best Spots for Public Restrooms [editorial]," *Seattle Times*, 8 October 1996.

163. "Finding the Best Spots [editorial]."

164. Terry McDermott, "The Mann, the Glen, and Yes, The Process," *Seattle Times*, 4 February 1997.

Chapter 8

Defining Revitalization in the Spectacular City

When Deputy Mayor Bruce Brooks informed LIHI on September 26, 1996 that the city had decided to kill the Glen site, they were absolutely stunned. Not only had Mayor Rice sent a letter expressing support for the Glen Hotel's Urban Reststop back in August,[1] but Bruce Brooks himself had told LIHI as late as September 6 that the mayor was foursquare behind the Glen site. At the same time, archived letters exchanged between Bruce Brooks and Rick Yoder's attorneys tell a different story. As these letters show, Brooks himself had been involved in the negotiations that would kill the Glen site since at least mid-August, and the deputy mayor had even received an update on Yoder's latest efforts to secure an alternative site two days *before* he reiterated to LIHI the mayor's support for the Glen site on September 6.[2] The only hint that anything was amiss was Brooks's admission that "the City is also in the process of exploring supplemental sites, including a women's only site in the Denny Regrade."[3] But Brooks had said *supplemental*, right? With the September 30 deadline for finding an acceptable alternative just days away, it looked to LIHI like the Urban Reststop at the Glen would finally become a reality. By October, the Glen site was dead on arrival.

To this day, LIHI's supporters feel absolutely betrayed by the mayor's turnaround, and, not surprisingly, they have in the meantime hatched a number of theories that attempt to explain why the mayor backtracked so suddenly on his support for the Glen. Perhaps the most prominent theory—eventually printed in the *Seattle Weekly*—tells of a late-night phone call Symphony benefactor Jack Benaroya allegedly placed to Norm Rice, in which the aging multimillionaire threatened to withdraw his financial support from Rice's 1996 gubernatorial campaign unless the mayor killed the Glen site.[4] In reality, however, the reasons for the mayor's turnaround were likely more prosaic, having more to do with the administration's fundamental commitment to the concept of a "cultural district" on Third Avenue and their concern that the city's hefty investment in the new concert hall might not generate as many benefits for the city (in terms of increased development and property tax revenue) with a hygiene center placed nearby. By building the Benaroya Hall with $40 million in public money, the city was in effect the newest property owner on Third Avenue, and as such the mayor's office shared many of the same concerns expressed by local landowners and businesses.

Finally, the decision may have made sense for purely political reasons as well. When compared to the financial and political clout of the downtown business community, the amount of leverage advocacy organizations can apply in city hall is quite modest. In addition to funneling money into political campaigns, the downtown business community hosts social functions that bring politicians in regular contact with downtown movers and shakers. Downtown business leaders can also offer politicians high-powered jobs upon their exit from public life, providing another incentive for public officials to stay close to the interests of the downtown establishment. Compared to this kind of clout, as one LIHI staffer argued, small nonprofits "have nothing to offer them." On certain occasions, advocates can "get a crowd of shouting, angry people in their face" which "can sometimes get us somewhere," but this kind of public pressure is difficult to sustain. Eventually, she conceded, the protests die off, and people go home.[5] But the influence of the downtown business community, while sometimes less overt, is ever-present and extremely powerful, like the hum of a high voltage wire. In short, she concluded, the Rice administration most likely looked at the political landscape and calculated the path of least resistance, and by September of 1996, that meant killing the Urban Reststop at the Glen Hotel.[6]

Back from the Ashes: LIHI's Master Negotiator

In any event, whatever political reasons the mayor had for nixing the Glen site, LIHI and their supporters were in no mood to sympathize. In the aftermath of Norm Rice's turnaround, some supporters reacted with incredulity and deep disappointment. In a tersely worded letter to the mayor's office, for example, Dan Merkle of the Urban Reststop Advisory Committee blasted the mayor for what he called his "cavalier, condescending, and unethical" last-minute maneuvering. "My frustration on this project," as Merkle concluded, "is that a very small group of downtown business owners were able to bully you and the City into making a decision that is not in the long-term best interests of the City or its citizens."[7] LIHI's supporters were particularly galled by the city's solicitation of the $350,000 grant from the Downtown Seattle Association—a grant that was forwarded only on the condition that the city kill the Glen site. As one LIHI staffer argued, such a move sets "a precedent for being able to buy [out] the community facilities in your neighborhood. . . . It basically set a price tag where if you have $300,000 you don't have to have homeless people in your neighborhood."[8]

Beyond their political objections to Rice's turnaround, LIHI's supporters also objected to the mayor's new plan on practical grounds. This "dual alternatives" plan—whereby hygiene services for men and women would be split between a Regrade site and the Muni Annex parking garage—simply would not work. First, LIHI pointed out that Rick Yoder's control of the Denny Regrade site was questionable. Yoder had only bought a lease *option* for the property, and it was by no means certain if either he or the city would actually follow through and secure the property over the long run.[9] The long-term prospects for the Muni Annex were similarly uncertain, as the city council had long been eyeing that property as a ripe site for redevelopment in the near future.[10] Moreover, LIHI argued that the DSA grant itself was a mere promise in the wind. The DSA had not yet raised the money, and the mayor had given them five years to pass the hat around.[11] By that time, of course, Yoder's lease option would have long since expired, and the Muni Annex might be a glittering new skyscraper. So, taken together, the financial future of the mayor's "dual alternatives" seemed murky at best, and this, in LIHI's view, hardly met the conditions of the settlement agreement which mandated that any alternative to the Glen site be "controlled and funded" by September 30, 1996.[12]

Furthermore, LIHI objected to the mayor's "dual alternatives" plan because it would once again let the retail core dodge its responsibility to host human services. As it stood, both of the mayor's alternatives were located well outside the retail core in neighborhoods that have historically hosted a large number of Seattle's human service facilities.[13] Finally, as part of this plan to exempt the retail core from human services, the mayor's selection of the Muni Annex was particularly galling. "Most users of the Garage site will have to walk up several of the steepest blocks in the City to use the facility," Merkle noted. Once they arrived, patrons would then encounter an "isolated," "dreary" and "dismal" parking garage. As Merkle concluded, choosing such a dismal location would surely ensure that only the most desperately homeless and poor would use the facility—provided, that is, that they had the stamina to make the steep climb up Cherry Street.[14] Under such a plan, LIHI's dream of a downtown "Urban Rest-stop" open to all members of the community—rich and poor, tourists and homeless alike—would be simply unachievable. For LIHI, then, the mayor's "alternatives" were, in a word, unacceptable.

So LIHI decided to fight back. Blocked by the mayor's office, LIHI turned their attention to the city council. In doing so, the advocates refined their tactics. If in the media LIHI's supporters continued to argue that the Glen Hotel was by far the best and most appropriate site for hygiene services, in council chambers, LIHI's Sharon Lee took a more pragmatic approach. As many consultants noted, Sharon Lee was a "master negotiator"[15] and was "always willing to make any kind of deal" that would still provide Seattle's low-income citizens with first-rate services and facilities. In this way, Lee's strategy was that, by using the Glen as a bargaining chip, "maybe we can end up with a better arrangement"[16] than that proposed at the Glen Hotel. If the council could be convinced to support the Glen Hotel site, this would force the mayor to either veto the council's resolution—thereby positioning him as the man who denied the homeless access to bathrooms—or to embrace the Glen site in the face of an agitated and organized business community. Faced with these two equally unattractive options, the mayor would likely return to direct negotiations with LIHI and the result would be a viable proposal for locating hygiene services downtown.[17]

To this end, LIHI met with a number of city councilmembers at the end of 1995 and argued forcefully against the mayor's "dual alternatives" proposal.[18] In these meetings, LIHI ran through all the practical arguments against the two locations, including the lack of site control, the uncertain funding, and the dismal appearance of the Muni Annex. Perhaps most importantly, they also appealed to the city council's sense of self-interest. LIHI knew, for example, that the city had long planned to redevelop the Muni Annex garage (which was located across from city hall, between the financial district and Pioneer Square) into a more lucrative commercial project—one that could fill city coffers with office and retail rents (in addition to new sales taxes).[19] The mayor's "dual alternatives" scheme, however, would stick the "men's only" hygiene center in the Annex, effectively putting off any such redevelopment plans. As one LIHI staffer recalled, Sharon Lee asked the city councilmembers, "Do you really want to take a 1,500-square-foot hygiene center at the corner of this incredible site and tie it up for years and years?"[20] Either way you looked at it, as LIHI concluded, the mayor's plan would end up costing the city dearly: either the Muni Annex hygiene center would mean no big-ticket redevelopment of the Annex site, or the City would go ahead with redeveloping the Annex in three or four years—thereby wasting the many thousands of dollars used to locate hygiene services there in the first place.

The city council was floored. As one LIHI executive recalled, the council's immediate reaction went something like "my god, we totally agree with you."[21] One councilmember put her objections to the mayor's Annex proposal this way: "why put money into something that's going to come down in a few years? By the time you build it and get the routine going, you're tearing it down. . . . Almost all of us felt it was wasted money."[22] In short, just two weeks after the mayor first proposed his "dual alternatives" plan, it lay in tatters. The Denny Regrade site had reportedly run into difficulties with its lease agreement, and now the city council had summarily rejected his Muni Annex proposal.

With the mayor's plan thoroughly discredited in the council, LIHI then began to lobby hard to return the hygiene center to the Glen Hotel. The mayor's office, they argued, broke their word. As part of the settlement agreement, "if they couldn't come up with an alternative site . . . after so many days . . . they were supposed to be back at the Glen."[23] As one LIHI staffer put it, the city should live up to its obligations. "We have a permit. We have funding [the HUD grant]. We've done our notification process," she said. "We have a right to build this."[24] If the city council refused to support the Glen, and if they did not come up with an alternative more acceptable than the mayor's cobbled-together Muni Annex/Denny Regrade plan, then all bets were off. LIHI might just try to build the Urban Reststop without the city's support.

All of this had a dramatic effect on the city council, particularly Cheryl Chow. First, LIHI's lobbying effort had thoroughly discredited the mayor's Regrade and Muni Annex proposals. Moreover, by threatening to move forward unilaterally on the Glen site, LIHI had forced the city's hand. If the city truly wanted to mollify the downtown establishment and stop the Urban Reststop from going in next to Benaroya Hall, they would have to find some alternative acceptable to Sharon Lee—or else LIHI would just build the Reststop anyway. Therefore, with the mayor's "dual alternatives" in tatters, the council, led by Cheryl Chow's housing and human services committee, decided to throw the entire process back to square one.[25] Nothing was off the table, as Chow announced officially in early January. Her committee would solicit proposals from all the interested parties, from LIHI to the Downtown Seattle Association to the mayor's office, and any and all legitimate sites—*including the once-dead Glen Hotel*—would be carefully reviewed over the next two months.[26] In February 1997, the committee would then make a recommendation to the larger council regarding where, finally, Seattle would locate its long-debated hygiene center.

By the end of January, all the proposals had arrived at Chow's office. In their submissions, LIHI pushed hard for the original Glen Hotel Urban Reststop, but, failing that, indicated they were also willing to entertain an alternative location, so long as it met the conditions of the original settlement agreement.[27] In a surprise move, the mayor's office continued to stick to its largely discredited "dual alternatives" proposal,[28] while, for their part, the DSA came to Chow's committee with a proposal that would simply expand the limited hygiene facilities available at three already-existing homeless shelters around the city.[29] As one member of Chow's committee later conceded, of all these proposals, LIHI's original Glen Hotel plan stood head and shoulders above the rest. "They had done their homework," said the councilmember. The Glen Hotel proposal was "further [along] than any other proposal."[30] With HUD's grant and the once-approved city grant, LIHI "had the funding lined up" and had even completed an extensive planning and outreach effort designed to mollify community concerns. Furthermore, it was not at all clear whether LIHI's $1 million HUD grant—which had been earmarked only for the Glen Hotel—could be applied to any other alternative.[31] In fact, the local HUD office was hinting that if the mayor or the council indeed followed through and killed the Glen without finding an alternative acceptable to LIHI, the city might lose the HUD grant forever and have to come up with the money itself.[32] As one councilmember recalled, the prospect of losing the HUD grant sent chills up and down city hall.[33]

So in late January 1997, Chow's committee informally issued their recommendation. In their view, the preferred site for hygiene services in Seattle was, once again, *the Glen Hotel.* As the committee argued, the other proposals were riddled with problems—either they were too expensive[34] or they lacked solid funding commitments and site control (DSA's "multiple sites" proposal).[35] And, although the committee agreed with the mayor's proposal to locate a "women's only" hygiene center in the Regrade, this site would not address the need to serve men or families (i.e., a mom with male children).[36] In the end, of all the suggestions submitted to the council, as the committee somewhat reluctantly concluded, the Glen Hotel site was by far the most viable.[37] On February 14, the committee would make their official recommendation to the larger council—which could then vote on the future of the Glen, up or down, once and for all. The Urban Reststop had officially risen from the ashes.

The Struggle to Define Urban Vitality

LIHI's supporters were predictably ecstatic. "Victory for the little people!" as Diana Lee, a LIHI board member, exclaimed to the *Post-Intelligencer*.[38] But the Glen's opponents were, of course, outraged. The Glen site had been declared DOA not once, but twice. And here it was again, in February 1997, threatening to be officially resurrected by the full city council.[39] "They've completely reversed all the work that's been done," complained Rick Yoder, who once again threatened to cancel his planned renovation of the Mann Building.[40] "It's a wrong-headed move," concurred the editors of the *Times*. Chow's move, they argued, "puts at risk a major rehabilitation proposed for the adjacent Mann Building . . . directly across from where the new Symphony Hall is being constructed. . . . That financing for Yoder's project could evaporate if the city allows a public hygiene center next door seems of no consequence to Chow."[41] With the decisive council meeting just two weeks away on Valentine's Day, the business community, headed once again by Yoder, DSA president Kate Joncas, and the Glen's other longtime opponents, mobilized one more time to kill the city's support for the Glen Hotel site. "The full city council has a chance February 14 to quash the Glen Hotel site once and for all," wrote *Puget Sound Business Journal* editor Don Nelson. Now is the time, he argued, to "send a clear message: not at the Glen. Not now, not later."[42]

As a result, during the three weeks from Chow's committee's announcement to the all-important February 14 council meeting, the longtime Third Avenue combatants geared up for one final public battle over the future of homeless services in the revitalizing retail core. Although the long-simmering debate had boiled up into public view a couple of times in the past, most notably after LIHI unilaterally announced their intention to build the Urban Reststop in late May of 1996, by the winter of 1997, both proponents and opponents had carefully sharpened their arguments and were ready for one last big push in city hall. To this end, the three-week debate leading up to the council's Valentine's Day meeting presents a good opportunity to step back and look more closely at the discursive and ideological dimensions of this divisive debate over hygiene, homelessness, and gentrification in downtown Seattle. What arguments did each side marshal during this debate? And what political discourses—that is, what specific "ways of seeing" and interpreting social reality, in this case, the future of downtown Seattle—were woven into these arguments?

The Reststop's Opponents: "It's the Wrong Place"

From the beginning of the debate, opponents of the Urban Reststop argued that they supported the concept of a city-funded homeless hygiene center and recognized the desperate need for the services. The problem was the location. Time and again, opponents—including, by 1997, the Downtown Seattle Association, the mayor's office, and BH Music Center (the private nonprofit set to manage the new Symphony Hall), and, of course, local landowners—claimed that the proposed Glen Hotel hygiene center would be "at odds"[43] with its surroundings, "ill-suited to Third and Pike,"[44] and "not compatible with planned upgrades"[45] in the neighborhood. The arrival of the Symphony on Third Avenue changed everything for opponents. The Glen site may have been acceptable before, but now, with the construction of Benaroya Hall now underway, Third Avenue was "coming alive."[46] The emergent health of the neighborhood was an achievement that must be protected.

In this way, opponents of the Glen location, like their CRORC counterparts in the Pine Street debate, drew heavily upon the trope of the organic city discussed previously (see chapter 5 for details). This time, however, the temporal context of the trope shifted slightly. If during the Pine Street debate, pro-Nordstrom forces depicted the retail core as a once-robust but now-sickly entity waiting for a "shot in the arm," opponents of the Glen site depicted Third Avenue as an at-risk infant, an emerging "cultural district"[47] that showed some promising "signs of life."[48] But the nascent life of this "cultural district" was "still fragile."[49] The long history of urban decay and deviance on Third Avenue—including chronic problems with loitering, drug dealing, and public drunkenness—would be difficult to overcome, but the impending arrival of the Symphony had endowed the area with a spark of life. Now it would be up to civic leaders to protect and nurture this spark. In short, if the organic city trope allowed pro-Nordstrom forces to write a compelling narrative about "saving" the health of the retail core, the Glen's opponents drew on the trope to craft a narrative in which a *new* life—the cultural district—was being created in a context of already-existing disorder and decline. To locate a homeless hygiene center in the midst of this "fragile piece of downtown"[50] would be tantamount to abandoning a defenseless infant threatened by a deadly disease. Such a decision would "effectively kill this fledgling area"[51] and allow urban decay on Third Avenue to proceed unperturbed.

At the same time, the connections between "the hygiene center" and "urban decay" are not intuitive. In fact, LIHI's supporters would argue exactly the opposite, that the hygiene center in fact contributes to the maintenance of social order on Seattle's streets. What explains, in short, the tight association between the hygiene center and the forces of urban decay? The problem, according to opponents, was not the facility itself, or even the bare fact that public showers and toilets will be located near the concert hall. The problem was who would be using these facilities. It is at this point that more abstract discussions of location and revitalization merge with the opponents' discourse on contemporary homelessness.

In short, in the political imaginary constructed by the Glen's opponents, "the homeless" have become intertwined with a whole host of other "urban problems," including especially the pathologies of mental illness, crime, and drug addiction. Often, this tight association between homelessness and urban deviance would be expressed in respondents' unsolicited lay theories that attempt to explain why people become homeless. As one opponent said, "[there are] three things, the reason why people are homeless [*sic*]. First is they're alcoholic. Second, they're drug-addicted, and third is they've got mental problems." Other opponents reinforced this equation between homelessness and deviance, with one anti-Glen councilmember noting that "the majority" of the "street population . . . is what they call dually diagnosed, and it's mental illness as well as drug addiction"[52] while one letter-writer argued more bluntly that "loitering, begging, littering, alcohol and drug abuse are a transient's greatest contributions."[53] Opponents also expressed this association in more subtle ways. For example, a question concerning why the respondent opposed the Glen Reststop would sometimes elicit impromptu stories about mentally ill people who went "crazy" and perpetrated violent crimes on unsuspecting civilians.[54] The implication was that "the hygiene center has the potential to attract more of this type of [deviant] behavior."[55]

The connections opponents drew between homelessness and deviance thus led them to conclude that the "Urban Reststop" would *inevitably* become a refuge for drugs and violent crime. By attracting homeless clients, the basement of the Glen would then become a "hang-out" or a "congregation point" for the homeless, thereby concentrating deviance and disorderly behavior in this now-crucial part of downtown. As one opponent put it:

> Our city has been over-taken by people that wander the streets, often either intoxicated or on drugs. The shelters become hang-outs for these people, and it intensifies the problem. . . . Now you want to add the Glen Hotel as a site for public restrooms and showers. It is beyond me as to the reason we want to proliferate the existing problems of crime and drugs in downtown Seattle.[56]

All in all, perhaps the most clearly articulated fear of "concentrated deviance" was the prediction that the Reststop's showers, urinals, and bathroom stalls would become "a mecca for drug activity."[57] Opponents on the whole had little faith in LIHI's ability to patrol the facility, and many were convinced that the Reststop would immediately become Seattle's most popular and accessible drug marketplace. "Every police officer who walks the beat will tell you that a hygiene center, no matter how well policed, will be a drug exchanging venue and will not be safe, no matter how much monitoring you do," explained one opponent.[58]

If the opponents were concerned that the basement of the Glen Reststop would become a "congregation" for street disorder and a "mecca" for the drug trade, they were doubly afraid that this concentrated deviance would somehow leak out into streets and "have an impact on the neighborhood."[59] The root of this fear lay in LIHI's initial proposal for the Reststop, which claimed that the facility would be open 24 hours and serve up to 800 people per day. Although, as one opponent noted, LIHI admittedly "scaled back" this number "as time went on"[60] (and the "800" number would even be described as "physically impossible" by city officials),[61] the effect of LIHI's "800 a day" proposal was immediate and long lasting. With this many clients, opponents asked, how would LIHI be able to patrol the facility? Where would these crowds stand as they waited to use the bathrooms or showers?

It was this last question that really had neighboring property owners and merchants worried. When combined with what opponents viewed as a lack of "waiting space" inside the proposed facility, the "800 a day" proposal had nearby landlords and retailers envisioning unruly crowds of homeless people hanging out in front of the Glen Hotel well into the evening, forming a formidable barrier to pedestrians, dinner theater guests, and symphony patrons making their way down Third Avenue. "Where were they going to queue?" asked one opponent. With its interior design devoted mostly to lockers, bathrooms, and showers, she continued, the Reststop looked like it would "spill crowds onto the street."[62] Looking back, it was exactly this fear of "crowds" and "queues" in front of the Glen that motivated Rick Yoder and Kate Joncas (DSA president) to demand that LIHI restrict the Reststop's hours of operation to daytime only, put strict time limits on using the facilities (five minutes in the stall, for example), and to move the main entrance from the street to the alley—anything to move these crowds out of sight.

Borrowing the language and imagery of broken windows theory (see chapter 6 for details), opponents therefore concluded that locating the hygiene center in the Glen would create a "critical mass" of street deviance that would quickly undermine the nascent health of the planned cultural district.[63] If you have two or three people involved in drug dealing, as one opponent explained, and there are still people walking the streets conducting legitimate business, "it is much easier for the neighborhood to deal with the problem." As long as there are still signs of life in the neighborhood, including "people walking to and fro," the dealers will feel exposed and can be intimidated into "moving along." "If you get, however, five or six people" or even more people hanging around, dealing drugs, engaging in disruptive behavior, "you get people saying 'ewwww'" and they abandon the area. Then, once the legitimate public abandons the neighborhood, "you get this crowd taking over the street" forcing average folks to "avoid the area."[64] By concentrating street deviance on Third Avenue, by acting as a "congregation point" for potentially unruly crowds of street people, the Urban Reststop would quickly become a destructive "broken window" in the neighborhood and would therefore inaugurate a rapid spiral of abandonment and decay.

Building on this tight association between homelessness, deviance, and neighborhood decay, the third theme of the anti-Glen campaign argued that the Reststop—and the crowds of homeless people drawn to it—*would inevitably frighten off the very people Seattle needs to attract back downtown.* Time and again, the anti-Glen campaigners would argue that, as one city staffer said, "it's the *perception* of danger, not necessarily the reality" that tourists, pedestrians, and investors use to determine where to visit and how to spend their money.[65] If something as innocuous as panhandling can frighten visitors to downtown, she said, imagine the effect a Glen Hotel Urban Reststop—with its crowds of homeless folks queued up outside—might have on potential shoppers, diners, and symphony patrons.[66] Another opponent put it this way:

> So if your wife has to walk adjacent to, or through, or whatever, a whole bunch of homeless downtrodden folks that are queued up on the sidewalk waiting to take a shower, is she going to go there? . . . It's a safety thing. I mean, it may not be unsafe . . . [but] there's still the perception that I might get accosted, I might get beat up, I might get robbed, I might get raped, or whatever.[67]

In short, for opponents, building a hygiene center next to a major cultural attraction would be tantamount to inviting tourists, shoppers, and suburbanites back downtown, only to scare them away again with a spectacle of street deviance, anchored by the Glen Hotel.[68]

Finally, with tourists, consumers, and pedestrians frightened away from Third Avenue, any future investment the city hoped might flow into the area would evaporate into Seattle's cold gray skies. In the end, the spark of life generated by the Symphony's arrival would be snuffed out in its infancy, bringing any dreams city officials entertained about a vibrant retail-cultural district on Third Avenue to an unceremonious end.[69] As one opponent concluded in his notes during a meeting with LIHI staff, "how can you expect the homeless to mingle with shoppers, commuters, and tourists? Why put them together? To what end? What if you are wrong? The Symphony will be stuck with a neighbor that hurts them."[70]

At this point, the Glen's opponents had one last question to answer. Given that they had conceded the need for hygiene services in Seattle, where did they propose to locate the facility, if not in the Glen? If the city's dreams of a "cultural district" on Third—and a world-class downtown more generally—required the isolation of the "target markets" of urban revitalization from unwonted contact with the urban poor, where then should hygiene services be located?

The opponents' most common solution to this dilemma drew upon, interestingly enough, technical language of urban planning. For opponents, the Urban Reststop (as well as other human services) should be viewed much like a truck parts factory or a toxic waste dump and "zoned" out to the fringes of the central city, far away from Seattle's revenue-generating and tourist-friendly retail core. As one opponent argued,

> This location [the Glen Hotel on Third Avenue] is in the middle of our retail core, and it's zoned appropriately as the middle of our retail core. And we spend thousands of dollars . . . to establish zoning codes and to establish areas for . . . specific events or activities. And putting a hygiene center in the middle of the retail core isn't logical.[71]

Or, as another opponent put it more vividly,

> I don't want to come across as an elitist . . . but it's like putting a garage dump next to the [Scottish] Highlands. Or it's like . . . a meat rendering plant next to a high-income residential area. . . . Planning says you don't do that.[72]

When pressed for specifics, a number of opponents argued that Seattle's industrial districts—particularly the industrial area south of the now-imploded Kingdome—would be the best location for the hygiene facilities and other human services. "Perhaps an industrial area south of Pioneer Square" would be the best place, wrote one opponent to the *Times*.[73] "Maybe other sites south of the Kingdome should be considered as well," agreed another opponent.[74] One property owner had an even more specific proposal: the city should erect a "warehouse-style" structure on the site of the old burned-out Sunny Jim Peanut Butter factory (near Boeing Field) to house the city's homeless and provide them with "facilities—kitchens, showers, all this jazz." You could help "500 people a night for the same amount of money" it took to rehab the Glen Hotel, he argued. The city could then "dedicate a bus" to get the clients back and forth from downtown. "Why aren't they doing stuff like that?" he asked.[75] Other opponents were less specific in their proposals. "I would argue that the homeless downtown don't do anything for anybody," one property said. "If [you need] any place to put a hygiene center, you put it where these people are living, which is under the freeway and all sorts of places . . . to be homeless and living in the middle of the city is, that doesn't fit."[76]

And so, again, in another political debate over the future shape of downtown Seattle, the organic city trope, with its strict dichotomies between *life/death* and *vitality/decay*, appears to be at work. This time, in the discourse of the downtown business community, it was the "emerging cultural district" that became the metaphorical entity threatened by the forces of urban decay—represented in this case by the proposed Glen Hotel hygiene center. This central conceit, in which Third Avenue was re-imagined as an infant struggling to survive, was further structured by a series of oppositions in a manner similar to those operating in the Pine Street debate.

VITALITY	DECAY
Benaroya Hall	Glen Hotel
Emerging Cultural District	Meat Rendering Plant
Lively Entertainment Core[77]	Drug "Mecca"
Coming Alive	"Kill this Fledgling Area"
LIFE	DEATH

Within the logic established by these oppositions, a decision to locate homeless services in the Glen would be equivalent to unleashing the forces of decay and disorder upon the struggling, still emerging, still infantile cultural district "entity." Opponents thus labored to present the question of the Glen Hotel site as a stark choice between "vitality" and "decay," between "life" and "death." Either you reject the Glen and nurture a thriving cultural and entertainment district anchored by Benaroya Hall, or you embrace the Glen and surrender this part of downtown once again to urban deviance and decay, concentrated this time in industrial strength proportions around the Glen Hotel.

The ultimate political trajectory of this particular application of the organic city trope is revealed in the opponents' final solutions to Seattle's hygiene dilemma. If the homeless are inextricably linked with deviance and disorder, and if human service facilities do little else but "concentrate" this deviance and spill it out onto the streets, then the rational response is a policy of enforced social apartheid. To protect the public's investment in the concert hall, and its interest in the larger dream of a cultural district on Third Avenue, homeless services should be "zoned out" of sections of cityspace slated for upscale consumption and leisure. To do otherwise would be to allow a spectacle of street deviance to frighten off the tourists, consumers, and patrons that breathe life into downtown commercial and public space. Within the logic set up by the Glen's opponents, this policy of social apartheid, of "zoning out," or, more euphemistically, "dispersing" homeless services out of the city's retail and financial core becomes more than sound policy. It becomes one's civic duty. It becomes simple common sense. As one opponent put it, as he searched for a metaphor that could describe the illogic of placing homeless services cheek-by-jowl against the new Symphony Hall, "it's kind of like mixing chocolate ice cream with horse manure. It doesn't hurt the horse manure . . . but it doesn't do much for the chocolate ice cream."[78]

The Reststop's Supporters: "Downtown Should be for Everyone"

LIHI's most fundamental argument for locating hygiene services in the Glen Hotel was perhaps their most straightforward. There is, as LIHI argued, a clear and desperate need for these services on the streets of Seattle, and providing these services is a simple matter of human compassion. To this end, building the Urban Reststop was, at base, a human rights issue. As one LIHI staffer said:

> Some things you have to take stands on . . . There are a lot of homeless people in the downtown core, and there are no public bathrooms. And there are no public hygiene facilities. You know, there you go. It's just basic decency and treating people well, giving people a chance to be clean [and to] have clean clothes.[79]

For LIHI, the city's lack of downtown public hygiene facilities is an affront to the dignity of street people and a violation of their most basic human rights. Bereft of these services, as one *Real Change* article put it,[80] the homeless are forced into a series of potentially humiliating options: they can either tend to their needs in public (bathing in public, public urination, and so on) or sneak into private facilities and risk getting unceremoniously bounced by private security guards.[81] Over time, this relentless search to find a place to wash up begins to take its toll on those trying to get off the streets, as one member of Seattle's homeless community explained. "You don't smell good. You don't look good . . . people look at you like you're a bum."[82] Providing free and easy access to toilets, showers, and washer/dryers would therefore help low-income people in downtown Seattle "maintain a level of dignity that the rest of us take for granted."[83]

Furthermore, LIHI's supporters argued that locating the Urban Reststop downtown would eventually help many in the homeless community find their way off the streets. As one supporter wrote in the *Times*, "those who have had trouble finding the motivation to start a job search may find more energy and self-esteem after they have taken a shower or washed their clothes."[84] Over time, the chronic dirtiness that accompanies life on the streets makes it less and less likely that a homeless man or woman will be able to find their way off the streets.[85] Locating a hygiene center in the heart of downtown—where it is easily accessible to the homeless—is in this way a crucial part of helping homeless people "step forward with their lives."[86]

On their face, these are compelling arguments. After all, few people truly oppose helping people get off the streets." But even while they were arguing that Seattle's most desperately poor needed hygiene services, LIHI still faced a thorny rhetorical problem. The main problem, as we've discovered, was that

LIHI's opponents immediately neutralized this "human rights" argument by cheerfully conceding that, yes, the city does indeed need hygiene services. "We're not opposed to a place for people to shower," as Paul Etsekson told the *Times*.[87] "We agree on the basics," claimed another opponent. "The services are needed."[88] But, as opponents argued, even if you grant that hygiene services are desperately needed, why should they be located in the heart of the retail core? Presumably, these services could be located *anywhere* in the city. Why place them in the middle of the revitalizing retail and entertainment core?[89]

To counter such arguments, and the implied assertion that the Urban Reststop would bring the "revitalization" of Third Avenue to a grinding halt, LIHI was forced to move beyond arguing that the services were needed and instead had to craft a compelling case for why hygiene services should be placed in the heart of downtown. To make this case, LIHI, in essence, was forced to demonstrate both *how* the Urban Reststop would fit into the city's expressed policy for "strengthening downtown" and *why* the Urban Reststop would not be "at odds" with the "emerging cultural district" or the larger post-Rhodes revitalization of Seattle's retail core. This was a daunting rhetorical challenge, because as we discovered during the fight over the Rhodes Project, the language of "revitalization" has never been the most friendly discursive terrain for housing, antipoverty, and antigentrification activists. In Seattle, the trope of the organic city has become one of the most effective arrows in the rhetorical quiver of the downtown establishment, and in this trope, "urban vitality" has been defined in narrow terms—terms that equate the city's "health" with growing property values and crowds of upscale shoppers.

In short, the ultimate success of LIHI's political strategy hinged on their ability to contest the business community's ideological stranglehold on what "urban revitalization" symbolizes within the public imagination. If they could appropriate the discourse of "revitalization" and redefine it in a way that did not by necessity preclude the presence of homeless people and human services in the retail core, then perhaps they could convince the city to move forward on the Glen Hotel Reststop. LIHI therefore faced a daunting project of discursive rearticulation.[90] As we discovered in the battle over Pine Street, and as Volosinov reminds us, there are no absolutes in language, no singular or permanently fixed meanings. Instead, all linguistic signs—"revitalization," for example—are *multiaccentual*, capable of divergent social "accents" or connotations depending on how they are articulated with other signs in relations of opposition and association.[91] The inherent multiaccentuality of language therefore opens the door to a political struggle over which social "accent" or which set of political connotations will be highlighted and activated within key cultural signs and symbols.[92]

An analysis of the LIHI's arguments in support of the Glen Hotel site reveals just such a struggle being waged over the meanings and images articulated with "revitalization." In many of their statements, in short, I discovered a halting but nonetheless explicit effort to *appropriate* the language of "urban revitalization" from its long association with the interests of the downtown business community. In this act of appropriation, LIHI first sought to argue that, far from undermining the "vitality" of downtown, the Glen Reststop could in fact play a key role in the "downtown renaissance" so actively pursued by public and property elites. But, as we will discover, in addition to merely appropriating the language of revitalization, LIHI also sought to expand this discourse, to *transform* it or *rearticulate* it in new and interesting ways—ways that did not exclude a priori the continuing presence of low-income people in areas of the city slated for middle-class consumption and leisure.

The first step of LIHI's strategy hinged on meeting the business community on its own ideological turf, appropriating the language of "urban revitalization," and convincing city officials that the Reststop could indeed play an important role in realizing elite dreams of a vibrant, world-class downtown. But how could a hygiene center help *revitalize* the commercial fortunes of downtown Seattle? To answer this question, LIHI's supporters noted that the original push for the hygiene center came largely from merchants' complaints about public urination in downtown alleys and streets. As one supporter wrote in a letter to the mayor, "nobody likes having people use alleys and streets as toilets, and this [the Urban Reststop] should be an answer to the area's prayers rather than a cause for concern."[93] John Fox of the Displacement Coalition put it this way: "What is better? Changing clothes and urinating on the street, or going into a shower and a restroom?"[94] As another supporter wrote, instead of fighting the Glen site, the Downtown Seattle Association should embrace a centrally located Reststop as a key part of the larger downtown renaissance.

> The facility would make our downtown a cleaner, more sanitary, less odorous place for everyone—office workers, merchants, shoppers, tourists, and, yes, street people. . . . The facility would, by any measure, make our downtown a more attractive place for commerce. Foul-smelling people and foul-smelling streets, sidewalks, and alleys are not a big drawing card for retail business.[95]

Other supporters explicitly sought to connect LIHI's Glen Hotel proposal to their opponents' hopes for a "vibrant cultural district" on Third Avenue, arguing that continued problems with public urination could drive away the very tourists and symphony patrons the city was trying to attract back downtown. "As you state, this area is 'on the cusp' of becoming a cultural district with the completion of the symphony hall and maybe a dinner theater. This area is going to be a magnet for people at night, including the homeless. Wouldn't it be better if there were public toilets at the Glen Hotel, so that the homeless would not be urinating in public as they hang around the symphony. . . ?"[96] Beyond merely cleaning up the streets, however, a number of LIHI's supporters argued that the Reststop would aid in the realization of elites' world-class dreams by proving once again to international audiences that Seattle is indeed a humane and "sophisticated" metropolis, one which does not focus on the interests of tourists or retailers to the exclusion of all "other aspects of the community."[97] As one supporter wrote in the *Times*, "Seattle rightfully strives to become a world-class city. Yet it is difficult to envision a progressive, world-class city with restrooms for the general public." For other supporters, Seattle's inability to address the most basic needs of its citizens thus placed its world-class status in jeopardy, revealing instead a provincial approach to social problems more worthy of Peoria than Paris.[98] As one *Real Change* reporter concluded, far from undermining the city's effort to draw tourists, shoppers, and investors back downtown, the Reststop would be a "world-class step" for Seattle. "The goal of the Urban Reststop is to provide hygiene services and to maintain the health and vitality of downtown Seattle for at least the next thirty years," she wrote. "It is a small part of the bigger picture, not glitzy or glamorous, but just as significant and important as a symphony hall or dinner theater and even more necessary."[99]

This being said, the political purchase of this strategy of appropriation was, in many ways, quite limited. City officials have long been conditioned by the sober realities of city budgets and limited taxation powers to think about "renewal" and "revitalization" in a particular way, one which frames "urban vitality" largely in economic terms (e.g., the "vitality" of property values or the "health" of retail sales).[100] When it comes to debates over the social and economic benefits of downtown projects and facilities, city officials are similarly accustomed to listening to the downtown business community—a community which not only wields much political influence, but which is also assumed to have expertise in such matters. As a result, the risk LIHI faced in arguing merely that the Reststop would *enhance* the commercial "comeback" of Third Avenue was that such assertions (i.e., "the Reststop is a 'world-class step'") would fall on deaf ears, especially considering that city officials were hearing precisely the opposite from the *de facto* experts on the "vitality of downtown"—the Downtown Seattle Association.

Therefore, to successfully promote the Glen site, LIHI had to do more than simply appropriate the language of revitalization and talk about how business-friendly the Reststop would be. If city officials continued to define "revitalization" from squarely within the dominant pro-growth frame of "healthy" property values, "vigorous" retail sales, and "growing" office rents, the Glen Hotel site likely had little chance of garnering much political support. Yet, if the language of revitalization could be *expanded* and *rearticulated* so that the prevailing image of "urban vitality" in city hall did not, by definition, exclude low-income people, then the Urban Reststop stood a better chance of winning allies in city hall. As a result, slowly, haltingly, in bits and pieces, LIHI and their allies began, over the course of the debate, to articulate a new way of thinking about urban revitalization, one in which a "vital" urban community would be measured by more than upscale retail sales and ever-rising office rents. Within this alternative definition of "revitalization," then, the Urban Reststop could be recast and redefined as an important asset in an *expanded* project of urban renewal and rebirth, rather than as a pernicious incubator of social disorder and urban decay. And if (and this was a big "if") such an alternative view of a "vital" downtown could take hold among enough decision-makers in city government, then LIHI had a fighting chance of seeing their dream of a Glen Hotel Reststop finally realized.

But how did LIHI attempt to create such an alternative discourse of urban vitality? First, LIHI began with a basic political premise: "this city is for everyone, not just for those with the biggest bankrolls."[101] Other supporters echoed this premise in their statements, arguing that "downtown should be for everyone"[102] and not simply reserved for shoppers, tourists, and symphony patrons.[103] As another supporter put it, "downtown is a public area—a place where any law-abiding citizen is allowed and where the homeless tend to congregate because it's amenable to their condition in a variety of ways."[104]

For supporters, the recent flap over hygiene services proved that this basic premise—downtown is for everyone—was under assault. The opponents of the Glen site were trying to re-create downtown as a "playground for the rich."[105] As one *Real Change* reporter quipped, "it seems clear that it is hard to put public toilets downtown because downtown is no longer for the public—that is, for the public who don't have a lot of money."[106] LIHI's supporters took an equally dim view of their opponents' call to "disperse" hygiene services throughout the city. The problem with such talk of "dispersal," according to *Eat the State!* was:

> that the DSA's intent isn't to disperse toilets and showers; it's to disperse the homeless by getting them out of downtown by whatever means possible. The DSA plan makes no sense from a service provider standpoint, but plenty of sense if you believe the rich have exclusive rights to downtown—and to buying off city policy.[107]

In the view of one LIHI staffer, the message of the Glen's opposition is clear. "You're not welcome downtown if you're not a shopper."[108] As one supporter concluded in *The Stranger*, "they're asserting that it's going to hurt their property values simply because poor people are nearby. They want to exclude these people from going downtown. That's not fair. It's certainly not legal, and it's not what Seattle is all about."[109]

Moreover, in the view of the Glen's supporters, this vision of a more inclusive and diverse downtown—one which tolerated, if not encouraged, the residence and patronage of rich and poor alike—was more than a mere pipe dream. In fact, it was a vision rooted in the history of downtown Seattle, a history that, until quite recently, had been characterized by extraordinary class diversity and the longtime residence of low-income individuals and families. As one supporter noted, "Seattle has worked hard to make sure its downtown is for everyone—a place where people regardless of income, age, or race could live, work or play. . . . We are proud of this record."[110] Sometimes discussions of Seattle's past would evoke fond memories of Third Avenue's working-class rooming houses and gathering places (now replaced by skyscrapers and upscale condos), including one consultant who recalled how his elderly uncles would tell stories, play checkers, and imbibe an impressive succession of $1 "steamrollers" just steps away from the current location of the Seattle Symphony. Now, observed this consultant wryly, when developers come in and say "we want to upscale this whole area . . . we want to get rid of 'those people'," he thinks to himself, "'those people' were my uncles!"[111]

For supporters without such a direct connection to downtown's working-class past, however, the most tangible symbol of downtown's social diversity has always been the Pike Place Market, located between the retail core and the waterfront. At the heart of this district, as one consultant described, is of course, the Public Market itself: a festive row of open-air shops, fruit stands, fish markets, and coffeehouses stretching along three cobblestone blocks. At the Market, he explained:

> You'll find tourists . . . going up to who knows what attractions . . . you'll find business people who are walking past in an agitated way, and you'll find maybe a street person or you'll find a street musician . . . playing a saxophone on the corner. And you just get that whole hodgepodge.[112]

For this consultant, the hodgepodge of the Market stands as a symbol for the diversity historically tolerated and even actively cultivated in Seattle's wider downtown. "The Market is really the heart of Seattle," he said, "and I think that that resonates out. I think that's why you find in Seattle such a mix . . . you have a compact area and people mix together. You don't have those wide boulevards that other cities have where people can drive by very quickly in their cars . . . [in Seattle] people are forced to intermingle." Far from being a source of concern, this diverse hodgepodge on downtown is what makes Seattle distinctive, in this consultant's view. "Personally," he said, "I sort of think that's the Seattle story."[113]

Unfortunately, for LIHI's supporters, this ideal of a lively, mixed-use, mixed-class downtown has been under assault for some years and is now mortally threatened by a massive wave of retail redevelopment and residential gentrification. "Consider the scope of downtown," wrote a reporter from *Real Change*:

> what used to be a diverse array of residences, including numerous apartment buildings, low-rent and artistic districts, has been replaced by loads of high-priced condominiums (interspersed with a half-dozen homeless shelters). A mix of retail establishments have been replaced by the likes of Niketown, Planet Hollywood, FAO Schwartz, and two glitzy malls.[114]

As downtown's low-income housing units and the traditional blue-collar gathering places are redeveloped and "revitalized," the celebrated downtown "hodgepodge" that made Seattle distinctive has begun to disappear, perhaps forever. This is a prospect which alarmed many LIHI supporters, who argued, as did one consultant, that Seattle is "in danger of losing its identity" and becoming "just like every other city" in the country. "Every city you go to looks the same," she said. You see "the same kinds of people downtown" with those who don't fit in "pushed to the margins."[115]

Still, all is not lost, argued LIHI's supporters. With some hard work, this dream of a more inclusive downtown can indeed be revived. To this end, the Urban Reststop at the Glen Hotel could play a crucial role in revitalizing the mixed-class, mixed-race hodgepodge that has long distinguished Seattle from "every other city" in America. A clean, well-run, centrally located Urban Reststop could act as a true public space—a space where all kinds of people would mix and where the boundaries of race and class would be transcended in the search for a warm shower or a clean bathroom. Rich or poor, as one LIHI executive quipped, "everyone needs to use toilets,"[116] and the whole intention of locating the Reststop downtown "was to have a place that would not be stigmatized [as a "homeless" facility], but would be a clean, safe refuge for *everyone*."[117] In this way, by placing the Urban Reststop in the heart of the retail core (on one of the busiest pedestrian streets in the city, no less), LIHI hoped to attract users from *all* walks of life—"not just homeless people, but visitors, travelers, bicyclists, and bus riders, anybody stuck inside our lovely downtown retail core with no place to go, and I mean *go*."[118]

Finally, by serving such a wide swath of Seattle's social fabric, LIHI's supporters hoped that a clean, well-run, centrally located Reststop would help counterbalance the seemingly unstoppable momentum toward a class-segregated and stratified downtown. In short, if the Reststop's opponents' message is that "you're not welcome downtown if you're not a shopper,"[119] then the Reststop itself becomes an especially important political symbol in the struggle to preserve the social diversity of downtown. Locating the Reststop near the retail core would show that, despite Seattle's billion-dollar exercise in world-class gentrification, downtown Seattle is indeed *still* "for everyone."[120] And maybe, just maybe, as one supporter mused, a well-run, well-used Urban Reststop could even help to "integrate different parts of the community, to start making people feel comfortable interacting with . . . people that are different from them."[121] Ideally, then, the Reststop might even serve as a "tool to break down xenophobia" on the streets of downtown and preserve the vital and lively hodgepodge that made downtown Seattle distinctive.[122]

In the end, what is revealed in the various discourses deployed by both supporters and opponents of the Glen Hotel Urban Reststop? What does this analysis tell us about the specific visions of the urban good life embedded in each campaign's arguments regarding the future place of homeless services in the

the heart of downtown Seattle? At this point it seems clear that a fundamental symbolic opposition lies at the heart of this discursive struggle over homelessness and gentrification in Seattle. At one end of this semantic divide lie symbols and images relating to "urban revitalization" and "urban vitality" while at the other end lie symbols and images of "urban decay" and "urban decline." The struggle between opponents and supporters, at least on one level, was waged over just *where* the city should place the Urban Reststop along this symbolic divide. Was the Reststop a world-class step for Seattle, a key contributor toward the goal of creating a clean, safe, and revitalized downtown for tourists, investors, and residents? Or would the Reststop become a concentration point for sundry street incivilities, undermining the emergence of a "fragile" and "fledgling" cultural district and sustaining the hold of blight and decay at the corner of Third and Union? If either side could successfully convince city officials to associate the Glen Reststop with a discourse of "revitalization" or, conversely, of "decay" then they would be in a better position to shape the future of Third Avenue.

At another level, however, the struggle between supporters and opponents was not confined merely to the question of whether the Reststop would be defined as an agent of decay or revitalization, but in fact moved haltingly toward a more fundamental political question: *How should "revitalization" be defined in the first place?* What constitutes a "vibrant" and "vital" urban community? And who is included and excluded from this vision of "revitalization"? Embedded within the speech of both supporters and opponents are important answers to these questions. Exploring the various definitions of "urban revitalization" woven into the arguments of opponents and supporters—and the social and political implications of these definitions—will be one of our main tasks in the concluding chapter. But before we can explore these implications, there is still one last chapter of Seattle's hygiene saga to tell.

The Julie Apartments and Bittersweet Compromise

When last we left the story, Seattle City Councilmember Cheryl Chow had resurrected the Glen Hotel site during a January 1997 meeting of her Housing and Human Services committee. Chow's decision to place the Glen site back on the table provided the hygiene combatants one last opportunity to reprise this struggle over how urban vitality would be defined and realized by downtown policy-makers. With a final vote on the Glen site scheduled for three weeks later, on Valentine's Day no less, each side met incessantly with council staff, littered council chambers with faxes and e-mails, and threw rhetorical fire at one another on the pages of the city's major dailies.[123] By February 11, however, there were some initial indications that the arguments of Rick Yoder and the Downtown Seattle Association were beginning to carry the day among Seattle's esteemed councilmembers. *Eat the State!* reported a rumor circulating around city hall that Cheryl Chow and DSA president Kate Joncas had met on several occasions in the week prior to the big council meeting, allegedly working on a deal that would kill the Glen site (yet again).[124] Joncas's newest proposal would transfer the $350,000 in private money previously committed to Rice's "dual alternatives" plan to fund a number of small hygiene centers (some in existing homeless shelters) sprinkled throughout the city—with, of course, the important exception of the downtown retail and financial core. According to *Eat the State!*, Chow was ready to sign off on the deal.[125]

And sign off she did. At the February 14 meeting, Chow jubilantly announced what she called a "win-win" solution to the hygiene debate. In fact, Chow's "win-win" plan was basically a reheated version of the DSA's "dispersed alternatives" proposal, but this time, Chow would split up men's facilities between the First United Methodist Church near Pioneer Square and the St. Regis Hotel in the Denny Regrade and would also locate a women's hygiene center in the Josephinum building, again in the Regrade. "You've made my Valentine's Day the most wonderful Valentine's Day ever," she gushed to the cooperative Methodists, reportedly much relieved to be rid of her position at the center of the hygiene war.[126] Citing the need to allow First United, St. Regis, and the Archdiocesan Housing Authority (who had volunteered to run the Josephinum facility) time to prepare more detailed plans, Chow then moved to put off the council's final vote on hygiene services for at least one more month.[127] It appeared that the Glen site—which had already lost the mayor's support and now had lost the council's support—had finally been taken off the table, this time for good.

At this point, LIHI had to face up to an unattractive reality. Their attempts to rearticulate the meaning of "urban revitalization" had utterly failed to take hold in Seattle's municipal hall. Although some councilmembers were sympathetic to LIHI's argument that a truly "vital" urban community should not, by definition, exclude either low-income people or the services they need to live with dignity, none seemed willing to buck the mayor or the DSA to embrace this expanded vision of "revitalization." With Chow's turnaround, the strategy of rearticulation was, at least for the moment, stymied. LIHI had lost the battle over what "urban vitality" would mean for the "emerging cultural district" at Third and Union.

But this did not mean that LIHI was ready to concede defeat and let Chow's "dispersed alternatives" plan move forward without a fight. From LIHI's perspective, this latest "dispersed alternatives" proposal was as unsatisfactory and objectionable as any of its predecessors. First, Chow's plan, which clustered hygiene facilities to the north and south of the downtown core, represented for LIHI another transparent attempt to exempt the retail core from hosting human services.[128] Beyond this, of all the proposed sites, only the women's site in the Josephinum seemed even remotely likely to actually break ground in the next two years. The nonprofit organizations tagged to run the First United Methodist site and the St. Regis Hotel site had really just promised to "look into" building men's hygiene services, and neither agency had officially applied for city or private funding.[129] In addition, according to *Real Change*, there was some early indication that the First United Methodist Church might even back out of their Valentine's Day commitment entirely. Even the Archdiocesan Housing Authority's proposal for the Josephinum building had some fairly big holes, not the least of which included a complete lack of capital funds to begin construction.[130]

In short, to LIHI, Cheryl Chow's latest "alternatives" seemed speculative at best.[131] In fact, there seemed to be a real danger that none of these "alternatives" would *ever* make it off the drawing table. By mid-April their sinking suspicion that the city might just drop the troublesome issue of hygiene services entirely had morphed into full-blown fear. For weeks, the council had hinted that its April 14 meeting on human services would decide once and for all (yet again) where Seattle would build its long-delayed homeless hygiene centers. But instead of actually approving funds for construction at one or more of Chow's (and the DSA's) alternative sites, the council merely passed a vaguely worded resolution directing the mayor's office to *evaluate* the siting, financing, and operation of hygiene services at a number of locations—including the First United, St. Regis, and Josephinum sites.[132] In essence, the council's April resolution said "Seattle to homeless: we're still looking into it." To be fair, however, the council's resolution did put *one* matter to rest. In an effort to assuage Rick Yoder's nervous dinner theater investors, the assembled councilmembers officially declared the Glen site DOA. "No alternative," the resolution intoned, "shall include showers or laundry at the Glen Hotel."[133]

For LIHI, the city's inability to decide on a suitable alternative for locating hygiene services was simply unacceptable.[134] In two long years, no other sites had managed to move beyond the most preliminary of planning stages, and the city seemed completely satisfied with extending this "evaluation" process indefinitely. Therefore, Sharon Lee (LIHI's executive director) decided in the spring of 1997 to force an endgame in Seattle's hygiene war.[135] But how could they force the city to come to a final decision? What leverage did they have? The answer in April of 1997 was the same as it was in October of 1996—they would play a risky game of "chicken" with the mayor's office and the city council. They still owned the Glen Hotel. They still had the HUD grant for operating funds. All they needed was a one-time grant for construction funds, and they could go forward with the long-delayed Reststop, with or without city approval.[136] Even if they did not actually follow through with this plan, the threat was credible. They could have a hygiene center up and running by the end of the year. This threat, at least, might force the city—now unified in defense of Symphony Hall and Rick Yoder's proposed Wild Ginger project—back to the table for a final showdown.[137]

So immediately after the April 14 council vote, LIHI announced publicly for the first time that, despite the now-official opposition of the *entire* city government (including both the mayor's office and now the city council), they were *still* moving forward with the Glen Hotel Urban Reststop.[138] To replace the city funds originally promised for construction, LIHI claimed to have secured a "bridge loan" from an anonymous donor.[139] With this loan, and with the HUD grant for operating expenses, LIHI promised that they would make the Reststop a reality on Third. Moreover, to increase the pressure on the mayor and city council, LIHI also hinted in many letters that they might try to force the city to release the city grants originally earmarked for the Glen Reststop back in 1994.[140]

Interestingly, in their final attempt to coerce the city into locating the hygiene center *somewhere*—either in the Glen or at a suitable alternative—LIHI found a willing and effective ally in the federal Department of Housing and Urban Development (HUD). For their part, officials at HUD's Seattle office felt the city's decision to kill the Glen site was a blatant cave-in to powerful downtown business interests.[141] Moreover, they were eager to fund hygiene services in downtown Seattle and continued to express confidence in LIHI's ability to run a successful facility at the Glen. For example, one HUD official described LIHI as a "good organization" and noted that LIHI's Glen Hotel hygiene center application had "won a national competition" against hundreds of other nonprofits around the country for one of the agency's grants. Upset with the city's foot-dragging and expressing support for LIHI's call for a final resolution of the issue, HUD officials in Seattle began to pressure the mayor and the city council to work with LIHI to find a quick solution to the city's hygiene dilemma. As one official recalled, HUD basically told the city, "unless you can find . . . an alternative [to the Glen], we will support LIHI and the Glen site."[142]

Together, the pressure applied from LIHI and their newfound allies in HUD had the desired effect. Without access to LIHI's HUD grant, the city would be forced to come up with an additional $1 million in its own budget to fund whatever "dispersed alternatives" eventually made it off the drawing board. And no one in the city was eager to take the blame for losing access to these funds, as one councilmember recalled.[143] To be sure, HUD officials *had* said that they were hypothetically willing to transfer the grant out of the Glen Hotel, but this was on the condition that LIHI *also* approved of the city's plans.[144] As it stood, LIHI was unwilling to simply hand over the HUD grant on the mere promise that the mayor's office would "someday" find a suitable alternative. For LIHI, the deal had to be just right, and the council's vague promise to "evaluate" a number of "dispersed" locations did not even come close to passing muster.[145] Therefore, to prevent LIHI from actually moving forward on the Glen Reststop, and to ensure continued access to the HUD grant, the mayor's office and city council reluctantly came back to the table in the summer of 1997. They would agree to work with LIHI to find a suitable and *viable* alternative to the Glen Hotel site.[146]

So it was during these negotiations during the summer of 1997 that the longtime adversaries—LIHI's Sharon Lee, Deputy Mayor Bruce Brooks, Rick Yoder, and DSA president Kate Joncas—reached a final, uneasy accord. As one LIHI executive recalls, the key moment in this negotiation came when "out of the goodness of our heart," LIHI proposed to once again look for a viable alternative.[147] But this time, there would be no further dickering, no extended "evaluation process." As the executive recalled, "we basically said . . . to the mayor's office, 'okay, look, Bruce, we're happy to go find another site. But if we find another site, you've got to buy into it . . . you have to agree to move [the city's] hygiene center money over.'"[148] As it turned out, it took only a few weeks of searching for LIHI to find a promising alternative—in this case, an unremarkable 1920s-era, five-story apartment building called "the Julie Apartments," located at the corner of Ninth and Stewart amidst a sea of parking lots and warehouses.

To be sure, the Julie Apartments stood on the outer fringe of downtown, two blocks *outside* the Metro Free Ride Zone—a violation of the 1995 settlement agreement. But still, at first blush, the Julie seemed to offer something for everyone at the negotiation table. For LIHI, the Julie's distance from the retail core was offset at least in part by its other crucial feature: in addition to containing more than enough space for a good-sized hygiene center, the Julie *also* contained another forty-seven units of "at risk" low-income housing. By agreeing to nix the Glen site in favor of the Julie, LIHI would therefore kill "two birds with one stone," as one staffer put it. "You can put the hygiene center in, and you can also save low-income housing."[149] For Rick Yoder, Kate Joncas, and other downtown boosters, the Julie had the singular advantage of being located "a polite distance from the Benaroya Symphony Hall and the Seattle Art Museum."[150] With hygiene services exiled to the warehouse district northeast of downtown proper, the "emerging cultural district" on Third Avenue could grow and prosper with the threat of an Urban Reststop just a distant, unpleasant memory. For Bruce Brooks, Norm Rice, and the rest of the mayor's office, the Julie primarily represented an opportunity to put these ugly hygiene wars behind them once and for all.[151]

On November 11, 1997, the longtime combatants made it official—the Julie Apartments would be the location for the city's first stand-alone hygiene center. As part of the deal, the city promised to give LIHI $1 million to buy the Julie, renovate the forty-seven units of housing, and install a half-dozen public showers, laundry machines, and toilets on the ground floor. HUD also came onboard and agreed to extend their grant to the new project, and, for their part, the Downtown Seattle Association forwarded its grant—originally tagged at $350,000 as part of the mayor's dual alternatives proposal but by this time down to $250,000—to LIHI as well.[152]

And so, in the waning months of 1997, over three years after their first public announcement in the lobby of the Glen Hotel, LIHI and their supporters were left with a bittersweet compromise. Although they had been unable to convince the city to think of the Glen Hotel Reststop as a crucial component of a "vital" and diverse urban community, there was still much to celebrate. Most importantly, their decision to play hardball with the city had paid off with some tangible gains for low-income people in Seattle. By threatening to move forward on the Glen with or without city approval, LIHI had forced a reluctant mayor's office back to the table and, as a result, there would be no more time wasted "evaluating" all manner of "dispersed sites." With the selection of the Julie site, the long-delayed homeless hygiene center was now certain to become a reality.[153] Moreover, LIHI still retained control of the Glen Hotel and the thirty-seven units of low-income housing inside, and now the Institute had an opportunity to save another forty-seven units in the upper floors of the Julie. If they had not forced the city and their opponents to make this compromise, these precious low-income units might have been lost to some future developer's wrecking ball.[154] By fighting tooth and nail over the past two years, LIHI had not only managed to build their hygiene center, but they also managed to save eighty-four units of low-income housing in the process.

Still, not everyone in LIHI was enthusiastic about the Julie Apartment compromise. First and foremost, LIHI was forced, in the end, to drop their dream for an Urban Reststop in the heart of downtown, a centrally located place which could serve to transcend class boundaries in the search for a public restroom and a warm shower. As one staffer conceded, LIHI and their supporters knew that the Julie would never live up to the dreams proponents had nurtured for the Glen Hotel.[155] "The Julie's not downtown. Tourists are not going to go to the Julie. Bike commuters are not going to find it convenient," she said. "So it doesn't have [all] that—it will only be a human service and homeless facility." As a result, "some people [among LIHI's supporters] don't feel right about the compromise because [the Julie] is not going be . . . a tool to break down xenophobia."[156] As another longtime Glen supporter noted, the Julie is "a good site and will have a good population to serve, but it's not convenient to the downtown retail area, and there are a tremendous number of people downtown that need a public restroom."[157] So although the Julie would have been a good location for an *additional* hygiene center, it should not have replaced the Glen Hotel. In the end, for some of LIHI's most vocal supporters, the Julie compromise "sends a very poor message" to Seattle's political establishment. "It has the effect of redlining the retail core . . . and says that those with political power and money can unfairly influence issues of significance to the larger community."[158]

Perhaps John Fox of the Seattle Displacement Coalition best summed up the advocacy community's ambivalence. "Quite honestly," he told the *Times*, "I have mixed feelings on this latest [Julie Apartment compromise]. But if they get the money and the cooperation of the city, then I guess I'd set aside my misgivings."[159] Still, the Third and Union area was much more convenient for Seattle's community of downtown low-income and homeless folks, he noted. Third Avenue may indeed become a trendy locale for symphony patrons, tourists, and investors. But, he explained, "before it was a gentrified community, it was a community for low-income people."[160]

Notes

1. August 1, 1996 letter from Norm Rice to Robert Siegel, Seattle City Archives, Jane Noland Subject Files (see methodological appendix for retrieval information).

2. Phone messages. Seattle City Council, Jan Drago's Office Files. See also: September 4, 1996 letter from Sally Clarke to Bruce Brooks, Seattle City Archives, Jane Noland Subject Files.

3. September 6, 1996 memo from Sharon Lee to Urban Reststop Advisory Committee, Low Income Housing Institute Files.

4. The theory, which circulated first as a closely guarded rumor before appearing full-blown in the *Seattle Weekly*, goes something like this: Jack Benaroya, the longtime Seattle real estate magnate who gave $15 million to the Symphony toward the construction of the new concert hall, was livid with the notion of a homeless hygiene center next to "his" concert hall. So, as the rumor alleges, sometime during the summer of 1996, Benaroya gave Norm Rice a call and issued an ultimatum: "If you kill the Glen, I will continue to help fund your campaign for Governor. If you move forward with the Glen, not only will I withdraw my support but I will also encourage other potential donors to jump ship." Seeing the writing on the wall, the theory goes, Rice caved in, and, in the days immediately prior to the all-important Democratic primary, killed his office's support for the Glen site (see Mark Worth, "Who Really Runs Seattle? A Who's Who of the City's Backroom Wheeler-Dealers," *Seattle Weekly*, 12 November 1998. This theory also appeared in numerous interviews with LIHI staff and supporters). Did this late-night call force Rice to kill the Glen Hotel? In my view, probably not. To be sure, Jack Benaroya was indeed upset at the idea that a hygiene center would be located so close to the new Symphony Hall. For instance, in a letter sent to Councilmember Jan Drago and copied to Jack Benaroya, one opponent noted that "Jack and I have been fighting this [the Glen site] for a couple of years now . . . " (10 July 1996 letter from downtown property owner to Norm Rice, Seattle City Council Files, Jan Drago's Office). Furthermore, it is true that BH Music Center (the nonprofit organization which operates Benaroya Hall) was active in the campaign to find an alternative site, even going so far as calling neighbors to convince them to contribute to the DSA grant which eventually turned the city against the Glen (Personal interview, BH Music Center, 8 January 1999). Finally, campaign disclosure forms reveal that Jack Benaroya and his wife indeed gave Norm Rice $2,200 toward his gubernatorial campaign—the highest possible donation under Washington State's campaign finance laws (*1996 Gubernatorial Campaign Contributions: Norman Rice*, Olympia, WA: Washington State Public Disclosure Commission). At the same time, in my view, this "Benaroya did it" theory overstates the developer's ultimate importance in the debate. For one, the Benaroyas donated the bulk

of their money to Rice's campaign back in March 1996, during the Hygiene Services Committee's "search for alternatives," and at that time most observers felt that the Glen site was a dead issue. Of course, Benaroya could have called Rice and threatened to withdraw support for the *general* election campaign in November, but on September 13, Rice lost his primary bid to Gary Locke. This left Rice with two weeks before the September 30 deadline to reverse his alleged promise to Benaroya and throw his support behind the Glen once more—a move which, as we've seen, Rice never made. Moreover, it is equally unclear if Rice would have behaved any differently with or without Benaroya's opposition or involvement. Rice's enthusiasm for high-profile downtown revitalization is the stuff of Seattle legend, and he has always had close ties to the downtown property establishment. By no means was Benaroya the only big-time Seattle developer to contribute to Rice's failed bid for governor. In addition to Benaroya's $2,200, members of the DSA's Board of Trustees collectively gave Rice nearly $25,000. Investors and managers from Pine Street Development (who developed the Rhodes Project) collectively gave Rice nearly $15,000, and the Alhadeff family—who also opposed the Glen site and at one point were even Rick Yoder's partners—contributed $6,600 (see *1996 Gubernatorial Campaign Contributions: Norman Rice*, Olympia, WA: Washington State Public Disclosure Commission). In politics, money does not necessarily buy policy, but it does buy access and empathy. At the very least, it buys you a hearing, and in most cases, it adds significant rhetorical weight to your point of view. Given the importance of such donations in a tightly contested political campaign, it is not outrageous to think that, when push came to shove over the Urban Reststop, Norm Rice would feel the plight of the downtown business community and their opposition to the Glen site with particular force and clarity. In this larger political context, then, it is probably safe to say that Rice was *already* predisposed to listen carefully to the concerns of downtown businesses regarding the Glen Hotel—*with or without* Benaroya's endorsement and his $2,200. Finally, in many ways, the Rice administration had high hopes for the potential spin-off effects of Benaroya Hall, arguing that adding key cultural institutions to the mix of retail and office development would "provide a major infusion of . . . energy" and "encourage great, thriving life in downtown." In this way, as the Rice administration would later admit, the selection of the Marathon Block as the site of the new Symphony Hall forever changed the mayor's thinking about the Glen Hotel hygiene center. No longer a decrepit stretch of downtown real estate, Third Avenue was now being reimagined as a cultural center. In this new context, the administration agreed with merchants that the hygiene center would be "at odds" or "out of place." This act of urban reimagination, perhaps more than anything else, turned the adminstration against the Glen (see especially Joe Mooney, "Hygiene Center Goes Down Drain," *Seattle Post-Intelligencer*, 13 December 1996).

5. Personal interview, Low Income Housing Institute, 11 November 1998.

6. Personal interview, Low Income Housing Institute, 11 November 1998.

7. October 2, 1996 letter from Dan Merkle to Bruce Brooks, Seattle City Archives, Jane Noland Subject Files.

8. Personal interview, Low Income Housing Institute, 11 November 1998.

9. September 26, 1996 letter from Bruce Brooks to Sharon Lee, Seattle City Archives, Jane Noland Subject Files.

10. Personal interview, Low Income Housing Institute, 9 February 1999. Also, Personal interview, Seattle City Council, 7 January 1998.

11. *1996 Annual Report: Urban Reststop at the Glen Hotel* (Seattle: Low Income Housing Institute, October 1996).

12. Bob Redmond, "Third and Long for Hygiene Center: Political Football Continues Downtown," *Real Change,* October 1996.

13. October 2, 1996 letter from Dan Merkle to mayor's office, Seattle City Archives, Jane Noland Subject Files.

14. October 2, 1996 letter from Dan Merkle to mayor's office.

15. Personal interview, Low Income Housing Institute, 20 November 1998.

16. Personal Interview, LIHI supporter, 13 January 1999.

17. Personal interview, LIHI supporter, 13 January 1999. See also, Personal interview, Low Income Housing Institute, 9 February 1999.

18. Personal interview, Low Income Housing Institute, 9 February 1999.

19. Personal interview, Low Income Housing Institute, 9 February 1999.

20. Personal interview, Low Income Housing Institute, 9 February 1999.

21. Personal interview, Low Income Housing Institute, 9 February 1999.

22. Personal interview, Seattle City Council, 7 January 1999.

23. Personal interview, Low Income Housing Institute, 9 February 1999.

24. Personal interview, Low Income Housing Institute, 9 February 1999.

25. Personal interview, Seattle City Council, 7 January 1999.

26. January 7, 1997 memo from Cheryl Chow to Seattle City Council, Seattle City Archives, Jane Noland Subject Files.

27. Linda Keene, "Restroom Protest at Nordstrom—Homeless Advocates Seek Downtown Hygiene Center," *Seattle Times,* 22 January 1997, 1(B).

28. January 8, 1997 memo from Bruce Brooks to Seattle City Council, Seattle City Archives, Jane Noland Subject Files.

29. February 13, 1997 memo from Kate Joncas to Jane Noland, Seattle City Archives, Jane Noland Subject Files.

30. Personal interview, Seattle City Council, 7 January 1999.

31. Personal interview, Seattle City Council, 7 January 1999.

32. Personal interview, Department of Housing and Urban Development, 15 December 1998.

33. Personal interview, Seattle City Council, 7 January 1999.

34. January 8, 1997 memo from Bruce Brooks to Seattle City Council, Seattle City Archives, Jane Noland Subject Files.

35. January 8, 1997 memo from Bruce Brooks to Seattle City Council, Seattle City Archives, Jane Noland Subject Files.

36. Personal interview, Low Income Housing Institute, 20 November 1998.

37. Linda Keene, "Glen Hotel Site Back in Hygiene Center Fray—Shocked Opponents Thought Plan was Dead," *Seattle Times,* 23 January 1997, 3(B).

38. Neil Modie, "Panel Favors Public Toilets at Hotel," *Seattle Post-Intelligencer,* 23 January 1997.

39. Linda Keene, "Glen Hotel Site Back in Hygiene Center Fray."

40. Linda Keene, "Glen Hotel Site Back in Hygiene Center Fray."

41. "Glen Hotel Basement Center of Bitter Battle [editorial]," *Seattle Times,* 9 February 1997.

42. Donald Nelson, "Time to Clean Up Hygiene Center Dispute," *Puget Sound Business Journal,* 31 January 1997.

43. Donald Nelson, "Time to Clean Up the Hygiene Center Dispute," *Puget Sound Business Journal*, 31 January 1997.

44. "Finding the Best Spot for Public Restrooms [editorial]," *Seattle Times*, 8 October 1996.

45. David Gellatly, "Users of Hygiene Center will Threaten Building Tenants," *Seattle Times*, 8 January 1996.

46. James Epes, "No Clean Resolution Yet in Hygiene Center Dispute," *Puget Sound Busines Journal*, 14 June 1996.

47. Mindy Cameron, "Hygiene Center Won't Wash in Climate of Fear, Mistrust," *Seattle Times*, 23 June 1996.

48. Leyla Kokmen, "Sale of Mann Building Near," *Seattle Times*, 10 April 1996.

49. "Finding the Best Spots for Public Restrooms [editorial]."

50. February 12, 1997 letter to Seattle City Council, Jan Drago Office Files.

51. January 23, 1997 e-mail to Seattle City Council, Jan Drago Office Files.

52. Personal interview, Seattle City Councilmember, 15 December 1999.

53. July 18, 1996 letter from B. Keller to Jane Noland, Seattle City Archives, Jane Noland Subject Files.

54. Personal interview, Seattle City Councilmember, 15 December 1998. As the councilmember said, "we've seen two incidents in this city in the last few months. One was a retired firefighter that was shot by a mentally ill man after a Mariner's game. The other one is the bus driver, the Metro bus driver [she is referring to a tragic incident were a disturbed man shot and killed a Metro bus driver, causing the bus to plunge off the side of the Aurora Bridge]. So people are kind of shaken now . . . " The "Metro Bus" incident was also mentioned by another respondent (personal interview, Downtown Property Owner, 3 December 1998). Another respondent referred to the infamous "Swordman" incident where a mentally ill man kept the Seattle Police Department at bay by waving a sword for 11 hours at the corner of Third and Pike (personal interview, Downtown Property Owner, 11 November 1998).

55. Linda Keene and Charles Brown, "New Name, Same Old Fight," *Seattle Times*, 18 June 1996.

56. February 13, 1997 letter from Don Meehan to Seattle City Council, Seattle City Archives, Jane Noland Subject Files.

57. Lewis Kamb, "A Place to Rest: Downtown Merchants and Homeless Hygiene," *The Stranger*, 12 July 1996.

58. Personal interview, Downtown Property Owner, 9 December 1998.

59. Personal interview, Downtown Property Manager, 8 January 1999.

60. Personal interview, Downtown Property Manager, 8 January 1999.

61. Personal interview, Seattle Department of Housing and Human Services, 15 December 1998.

62. Personal interview, Downtown Property Manager, 8 January 1999.

63. Personal interview, Downtown Property Manager, 8 January 1999.

64. All quotes: Personal interview, Downtown Property Manager, 8 January 1999.

65. Personal interview, Seattle City Council Staff, 15 December 1998.

66. This theme came up in a number of interviews. Crowds of homeless would be "intimidating" (Seattle City Council, 15 December 1998). "I mean, they're going to have people lining up around the block, flooding the streets in an area now that is already impacted by . . . the highest amount of 911 calls in Washington state" (Downtown

Property Owner, 11 November 1998). If the Glen site is chosen, hotel employees will continue to tell tourists to "go down Pine Street . . . Don't go down Pike, which is the main entrance to the place . . . because it's such a seedy street" (Downtown Property Owner, 13 November 1998). One city councilmember recalled small business owners in her office weeping openly because "they were just so sad and frustrated that . . . here they've worked all their lives to be able to have a business, and [they had] this fear that their business depended on the walking pedestrian. And if this situation [the Urban Reststop] had people walking one block around just not to have to . . . go past a site they might have perceptions of . . . it goes down to perceptions" (personal interview, City Councilmember, 7 January 1999).

67. Personal interview, Downtown Property Owner, 9 December 1998.

68. Personal interview, Downtown Property Manager, 13 November 1998. Given their belief that the Reststop would inevitably frighten off shoppers, tourists, and symphony patrons, it is perhaps not surprising that opponents also openly ridiculed LIHI's notion that the Urban Reststop could serve as a diverse mixing-place for Seattleites of all social classes—everyone from the homeless to "well-heeled shoppers" and "Moms from Bellevue [and upscale suburb] with kids." *"We* knew," as one opponent said, "that the 'Mom from Bellevue,' the well-heeled shoppers and the rest ain't gonna use it. That's just the way it is. However you feel about it, that's the way it is." Given that, as one opponent said, "people feel comfortable being in places . . . that have like-minded people . . . you know, a normal environment," LIHI's dream of a "mixed-class" facility was said to simply stand outside the boundaries of common sense. As one opponent concluded, to expect that people with "actual functioning things to do downtown" would choose to use the same facilities as the city's homeless would be tantamount to expecting that the laws of physics and nature could be summarily repealed. "To have a homeless guy, who's maybe been on the street for a week . . . to go in and use the same facility as a shopper or a commuter is, is just unrealistic," he said. "I mean, maybe some people find that natural, but it's just not natural" (personal interview, Downtown Property Manager, 13 November 1998).

69. Personal interview, Downtown Property Owner. As one opponent argued, if shoppers and tourists learn to avoid the Reststop for fear of being accosted by its clients, no potential retailer or investor in his or her right mind would sink their hard-earned capital into the block, even with the Symphony Hall located just across the street. "I mean, we were talking to some tenants that, you know, there isn't a chance that they were going to spend good money to lease a storefront with not only the possibility but the . . . probability that there was going to be homeless folks and what have you hanging out on the sidewalk out front" (personal interview, Downtown Property Owner, 9 December 1998).

70. Personal interview, Downtown Property Manager, 13 November 1998.

71. Personal interview, Urban Reststop Advisory Committee, 11 November 1998.

72. Personal interview, Downtown Property Owner, 3 December 1998.

73. John Nelson, "Liberal Bureaucrats at Work," *Seattle Times*, 6 January 1996.

74. January 23, 1997 e-mail from Michael Kann to Seattle City Council, Seattle City Archives, Jane Noland Subject Files.

75. Personal interview, Downtown Property Owner, 11 November 1998.

76. Personal interview, Downtown Property Owner, 3 December 1998.

77. Full quote: "the city has a chance to create a lively entertainment core that would bustle with office workers by day and arts and entertainment patrons by night."

"Music-Theater Complex and the Hygiene Center [editorial]," *Seattle Times*, 13 November 1995.

78. Personal interview, Downtown Property Owner, 3 December 1998. I borrow the phrase "social apartheid" with many thanks to Mike *Davis, City of Quartz: Excavating the Future in Los Angeles* (New York: Verso, 1992).

79. Personal interview, Low Income Housing Institute, 11 November 1998.

80. Jill Curtis, "A Pot to Piss in: Construction on LIHI's Urban Reststop Begins," *Real Change*, February 1999.

81. As John Fox told the *Times*, "what is better, changing clothes and urinating on the street in front of a business, or going into a shower and restroom?" Linda Keene, "Hygiene Center for Homeless has Retailers Hot, and Suing," *Seattle Times*, 4 November 1995, 1(A). Or, as another supporter wrote in a letter to the mayor's office: "The Reststop would give street people a bit of dignity by allowing them to clean their clothes and bodies, and use a bathroom without having to sneak into the restrooms of stores, restaurants, or offices—where they're obviously not wanted." September 27, 1996 letter to Mayor Rice, Low Income Housing Institute Files.

82. David Fahrenthold, "Hygiene Center for Homeless: New Facility to Open in April," *Seattle Times*, 3 August 1998, 1(B).

83. November 5, 1996 letter to Councilmember Jan Drago, Seattle City Archives, Jane Noland Subject Files.

84. Dan Merkle, "Reststop's a World-Class Step for Seattle," *Seattle Times*, 1 July 1996, 5(B).

85. David Fahrenthold, "Hygiene Center for Homeless: New Facility to Open in April."

86. Dan Merkle, "Reststop's a World-Class Step for Seattle," *Seattle Times*, 1 July 1996, 5(B).

87. "Groups Debate Plan for Hygiene Center," *Seattle Times*, 30 May 1996, 2(B).

88. Personal interview, Downtown Property Manager, 8 January 1999.

89. Personal interview, Downtown Property Manager, 13 November 1998.

90. For discussions of the concept of "articulation" and "rearticulation," see Lawrence Grossberg, *We Gotta Get Out of This Place*, chapter 4 (London: Routledge, 1992) and Stuart Hall, "On Postmodernism and Articulation: An Interview," *Journal of Communication Inquiry* 10 (1986): 45-60; Ernesto Laclau and Chantal Moufee, *Hegemony and Socialist Strategy* (London: Verso, 2001).

91. V. N. Volosinov, *Marxism and the Philosophy of Language* (London: Seminar Press, 1973).

92. Consider for a moment the discursive struggles that have taken place over the symbol "black" during the post–Civil Rights era. As Stuart Hall, a British social theorist notes, the political meaning of "black" is not inherent in the sign itself, but rather depends upon its insertion within a particular chain of connotative meanings. It is this discursive context that gives the sign "black" its particular historical "accent" or sociopolitical meaning—an "accent" which can change radically under different social and historical circumstances. In this way, black liberation movements have worked long and hard over the last three decades to detach "black" from its previous context within white supremacist discourse, so that the symbol could be rearticulated with a new set of connotations, including those evoking images of dignity, beauty, and struggle. For more details, see Stuart Hall, "The Rediscovery of 'Ideology': Return of the Repressed in

Media Studies," in *Culture, Society, and the Media,* ed. M Gurevitch et al. (London: Methuen, 1982).

93. September 17, 1996 letter from James McGrath to Norm Rice, Seattle City Archives, Jane Noland Subject Files.

94. Linda Keene, "Hygiene Center for Homeless has Retailers Hot, and Suing," *Seattle Times,* 4 November 1995.

95. September 27, 1996 letter from Roger Thompson to Norm Rice, Seattle City Archives, Jane Noland Subject Files.

96. Dennis MacCoumber, "Homeless Will Come—and They Will Go—With or Without Toilets," *Seattle Times,* 4 April 1997, 5(B).

97. Personal interview, Urban Reststop Advisory Committee, 11 November 1998.

98. Personal interview, Low Income Housing Institute, 20 November 1998.

99. Keoki Kauanoe, "Still Waiting: Red Tape and Politics Stall Downtown Bathroom Project," *Real Change,* February 1997.

100. John Logan and Harvey Molotch, *Urban Fortunes: The Political Economy of Place* (Berkeley, CA: University of California Press, 1987), 66-69.

101. David Bloom, "Urban Living—Change in Hygiene Center Ignores Civic Responsibility," *Seattle Times,* 10 October 1996, 7(B).

102. Personal interview, Low Income Housing Institute, 20 November 1998.

103. Personal interview, Low Income Housing Institute, 20 November 1998.

104. Percy Hilo, "Business Owners Appear Willing to Sacrifice Homeless People to Preserve Bottom Line," *Seattle Times,* 14 November 1995, 5(B).

105. "The Right Questions: Talking Sense About Seattle's Toilets," *Real Change,* December 1996.

106. "The Right Questions."

107. "Money Changes Everything, Again," *Eat the State!* 11 February 1997.

108. Bob Redmond, "'No Comment': Hygiene Center Stalled and Stonewalled," *Real Change,* October 1996.

109. Lewis Kamb, "A Place to Rest," *The Stranger,* 12 July 1996.

110. Anne Fennessy, "City Should Open Facility, Hold Operators Accountable," *Seattle Times,* 30 June 1996.

111. Personal interview, Department of Housing and Urban Development, 15 December 1998.

112. Personal interview, Seattle-King County Convention and Visitors Bureau, 4 February 1999.

113. Personal interview, Seattle-King County Convention and Visitors Bureau, 4 February 1999.

114. "The Right Questions: Talking Sense."

115. Personal interview, Low Income Housing Institute, 20 November 1998. Interestingly, this sense of dissatisfaction with the social consequences of downtown gentrification also registered in the focus groups conducted by proponents of the Rhodes Project back in 1995. See especially the discussion in Chapter 5 and Citzens to Restore Our Retail Core, Focus Group Notes, Seattle City Council, Jan Drago's Office Files.

116. Personal interview, Low Income Housing Institute, 9 February 1999.

117. Ben Jacklet, "Business, as Usual," *The Stranger,* 10-16 October 1996.

118. Ben Jacklet, "Business, as Usual."

119. "The Right Questions."

120. Personal interview, Low Income Housing Institute, 20 November 1998.

121. Personal interview, Urban Reststop Advisory Committee, 11 November 1998.

122. Personal interview, Low Income Housing Institute, 13 November 1998.

123. See especially, Rick Yoder, "Hygiene Center Backers Muddy the Facts," *Seattle Times*, 12 February 1997; Robert Siegel, "Meeting Public Needs at the Glen Hotel," *Seattle Times*, 21 February 1997.

124. "Money Changes Everything, Again," *Eat the State!* 11 February 1997.

125. "Money Changes Everything, Again."

126. Debera Carlton Harrell, "New Homeless Hygiene Plan Proposed," *Seattle Post-Intelligencer*, 15 February 1997.

127. Debera Harrell, "New Homeless Hygiene Plan Proposed."

128. Personal interview, Urban Reststop Advisory Committee, 11 November 1998. See also, Marla Williams, "Hygiene Center to Proceed at Glen Hotel," *Seattle Times*, 15 April 1997.

129. March 27, 1997 letter from First United Methodist to DHHS, City of Seattle, DHHS Office Files. See also 20 May 1997 fax from Kate Joncas to DHHS, Seattle City Council, Jan Drago Office Files.

130. Keoki Kaunoe, "Still Waiting: Red Tape and Politics Stall Downtown Bathroom Project," *Real Change*, February 1997.

131. Personal interview, Low Income Housing Institute, 20 November 1998. This informant called the council's "dispersed alternatives" plan a collection of "little pretend solutions."

132. Seattle City Council Resolution 29559, Seattle City Archives, Legislative Information Service.

133. Seattle City Council Resolution 29559, Seattle City Archives: Legislative Information Services.

134. Personal interviews, Low Income Housing Institute, 9 February 1999; LIHI Supporter, 13 January 1999.

135. Personal interview, Low Income Housing Institute, 9 February 1999.

136. Personal interview, Low Income Housing Institute, See also 31 March 1997 letter from Sharon Lee to Seattle City Council, Seattle City Council, Jan Drago Office Files.

137. Personal interview, Low Income Housing Institute, 9 February 1999. See also, James Bush, "Hotel Rag," *Seattle Weekly*, 23 April 1997.

138. Marla Williams, "Hygiene Center to Proceed at Glen Hotel," *Seattle Times*, 15 April 1997.

139. March 31, 1997 letter from Sharon Lee to Seattle City Council, Seattle City Council, Jan Drago Office Files.

140. March 31, 1997 letter from Sharon Lee to City Council, Seattle City Council, Jan Drago Office Files. And, as was the case back in October 1996, LIHI's complaint seemed to be legitimate. As LIHI reminded the city, the settlement agreement signed by the city "provided that, if a suitable alternative site was not identified by March 15, 1996 and *funded* by September 30, 1996, LIHI would be free to go forward with its project at the Glen Hotel," armed with the city's original construction grants (see James Bush, "Hotel Rag," *Seattle Weekly*, 23 April 1997). Here we are in the spring of 1997, LIHI argued, and a suitable alternative for both men and women has neither been concretely identified nor funded. The city should simply live up to its agreement and re-

lease the funds originally promised to the Glen Hotel. See also, 26 March 1997 letter from Connie Proctor to Bruce Brooks, Seattle City Council, Jan Drago Office Files.

141. Personal interview, Department of Housing and Urban Development, 3 February 1999.

142. Personal interview, Department of Housing and Urban Development, 3 February 1999.

143. Personal interview, Seattle City Council, 7 January 1999.

144. Personal interview, Department of Housing and Urban Development, 3 February 1999.

145. March 31, 1997 letter from Sharon Lee to City Council, Seattle City Council, Jan Drago Office Files.

146. Personal interview, Low Income Housing Institute, 9 February 1999.

147. Personal interview, Low Income Housing Institute, 9 February 1999

148. Personal interview, Low Income Housing Institute, 9 February 1999.

149. Personal interview, Low Income Housing Institute, 9 February 1999.

150. "The Working Homeless [editorial]," *Seattle Times*, 6 August 1998.

151. Personal interview, Low Income Housing Institute, 9 February 1999.

152. Steven Goldsmith, "Search for Homeless Hygiene Center May be Over," *Seattle Post-Intelligencer*, 11 November 1997.

153. Personal interview, Low Income Housing Institute, 9 February 1999.

154. Personal interview, Low Income Housing Institute, 9 February 1999.

155. Personal interview, Low Income Housing Institute, 11 November 1998. As one staffer said, the demise of the Glen Hotel Urban Reststop shows the power of the downtown business establishment in city politics. Even though LIHI owned the Glen Hotel, she said, "we were prevented from fulfilling a dream"—that is, the dream of the multiclass, multiuse Urban Reststop in the heart of the city.

156. Personal interview, Low Income Housing Institute, 11 November 1998.

157. Personal interview, Urban Reststop Advisory Committee, 11 November 1998.

158. Marla Williams, "Hygiene Center to Proceed at Glen Hotel: Group to Go Ahead Despite Council Vote," *Seattle Times*, April 15, 1997.

159. Steven Goldsmith, "Search for Homeless Hygiene Center May be Over."

160. Steven Goldsmith, "Search for Homeless Hygiene Center May be Over."

Chapter 9

Building A City that Truly Lives

There has been something remarkable about the intensity of boom and bust in downtown Seattle since 1970. From the "Boeing Bust" of Northwest legend to the millennial hysteria of the "dot-com" boom, Seattle's civic leaders have vacillated wildly between chest-thumping celebrations about the city's world-class status and frenzied panics over the city's imminent decline. Haunted by fears of decay, Seattle's downtown elites have pursued dreams of vitality and growth with single-minded persistence. This book has chronicled the most recent chapter in their long pursuit of the world-class city: the bust and boom period of the 1990s. During this time, officials and their allies in the Downtown Seattle Association seized upon the strategy of big-ticket, retail-cultural redevelopment—symbolized most profoundly by the Nordstrom/Rhodes Project—as a way to enhance both downtown property values and Seattle's international competitiveness as a center of consumption, tourism, and global trade. By building the spectacle, they would make their world-class dreams come true.

And what a decade it was. After eight frenzied years of downtown redevelopment, Norm Rice would step down in 1998 and claim the revitalization of downtown Seattle as his most important legacy. To be sure, the list of new downtown amenities left in Rice's wake is impressive: two new sports stadiums, a new art museum, a new concert hall, the redevelopment of the retail core, an expanded convention center, and an increase in the number of upscale residents who not only work downtown, but live downtown as well. By the year 2000, Rice administration officials could look back on their tenure in city hall and declare victory. "We had a multi-pronged strategy to try to encourage great, thriving life in downtown, [and] I think you have to say it worked. To be flat bold about it, it worked."[1]

Yet for all the boosterism of city leaders, it is clear that the recent flurry of investment in downtown redevelopment in Seattle and in other U.S. cities has its roots in more than city pride and mayoral ego. As Mayor Paul Schell, Norm Rice's successor, noted, under conditions of rapid globalization (i.e., what some have termed the post-Fordist regime of accumulation), "most major cities have come to depend in one way or another on access to international markets for goods services and capital."[2] The result, discussed in part I, has been the ascendance of a cutthroat international competition between cities for whatever economic growth and investment can be squeezed out of a mobile and fickle multinational marketplace. As Schell continued, "now that people, capital,

[and] technology have become increasingly mobile, the stakes have risen. . . . News of [Seattle's] successes or failures will travel quickly around the world, and we are judged by an increasingly global standard." [3] If Seattle can succeed in this international competition, the city—particularly those highly educated residents well positioned to take advantage of new economic growth—will be rewarded with a disproportionate share of the global economic pie. But if Seattle fails, as boosters often cautioned during the struggles of the 1990s, the city could face a future of decline like that endured by Buffalo, Detroit, and other the infamous notches on the American rust belt.[4]

Facing this competition, Seattle's elites, like those in other cities, have thrown themselves into the task of presenting the kind of "business climate" that can position Seattle favorably in the global scramble for investment, jobs, and international tourism. This book has examined one crucial dimension of this strategy—the effort to cultivate an attractive international "image" through the redevelopment of downtown cityspace—and has documented some of the social and political consequences of Seattle's $1.4 billion commitment to spectacular retail-cultural urban revitalization. The arguments in support of publicly subsidized downtown redevelopment are well-known. Elaborate sports stadiums, concert halls, art museums, convention centers, and downtown department stores are more than morale boosters for existing residents. These amenities draw in free-spending visitors from the suburbs and beyond, generating jobs and much-needed tax revenue for basic services. As downtown becomes a better place to shop and visit, it also becomes a better place to live. If new residents from the suburbs can be enticed back into the city, this would add more middle-class incomes to the city tax base and would also up property tax revenues as city housing markets increase in value. If everything goes according to plan, a vibrant downtown "scene" emerges amidst the playground of newly built retail-cultural amenities, a scene that projects an image of vitality and growth to the global' marketplace. In the end, Seattle would move up the international hierarchy of "places to invest" among multinational corporate decision-makers.

Any one of these claims regarding the fantastic economic benefits that accrue from spectacular retail-cultural redevelopment can be, and have been, contested (i.e., do sports stadiums really pay off in terms of jobs and tourism? Do corporate decision-makers scouting out regions for new investment really care if the city has a world-class art museum? Each one of these questions has a rich debate raging behind it). Yet what cannot be contested is that urban elites around the United States, and particularly in Seattle, have embraced the logic of building the spectacular city chapter and verse. Whatever the merits of the economic analysis, Seattle's city leaders fervently believed that spectacular, public-private, retail-cultural revitalization was necessary to sustain a future of economic prosperity for Seattle residents, business owners, and property-holders. They believed with all their hearts: if you build it, they will come. The shoppers will come; the affluent arts patrons will come; the sports fans will come; the tourists will come; the international investment will come.

This book has therefore explored the social and political consequences of this policy, this faith that building the spectacular city is necessary for the future economic prosperity of the region. In particular, the book has interrogated the explicit claim that *all* of Seattle will benefit from the policy of diverting public resources to build spaces for upscale consumption and leisure. To this end, particularly in part III, I have explored some of the less celebrated dimensions of the city's revitalization strategy, including the explicit attempt to *reassure* potential shoppers and tourists that downtown streets were vibrant and safe places to be, and to *secure* this renaissance from the corrosive effects of street disorder and incivility. In this regard, this book is an attempt to open up larger questions concerning the specific kind of urban experience pro-development leaders are cultivating within Seattle's spectacular downtown, including questions of who is *included* in, or *excluded* from, this emerging vision of downtown cityspace.

In short, this book has been about widening the discussion of the social and political costs and benefits of contemporary urban revitalization. We hear often about the celebrations of the "comeback" of the American city. It is time to count the social and ethical costs as well. To this end, in this final chapter, I will begin by discussing how the sharp discursive distinction urban elites draw between "urban vitality" and "urban decay" works to confine the political imagination, thereby serving the priorities of the powerful downtown business community. My final remarks will discuss the prospects for promoting political values like class equity, democratic dialogue, and social diversity within the contemporary U.S. urban environment.

The Organic City Trope and the Spectacular City

Throughout the myriad struggles waged over revitalization and homelessness in downtown Seattle, the key players would, again and again, speak of "the city" through the binary categories of the organic city trope. For my consultants, the city was a living being—an entity with a life of its own, and therefore, potentially, a death. This was particularly true of downtown business leaders and pro-development city officials, who drew heavily and effectively from the organic city trope to frame their political and rhetorical strategies. During the Pine Street debate, for example, the pro-Nordstrom coalition depicted the retail core as a once-vital but now-ailing patient, teetering on the brink between renewed vigor and accelerating illness. In this application of the trope, Seattle voters were then cast as awaiting physicians poised to administer a life-giving infusion. A vote to open Pine Street to traffic would "pump new life" into the ailing retail core, opening up a future of vitality and health for the city and the region.

Likewise, when confronted with the possibility that a "hygiene center" for Seattle's homeless citizens might be installed across from the future site of Benaroya Hall, downtown business leaders again mobilized the organic city trope. This time, the "life" at stake was not the once-robust retail core, but instead a "long-neglected" and "struggling" stretch of Third Avenue. For the downtown business community, the battle to dislodge the Urban Reststop was a battle to nurture an emerging life—the embryonic "cultural district" anchored around the Seattle Art Museum, the incoming Benaroya Hall, and Rick Yoder's proposed Wild Ginger dinner theater. In this application of the trope, to install homeless services in the midst of this nascent cultural district would therefore be to introduce a concentrated pathogen of urban deviance into the body of the emerging entity. The resulting spread of disorder and deviance would quickly overwhelm the attempts of city leaders to revive this section of Third Avenue, killing the cultural district in its infancy.

Figure 9.1
Binary Oppositions: The Trope of the Organic City

VITALITY	DECAY
Benaroya Hall	Glen Hotel
Emerging Cultural District	Meat Rendering Plant
Lively Entertainment Core[5]	Domain of Crime[6]
Coming Alive	"Kill this Fledgling Area"
Rhodes Project	Westlake Park
Nordstrom	Pine Street Pedestrian Mall
Vibrant Downtown	Wretched Decay
Jazzy Downtown	Ghost Town[7]
Renaissance	Cancer
LIFE	DEATH

The organic city trope is therefore quite adaptable. For downtown boosters, it can be used to mobilize support for public subsidies, to privatize public spaces, and to ensure that zones of the city slated for upscale consumption remain unencumbered by human service facilities servicing low-income communities. At the same time, while morphing strategically to adapt to these divergent political circumstances, certain features of the trope remained constant. Beyond the basic metaphor that imbues urban space with life, the trope further categorizes urban spaces, personae, and experiences within a series of binary oppositions—*life/death, vitality/decay, health/blight, renewal/decline*—with one side of the dichotomy expressing a desire for "life" and "health" and the other articulating a fear of "death" and "decay" (see Figure 9.1). These binary oppositions are as discursively powerful as they are adaptable. The political calculus involved is simple—merely associate your preferred policy with the forces of urban health and your opponents' policies with the forces of blight and decay. Once these associations are formed, the binary logic of the oppositions can exert its force on the urban imagination: *of course* we wish to nurture "life" in the heart of the city, and who wouldn't wish to prevent cityspaces from descending into a spiral of decay and blight? We would never choose death and decay for ourselves, so why would we choose it for our city?

In both the Pine Street and Urban Reststop debates, the discursive power of the organic city trope was further strengthened when pro-development forces invoked the thoroughly mythologized history of American postwar urban decline. Replayed incessantly in television cop dramas and late-night newscasts, the cultural imagery of urban decay—the boarded-up store, the abandoned lot, the aggressive panhandler, the police tape around the crime scene—inspires a potent mix of fear, loathing, and pathos as it conjures up the social and physical wreckage left behind by fifty years of postwar urban abandonment. As we discovered, pro-development forces in Seattle drew often and effectively upon these powerful, almost mythic, images to dramatize the consequences of defying the political priorities of downtown business leaders. Look at other cities that let their downtowns "die," city boosters would inevitably caution. Do you want to see "our city" turn into another "Detroit"? Don't be smug, Seattle. It *can* happen here.

In the end, the organic city trope functioned as a powerful tool in the pro-development coalition's rhetorical utility belt. In the campaign to reopen Pine Street, in the push to enact Mark Sidran's incivility statutes, and in the fight to stop the Urban Reststop, the trope of the organic city functioned effectively, if ideologically: it allowed pro-development forces in each case to present what was in fact a specific social-economic interest (smooth traffic flow, restrictions on the homeless in commercial areas, a "human service free" zone in the retail core) as a universal, civic interest.[8] As argued in chapter 5, the representation of downtown Seattle as an (ailing, fragile, or "still emerging") organism acted as a hegemonic suture, stitching together a cacophony of competing social and political interests under a spurious assertion of a universal civic "good"—the preservation of "health" and "vitality" within the city-body.[9]

To be sure, the trope of the organic city would not be so compelling in the hands of pro-development forces if it did not capture a legitimate desire to nurture urban environments that are diverse, engaging, and economically viable. Who, after all, wants to see their city's retail core gripped by economic stagnation, abandonment, and social disorder? At the same time, to presume that a general desire to nurture economic prosperity and a lively downtown social scene necessarily entails an unqualified endorsement of the priorities of the business community is to presume too much. As always, the devil is in the details. One can generally endorse the idea of building a new downtown concert hall without agreeing that nearby human services must be exiled to an urban warehouse district. Likewise, one can generally endorse the idea of attracting new retailers to downtown without buckling under retailers' demands for tax concessions or for control over adjacent public spaces. But if city officials and the public can be persuaded that the "health" of the downtown entity is at stake, and if the policies of the Downtown Seattle Association can be presented as the only cure for what ails "our city," then the downtown business community can create a hospitable ideological terrain for the realization of their political agenda.

The reality of urban policy-making, however, is that there is no universal interest to pursue. Instead, urban policy emerges out of a complex, muddled dialogue and debate among a constellation of competing social interests. The developer on the twenty-fourth floor of a downtown office tower, the pensioner in the Pioneer Square efficiency, the social worker in the Pike Place Market Medical Clinic, the homeless panhandler standing at the corner of Pike and Third: each of these actual living human beings pursues a variety of overlapping and contradictory interests, some of which will be served by, for example, the passage of antivagrancy laws or the private appropriation of public spaces, while others will not. What was required during these debates over revitalization and homelessness, in short, was a vigorous public discussion among competing social interests about the gains and losses associated with Seattle's long pursuit of world-class status. But, as articulated by Seattle's pro-development coalition, the trope of the organic city neatly supplanted this confrontation of competing and complementary interests, and instead worked to unify the urban polity around a spurious political consensus—the effort to save "our downtown" from a future of urban decay and ill-health.[10] To this end, in the next section, I will attempt to pull open this ideological suture by discussing the social and ethical costs generated by downtown's spectacular renaissance.

Counting the Costs—The Transfer of Public Resources

So what were the social costs generated by this decade-long effort to save downtown Seattle from a future of urban decay? In the first instance, Seattle's pro-development coalition drew upon the organic city trope to justify the transfer of public resources into the hands of some of the wealthiest private actors in the Pacific Northwest. During the Rhodes Project negotiations, for example, the *either/or* logic of the organic city trope operated as both a motive *for* and a tactic *in* the drive to secure public subsidies for downtown redevelopment. Not only did the dramatic discourse regarding the ill-health of downtown provide a powerful motive for the Rice administration to actively search for developers interested in a public-private redevelopment partnership, but, once Jeff Rhodes proposed his ambitious Rhodes Project, the organic trope gave the city's private partners a powerful negotiating tactic in their discussions with city officials over the scope of public involvement.

In retrospect, it seems clear that the sense of urgency felt in city hall over the "health" of downtown in the early 1990s played to the advantage of private-sector negotiators. Within a discursive climate structured by the *vitality/decay* dialectic, Mayor Rice had plenty to lose if the Nordstrom-Rhodes plan fell through. Not only would he face the political ire of a powerful downtown business community, but, given the prevailing assumption within city hall and on the op-ed pages of the city's newspapers that this project represented the last and best chance to "keep downtown alive," Rice risked being blamed for the continued "decay" of downtown if the negotiations with Rhodes and Nordstrom failed. As a result, when Deputy Mayor Bob Watt sat down with Jeff Rhodes and the Nordstrom family, he was ready to deal.

The result was the complex redevelopment agreement that transferred an astonishing $100 million in public resources to some of the wealthiest investors and developers in the city. First, even if the city's decision to pay $73 million for a $50 million parking garage eventually pays off (if parking revenues keep up their late-1990s pace), by issuing $73 million in municipal bonds to build the garage, the city used up nearly one-third of the funds available for long-term, nonvoted debt.[11] These are funds that could have been used for other city projects. Likewise, the $24 million federal "urban blight" loan forwarded to Pine Street Development to help the developers purchase the Frederick & Nelson building could have been devoted to other social priorities as well—if not in Seattle, the perhaps elsewhere in urban America where the need is arguably greater than in Seattle's retail core.

The city's financial concessions to the project of retail-cultural redevelopment did not end with the Rhodes Project, of course. The construction of Benaroya Hall, for example, was made possible with $40 million in municipal bonds—representing yet another dip into the city's trough of long-term, nonvoted debt.[12] In addition, a host of other projects, including the two new sports arenas, the Seattle Art Museum, and the newly expanded Convention Center all included some combination of municipal, state, and federal funding. Taken together these projects represented nearly $700 million in public funds—funds that could have been spent on other social and economic priorities, but were instead funneled into the project of keeping downtown "alive" through retail-cultural redevelopment targeted to upscale shoppers, tourists, and convention-eers.

In addition, the public concessions forwarded to the private sector during the 1990s included more than financial resources. The city's decision (ratified by a public vote) to reroute traffic through the heart of Westlake Park obliterated nearly 40 percent of the park in the interest of improving traffic flow past

Nordstrom's new flagship store. Furthermore, the final agreement between Nordstrom and the city government contained a promise that the city would never again close the street to traffic, so long as any retailer (not just Nordstrom) occupies the Frederick & Nelson building. In other words, the city's promise to keep Pine Street open has now become a commodity that can be "sold" to a future buyer, so long as Nordstrom sells out to another retailer.[13] And finally, the city's eventual decision to withdraw support for the Glen Hotel Urban Reststop represented a concession of a different kind—this time a transfer of decision-making responsibility from public to private hands. As the hygiene center saga suggests, when push came to shove, the city's desire to mollify the downtown business community led officials to reverse themselves and oppose an already-approved and already-permitted Glen Hotel site, leaving the distinct impression that, at least when it comes to the retail core, municipal policy is subject to a veto from the Downtown Seattle Association.

To be fair, it is understandable why Seattle city officials were so willing to make these concessions and transfer these resources. As city officials point out, the municipal budget largely depends upon property and sales taxes, and within these revenue streams, the downtown core looms large (contributing, in one estimate, close to 25 percent of the city's total tax haul, even though downtown represents only 12 percent of the city's geography).[14] Moreover, it is difficult to overestimate the political clout of the downtown business community in municipal affairs, represented most effectively by the ever-present Downtown Seattle Association.[15] Even if the Rice administration was ideologically disposed to defy the redevelopment priorities of downtown developers and retailers, the combined power of pro-business campaign contributions, an aggressively pro-development mainstream media,[16] and the coordinated lobbying campaigns of downtown business leaders would likely blunt or at least moderate such municipal defiance.

But, as it turned out, most of Seattle's public officials in office during the 1990s were by no means ideologically disposed to counter the priorities of the downtown business community. Far from it. Throughout the decade, the mayor's office and a clear majority of the city council were immersed in the binary logic of the organic city trope, and believed sincerely that the quickest path to a world-class future of vitality lay in spectacular retail-cultural redevelopment. Though officials may be faulted for assuming that the benefits of an investment in upscale leisure amenities would "trickle down" to all Seattleites, the sincerity of their beliefs is not in question. Yet, it is also clear that the sense of urgency that gripped pro-growth city officials during the early 1990s—an urgency amplified by their immersion in the categories of the organic city trope—put the public sector at a disadvantage when it came to negotiating the terms of Seattle's downtown redevelopment. Taken together the ideological pressure applied by the organic city trope (*either/or, vitality/decay, life/death*), the political pressure of the Downtown Seattle Association, and the economic pressure of falling tax revenues all conspired to give public negotiators precious little room to maneuver when faced with the tenacious demands of the likes of Jim Nordstrom and Jeff Rhodes. In the end, this amplified sense of urgency allowed private developers and retailers to play "hard to get" and forced municipal players into all manner of public concessions.

Still, would the Rhodes Project negotiations have turned out differently if the mayor's office and the city council had not been gripped within this binary logic and the fear that they might be presiding over the "death" of downtown? In this regard, it should be noted that the transfer of public resources could have been even more dramatic. For instance, the city could have paid Jeff Rhodes his initial asking price of $100 million for the Pacific Place parking garage.[17] Additionally, the city could have paid for the parking garage with no strings attached, but instead they managed to force Rhodes to accept a "no financial risk" clause (which states that the city could force the developers to buy back the garage after twenty years, provided the developers had not filed for bankruptcy in the interim) and a series of design changes that made the project more likely to generate tax revenue for the city.[18] In the context of redevelopment negotiations taking place across urban America, these are significant victories for Seattle's officials. Many cities simply cut a check and demand little in return.

But in my view, the evidence suggests that the city was actually in a fairly strong bargaining position during the 1990s—breathless fears of imminent decay notwithstanding. For example, although Nordstrom continually raised concerns about the financial wisdom of occupying the "crumbling" F&N site, once the deal was struck, and once the Pine Street question was resolved in their favor, the retailer's tune changed dramatically. At a shareholder meeting held just two months after the Pine Street vote, executives bought back nearly $100 million in company stock, and shareholders burst into excited applause when executives officially announced their intention to build the new flagship store.[19] This suggests that the company was more optimistic about the prospects of success in the F&N site than they initially let on, and perhaps did not need to be bribed into the building with subsidies and concessions.

Moreover, despite the strategic mobilization of the organic city trope and the cunning references to the postwar misery of the American rust belt, Seattle is simply not Detroit. Even during the dark days of the early 1990s, the city boasted a strong, if slowly declining, manufacturing base, a well-educated work force, a rising concentration of software and biotechnology firms, and a stunning natural inheritance that includes a deep water seaport. Given this larger economic and geographical context, Seattle has a number of built-in advantages in the global competition for tourists and future capital investment. For this reason, Seattle's city officials were arguably in a strong position to bargain with the private sector when it came to funding downtown projects based on projections of overall urban growth. In other words, while Detroit may need to offer dramatic incentives to build big-ticket projects, Seattle's officials should feel more emboldened to walk away from developers' demands. In any event, what does seem clear is that, their immersion in hyperbolic, binary discourse of the organic city trope—one that presented each policy decision as a choice between *vitality/decay, life/death*—did very little to strengthen the city's hand when it came to negotiating the scope of public involvement in upscale retail-culture redevelopment.

Counting the Costs—A Narrow Vision of Urban Vitality

In the end, Seattle city officials devoted these public resources to the pursuit of a very specific vision of urban vitality. In one sense, the breadth and scope of their vision is remarkable. Politicians and boosters from other cities often focus their redevelopment efforts around a single organizing theme or basic urban strategy. Mayor William Hudnut built an array of athletic training facilities to promote Indianapolis as the "amateur sports capital" of America.[20] Cleveland's city leaders focused on professional sports, building three new sports stadiums in close proximity to create a massive sports-entertainment complex in the heart of downtown. New Orleans's growth strategy has long hinged on promoting the city as a hedonistic playground.[21] New York promotes an image of sophistication and high culture.[22] Orlando trades on family fun. Las Vegas trades on sin.[23] That city leaders are jockeying to present a single, distinct profile to the global marketplace is not surprising—the intense competition for tourism and investment forces city marketers to think in positional terms, to find ways to break through the clutter and promise consumers and investors a unique set of experiences and amenities that cannot be obtained elsewhere.[24]

Yet in Seattle during the 1990s, the pro-development coalition pursued a number of these same strategies *simultaneously*. Like Cleveland and Indianapolis, Washington State officials invested heavily in creating a sports-entertainment district—complete with new bars, restaurants, and even some residential development—around two elaborate new sports arenas constructed almost entirely at taxpayer expense. Like New York, Seattle officials embraced the importance of the arts in the city's larger accumulation strategy, pouring municipal bonds into a nascent cultural district anchored by the Seattle Art Museum and, of course, the new Benaroya Hall. The Rhodes Project reestablished downtown Seattle as the center of the regional retail scene, drawing in crowds of shoppers to mingle both with conventioneers from the convention center and tourists visiting Pike Place Market. By the end of the 1990s, city leaders had turned their attention to downtown's housing market, looking for ways to encourage trendy, upmarket residential development along the waterfront and in neighborhoods immediately adjacent to the downtown core.

This is a bold vision of urban vitality as a "critical mass"[25] of upscale consumption, recreation, and leisure. The hope is that, by assembling this "critical mass" of upscale retail-cultural amenities and concentrating them downtown, city leaders will spark a dynamic chain reaction where suburban shoppers, free-spending conventioneers, regional sports fans, and gawking global tourists jostle together in a bustling, engaging, and provocative urban scene. Once this critical mass of upscale consumption begins to build, city leaders can then use this lively urban scene in their future promotional strategies—in their pamphlets, in their websites, in their pitch-sessions with travel magazine editors and visiting business delegations—to draw in even more tourists, shoppers, sports fans, and, potentially, globe-trotting capital investment. Eventually, the critical mass of retail-cultural amenities generates a self-sustaining cycle of urban economic growth.

For those who can afford to participate fully in this spectacular downtown scene, it can be a grand experience indeed. In the heart of downtown, affluent tourists, white-collar professionals, suburban shoppers, and business travelers are now confronted with a breathtaking array of retail, cultural, and entertainment environments. They can sample the world's cuisines and imbibe an endless diversity of microbrews at the expanding legion of downtown restaurants. They can wander through Nordstrom's flagship store or the airy spaces of Pacific Place and peruse a range of luxury merchandise unavailable anywhere else in the Pacific Northwest. They can catch a play at the Eagles Auditorium, a broadway musical at the Paramount, or a concert at Benaroya Hall. Within this new downtown, crowds of tourists and shoppers are presented with a dramatic spectacle of surfaces, colors, sounds, and styles—all within walking distance, and all available at a price.

Such is the vision of urban vitality promoted within the policies of Seattle's downtown establishment. And, to be sure, there are real pleasures to be found in this conception of "urban vitality as urban spectacle." It is indeed pleasurable to be swept up in the jostling urban crowd, and, although the experiences offered within this new downtown come with a steep price tag, few of us would prefer to live in places that lack spaces devoted to spectacle, fantasy, and play.

Yet, despite the commercial ambition and creativity of elite Seattle's redevelopment strategy, this bold urban vision embraces a very specific, and in many respects, a very limited definition regarding what constitutes a "vital" urban community. In this vision, as Don Mitchell has argued, visitors to Seattle are encouraged to experience downtown space as a theater, within which the "public as audience" basks in "the grandeur of a carefully orchestrated corporate spectacle."[26] The spectacular city thus enacts a particular vision of the urban good life—a vision that promotes and celebrates the pleasures of losing one's self in a breathtaking diversity of commodities, images, services, and experiences unavailable in a typical suburban shopping mall.

In building and securing this new urban spectacle, Seattle's pro-growth establishment simply followed the well-worn advice of the nation's most prominent urban planners and retail analysts. As these urban revitalization consultants now routinely counsel, the surest path to urban vitality lies in creating urban environments where the kinds of activities and amenities offered are painstakingly screened to appeal to the desires of *high-end* consumers. The downtown renaissance, in other words, is a positional good aimed at the upscale market. It has been brought to you by Nordstrom, not Wal-Mart, and the reason for this is straightforward. Downtown retail cannot compete with suburban big box stores like Target for the mass of middle- to low-income consumers for whom the price of commodities is the primary consideration. Upscale consumers, on the other hand, are more likely to be lured downtown with the promise of purchasing commodities of distinction, commodities whose associations with luxury and sophistication allow the affluent to project an image of power and status. And if the excursion to Nordstrom can be combined with some sushi and a concert at Benaroya Hall, then so much the better.

By limiting the attractions offered in downtown to those that will likely appeal to upscale consumers—including such middlebrow but still quite expensive attractions like brewpubs and sporting events—city leaders will be more likely to convince this primary target market that downtown is "the type of place 'respectable' people like themselves tend to frequent . . ."[27] In this way, a vital downtown indeed offers a jazzy diversity of amenities, but it is a diversity that contains some fairly strict limits, lest it disrupt or distract from the overall message to upscale consumers that "this is *your* kind of place." As Don Mitchell concludes, the cultivation of diversity—both in terms of the attractions and amenities built into downtown spaces and the character of the public realm enacted within these spaces—is all well and good, but it is controlled diversity that creates marketable landscapes.[28]

So it can indeed be stimulating and engaging to wander through the streets of downtown surrounded by crowds of shoppers and tourists, all carrying steaming designer coffees and bags of upscale merchandise. Yet, underneath this surface diversity of images and commodities lies a numbing sameness of purpose. Traveling through Seattle's new downtown, one gets the sense that the entire point of downtown space is to grab upscale consumers, turn them upside down, and shake them vigorously until their money falls out.[29] For this reason, activities and uses of space that advance the commercial priorities of powerful downtown retailers and developers are supported vigorously with private and public resources. Activities and uses of urban space that fit uneasily with the priorities of downtown retailers and developers, especially insofar as they seem to disrupt the process of spectacular upscale consumption and recreation, are subject to elimination or increased surveillance and control.[30] Ultimately, the diversity of surfaces and images presented to upscale visitors constitutes a truncated and programmed diversity, within which anything that might distract from the spectacular experience of high-end consumption can be carefully screened out at the behest of Seattle's downtown business community.[31]

Counting the Costs—Social and Spatial Exclusion

If upscale consumers have gained a spectacular new series of consumption and cultural environments, who has shouldered the social costs of this achievement? Who, in other words, has not been invited to celebrate the realization of downtown Seattle's world-class dreams? In the first instance, it is clear that Seattle's community of low-income tenants and residents, both inside and outside of downtown proper, now find themselves largely excluded from any meaningful participation in the spectacular urban experience so laboriously constructed in the city's core. For example, although downtown Seattle has historically been the locus of the city's low-income and SRO (single-room occupancy) housing, the rush of office development in the 1980s and the massive retail-cultural redevelopment of the 1990s has begun to radically transform the class character of downtown's residential population.

According to housing advocates, this explosion of commercial real estate investment has directly led to the demolition or redevelopment of thousands of units of low-income housing in the downtown core, as developers hope to take advantage of downtown's emergence as a center of culture and recreation.[32] But in Seattle, the gentrification of downtown neighborhoods has been driven by more than impersonal market forces. In fact, it has been the explicit goal of the Rice and Schell administrations (1990-2002) to attract more middle-class and upper-income residents to downtown districts.[33] As a result, the neighborhood's long-term and mostly blue-collar residents (including many low-income seniors) have increasingly been displaced by a steady flow of more affluent young professionals looking to move close to downtown's new retail-cultural renaissance.[34] As Neil Smith has argued, any new office or residential development sparked by the redevelopment of downtown has to be located somewhere, and the most profitable route for developers typically involves buying up centrally located, but "underutilized," properties and redeveloping them into a "higher and better" use.[35] This practice often puts low-income housing directly in the path of the developer's wrecking ball, with the ultimate effect of either scattering communities of low-income people across the metropolis or potentially adding more souls to the ranks of the downtown homeless.

For those low-income residents who remain downtown (i.e., the lucky few able to snatch up the city's supply of subsidized downtown housing), they now confront a new downtown landscape that in many respects is simply not meant for them. Though the new Seattle experience may indeed be grand, it comes with a hefty price tag. The new retailers purposefully recruited to occupy downtown spaces offer wares and services targeted to upmarket consumers—so much so that the venerable Bon Marche department store, which once seemed luxurious when surrounded by competitors like JCPenney and Woolworth's, now seems downright proletarian. Furthermore the new cultural amenities located downtown all target a similarly affluent audience. So while many low-income Seattleites might love to catch a play at the ACT, a ball game at Safeco Field, or a concert at Benaroya Hall, the price of admission would make such trips a rare, and perhaps even inaccessible, luxury. If the explicit purpose of downtown space is now to nurture a spectacular urban experience featuring first-class retail, culture, and recreation, it is an experience largely beyond the reach of many, if not most, of the city's citizens.

However, events in Seattle during the 1990s have shown that the *most* unwelcome outsiders within this vision of downtown space are the city's community of homeless citizens. If low-income Seattleites have simply been priced out of downtown cityspace, the downtown homeless have found themselves symbolically and politically "zoned out" of downtown and increasingly subject to calls for their "dispersal" from "revitalizing" but "still fragile" sections of Seattle's metropolis. As discussed in chapter 6, in many respects, the genesis of this call to "disperse" the homeless and their human services out of revitalizing parts of the city lies in civic leaders' embrace of the broken windows theory.[36] Broken windows theory suggests that sparking a downtown "comeback" takes more than simply *building* the amenities and attractions that appeal to "people of the right sort."[37] Instead, middle-class and upscale consumers and tourists must also be *reassured* that downtown streets are once again interesting, vibrant, and most of all, safe places to be. In Seattle, this led to a notable crackdown on any activities that threaten the overall sense of safety and well-being on city streets—especially in the all-important commercial, retail, and cultural districts.

The problem for Seattle's downtown homeless (and the homeless in other cities, I would suspect) is that, because they necessarily must attend to private needs in public, they have become defined as *inherently* "disorderly" and therefore become viewed as an *inherent* threat to the city's vitality.[38] Furthermore, my discursive analysis of the Glen Hotel hygiene center debate in Seattle shows the extent to which the homeless has become, at least within a significant segment of the downtown business community, tightly associated with disturbing images of deviance and disorder. Local property owners would often note how homelessness is, in the final analysis, largely caused by some individual form of deviance—especially alcoholism, drug-addiction, and mental illness ("the crazies," as one city councilmember put it).[39] Thus, any facility specifically targeted to the homeless would inevitably concentrate this deviance and would quickly become a refuge for disorderly behavior, street crime, and drug-dealing. Such a spectacle of concentrated street deviance would also inevitably frighten off the very people the city needs to attract downtown—symphony patrons, suburban shoppers, and free-spending tourists. Within this logic, the homeless in Seattle came to represent, metaphorically, the first "broken window," which, if left "unrepaired," would eventually undermine the "health" and "vitality" of downtown.[40]

The call to fix Seattle's metaphorical broken windows in the interest of "urban vitality" provided a powerful ideological justification for the promotion of social apartheid.[41] Within Seattle's newly "revitalized" cultural and retail districts, the consuming classes are now offered any array of retail and recreation opportunities, all in an urban environment patrolled by private security, cleaned by private street sweepers, and policed by civic leaders who will take steps to protect them from undue exposure to the city's marginalized and poor.[42] As for the city's homeless citizens, because they are defined as inherently disorderly and linked discursively to all manner of social problems and pathologies, they are increasingly an easy target for loud calls to "disperse" them away from downtown streets for the benefit of white-collar workers and upscale shoppers.[43]

In the final analysis, I want to argue that Seattle's decade-long exercise in upscale revitalization has in this way resulted in a significant *narrowing of the public imagination* regarding what constitutes a healthy and vital downtown. As city officials and boosters love to say, it is in *all of our* interests to nurture "great, thriving life" in the heart of the city. And there is some truth to such claims. No one, least of all low-income residents, wishes to see downtown streets marked by abandoned stores, escalating incivility, and violent street crime. Likewise, no one wishes to see the streets evacuated of shoppers, tourists, or white-collar workers. All citizens have an interest in downtown spaces that are alive with economic activity and characterized by civility and order. As a result, policies that promise to restore or maintain order and generate pedestrian activity on city streets are bound to enjoy some measure of popular support.

Still, the problem with Seattle's revitalization effort is that, in the dominant vision, a "healthy" downtown is largely a *one-dimensional* downtown. It is a downtown organized almost wholly around the promotion and consumption of commodities—including especially the consumption of luxury goods, but also cultural commodities like films, concerts, and other artistic performances. Furthermore, it is a downtown tailored precisely to the needs, tastes, and desires of a particular class of shoppers, tourists, and business travelers, and within this one-dimensional downtown "renaissance," anything which seems "at odds" or "ill-suited" to the promotion of upscale consumption and leisure can be quickly redlined out of the retail core and "dispersed" to the fringes of the new downtown experience.[44]

Finally, and perhaps most disturbingly, it appears that the final decision-making authority regarding what "fits in" and what is "ill-suited" to this commodified vision of urban vitality resides less in city hall and more in the offices of the Downtown Seattle Association. Throughout the 1990s, it was the intervention of the downtown business community that was decisive in turning the public sector away from a more expansive notion of urban community and toward the promotion of "renewal by Nordstrom" and "vitality by Symphony." In many respects, during the 1990s, the public sector in Seattle ceded much of its authority regarding what constituted a "healthy" downtown to its allies within the downtown property and retail establishment. This cession of decision-making authority not only represented a failure of public leadership but also laid the groundwork for a future where alternative and potentially more inclusive notions of downtown "vitality" will find it increasingly difficult to gain a political foothold.

Rearticulating Urban Vitality

This one-dimensional vision of urban vitality—a vision in which a series of spectacular consumption environments are presented to upscale "target markets" in an environment policed to minimize unpleasant reminders of poverty and inequality—thoroughly dominated the political imagination in Seattle during the 1990s. And Seattle was by no means alone. There is a poignant moment in one of Sharon Zukin's recent books on redevelopment in New York when she describes a local Brooklyn developer gazing across a canal at an abandoned industrial district. Speaking to a reporter, the developer describes his dream of waterfront promenades lined by high-end apartments, art galleries, boutiques, and gourmet restaurants. As Susan Christopherson notes in her review of Zukin's work, this developer's imagination had been utterly colonized by the only successful model of urban vitality available to him—"the city of privatized commercial space."[45] In short, the concern is not merely that the pursuit of spectacular urban revitalization carries social and economic costs not routinely acknowledged in the pronouncements of downtown boosters, but that, in contemporary urban politics, it is increasingly difficult to imagine urban vitality outside the discursive categories of pro-development urban elites.

It would be tempting to conclude at this point that the organic city trope itself is to blame for this colonization of the urban imagination, that the binary logic of *either/or, vitality/decay, life/death* itself forces the public to view urban health and vitality through the narrow priorities of the downtown business community. Yet, I think this would be a mistake. As the work of urban activist and scholar Jane Jacobs shows, the language of the "living city" can be turned against the plans and priorities of developers and pro-growth officials. Jacobs not only drew on organic metaphors to argue that the cult of postwar "urban renewal"—with its emphasis on "slum clearance," highway construction, and aggressive zoning—actually killed the cities it attempted to "save" (hence the title: *The Death and Life of Great American Cities*), but she and her fellow activists drew on the language of the living city to prevent highway construction from obliterating historic neighborhoods in New York and Toronto.[46] Roberta Brandes Gratz and Norman Mintz similarly deploy organic metaphors in their call to replace authority-driven central planning with what they call "urban husbandry," where city planners work closely with residents to nurture the health of urban spaces. In their application of the organic trope, citizen-planners work with authorities as urban "gardeners," irrigating cityspace with mass transit, selectively thinning out spaces that have been abandoned, and fighting the proliferation of invasive and destructive "weeds" like multilane highways and suburban big box stores.[47]

In other words, the organic city trope is by no means hopelessly tethered to the interests of dominant commercial interests. To speak of the city as a living being is not necessarily to subordinate one's consciousness to the priorities of the downtown business community. In fact, if Lakoff and Johnson are correct and ontological metaphors are fundamental components of human cognition, we may simply be unable to grasp the complexities of urban economic and social life without recourse to the organic city trope.[48] Whatever its limits—including an inability to grasp those dimensions of urban experience that fit only uneasily within biological discourse—the trope has the singular advantage of recasting abstract urban phenomena within terms that emerge out of our concrete experiences as embodied beings. Speaking of the city as a living being is likely here to stay.

The urgent political task ahead, then, is not to jettison the organic city trope, but to recapture it, to rearticulate its key terms in ways that challenge the monopoly powerful commercial interests hold over how "urban vitality" should be defined and pursued.[49] The problem, in this way, is *not* that Seattle's downtown now hosts a Pottery Barn, a Hard Rock Café, and a ballpark with a retractable roof. Spectacle and play are part of any definition of the urban good life, and without rising revenue from sales and property taxes few city anti-poverty programs would survive the municipal budget axe. Instead, the problem is that urban vitality has become in the current political context wholly *equated* with these spaces of upscale consumption, spectacle, and play. It is as if, after securing the spectacular city, civic leaders and even city residents suffer from ideological exhaustion, unable to think of urban vitality in more expansive, inclusive, or noncommercial terms. For this reason, the political task ahead is to exploit what Volosinov called the multiaccentuality of signs like "vitality" and "decay," and to rearticulate these terms within different chains of semiotic association and difference.[50] These two powerful poles of the organic city trope, in other words, need to be detached from their current association with the policy priorities of the downtown business community and rearticulated to a new set of meanings, where our fears of urban decay inspire more than a desire to subsidize value-free development and where urban vitality comes to mean more than expanding retail sales. Easier said than done, to be sure. Yet the result of this process would be the cultivation of an ideological terrain more hospitable for urban policies that promote both economic equity and social comity.

To this end, the political struggle over revitalization and homelessness in Seattle suggests two principles that could guide the articulation of an alternative vision of urban health and vitality. These principles are offered merely to contribute to a dialogue about the values that should shape an inclusive and egalitarian definition of urban vitality. As such a contribution, these principles certainly do not exhaust the alternatives available to those who wish to contest the ideological monopoly that value-free development currently enjoys within contemporary urban politics. Yet at the same time, I think these principles capture not only some of the lessons of Seattle's own struggles with revitalization, but they also address dilemmas that are shared across the American urban landscape, especially as cities struggle to balance the priorities of growth and equity within an increasingly interdependent global economy.

The First Principle: Preserve and Nurture Civic Space

The first principle of an alternative definition of urban vitality asserts that, to borrow a phrase from the Friends of Westlake Park, "there is more to downtown than shopping."[51] Although a prosperous retail core is undoubtedly crucial in the economic health of the city, a more expansive notion of the urban good life depends upon preserving space for activities unrelated to the single-minded pursuit of upscale consumption dollars. In their campaign, the Friends drew voters' attention to the diversity of uses hosted in Westlake Park since its creation, including everything from large political rallies to cultural festivals to the everyday pleasures of walking in a public street without dodging auto traffic. Over the previous six years of the Park's existence, Seattleites had therefore appropriated the Park through this rich diversity of uses, thereby transforming this unremarkable patch of tiled urban space into the city's most important civic space. In other words, through use, the public had invested this urban space with "life," with cultural and political significance. The fear was that, by allowing cars to slice through the center of the park, city officials would leave citizens with insufficient space to conduct a wide variety of activities, including larger-scale political rallies and cultural celebrations—an act that would eventually drain the park, and the larger city, of much of its vitality.

In short, in the Friends' campaign, what makes a city "live" is the way in which collective performance—including especially the performance of democratic and cultural rituals—breathes life into raw physical space, endowing it with collective memories of struggle and celebration. Drawing on the Friends' discourse, the first principle of urban vitality therefore asserts that these urban spaces—spaces which have come to take on collective significance through their appropriation as sites of diverse political struggles, cultural celebration, and mundane daily life—must be preserved and nurtured.

The question is how to proceed. What concepts can guide our attempts to preserve spaces invested with political and cultural significance? For her part, Lyn Hollen Lees argues that the question of preserving these spaces has little to do with the distinction critical scholars often draw between "public and "private" space.[52] First, this distinction between "public" and "private" space most likely means little to urban residents who travel freely between these boundaries without even realizing it. Moreover, the strict classification of urban spaces into (progressive) public and (exclusionary) private categories usually obscures the ways in which "the public" and "the private" have historically been inter-twined.[53] For instance, public parks and squares have for centuries hosted all manner of private commercial activity, while ostensibly private spaces like pubs, churches, and union halls offer gathering places for a public more diverse in many ways than that found within strictly public spaces like government buildings and universities.

What is important, then, is *not* the classification of urban spaces as "public" and "private," but rather an assessment of how particular spaces are used and signified in the process of daily life. The crucial political question then becomes one of *use*. What sorts of activities are sanctioned within a particular space (public or private)? What range of uses does urban space, say, in downtown Seattle, afford? Are there places for consumption, play, and spectacle? Are there spaces for communal celebration and political participation? Are the rules governing the use of these spaces arrived at democratically, or does private ownership and unequal access to economic power confer monopoly control over decisions governing the use of urban space?

In my view, such questions provide a much-needed way to focus attention on what is worth fighting for in the contemporary urban landscape. In other words, the central issue in struggles like that waged over Pine Street is not a battle against privatization *per se*, but rather the need to defend what Lees calls *civic space*. For Lees, civic spaces are defined not by their ownership status (i.e., "public" or "private"), but rather through their use. Civic spaces are spaces, either publicly or privately owned, with a history of hosting particular forms of democratic and cultural practice. They are spaces in which citizenship is asserted through joint participation in the public rituals of democracy and cultural celebration.[54] Although Seattle has many spaces set aside for spectacu-lar consumption, where members of the public are addressed not as citizens but as consumers, the city has few civic spaces defined by their history of hosting the public rituals of democratic practice. And now, with the closure of the Pine Street pedestrian mall, Seattle has less civic space today than in the past.

In this way, the concept of civic space becomes a useful orienting principle. On the one hand, it enables a critique of privatized spaces like shopping malls and corporate plazas, not merely on the grounds of privatization, but rather on the grounds that, in many cases, private control is used to limit access to urban space, to tightly regulate the kinds of activities allowed within urban space, and to exclude democratic participation in decisions that regulate the use of space. Corporate owners of consumption spaces have not been known for their willingness to host political rallies and demonstrations.[55] But these are the kinds of events that, in Lees's view, create the collective memories that breathe life into urban space. For this reason, the extension of retailers' influence over spaces like Pine Street and Westlake Park is to be resisted, if only because corporate owners rarely allow the sorts of uses necessary to endow urban space with civic significance.

Finally, in this way, the concept of civic space allows for a more robust and defensible definition of "urban vitality." For, as Lees argues, civic spaces like Westlake Park are not just "built." They acquire their meaning through their history of facilitating collective political and cultural performances. A living city, in other words, is a city that preserves spaces for civic representation, for the joint enactment of democratic and cultural action. Thus the first principle of urban vitality asserts that the spaces in the city that are most "alive" are those that have been *animated* by historical, political, and cultural performance and struggle. For this reason, the first political task is therefore to preserve the civic spaces already invested with "life" and to carve out more living civic space within an otherwise commercialized and individualistic urban landscape.

The Second Principle: Nurture Democratic Participation in Urban Life

If the first principle focuses attention on the urgent need to preserve space for the collective assertion of political and cultural citizenship, the second principle attempts to reverse the current trajectory toward social homogeneity in districts slated for upscale consumption and leisure. As discussed in part III, city officials and boosters have been quite anxious to reassure tourists, shoppers, and potential businesses that downtown is once again a clean and safe place to visit, spend, and invest. To this end, they have embraced social and spatial policies that cultivate social apartheid in downtown spaces, including the tacit decision to redline human services out of the retail core and the enforcement of antivagrancy laws that expand police authority over the behavior of homeless citizens in commercial districts.

Against this trajectory of social exclusion and homogeneity, urban policy should affirm, in deed as well as in rhetoric, that downtown is indeed "everybody's neighborhood."[56] To this end, the principle of democratic participation recognizes, first of all, that a variety of economic and social groups lay claim to downtown space. To be sure, downtown districts have always served as playgrounds for the rich, and the poor were as unwelcome amidst the spectacle of upscale consumption during the 1920s as they seemingly are today. Yet it is also true that poor and working-class citizens exert their own historical claim on downtown as well. For example, elderly residents in the shrinking number of affordable efficiencies reminisce about a downtown very different than the one being created today.[57] Their downtown was a functioning blue-collar neighborhood, complete with greengrocers, hardware stores, discount shops, and working-class pubs. Seattle was a port and resource city, a city of loggers, fishers, dockworkers, and sailors with a boisterous and irreverent nightlife and a history of labor radicalism (as well as, sadly, anti-immigrant nativism).[58] Even today, the fading outlines of this past—the portion of it not repackaged for touristic consumption—can be observed here and there, in a select few pubs in Pioneer Square, the community aid societies of the international district, and the comparatively robust rates of unionization across the region.

The principle of democratic participation thus begins with the premise that economic power alone (mediated through the rent mechanism) should not determine whose claim on downtown should be recognized as legitimate. Instead, city policy should actively create the conditions within which a broad cross-section of the urban community can exert their sometimes competing, sometimes overlapping claims on the pleasures and opportunities inherent in downtown space. Downtown space, in other words, should be able to meet more than the consumption needs of the affluent. If downtown is to be a playground, it needs to be more than a playground for the rich. If downtown is to be a renewed residential district, it should provide housing opportunities for more than wealthy empty nesters. If downtown is to host world-class cultural amenities, let the definition of "culture" be wide-ranging and let it be affordable and accessible. To pursue urban policies that underwrite economic exclusion would be to embrace a truncated notion of urban vitality—one that substitutes a single-minded calculus of profit for the historically rich jockeying and dialogue between Seattleites from different class positions and ethnic communities who have pursued, and will continue to pursue, their own interests within downtown spaces.

So what are the basic conditions necessary to balance these competing claims on downtown space and to ensure that participation in the opportunities and pleasures of downtown space are distributed democratically? The first condition is public safety. Let there be no confusion on this point. Without a fundamental sense of safety and well-being, no one—rich or poor—will choose to invest their time, spend their money, or pursue their desires in downtown space. The public therefore has a right to expect that certain minimal standards of behavior will be maintained in public spaces. The public has a right to expect that streets, parks, and promenades will be free of disorder, intimidation, and incivility. Mark Sidran was absolutely correct when he noted that low-income people living downtown have the most to loose if public streets and parks become disorderly zones of aggressive panhandling, public drinking, and prostitution.[59] The affluent can always move away, or they can deploy a phalanx of private security guards for protection. However, if disorder escalates on city streets, the poor are stuck. Unable to purchase their escape, low-income families become prisoners in their own homes.

This being said, cracking down on street disorder without a simultaneous commitment to public services gives authorities carte blanche to clear the homeless out of commercial public spaces. The homeless may indeed offend middle-class conceptions of stability and order. Yet it is unfair to punish those who transgress middle-class distinctions between public and private behavior, with jail time in some cases, without providing the means for maintaining these private/public boundaries. The solution is not to push the homeless out of sight. It is to provide the homeless with clean and safe public services such as, for starters, public bathrooms, showers, and laundry facilities. With the construction of the first hygiene center in the Julie Apartments, Seattle has taken an important step in this direction.

Yet this is only a beginning. Long-term solutions would address the fundamental conditions that generate homelessness in the first place—including a renewed commitment to emergency housing, on-demand addiction services, and universal mental health coverage. The goal should be the elimination of forced homelessness itself, for unless the city's most impoverished citizens achieve the basics of private life—a home and enough income for necessities—effective and equal participation in urban public life is impossible. However, until then, there is no *a priori* reason why much-needed homeless services should not be located downtown, even in the retail core. The homeless exert their own claims on downtown space, and this should be respected in policy-making circles.

A second condition for democratic participation in urban life is affordable housing. Contemporary urban policy in Seattle and elsewhere has put renewed emphasis on encouraging residents to move back downtown. But in the absence of a strong commitment to public, subsidized, and affordable housing, this means that the overwhelming majority of these new downtown units will be priced well beyond the means of low-income, working families (see chapter 6 for details on the housing affordability crisis in Seattle and across urban America). If downtown is to be "everybody's neighborhood" in more than rhetoric, and if the competing claims of upscale and working-class communities on downtown space are to be respected, downtown housing must be available regardless of one's class position. Urban policy must therefore recognize that the marketplace cannot be relied upon to provide low-income housing downtown (or anywhere else in the metropolis). Local, state, and federal governments should redouble their efforts to address the affordability crisis, perhaps by expanding existing programs that link approval of upscale housing and retail development with the provision of affordable units.

Next, while there may be "more to downtown than shopping," retail, spectacle, and play should have a prominent role in any progressive vision of urban vitality. For this reason, the principle of democratic participation embraces the role of recreation and leisure in the life of downtown, but at the same time encourages policy-makers and planners to expand the range of recreational, retail, and cultural activities beyond those that merely serve the interests of upscale visitors and shoppers. In the retail sector, this could be achieved in part through a program of subsidies to longtime retailers and merchants who serve clients unlikely to shop at Nordstrom or Williams-Sonoma. It is a simple matter of fair play. If urban policy commits to extending subsidies to upscale national retail chains, then policy-makers should find a way to help locally owned drugstores, hardware stores, and greengrocers (and other merchants who serve downtown's blue-collar community) cope with the inevitable rise in retail rents that accompanies spectacular revitalization.

With regard to culture and recreation, city policy-makers could build upon their already-significant investment in downtown culture—represented by Benaroya Hall and the Seattle Art Museum—by challenging these institutions to place community arts programs, in downtown and elsewhere throughout the city, at the very heart of their organizational mission. There are dedicated artists, musicians, and educators already pursuing this goal within most downtown cultural organizations. A little more help from the city, in coordination with art and music educators in the public schools, would go a long way in expanding the reach of the arts throughout the polity. Other ideas for broadening what "leisure" means in downtown districts could include building more public recreational facilities (pools, parks, playgrounds, bike paths, etc.) available free of charge downtown. In this way, urban policy could ensure that downtown spaces will better the leisure needs of its many constituencies—from upscale tourists to blue-collar pensioners, from free-spending empty nesters to young families on a budget.

Finally, the principle of democratic participation would suggest that the policy-making and city planning apparatus itself must be democratized if these alternative principles of "urban vitality" are to be achieved. In Seattle, many of the important decisions that built and secured the spectacular (if one-dimensional) downtown were made behind closed doors with minimal public discussion. Often, members of the Rice administration met with developers and landowners from the Downtown Seattle Association, crafted a proposal, then presented the already-negotiated deal to the overwhelmingly pro-development city council for an up-or-down vote. To protect the interests of communities who do not own or control downtown space, but who still exert a historical and social claim on downtown, citizens groups need to find a seat at the planning table earlier in the policy-making process. One initial step toward democratization would be to establish a downtown citizens' roundtable that would subject future redevelopment decisions to an "urban community impact" review. Under this process, development proposals would be reviewed to determine whether they enhance (or undermine) both the city's stock of civic space and its obligation to balance competing social claims on downtown space.

At heart, these two principles are motivated by a simple desire for a notion of urban vitality based on fairness and equity. Yet I will concede that they also rest on an additional, contestable, but I think defensible moral claim as well: urban life is at its most "vital" when downtown space serves a broad range of social needs, when downtown provides a lively forum for the pursuit of a wide range of individual dreams and desires, and when the widest possible range of citizens share in the decisions that shape the future of the downtown landscape. By contrast, it is when downtown becomes shaped by the single-minded pursuit of profit that it is drained of its vitality and life.

In the end, it is my hope that these principles can help loosen the tight grip that spectacular retail-cultural redevelopment holds on the contemporary urban imagination. To be sure, contesting the ideological monopoly of one-dimensional urban revitalization will not be easy. Powerful commercial interests, including those assembled in pro-development organizations like the Downtown Seattle Association and the Greater Seattle Chamber of Commerce, have an inherent stake in publicly subsidized, privately controlled, value-free redevelopment. These commercial interests enjoy the kind of institutional legitimacy that comes from decades of speaking on behalf of "our downtown." They are also well-funded, well-organized, and accustomed to having their way within city hall.[60] Contesting their ideological stranglehold over how policymakers define "urban vitality" will therefore require more than articulating principles and visions. It will require a sustained struggle that draws not just on rhetorical resources, but also on whatever financial and organizational resources antipoverty and community advocacy groups can bring to bear. Still, advocates for an alternative vision of urban vitality are not without such resources, and, as the Low Income Housing Institute demonstrated, tenacious struggle can achieve important concessions from powerful interests— concessions that advance the interests of low-income residents with long-standing claims to downtown space.[61] The task ahead is therefore to build on these past achievements and to secure, through both word and deed, an urban future where the desire for economic growth is balanced against the values of social inclusion, economic equity, and democratic dialogue.

Postscript—Globalization and the Battle for Seattle

In the final analysis, neither the benefits nor the costs of the decade-long push to create a world-class Seattle have been distributed equally. In Seattle, as in most cities across the United States, the disparity between rich and poor has accelerated since the 1970s, as the number of family-wage jobs accessible to working-class, high-school-educated people has declined considerably. As these family-wage jobs have disappeared, they have been replaced by either lower-wage service work or high-wage, high-skill professional jobs well beyond the reach of most working-class citizens. The result has been a widening gap in living standards and the creation of *two* Seattles—one prosperous and the subject of countless fawning news stories at the height of the dot-com boom, and the other struggling to make ends meet even during the most favorable economic climate in the history of the Republic.

What can be done to address such expanding inequality on the streets of Seattle, and across urban America? Many critical scholars argue that the struggle for more egalitarian and equitable urban communities will continue to face almost overwhelming challenges in the foreseeable future due to the pressures of contemporary economic globalization and the industrial strategies associated with post-Fordism and flexible accumulation.[62] As we have seen, the pressure on city officials to "do whatever it takes" to present the best possible business climate can be immense. Multinational corporations now have many options regarding where to invest their capital, and so city officials all over the world are striving to find some way to capture their share of this global economic pie. The resulting strategies can run the gamut from promises to keep taxes low (which drains resources away from public services and redistributive programs) to, as we have focused upon, the redevelopment of key urban spaces in the interests of a small elite of tourists, shoppers, and investors (which also drains resources and can lead to the creation of socially homogeneous urban spaces).

Taken together, it would seem that few of these strategies for securing growth and investment benefit low-income people in any meaningful way. Therefore, to truly address the gaping inequality in our contemporary urban communities, we need to address the global context of cutthroat interurban competition for footloose global investment. As long as corporate investors can play one city off another, urban officials will be forced to enact the kinds of economic and social policies that distribute public resources (including access to public spaces) unevenly across the urban economic ladder.

I have few suggestions on how this global interurban competition can be muted or diffused. That is the topic of another book. But I did take some measure of hope from watching the protesters at the 1999 meeting of the World Trade Organization (WTO), held in none other than Seattle, Washington. The main themes of these massive—and largely peaceful—labor and environmental protests were "fair trade *not* free trade" and "if the WTO doesn't work for working families, it doesn't work." In essence, the protesters demanded that international organizations like the WTO should work to raise living and environmental standards for *all* cities and regions, rather than support the oft-cited "race to the bottom" as regions attempt to attract capital by undercutting their own labor and environmental regulations.[63] Although the ultimate influence of this remains unclear, at least for a week the demand for a more equitable world economic order was front and center in the public sphere.

Still, in my view, perhaps the most hopeful (and most poignant) sign of all was that the WTO protesters' Independent Media Center—the place where they sought to spread their message to the mainstream and alternative press—was housed in none other than the Glen Hotel on Third Avenue. And so, in my travels downtown, the Glen Hotel happily continues on not merely as a symbol of an increasingly polarized downtown community, but more importantly as a reminder that, when it comes to the struggle for more social and political equity, one must think of "the global" and "the local" as a fused and indistinguishable whole.

Notes

1. Personal interview, Downtown Task Force, 24 March 1999.

2. Paul Schell, "Letter from Seattle Mayor Paul Schell," *Crossroads: Seattle Trade Development Alliance* 7, no. 3.

3. Paul Schell, "Letter from Seattle Mayor Paul Schell."

4. Bill Stafford and Sam Kaplan, "Greater Seattle's Secrets of the Trade," *The Regionalist* 2, no. 3 (1997): 3.

5. Full quote: "the city has a chance to create a lively entertainment core that would bustle with office workers by day and arts and entertainment patrons by night." For details, see, "Music-Theater Complex and the Hygiene Center," *Seattle Times*, 13 November 1995.

6. Full quote: "[Rick Yoder's proposed redevelopment of the Mann Building is a] daring attempt to 'reclaim land' that has been formerly the domain of crime." February 3, 1997 letter from Rick Yoder to Jan Drago, Seattle City Council, Jan Drago Office Files.

7. When asked to explain why she supported the decision to reroute traffic on Pine Street, one city official described what she saw as a retail core in desperate circumstances. "There were no people [downtown]. There were no pedestrians...the buildings were all vacant. . . . It was just a ghost town there" (personal interview, Seattle City Council, 15 December 1998).

8. By ideology, I mean the practice of mobilizing meanings that reproduce relations of domination. See John Thompson, *Studies in the Theory of Ideology* (Berkeley, CA: University of California Press, 1984).

9. Michelle Barrett, "Ideology, Politics, Hegemony: From Gramsci to Laclau and Mouffe," in *Mapping Ideology*, ed. S. Zizek (New York: Verso, 1994). See also, Ernesto Laclau and Chantal Mouffe, *Hegemony and Socialist Strategy* (London: Verso, 2001).

10. For another discussion of how organic-medical metaphors were used to promote the political aims of developers and retailers, see David Wilson, "Metaphors, Growth Coalitions, and Black Poverty in a U.S. City," *Antipode* 28 (1996): 72-96.

11. Barbara Serrano and Deborah Nelson, "City Overpaid Pine Street Developer," *Seattle Times*, 21 December 1997, 1(A).

12. Melinda Bargreen, "Rice Wants New Concert Hall Downtown," *Seattle Times*, 15 July 1994 3(B).

13. Seattle City Archives, City Ordinance Files.

14. Personal interview, Downtown Task Force, 24 March 1999.

15. Walter Hatch and Joni Balter, "DSA: Seattle's Most Powerful Lobby," *Seattle Times*, 2 April 1989 1(B).

16. For more details on the pro-development coverage offered by the two major dailies in Seattle, see Timothy A. Gibson, "Watch Dog or Lap Dog? Seattle's Local Media and the Politics of Urban Redevelopment" (paper presented at the annual meeting of the Eastern Communication Association, Washington, DC, April 2003).

17. Serrano and Nelson, "City Overpaid Pine Street Developer."

18. Personal interview, Downtown Task Force, 24 March 1999.

19. Sylvia Nogaki, "Nordstrom: Downtown Excitement Building," *Seattle Times*, 17 May 1995.

20. William H. Hudnut, *Cities on the Rebound: A Vision for Urban America* (Washington, D.C.: Urban Land Institute, 1998).

21. Kevin Fox Gotham, "Marketing Mardi Gras: Commodification, Spectacle, and the Political Economy of Tourism in New Orleans," *Urban Studies* 39, no. 10 (2002): 1735-56.

22. Sharon Zukin, *The Cultures of Cities* (New York: Blackwell, 1995). For an insightful discussion of the role of the arts in urban growth strategies, with a focus on how Newark, New Jersey is currently attempting to establish its downtown as part of the "arts scene" in the New York City region, see Elizabeth Strom, "Let's Put on a Show! Performing Arts and Urban Revitalization in Newark, New Jersey," *Journal of Urban Affairs* 21, no. 4 (1999): 423-35.

23. David Gladstone, "Tourism Urbanization in the United States," *Urban Affairs Review* 34 (1998): 3-27. For a more general discussion of tourism and urban revitalization see Susan Fainstein and Dennis Judd, ed., *The Tourist City* (New Haven, CT: Yale University Press, 1999).

24. Kevin Fox Gotham, "Marketing Mardi Gras." See also, Susan Fainstein and Dennis Judd, ed. *The Tourist City* (New Haven, CT: Yale University Press, 1999).

25. The term "critical mass" emerged several times in interviews with pro-development officials and business leaders.

26. D. Crilley, "Megastructures and Urban Change: Aesthetics, Ideology, and Design," in *The Restless Urban Landscape*, ed. P. Knox (Englewood Cliffs, NJ: Prentice Hall, 1993), as cited in Don Mitchell, "The End of Public Space? People's Park, Definitions of the Public, and Democracy," *Annals of the Association of American Geographers* 85, no. 1 (1995): 120.

27. From an Urban Land Institute report on how to revitalize downtown districts. Cited in Mike Davis, *City of Quartz: Excavating the Future in Los Angeles* (New York: Vintage, 1992), 231.

28. Mitchell, "The End of Public Space?" 119. Seattle developers explicitly acknowledged the need to cultivate a sense of social order and control within urban spaces. As Matt Griffin, a co-developer of the Rhodes Project, told the *Puget Sound Business Journal*, building a parking garage within the Pacific Place complex—and then linking the complex to the adjacent Nordstrom store via a skybridge—was an explicit attempt to lure wary suburbanites back into city districts increasingly charged with connotations of disorder and incivility. In this way, the timid suburbanite could drive downtown, park in the garage, cross the skybridge, and never once set foot on a city

street. See Alex Fryer, "Strong-Arming a Retail Rebirth," *Puget Sound Business Journal*, 14-20 July 1995.

29. I first came across this contrast between surface diversity and a more fundamental homogeneity in Susan Christopherson, "The Fortress City: Privatized Spaces, Consumer Citizenship," in *Post-Fordism: A Reader*, ed. A. Amin (Cambridge, UK: Blackwell, 1994). Chrisopherson offers a terrific application of the Marxian concept, "commodity fetishism," to contemporary urban development.

30. Even urban parks are viewed with suspicion, mostly because the city cannot prevent certain individuals (letter-writers refer to drug dealers, panhandlers, gang members, and the homless) from using park space. See 12 December 1994 letter from Mark Houtchens to Seattle City Council, Seattle City Archives, Tom Weeks Subject Files.

31. For more on this point, see Susan Christopherson, "The Fortress City: Privatized Spaces, Consumer Citizenship."

32. Personal interview, Seattle Displacement Coalition, 3 February 1999.

33. Personal interview, Seattle Displacement Coalition, 3 February 1999.

34. Joe Martin, "Belltown Remembers: Seattle's Incredibly Disappearing Poor," *Real Change*, 15 May 2000. The increase in retail rents downtown has also pushed out locally owned retailers, who cannot compete with national chains in the intense bidding for downtown space. This further intensifies the ongoing class transformation of downtown Seattle. See S. Holmes, "Rebirth is Driving Up Rents that Some Shop Owners Cannot Afford," *Seattle Times*, 2 October 1995.

35. Neil Smith, *The New Urban Frontier: Gentrification and the Revanchist City* (London: Routledge, 1996).

36. George Kelling and Catherine Coles, *Fixing Broken Windows: Restoring Order and Reducing Crime in our Communities* (New York: Martin Kessler, 1996).

37. The phrase "people of the right sort" borrowed from David Harvey, *The Condition of Postmodernity* (New York: Blackwell, 1990).

38. Mitchell, "The End of Public Space?" 118.

39. Personal interview, Seattle City Council, 15 December 1998.

40. "Looking for Better Ways to Curb Unruly Street Life," *Seattle Times*, 26 July 1993, 4(B).

41. I use the term "social apartheid," following Mike Davis's use of the term in *City of Quartz* (New York: Vintage, 1992).

42. The Downtown Seattle Association has in recent years transformed the entire downtown core into one large "business improvement district." Within this district, local landowners and businesses pay a "fee" to the DSA. In return, the DSA hires private security guards and street cleaners to supplement city services. See the DSA's latest annual report, *To Champion a Healthy, Vital Downtown Core* for more details.

43. "Dispersal" of human services emerged as an explicit city policy in the wake of the hygiene center wars. Interview, Seattle Department of Housing and Human Services, 15 December 1998.

44. "At odds" was the term used by Donald Nelson in "Time to Clean up Hygiene Center Dispute," *Puget Sound Business Journal*, 31 January 1997. *The Seattle Times* used the term "ill-suited" in their anti-Glen editorial entitled, "Finding the Best Spots for Public Restrooms [editorial]," *Seattle Times*, 8 October 1996. A critique of the policy of "dispersal" can be found in "The Right Questions: Talking Sense About Seattle's Toilets," *Real Change*, December 1996.

45. Susan Christopherson, "The Cultures of Cities," *Journal of the American Planning Association* 62, no. 4 (1996): 533.

46. Jane Jacobs, *The Death and Life of Great American Cities* (New York: Random House, 1961).

47. Roberta Brandes Gratz and Norman Mintz, *Cities Back from the Edge: New Life for Downtown* (New York: John Wiley & Sons, 1998).

48. George Lakoff and Mark Johnson, *Metaphors We Live By* (Chicago: University of Chicago Press, 1981).

49. For a discussion of the concept of "articulation" in critical social thought, see Stuart Hall, "The Rediscovery of Ideology: Return of the Repressed in Media Studies," in *Culture, Society, and the Media*, ed. Gurevitch et al. (London: Methuen, 1982); Lawrence Grossberg, *We Gotta Get Out of This Place: Popular Conservatism and Postmodern Culture* (London: Routledge, 1992); Ernesto Laclau and Chantal Mouffe, *Hegemony and Socialist Strategy* (London: Verso, 2001)

50. V. N. Volosinov, *Marxism and the Philosophy of Language* (New York: Seminar Press, 1973).

51. Rick Aramburu letter to City Council, 29 November 1994, Seattle City Archives, Tom Weeks Subject Files.

52. Lyn Hollen Lees, "Urban Public Space and Imagined Communities in the 1980s and 1990s," *Journal of Urban History* 20 (1994): 443-65.

53. Sharon Zukin, *Landscapes of Power: From Detroit to Disney World* (Berkeley, Calif.: University of California Press, 1991). Peter Jackson, *Maps of Meaning* (London: Unwin Hyman, 1989).

54. Lyn Hollen Lees, "Urban Public Space and Imagined Communities in the 1980s and 1990s."

55. Anastasia Loukaitou-Sideris and Tridib Banerjee, *Urban Design Downtown: Poetics and Politics of Form* (Berkeley, CA: University of California Press, 1998).

56. In their most recent Annual Report, the Downtown Seattle Association adopted "downtown is everybody's neighborhood" as their slogan.

57. Personal interview, Department of Housing and Urban Development, 15 December, April 9, 1999; Personal interview, Elderly Seattle Resident, 8 February 1999.

58. Murray Morgan, *Skid Road: Seattle—Her First 100 years* (New York: Ballantine, 1971).

59. Personal interview, Seattle City Attorney's Office, 9 February 1999.

60. Hatch and Balter, "DSA: Seattle's Most Powerful Lobby." John Thompson argues persuasively on the limits of ideological or discursive struggle. For Thompson, anyone can present a compelling and alternative vision for structuring social relations, and can advocate for this vision persuasively through discursive struggle. But this is merely a first step. Anyone, in other words, can "make meaning." The challenge is "making meaning stick." Powerful interests have the financial and organizational resources to have their political visions "take hold" in state policy. The success of alternative visions depends on the ability of advocates to mobilize extradiscursive financial and organizational resources of their own. See John Thompson, *Studies in the Theory of Ideology* (Berkeley, CA: University of California Press, 1984).

61. Other victories against the forces of value-free development could be mentioned. For a particularly insightful study of one successful struggle to preserve open

space from spectacular redevelopment, see Mark Lowes, *Indy Dreams, Urban Nightmares* (Toronto: University of Toronto Press, 2002).

62. See especially the pessimistic take of Jamie Peck and Adam Tickell, "Searching for a New Institutional Fix: The After-Fordist Crisis and the Global-Local Disorder," in *Post-Fordism: A Reader*, ed. A. Amin (Cambridge, UK: Basil Blackwell, 1994): 280-315. Or, A. Sivanandan, "All That Melts into Air is Solid: The Hokum of New Times," *Race & Class* 31, no. 3 (1989): 1-30.

63. Peck and Tickell, "Searching for a New Institutional Fix," 294. For a compelling description of how unfettered, value-free international trade cultivates a "race to the bottom" regarding labor standards in the athletic shoe industry, see T. Connor and J. Atkinson, "Sweating for Nike: A Report on Labor Conditions in the Sport Shoe Industry," *Community Aid Abroad Briefing Paper*, no. 16 (November 1996).

Methodological Notes

In writing and researching this manuscript, I employed a wide-ranging, qualitative methodological approach that drew primarily upon three sources of data: in-depth interviews, close analyses of mainstream and alternative press reports, and intensive archival research. The first source of data was derived from extensive archival research, conducted at a variety of locations in and around Seattle. Most notably, I was able to access city documents and memoranda regarding the hygiene center and Rhodes Project debates through the city council "subject files" at Seattle City Archives (see endnote for retrieval information).[1] These city council records included citizens' letters to the city council, memoranda and letters sent to the city council from key interest groups (including downtown business leaders and antipoverty nonprofits), and internal government memos, phone messages, and reports. With permission, I also was able to gain access to similar material in the office files of a current city councilmember. These records provided the essential materials I needed to fill in the details of the behind-the-scenes political debates and negotiations between city officials, advocates, and property owners. They also provided another corpus of political speech to include in the analysis of each group's discursive "way of seeing" issues of gentrification and homelessness.

In addition, I accessed the government documents collections at the University of Washington and Western Washington University in order to collect U.S. Census data on poverty, income inequality, and changes in employment patterns in King County and the City of Seattle. Statistics on homelessness and housing affordability were collected largely through the City of Seattle's Department of Housing and Human Services, and through recent reports produced by the Center for Budget and Policy Priorities. These government statistics proved quite helpful in detailing the larger economic context framing the more immediate debates over revitalization and homelessness in Seattle. Taken together, I collected approximately 182 different letters, memos, documents, and reports in my archival research.

During the course of the research, I also conducted twenty-five in-depth interviews, most of which were audiotaped and fully transcribed. Eight interviews were transcribed from hand-written notes when respondents refused to consent to being audiotaped. These interviews ranged between 20 minutes and 120 minutes in length, with the typical interview logging in at around 60 minutes in length. Each interview was conducted using a semistandardized format, where I went in with a predetermined schedule of questions (depending upon whether I was interviewing an advocate, a city official, or a member of the downtown business community), but would allow for unscheduled probes and follow-up questions.

My respondents were recruited purposefully. After familiarizing myself with the debates discussed in this manuscript—particularly by reading press reports about the Rhodes Project and the dispute over the Glen Hotel hygiene center—I was able to discover the key players in these debates, both within the local advocacy and business communities as well as within the city government. As a result, my respondents included many of these key players, including ten members of the downtown business community, seven antipoverty and housing advocates, and eight city officials (both present and recently retired). In the end, the interview data proved to be rich and valuable, particularly in the analysis of the political discourses deployed to both marshal support for and opposition to Seattle's ongoing exercise in downtown revitalization.

Finally, my last source of data was derived from a comprehensive analysis of approximately 350 published press reports concerning downtown Seattle's decade-long project of urban revitalization, the debates over the use of public subsidies in the Rhodes Project, and the bitter disputes over the proposed Glen Hotel hygiene center. By far, the majority of these reports came from the two major daily newspapers in Seattle—the *Seattle Post-Intelligencer* and the *Seattle Times*. For the most part, these mainstream press reports were accessed via full-text computerized searches conducted in the University of Washington and Western Washington University libraries. However, some reports were clipped from original copies of these major dailies, and I received other reports from accommodating friends and family members.

Although the *Times* and *P-I* formed the most important source of articles, I also collected a number of articles from the weekly business newspaper in Seattle, the *Puget Sound Business Journal.* In addition, I managed to collect close to forty articles on the politics of downtown gentrification and homelessness from Seattle's vibrant alternative press, including especially *The Stranger, Seattle Weekly, Eat the State!, Washington Free Press,* and *Real Change,* a weekly paper run by Seattle's homeless community (which provided perhaps the most insightful coverage of downtown issues and debates). As with the archival documents, the press reports provided an important source of historical data, which enabled me to fill in the details of the debates over revitalization and homelessness detailed in the pages below. At the same time, the press reports—and particularly the verbatim quotes of key participants included in the reports—formed another source of discursive data, from which I could infer how particular social groups were "making sense" of the debates and the larger project of urban revitalization in downtown Seattle.

These three sources of data formed the body of evidence from which my overall analysis is derived. In other words, the historical and economic context of contemporary urban redevelopment in Seattle (and its political and social fallout) is pieced together largely from information gleaned from archived documents, press reports, and firsthand accounts provided by key players in Seattle's political scene. The interpretations I offer of the political discourses woven into the speech of city officials, downtown boosters, and antipoverty advocates were derived inductively, using the interpretive tools of qualitative discourse analysis (as elaborated within cultural studies, cultural anthropology, and qualitative approaches to sociological research).

In this approach to qualitative discourse analysis, the patterns of symbols and meanings expressed by respondents are treated as potential evidence for a cultural system of meaning that provides individuals with a particular way of understanding themselves and their social world.[2] In short, as James Anderson writes, qualitative discourse analysis begins with the premise that the causes of human behavior are not in objectified attributes that can be measured in surveys and tabulated in charts. Instead, human behavior is guided and patterned by the meanings that are created in communities and held by individuals.[3] In order to come to grips with these cultural systems of meaning, then, analysts must at some point immerse themselves within the discourse generated by their participants. We must, as Clifford Christians and James W. Carey write, "study the human spirit as expressed through symbolic imagery," and, in the qualitative tradition, this is most productively accomplished by collecting and analyzing actual instances of discourse recorded through fieldwork, in-depth interviews, and detailed archival research.[4]

Furthermore, in my own work, I attempt to marry this largely anthropological approach to discourse analysis with the theoretical commitments of critical/cultural studies. This is a move that could be construed as controversial among some within the anthropological or ethnographic tradition who view the task of analysis to end with the explication of the "participants' points of view"—without attempting to discuss the political *implications* of these cultural systems of meaning. In critical/cultural studies, however, the analyst is theoretically challenged to explore the links between the cultural discourses as expressed by one's respondents and the social, political, and economic forces at play within their communities and within the wider social formation. In short, as Stuart Hall has argued, the meanings our respondents use to grasp and understand their social realities are not divorced from the wider economic and political relations which animate a particular social formation. Cultural systems of meaning have their origins within (especially in the case of the United States) a complex social totality, riven by political struggles over the distribution of economic and cultural resources and too often characterized by relations of subordination and domination. For that reason, it is important to recognize that cultural systems of meaning may well work in an ideological manner in certain contexts to reinforce dominant social relations.[5]

While these historically based contradictions and cleavages within the social formation may not have an immediate bearing upon *every* question asked
by scholars of discourse and communication, to *refuse* to explore the potential
relationship between a particular discourse and the wider economic and political context seems, in the critical tradition, quite counterproductive and limiting. And if the analysis of the wider social-historical context of discursive for-
mations (as well as the implications of participants' points of view on relevant
social struggles and relations of power) is, within a critical/cultural studies perspective, actively encouraged, it is, in my view, *required* in the study of overtly
political disputes, such as the urban struggles analyzed in this manuscript.

Following this critical/cultural approach, the discourse analyses included
in this manuscript focus primarily on the various political arguments expressed
within two debates over the future social and physical landscape of downtown
Seattle: (1) the Rhodes Project and the larger redevelopment of the retail core,
and (2) the two-year dispute over a proposal to locate homeless hygiene services
in the retail core, adjacent to the new downtown Symphony Hall. To conduct
this analysis, I first compiled the interview transcripts, press reports, and letters
from Seattle City Archives. This material was then organized, coded, and categorized with a focus on inferring the discursive themes encoded within the
speech of the participants—particularly those themes relating to: (1) the various
political arguments forwarded by participants in these two debates, and (2) the
various discursive strategies and rhetorical devices deployed to promote these
arguments in the public sphere, including especially the participants' metaphors, images, and narratives concerning what "urban future" awaits Seattleites
should the participants' preferred policy solution be adopted or rejected.

More specifically, the interview transcripts, press reports, and archival data
were initially scanned, organized, and categorized using an "open coding"
process adapted from the pioneering grounded theory work of Strauss and Cor-
bin.[6] In this initial stage of the analysis, I began by examining each utterance
that appeared in interviews, letters, and press reports, looking for instances of
discourse that in some way addressed these two debates. During this examination, I attached a "label" or "code" to each utterance that seemed to describe the
meaning of the utterance. For the most part, the language of the participants
themselves guided the development of these category labels. So, for example,
when analyzing the discourse of those supporting the reopening of Pine Street
to auto traffic, I encountered utterances that I labeled as "downtown on the
brink" and "no vote=decay." Conversely, when pouring over the discourse of
those who wished to protect Westlake Park, I encountered utterances that I labeled as "Westlake=civic space," and "versus 'special interests.'"

Eventually, in the analysis of both debates, I derived a multitude of categories from this process of coding and labeling. Some of these categories were
quite thin, indicating the utterances contained in this category were most likely
idiosyncratic in some way (and therefore not a candidate for closer analysis).

But a number of these categories were *thick* with quotes and utterances, approaching the saturation point described by qualitative research texts (i.e., the point at which further coding adds nothing new to the analysis of the category). This indicated the potential discovery of a more central *theme* or *pattern* within the discourse of the various protagonists in these two debates. My discourse analysis of these two political debates is therefore based upon those themes that reached this saturation point. And by organizing, comparing, and contrasting these thickly supported discursive patterns, I was eventually able to describe both the general logic of the participants' arguments (i.e., the claims each group made and how these claims held together to present a coherent way of seeing the issue in dispute) as well as the discursive imagery they used to dramatize their perspectives.

The discourse analysis presented in the conclusion was derived from one such pattern that emerged from this "open coding" process. When pouring over this discourse generated by developers, pro-business groups, and city officials, I discovered that many of these participants would use a biological metaphor when discussing these debates over the use of urban space. In short, they would speak of the city as if it were a biological being, as if it had a "life" and perhaps even a "death." My theoretical training in cultural studies has taught me to pay close attention to the use of such tropes in everyday speech. Lakoff and Johnson, for instance, have long argued that human linguistic systems are fundamentally metaphorical in nature, allowing us to grasp abstract concepts (such as urban change) through the lens of concrete experiences (such as our experiences as biological beings).[7] Indeed, as Shearing and Ericson have written, verbal tropes (such as metaphors and analogies) "create a world by permitting it to be seen and experienced in new ways which, once brought to life, persist."[8] Guided by this theoretical perspective, the repeated appearance of this biological metaphor in my data was hard to miss, and even more difficult to ignore. The analysis in the conclusion therefore reports my attempt to explore this metaphor about urban change, especially the symbols (i.e., terms/words) associated with "healthy" cities and, conversely, "decayed" cities.

In summary, by immersing myself in this corpus of discursive data, I would ask questions such as: How were the participants talking about these issues? What kinds of language—metaphors, images, narratives, for example—did they use to both express their political perspectives and to promote their adoption within the public sphere? And finally, what is the underlying vision of "the urban good life" invoked in their statements, and who, if anyone, seems to be included in (or excluded from) this vision? The main arguments and discursive strategies employed by both proponents and opponents of publicly subsidized, world-class redevelopment in downtown Seattle are reported in chapter 5 (Rhodes Project debate) and chapter 8 (hygiene center debate). The political implications of these discourses—with a particular focus on the discourses of Seattle's pro-development elite—are discussed in detail in the conclusion.

Notes

1. For the debate over Pine Street, I accessed the following files: (1) Sue Donaldson Subject Files (4623-02, boxes 20-21, folders 3-11); (2) Tom Weeks Subject Files (4691-02, box 26, folders 5-6 and box 21, folder 13); (3) Jan Drago Subject Files (4624-02, box 20, folders 1-3), and (4) Jane Noland Subject Files (4663-02, box 55, folders 10-11, and box 56, folders 1-3). For the debate over the Glen Hotel hygiene center, I accessed the following files: (1) Jane Noland Subject Files (4663-02, box 108, folders 11-14), and (2) Jan Drago's Office Files (two folders of material on both debates that Ms. Drago graciously lent me from her own office). Also, a note on Seattle's Department of Housing and Human Services: in 1999, this agency was split in two. As of 2003, the Office of Housing collects statistics on low-income housing issues, and the Human Services Department coordinates city antipoverty and homeless services.

2. Clifford Geertz, *The Interpretation of Cultures* (New York: Basic Books, 1973). For other classic treatments of an ethnographic approach to discourse analysis—sometimes called the "ethnography of communication model"—see Dell Hymes, "The Ethnography of Speaking." *Anthropology and Human Behavior*, ed. T. Gladwin and W. C. Sturtevant (Washington, D.C.: Anthropological Society of Washington, 1962); Clifford Geertz, "From the Native's Point of View: On the Nature of Anthropological Understanding," in *Meaning in Anthropology*, ed. K. Basso and H. Selby (Albuquerque, NM: University of New Mexico Press, 1976); Gerry Philipsen, *Speaking Culturally: Explorations in Social Communication* (Albany, NY: SUNY Press, 1992); Donal Carbaugh, *Situating Selves: The Communication of Social Identities in American Scenes* (Albany, NY: SUNY Press, 1996).

3. James Anderson, *Communication Research: Issues and Methods* (New York: McGraw-Hill, 1987): 244-45.

4. Clifford Christians and James W. Carey, "The Logic and Aims of Qualitative Research," in *Research Methods in Mass Communication*, ed. Guido Stempel and Bruce Westley (Englewood Cliffs, NJ: Prentice Hall, 1981).

5. See Stuart Hall, "Gramsci's Relevance for the Study of Race and Ethnicity," *Journal of Communication Inquiry* 10, no. 2 (Summer 1986), and Stuart Hall, "Cultural Studies and the Centre: Some Problems and Problematics," in *Culture, Media, Language: Working Papers in Cultural Studies, 1972-1979*, ed. S. Hall, D. Hobson, A. Lowe, and P. Willis (London: Hutchinson, 1980); Janice Radway, "Identifying Ideological Seams: Mass Culture, Analytical Method, and Political Practice," *Communication* 9 (1986): 93-125. For a classic example of critical ethnography, see Paul Willis, *Learning to Labour: How Working Class Kids Get Working Class Jobs* (New York: Columbia University Press, 1981).

6. As adapted by Sandra Kirby and Kate McKenna, *Experience, Research, Social Change: Methods from the Margins* (Toronto: Garamond Press, 1987).

7. George Lakoff and Mark Johnson, *Metaphors We Live By* (Chicago: University of Chicago Press, 1981), 115.

8. Clifford Shearing and Richard V. Ericson, "Culture as Figurative Action," *British Journal of Sociology* 42 (December 1991): 494.

Bibliography

Abbott, Carl. *The Metropolitan Frontier: Cities in the Modern American West.* Tucson, AZ: The University of Arizona Press, 1993.
―――. "Regional City and Network City: Portland and Seattle in the Twentieth Century." *Western Historical Quarterly* (August 1992): 293-319.
Alkire, John. "Pine Street Tied to City's Future." *Seattle Times,* 4 February 1995.
Althusser, Louis. *Lenin and Philosophy and Other Essays.* London: New Left Review, 1971.
Amin, Ash. "Post-Fordism: Models, Fantasies, and Phantoms of Transition." In *Post-Fordism: A Reader,* edited by Ash Amin. Oxford: Blackwell, 1994.
Amin, Ash, and Kevin Robins. "The Re-emergence of Regional Economies? The Mythical Geography of Flexible Accumulation." *Environment and Planning D: Society and Space* 8 (1990): 7-34.
"An Important Milestone for Downtown Seattle [editorial]." *Seattle Times,* 4 July 1995.
Anderson, James. *Communication Research: Issues and Methods.* New York: McGraw-Hill, 1987.
Angelos, C. "Sidran Plan Recommended to City Council." *Seattle Times,* 24 Sept. 1993.
Angelos, C., and D. Birkland. "Homeless Take to the Streets: Protestors, ACLU Decry New City Laws Meant to Curb Public Drinking, Begging." *Seattle Times,* 9 November 1993.
Aramburu, J. Richard. "Downtown Development: Obvious Public Subsidy." *Seattle Times,* 21 February 1995.
Aramburu, J. Richard, Daniel Norton, Jan Drago, Kay Bullitt, and Ron Judd. "Should Pine Street Be Re-Opened? Pro/Con." *Seattle Times,* 5 March 1995.
Bargreen, Melinda. "Will Seattle Take the Ball and Go the Distance?" *Seattle Times,* 16 May 1993.
Bargreen, Melinda. "Symphony Site: Getting Close." *Seattle Times,* 15 June 1994.
―――. "Symphony Could Bring Oomph to Downtown: Marathon Property Hits Right Chord with Panel, not Center Site." *Seattle Times,* 8 July 1994.
―――. "The Making of a Great Place for Music." *Seattle Times,* 1 September 1998.
Bargreen, Melinda, and Peter Lewis. "Rice Wants New Concert Hall Downtown." *Seattle Times,* 15 July 1994.
Barrett, Michelle. "Ideology, Politics, Hegemony: From Gramsci to Laclau and Mouffe." In *Mapping Ideology,* edited by S. Zizek. New York: Verso, 1994.
Berman, Marshall. *All That is Solid Melts into Air: The Experience of Modernity.* New York: Penguin, 1982.

Bloom, David. "Urban Living—Change in Hygiene Center Ignores Civic Responsibility." *Seattle Times,* 10 October 1996.

Bluestone, Barry, and Bennett Harrison. *The Deindustrialization of America: Plant Closings, Community Abandonment, and the Dismantling of Basic Industry.* New York: Basic Books, 1982.

Boren, Rebecca. "Pine Street Debate Opens Old Wounds." *Seattle Post-Intelligencer,* 2 December 1994.

Bourdieu, Pierre. *Distinction: A Social Critique of the Judgement of Taste.* Cambridge, MA: Harvard University Press, 1984.

"Bright Lights, Empty Space." *Seattle Times,* 10 July 1992.

Brown, Edward. "Seattle." *Fortune,* 24 November 1997.

Bryant, H. "Seattle in Transition: Manners and Morals." *Seattle Post-Intelligencer,* 27 January 1976.

Buck, R. "F&N Plan is Called Tax Boon." *Seattle Times,* 19 August 1994.

Budd, Mike, Steve Craig, and Clay Steinman. *Consuming Environments: Television and Commercial Culture.* New Brunswick, NJ: Rutgers University Press.

"Build the Concert Hall in Downtown Seattle [editorial]." *Seattle Times,* 17 June 1994.

Bush, James. "Hotel Rag." *Seattle Weekly,* 23 April 1997.

Byrnes, Susan. "Criminal Probe Clears Rice over HUD Loan: But Application Process Under Question." *Seattle Times,* 30 July 1997.

Cameron, Mindy. "Hygiene Center Won't Wash in Climate of Fear, Mistrust." *Seattle Times,* 23 June 1996.

Carbaugh, Donal. *Situating Selves: The Communication of Social Identities in American Scenes.* Albany, NY: SUNY Press, 1996.

Carlson, John. "City Needs Homeless Laws That'll Send Them Packing." *Seattle Times,* 17 August 1993.

Christians, Clifford, and James W. Carey. "The Logic and Aims of Qualitative Research." In *Research Methods in Mass Communication,* edited by Guido Stempel and Bruce Westley. Englewood Cliffs, NJ: Prentice Hall, 1981.

Christopherson, Susan. "The Fortress City: Privatized Spaces, Consumer Citizenship." In *Post-Fordism: A Reader,* edited by Ash Amin. Oxford: Blackwell, 1994.

———. "The Cultures of Cities." *Journal of the American Planning Association* 62, no. 4 (1996): 533.

"City Hygiene Plan Deserves Support [editorial]." *Seattle Post-Intelligencer,* 29 March 1997.

"City of Broad Sidewalks [editorial]." *Seattle Times,* 21 May 1994.

City of Seattle, Department of Community Development. *Seattle Downtown Housing, 1983.* Seattle: City of Seattle, 1984.

City of Seattle, Department of Housing and Human Services. *1999-2000 Consolidated Plan for Housing and Community Development.* Seattle: City of Seattle, 1999.

"City's Pine Street Deal Violated Public Trust [editorial]." *Seattle Times,* 23 December 1997.

"Closing Pine Street: On to the Ballot Box [editorial]." *Seattle Times,* 24 January 1995.

Coates, Daniel, and Brad Humphries. "The Growth Effects of Sports Franchises, Stadia, and Arenas." *Journal of Policy Analysis and Management* 18, no. 4: 601-24.

Collins, Doug. "Seattle to Nordstrom: Try on Anything You'd Like." *The Washington Free Press,* June/July 1995.

"Coming to Life: Seattle's Retail Center Could Become a Destination Spot with More Shopping, Nightlife." *Seattle Times*, 8 January 1995.

Conklin, Ellis. "Cheering at Third and Union: Mann Building Sold, Will be Revitalized into Theater, Shops." *Seattle Post-Intelligencer*, 10 April 1996.

Connor, T., and J. Atkinson. "Sweating for Nike: A Report on Labor Conditions in the Sport Shoe Industry." *Community Aid Abroad Briefing Paper, No. 16*, November 1996.

Crane, P. "Homeless in Seattle: Eliminate 'Charlie Show.'" *Seattle Times*, 24 August 1993.

Crawford, Margaret. "The World in a Shopping Mall." In *Variations on a Theme Park: The New American City and the End of Public Space*, edited by Michael Sorkin. New York: Noonday Press, 1992.

Crilley, David. "Megastructures and Urban Change: Aesthetics, Ideology, and Design." In *The Restless Urban Landscape*, edited by P. Knox. Englewood Cliffs, NJ: Prentice Hall, 1993.

Crowley, Walt. *Rites of Passage: A Memoir of the Sixties in Seattle*. Seattle, WA: University of Washington Press, 1995.

Curtis, J. "A Pot to Piss in: Construction on LIHI's Urban Reststop Begins." *Real Change*, February 1999.

"Cyber Seattle: Software Capital." *Crossroads: Newsletter of the Trade Development Alliance of Greater Seattle* 5, no. 1 (Winter 1996).

Daskal, Jennifer. *In Search of Shelter: The Growing Shortage of Affordable Rental Housing*. Washington, DC: Center for Budget and Policy Priorities, 1998.

Davila, F. "Hygiene Center Won't Go in Hotel." *Seattle Times*, 2 October 1996.

Davis, Mike. *City of Quartz: Excavating the Future in Los Angeles*. New York: Vintage, 1992.

———. *Ecology of Fear: Los Angeles and the Imagination of Disaster*. New York: Vintage, 1998.

Debord, Guy. *The Society of the Spectacle*. Detroit: Red & Black Books, 1983.

Dickens, Ishbel. "Urban Reststop: City Should Embrace Plans for Downtown Hygiene Center." *Seattle Times*, 23 June 1996.

Dolbeare, Cushing. *Out of Reach: The Gap Between Housing Costs and the Income of Poor People in the United States*. Washington, DC: National Low-Income Housing Coalition, 1999.

Downtown Seattle Association. *Survey of Downtown Users: Executive Summary*. Seattle, WA.: Elway Research, Inc., 1993.

Economic Research Associates. *An Economic Evaluation of the Rhodes/Nordstrom Project*. San Francisco: Economic Research Associates, 1994.

Enbysk, Monte. "Destination: Downtown Seattle." *Washington CEO*, November 1996, S-4.

Entman, Robert, and Andrew Rojecki. *The Black Image in the White Mind*. Chicago: University of Chicago Press, 1999.

Epes, James. "Mann Building Rehab Plan Includes Nightclub, Shops." *Puget Sound Business Journal*, 17 March 1995.

———. "Hygiene Center Riles Downtown Landlords." *Puget Sound Business Journal*, 11-17 August 1995.

————. "'Hygiene Center' for Homeless Faces Legal Challenge." *Puget Sound Business Journal,* 25 August 1995.

————. "No Clean Resolution Yet in Hygiene Center Debate." *Puget Sound Business Journal,* 4 June 1996.

Erickson, J. "Nordstrom to Go to F&N Building: Key Pieces of $400 Million Plan in Place." *Seattle Post-Intelligencer,* 27 June 1995.

Etsekson, Paul. "Campaign for Hygiene Center Misleads." *Seattle Times,* 12 July 1996.

Ewen, Stuart. *All Consuming Images.* New York: Basic Books, 1988.

Fainstein, Susan, and Dennis Judd, eds. *The Tourist City.* New Haven, CT: Yale University Press, 1999.

Fahrenthold, D. "Hygiene Center for Homeless—New Facility to Open in April." *Seattle Times,* 3 August 1998.

Featherstone, Mike. "City Cultures and Postmodern Lifestyles." In *Post-Fordism: A Reader,* edited by Ash Amin. Oxford: Blackwell, 1994.

Fefer, M. "Is Seattle the Next Silicon Valley?" *Fortune,* 7 July 1997.

Fennessy, A. "City Should Open Facility, Hold Operators Accountable." *Seattle Times,* 30 June 1996.

"Finding the Best Spot for Public Restrooms [editorial]." *Seattle Times,* 8 October 1996.

Findlay, John. "The Off-center Seattle Center: Downtown Seattle and the 1962 World's Fair." *Pacific Northwest Quarterly* 80 (January 1989): 2-11.

Flores, Michele. "What's Up Downtown: An Oversupply of Office Space Leaves Developers Stretching to Cover Costs." *Seattle Times,* 28 October 1990.

————. "Downtown Dealmaker: Frederick & Nelson Heir Holds the Key to Revitalizing Seattle's Retail Core." *Seattle Times,* 16 January 1992.

————. "End of a Dream: Developers Lost Millions of Dollars, Titles to Homes." *Seattle Times,* 15 October 1992.

————. "Downtown ACT Plans Dashed by Sale: Buyers Have Hope for Downtown Retail." *Seattle Times,* 26 March 1994.

Fox, John. "A Very Big Deal: Displacement Coalition Responds to Nordstrom 'Revelation.'" *Real Change,* January 1998.

Fox, John, and John Reese. "Rude Behavior: Seattle's Harrassment of Homeless Found Intolerable." *Real Change,* October 1994.

————. "Whose Seattle?" *Real Change,* October 1994.

Fyer, Alex. "Action on Several Fronts Paves Way for Pine Street Vision." *Puget Sound Business Journal,* 9 June 1995.

————. "Strong-Arming a Retail Rebirth: The Build It and They Will Come Credo May Have Some Flaws." *Puget Sound Business Journal,* 14-20 July 1995.

————. "Sidran: The City Attorney as Street Cleaner." *Puget Sound Business Journal,* 21 July 1995.

Geertz, Clifford. *The Interpretation of Cultures.* New York: Basic Books, 1973.

————. "From the Native's Point of View: On the Nature of Anthropological Understanding." In *Meaning in Anthropology,* edited by Keith Basso and H. Selby. Albuquerque, NM: University of New Mexico Press, 1976.

Gellatly, David. "Users of Hygiene Center Will Threaten Building Tenants." *Seattle Times,* 8 January 1996.

Gerbner, George. "Foreword: Telling All the Stories." In *Consuming Environments: Television and Commercial Culture*, Mike Budd, Steve Craig, and Clay Steinman. New Brunswick, NJ: Rutgers University Press, 1999.

Gibson, Timothy. "Watch Dog or Lap Dog? Seattle's Local Media and the Politics of Urban Redevelopment." Paper presented at the annual meeting of the Eastern Communication Association, Washington, DC, April 2003.

Gilroy, Paul. *There Ain't No Black in the Union Jack*. London: Hutchinson, 1987.

Gladstone, David. "Tourism Urbanization in the United States." *Urban Affairs Review* 34 (1998): 3-27.

"Glen Hotel Basement Center of Bitter Battle [editorial]." *Seattle Times,* 9 February 1997.

Goldsmith, S. "Search for Homeless Hygiene Center May Be Over." *Seattle Post Intelligencer,* 11 November 1997.

Gotham, Kevin Fox. "Marketing Mardi Gras: Commodification, Spectacle, and the Political Economy of Tourism in New Orleans." *Urban Studies* 39, no. 10 (2002): 1735-56.

Gratz, Robert Brandes, and Norman Mintz. *Cities Back from the Edge: New Life for Downtown*. New York: John Wiley & Sons, 1998.

Greene, Harold. "Chairman's Report." In *1996-1997 Annual Report of the Downtown Seattle Association*. Seattle, WA: Downtown Seattle Association.

Grossberg, Lawrence. *We Gotta Get Out of This Place: Popular Conservatism and Postmodern Culture*. London: Routlegde, 1992.

"Groups Debate Plan for Hygiene Center." *Seattle Times,* 30 May 1996.

Habermas, Jurgen. *Legitimation Crisis*. Boston: Beacon Press, 1975.

Haberstroh, J., and Polly Lane. "A 'Rookie' to the Rescue." *Seattle Times,* 28 May 1994.

Hall, Stuart. "Cultural Studies and the Centre: Some Problems and Problematics." In *Culture, Media, Language: Working Papers in Cultural Studies, 1972-1979*, edited by Stuart Hall, Deborah Hobson, A. Lowe, and Paul Willis. London: Hutchinson, 1980.

———. "The Rediscovery of Ideology: Return of the Repressed in Media Studies." In *Culture, Society, and the Media*, edited by M. Gurevitch, T. Bennett, and J. Wollacott. London: Methuen, 1982.

———. "Gramsci's Relevance for the Study of Race and Ethnicity." *Journal of Commnication Inquiry* 10 (Summer 1986).

———. "On Postmodernism and Articulation: An Interview," *Journal of Communication Inquiry* 10 (Summer 1986): 45-60.

Hannigan, John. *Fantasy City: Pleasure and Profit in the Postmodern Metropolis*. London: Routledge, 1998.

Harrell, Debera. "New Homeless Hygiene Plan Proposed." *Seattle Post-Intelligencer,* 15 February 1997.

Harvey, David. *The Urbanization of Capital*. Baltimore: Johns Hopkins University Press, 1985.

———. *Consciousness and the Urban Experience*. Baltimore: Johns Hopkins University Press, 1985.

———. *The Condition of Postmodernity*. Cambridge, MA: Blackwell, 1990.

————. "Flexible Accumulation Through Urbanization: Reflections on 'Postmodernism' in the American City." In *Post-Fordism: A Reader*, edited by Ash Amin. Oxford: Blackwell, 1994.

Hatch, Walter. "City Limits." *Seattle Times*, 30 April 1989.

Hatch, Walter, and Joni Balter. "DSA: Seattle's Most Powerful Lobby." *Seattle Times*, 2 April 1989.

Higgins, Mark. "Rice Does Pine Street U-Turn." *Seattle Post-Intelligencer*, 22 November 1994.

————. "Pine Street Project Gridlock: Group's Initiative Would Permanently Close Road to Cars." *Seattle Post-Intelligencer*, 9 January 1995.

————. "Public Vote Likely on Pine Street." *Seattle Post-Intelligencer*, 21 January 1995.

————. "Last Round for Pine Street Fight: Both Sides Push Their Views on Re-opening Before Voters Decide March 14th." *Seattle Post-Intelligencer*, 2 March 1995.

————. "Pine Street Vote One Week Off: The Great, and Greatly Uneven, Debate Nears End." *Seattle Post-Intelligencer*, 7 March 1995.

Hilo, P. "Business Owners Appear Willing to Sacrifice Homeless People to Preserve Bottom Line." *Seattle Times*, 14 November 1995.

Hirsch, J. "From the Fordist to the Post-Fordist State." In *The Politics of Flexibility: Restructuring State and Industry in Britain, Germany, and Scandinavia*, edited by Bob Jessop, H. Kastendiek, Klaus Nielsen, and O. Pedersen. Brookfield, VT: Edward Elgar, 1991.

Hoffman, John. "Court Gestures: Seattle's Sidran Ordinance Has Its Day(s) in Court." *Real Change*, November 1994.

Holmes, S. "Rebirth is Driving Up Rents that Some Shop Owners Can't Afford." *Seattle Times*, 2 October 1995.

"Homeless Protest." *Seattle Times*, 21 July 1993.

Hopper, K., and J. Hamberg. "The Making of America's Homeless, from Skid Row to New Poor, 1945-1984." In *Critical Perspectives on Housing*, edited by Rachel Bratt, Chester Hartman, and Ann Meyerson. Philadelphia, PA: Temple University Press, 1986.

Houston, E. "Alice Worries About Eviction: Low-Income Housing Vanishing." *Seattle Post-Intelligencer*, 19 July 1993.

"Howl: Sidranesque 'Civility' Rhetoric Misdirects Debate." *Real Change*, August 1996.

Hudnut, William H. *Cities on the Rebound: A Vision for Urban America*. Washington, DC: Urban Land Institute, 1998.

Hymes, Dell. "The Ethnography of Speaking." In *Anthropology and Human Behavior*, edited by T. Gladwin and W. C. Sturtevant. Washington, DC: Antropological Society of Washington, 1962.

Jacobs, Jane. *The Death and Life of Great American Cities*. New York: Random House, 1961.

Jacklet, B. "Business, as Usual." *The Stranger*, 10-16 October 1996.

Jencks, Christopher. *The Homeless*. Cambridge, MA: Harvard University Press, 1994.

Jessop, Bob. *State Theory: Putting the Capitalist State in its Place*. Oxford: Blackwell, 1990.

————. "Post-Fordism and the State." In *Post-Fordism: A Reader*, edited by Ash Amin. Oxford: Blackwell, 1994.

Joncas, Kate. "Pacific Place Garage: Responsible Debate Poisoned." *Seattle Times*, 4 January 1998.

Judd, Dennis, and Todd Swanstrom. *City Politics: Private Power and Public Policy*. New York: HarperCollins, 1994.

Kamb, Lewis. "A Place to Rest: Downtown Merchants and Homeless Hygiene." *The Stranger*, 12 July 1996.

Katz, Bruce J. "Reviving Cities: Think Metropolitan." In *Policy Brief #33, The Center on Urban and Metropolitan Policy, Brookings Institution*. Available from the Brookings Institution website: www.brookings.edu.

Kauanoe, K. "Still Waiting: Red Tape and Politics Stall Downtown Bathroom Project." *Real Change*, February 1997.

Keene, Linda. "Hygiene Center for Homeless Has Retailers Hot, and Suing." *Seattle Times*, 4 November 1995.

———. "Hygiene Center Debate Unabated." *Seattle Times*, 3 October 1996.

———. "Restroom Protest at Nordstrom—Homeless Advocates Seek Downtown Hygiene Center." *Seattle Times*, 22 January 1997.

———. "Glen Hotel Site Back in Hygiene Center Fray—Shocked Opponents Thought Plan was Dead." *Seattle Times*, 23 January 1997.

Keene, Linda, and Charles Brown. "New Name, But Same Old Fight." *Seattle Times*, 18 June 1996.

Kelling, George, and Catherine Coles. *Fixing Broken Windows: Restoring Order and Reducing Crime in Our Communities*. New York: Free Press, 1995.

Kelling, George, et al. "Crime Solutions: 18 Things We Can Do Now to Fight Back." *The American Enterprise*, May/June 1995.

"Key Loan Bolsters Downtown Project." *Seattle Times*, 15 September 1994.

Kim, N. "New Hall is Stage for Downtown Expansion." *Puget Sound Business Journal*, 4-10 September 1998.

Kirby, Sandra, and Kate McKenna. *Experience, Research, Social Change: Methods from the Margins*. Toronto: Garamond Press, 1987.

Kokmen, Lela. "Sale of Mann Building Near." *Seattle Times*, 10 April 1996.

———. "HUD Chief Lauds Creativity Downtown." *Seattle Times*, 11 May 1996.

Kraut, A. *Silent Travelers: Germs, Genes, and the "Immigrant Menace."* New York: Basic Books, 1994.

Labor Market Economic Analysis Branch. In *Washington State Labor Area Summary, November 1998*. Olympia, WA: Washington State Economic Security Department, 1998.

———. "Economic History: King County." In *County Profiles*. Olympia, WA: Washington State Economic Security Department, 1996.

Lacitis, Eric. "Ground Zero: What Does Downtown Mean to You?" *Seattle Times*, 11 July 1993.

Laclau, Ernesto, and Chantal Mouffe. *Hegemony and Socialist Strategy*. London: Verso, 2001.

Lakoff, George, and Mark Johnson. *Metaphors We Live By*. Chicago: University of Chicago Press, 1981.

Lane, Polly. "Full Steam Ahead for Flagship Downtown." *Seattle Times*, 2 November 1994.

Lane, Polly, and Sylvia Nogaki. "Downtown Merchants Want Action on Parking, Crime." *Seattle Times*, 23 April 1993.

Lange, Gentry. "Criminalization of Homelessness is On the Rise." *Real Change*, March 1997.

Large, J. "Seattle's Brilliant Bulldog: Friends, Foes Agree on Little Else about City Attorney Sidran." *Seattle Times*, 18 August 1994.

Larin, Kathryn, and Elizabeth McNichol. *Pulling Apart: A State-by-State Analysis of Income Trends*. Washington, DC: The Center on Budget and Policy Priorities, 1997.

Lash, Scott, and John Urry. *The End of Organized Capitalism*. Madison, WI: University of Wisconsin Press, 1987.

Law, Robin, and Jennifer Wolch. "Homelessness and Economic Restructuring." *Urban Geography* 12, vol. 2 (1991).

Lawhead, Terry. "Pacific Center Draws Interest." *Seattle Times*, 28 December 1989.

————. "Downtown Vacancies, Rents Hurting Developers." *Seattle Times*, 26 April 1990.

Leach, William. *Land of Desire: Merchants, Power, and the Rise of a New American Culture*. New York: Pantheon, 1993.

Le Corbusier. *Towards a New Architecture*. New York: Payson and Clarke, 1927.

Lefebvre, Henri. *The Production of Space*. Oxford: Blackwell, 1991.

Lees, Lyn Hollen. "Urban Public Space and Imagined Communities in the 1980s and 1990s," *Journal of Urban History* 20 (1994): 443-65.

Leiss, William, Steve Kline, and Sut Jhally. *Social Communication in Advertising: Persons, Products, and Images of Well-Being*. New York: Routledge, 1990.

Levine, Paul, ed. *Georg Simmel: On Individuality and Social Forms*. Chicago: University of Chicago Press, 1971.

Lewis, P. "Pine Street on Road to Redevelopment." *Seattle Times*, 15 March 1994.

Ley, David. "Liberal Ideology and the Postindustrial City." *Annals of the Association of American Geographers* 70 (1980): 238-258.

Licata, Nick. "Put Westlake Debate to Rest: Close Pine." *Seattle Times*, 6 December 1994.

Liebman, L. "Downtown's Supporters Hopeful for Good News." *Puget Sound Business Journal*, 13 May 1994.

Lilly, Dick. "Sidran Details Proposals to Control Street People." *Seattle Times*, 3 August 1993.

————. "Keeping Downtown Alive." *Seattle Times*, 19 August 1993.

Logan, John, and Harvey Molotch. *Urban Fortunes: Toward a Political Economy of Place*. Berkeley, CA: University of California Press, 1987.

Lonquist, Judith. "Disorder in the Streets: City Attorney's Proposals Fail to Address Human Suffering." *Seattle Times*, 3 October 1994.

"Looking for Better Ways to Curb Unruly Street Life [editorial]." *Seattle Times*, 26 July 1993.

Lord, George, and A. Price. "Growth Ideology in a Period of Decline: Deindustrialization and Restructuring, Flint Style." *Social Problems* 39, (May 1992).

Loukaitou-Sideris, Anastasia, and Tridib Banerjee. *Urban Design Downtown: Poetics and Politics of Form*. Berkeley, CA: University of California Press, 1998.

Low Income Housing Institute. *Urban Reststop at the Glen Hotel: Annual Report*, 14 October 1996.

Lowes, Mark. *Indy Dreams and Urban Nightmares*. Toronto: University of Toronto Press, 2002.

Lucas, Eric. "Plane Facts About Boeing." In *Insight Guides: Seattle*, edited by John Wilcock. Boston: Houghton Mifflin Company, 1993.

MacCoumber, D. "Homeless Will Come—and They Will Go—With or Without Toilets." *Seattle Times*, 4 April 1997.

Macek, Steve. "Television and the Process of Urban Decline." Paper presented at the 1999 Conference of the Union for Democratic Communications. Eugene, OR: University of Oregon.

Mair, Andrew. "The Homeless and the Post-Industrial City." *Political Geography Quarterly* 5 (October 1986): 351-68.

Marcuse, Herbert. *One-Dimensional Man*. London: Abacus, 1972.

Marcuse, Peter. "Neutralizing Homelessness." *Socialist Review* 18 (1988): 69-96.

Martin, Joe. "Belltown Remembers: Seattle's Incredible Disappearing Poor." *Real Change*, 15 May 2000.

Marx, Karl, and Fredrich Engels. "The Manifesto of the Communist Party." In *The Marx-Engels Reader*, edited by Robert Tucker. New York: Norton, 1978.

Massey, C. "No Room for the Poor: Over Half of Homeless Turned Away from Shelter." *Real Change*, February 1996.

Mayer, Margit. "Post-Fordist City Politics." In *Post-Fordism: A Reader*, edited by Ash Amin. Oxford: Blackwell, 1994.

McChesney, Robert. *Rich Media, Poor Democracy*. Urbana, IL: University of Illinois Press, 1999.

McDermott, Terry. "High Rise: Making the Deal—Seattle Developer Digs into Foreign Pockets for Millions of Dollars to Get Gateway Going." *Seattle Times*, 9 July 1989.

———. "The Mann, the Glen, and Yes, the Process." *Seattle Times*, 4 February 1997.

Merkle, Dan. "Reststop's a World-Class Step for Seattle." *Seattle Times*, 1 July 1996.

Mihalopoulos, S. "From Skid Row to Vibrant City on the Sound: St. Louis Leaders See What a 24-hour Downtown is Really Like." *St. Louis Post-Dispatch*, 5 October 1997.

Miletich, Steve. "Old Glen Hotel to be Spruced Up: Face-Lift Will Be Part of Low Income Housing Plan." *Seattle Post-Intelligencer*, 21 January 1994.

Millspaugh, Martin L., "The Inner Harbor Story," In *Urban Land Archives, April 2003*, retrieved from the Urban Land Institute website: http://research.uli.org.

Mitchell, Don. "The End of Public Space? People's Park, Definitions of the Public, and Democracy." *Annals of the Association of American Geographers* 85 (1995): 108-33.

Modie, L. "Panel Favors Public Toilets at Hotel." *Seattle Post-Intelligencer*, 23 January 1997.

"Money Changes Everything, Again." *Eat the State!*, 11 February 1997.

Mooney, Joe. "Hygiene Center Goes Down Drain: Homeless Advocates Say Pressure from Merchants Led City to Renege on Facility." *Seattle Post-Intelligencer*, 13 December 1996.

Morgan, Murray. *Skid Road: Seattle—Her First Hundred Years*. New York: Ballantine, 1971.

Moriwaki, Lee. "Boom Times: Seattle's Downtown is Evolving." *Seattle Times*, 18 January 1998.

——. "Downtown Urged to 'Retain Our Soul.'" *Seattle Times*, 30 May 1998.

——. "Pacific Place: Will Opening of Downtown's Newest Shot in the Arm Be Clouded by Recession?" *Seattle Times*, 25 October 1998.

Moriwaki, Lee, and J. Heim. "High-Fives Greet New Nordstrom: 5,000 at the Door as Flagship Store Opens Today." *Seattle Times*, 21 August 1998.

Mosco, Vincent. "New York.Com: A Political Economy of the 'Informational' City." *Journal of Media Economics* 12 (1999): 103-16

Moulton, Jennifer. "Ten Steps to a Living Downtown: A Discussion Paper Prepared for the Brookings Institution Center on Urban and Metropolitan Policy." Available on the Brookings Institution website: www.brookings.edu.

"Music-Theater Complex and the Hygiene Center [editorial]." *Seattle Times*, 13 November 1995.

National Low Income Housing Coalition. *1998 Advocates Resource Handbook*. Washington, DC: NLIHC, 1998.

Nelson, Deborah. "Time to Clean Up Hygiene Center Dispute." *Puget Sound Business Journal*, 31 January 1997.

Nelson, John. "Liberal Bureaucrats at Work [letter to the editor]." *Seattle Times*, 6 January 1996.

Nelson, Robert. "Pedigree, Ambition Put Cuomo Past Rice: Campaign for HUD Job Too Late for Seattle Mayor." *Seattle Times*, 20 December 1996.

Nielsen, Klaus. "Towards a Flexible Future: Theories and Politics." In *The Politics of Flexibility: Restructuring State and Industry in Britain, Germany, and Scandinavia*, edited by B. Jessop, H. Kastendiek, K. Nielsen, and O. Pedersen. Brookfield, VT: Edward Elgar, 1991.

Nogaki, Sylvia. "Retailing Talk of the 'Town': Uptown Mosquito Fleet is Part of Plan to Save Vitality of Downtown." *Seattle Times*, 22 June 1992.

——. "Downtown Wonderland? Retailers are Determined Not to Have a Blue Christmas Without F&N." *Seattle Times*, 23 November 1992.

——. "Task Force to Coax Retailers Downtown." *Seattle Times*, 7 August 1993.

——. "Reluctant Inhabitant of Seattle Limelight." *Seattle Times*, 20 December 1994.

——. "Solving the Pine Street Puzzle." *Seattle Times*, 28 November 1994.

——. "Local Investors Back Rhodes Project: Group Provides a Big Chunk of Venture Capital." *Seattle Times*, 29 November 1994.

——. "Growing List of Shops, Eateries Ready to Go Downtown." *Seattle Times*, 6 May 1995.

——. "Nordstrom: Downtown Excitement Building." *Seattle Times*, 17 May 1995.

Nogaki, Sylvia, and Polly Lane. "Panhandler's Among Area's Problems." *Seattle Times*, 24 March 1993.

Nogaki, Sylvia, and Peter Lewis. "Vote Energizes Downtown Deals." *Seattle Times*, 16 March 1995.

Norman, James. "Contrary to Your Assertions, Praise is in Order, Not Blame." *Seattle Times*, 8 January 1998.

"Nordstrom Project Clears Big Hurdles [editorial]." *Seattle Post-Intelligencer*, 28 June 1995.

Norton, D. "Hotel Becomes Home to Needy." *Seattle Times*, 22 November 1996.

O'Corr, Casey. "Pine Street Not Only Hurdle for Investors." *Seattle Times*, 15 December 1994.

Office of Financial Management. *Washington Trends: Economy, Population, Budget Drivers, Revenues, Expenditures*. Olympia, WA: State of Washington, 1996.

Paulson, M. "Rice Unveils Plan to Rev Up Downtown." *Seattle Post-Intelligencer*, 19 August 1993.

Peck, Jamie, and Adam Tickell. "Searching for a New Institutional Fix: The After-Fordist Crisis and the Global-Local Disorder." In *Post-Fordism: A Reader*, edited by Ash Amin. Oxford: Blackwell, 1994.

Philipsen, Gerry. *Speaking Culturally: Explorations in Social Communication*. Albany, NY: SUNY Press, 1992.

"Pine Closure Senseless Effort [editorial]." *Seattle Post-Intelligencer*, 5 December 1994.

Piore, Michael, and Charles Sabel. *The Second Industrial Divide*. New York: Basic Books, 1984.

"Probe Stalls Rice's Possible HUD Nomination: Nomination Seems on Hold as HUD Looks into Project." *Seattle Times*, 13 December 1996.

Putnam, Robert. *Bowling Alone: The Collapse and Revival of American Community*. New York: Touchstone, 2000.

Radway, Janice. "Identifying Ideological Seams: Mass Culture, Analytical Method, and Political Practice." *Communication* 9 (1986): 93-125.

Redmond, Bob. "Third and Long for Hygiene Center: Political Football Continues Downtown." *Real Change*, October 1996.

————. "No Comment: Hygiene Center Stalled and Stonewalled." *Real Change*, October 1996.

Reich, Robert. *The Work of Nations*. New York: Basic Books, 1991.

"Rice Backs Downtown Site for Symphony Hall." *Seattle Times*, 14 July 1994.

Rice, Norm. "Seattle—A First-Class Downtown Community." *Downtown: The Newsletter of the Downtown Seattle Association*, Winter 1996.

Rosen, G. "Books in Review." *Commentary*, December 1996.

Ruddick, Susan. *Young and Homeless in Hollywood: Mapping Social Identities*. New York: Routledge, 1996.

Sassen, Saskia. *The Global City: New York, London, Tokyo*. Princeton, NJ: Princeton University Press, 1991.

————. "Economic Restructuring and the American City." *Annual Review of Sociology* 16 (1990): 465-90.

Sather, J. "No Pine Street, No Deal, Rhodes Says." *Puget Sound Business Journal*, 10 March 1995.

Sayer, Andrew. "The 'New' Regional Geography and Problems of Narrative." *Environment and Planning D: Society and Space* 7: 251-76.

Schell, Paul. "Letter from Seattle Mayor Paul Schell." *Crossroads* 7, 3 (Summer 1998).

Schumpeter, Joseph. *Capitalism, Socialism, and Democracy*. New York: Harper and Row, 1950.

Schwarz, Amy, and Ingrid Ellen, "Cautionary Notes for Competitive Cities." A working paper available on the Brookings Institution website: www.brookings.edu.

Schwarz, Gerald. "Benaroya, Hallmark of City's Awakening." *Seattle Times*, 2 February 1999.

"Seattle in Transition: 1965: Growth in the Air." *Seattle Post-Intelligencer,* 25 January 1976.

Serrano, Barbara. "City Clears Legal Review on Pine Street Garage Deal: Money to Developer Deemed Constitutional." *Seattle Times,* 23 April 1998.

Serrano, Barbara, and Deborah Nelson. "City Overpaid Pine Street Developer." *Seattle Times,* 21 December 1997.

————. "City Spent Little Time Questioning Garage Cost: But Some on Council Were Uneasy with Deal." *Seattle Times,* 13 January 1998.

————. "City, Mayor Cleared in Loan Deal: But Report Says Public Communication About F&N Project Fell Short." *Seattle Times,* 17 November 1998.

Shearing, Clifford, and Richard V. Ericson. "Culture as Figurative Action." *British Journal of Sociology* 42 (December 1991): 481-506.

Shields, Rob. "Social Spatialization and the Built Environment: The West Edmonton Mall." *Environment and Planning D: Society and Space,* 7 (1989): 147-64.

Shropshire, K. L. *The Sports Franchise Game: Cities in Pursuit of Sports Franchises, Events, Stadiums.* Philadelphia: University of Pennsylvania Press, 1995.

Sidran, Mark. "This is the Best of Times to Keep This City Livable." *Seattle Times,* 10 August 1993.

————. "Establishing Standards of Civil Behavior." *Seattle Times,* 10 August 1994.

Siegel, Robert. "Meeting Public Needs at the Glen Hotel." *Seattle Times,* 27 February 1997.

Sieverling, Bill. "City's Population in Major Shifts." *Seattle Post-Intelligencer,* 26 January 1976.

————. "Seattle in Transition: Downtown's 1,000 Acres." *Seattle Post-Intelligencer,* 1 February 1976.

————. "Seattle in Transition: What Will Seattle Be Like in 1985?" *Seattle Post-Intelligencer,* 25 January 1976.

Sivanandan, A. "All That Melts into Air is Solid: The Hokum of New Times." *Race & Class* 31, vol. 3 (1989): 1-30.

Skogan, Wesley. *Disorder and Decline: Crime and the Spiral of Decay in American Neighborhoods.* New York: The Free Press, 1992.

Smith, Neil. *The New Urban Frontier: Gentrification and the Revanchist City.* London: Routledge, 1996.

————. "Gentrification, the Frontier, and the Restructuring of Urban Space." In *The Gentrification of the City,* edited by Neil Smith and Peter Williams. Boston: Allen & Unwin, 1986.

————. "New City, New Frontier: The Lower East Side as Wild, Wild West." In *Variations on a Theme Park,* edited by Michael Sorkin. New York: Hill and Wang, 1992.

Soloman, J. "Whose Game is it Anyway?" *Washington Monthly* 31 (December 1999).

Sontag, Susan. *Illness as Metaphor.* New York: Farrar, Straus, and Giroux, 1978.

Sperry, Sam. "Pine Street: Council Cuts to the Chase." *Seattle Post-Intelligencer,* 22 January 1995.

Stafford, Bill, and Sam Kaplan. "Greater Seattle's Secrets of the Trade." *The Regionalist* 2 (Fall 1997).

Strom, Elizabeth. "Let's Put on a Show! Performing Arts and Urban Revitalization in Newark, New Jersey." *Journal of Urban Affairs* 21, no. 4 (1999): 423-35.

Swanstrom, Todd. "Urban Populism, Uneven Development, and the Space for Reform." In *Business Elites and Urban Development: Case Studies and Critical Perspectives*, edited by Scott Cummings. Albany, NY: SUNY Press, 1988.

Tang, Terry. "Pine Street: Twisted Aims and Fractured Policies." *Seattle Times*, 25 January 1995.

"The Right Questions: Talking Sense About Seattle's Toilets." *Real Change*, December 1996.

"The Working Homeless [editorial]." *Seattle Times*, 6 August 1998.

Thompson, John. *Studies in the Theory of Ideology.* Cambridge, UK: Polity Press, 1984.

Toffler, Alvin, and Heidi Toffler. "Getting Set for the New Millenium." *The Futurist* (March-April 1995).

Tomlinson, John. *Cultural Imperialism: A Critical Introduction.* Baltimore, MD: Johns Hopkins University Press, 1991.

Trade Development Alliance of Greater Seattle. *International Promotion Plan,* December 1998.

U.S. Bureau of Census. *General Social and Economic Characteristics, Washington State (1970-1990).* Washington, DC: Bureau of Census, 1990.

VanKempen, Ronald, and Peter Marcuse. "A New Spatial Order in Cities?" *The American Behavioral Scientist* 41 (November/December 1997): 285-98.

Veblen, Thorstein. *The Theory of the Leisure Class.* New York: New American Library, [1899] 1953.

Volosinov V. N. *Marxism and the Philosophy of Language.* New York: Seminar Press, 1973.

"Vote Yes to Reopen Pine for a Healthy Downtown [editorial]." *Seattle Times,* 12 March 1995.

Washington State Public Disclosure Commission. *1996 Gubernatorial Campaign Contributions: Norman Rice.* Olympia, WA: Washington State Public Disclosure Commission, 1996.

Wells, R. "Uptown, Downtown: The Players Get Richer and the Stakes Get Higher." *Seattle Times,* 12 September 1999.

West, W. "Modell Hands Off to Glendening, But Fans Left Holding the Ball." *Insight on the News* 12, no. 3 (January 1996): 48.

Westlake Management Review Task Force. *Recommendations Report.* Seattle: City of Seattle, July 1996.

Whitley, P. "'Keep Downtown Healthy,' Supporters Urge at Rally Boosting Pine Street Vote." *Seattle Times,* 5 March 1995.

Wilcock, J. "A Livable City." *Seattle: Insight Guides.* Boston: Houghton Mifflin Company 1993.

Williams, M. "Hygiene Center to Proceed at Glen Hotel." *Seattle Times,* 15 April 1997.

Williams, Rosalind. *Dreamworlds: Mass Consumption in Late Nineteenth Century France.* Berkeley, CA: University of California Press, 1983.

Williamson, David. "What Toll are We Willing to Pay to Walk the Street?" *Seattle Times,* 15 August 1993.

Willis, Paul. *Learning to Labour: How Working Class Kids Get Working Class Jobs.* New York: Columbia University Press, 1981.

Wilson, David. "Metaphors, Growth Coalition Discourses, and Black Poverty in a U.S. City." *Antipode* 28 (1996): 72-96.

Wilson, James Q., and George Kelling. "Broken Windows." *The Atlantic Monthly,* March 1982.

Wilson, William J. *The Truly Disadvantaged: The Inner City, the Underclass, and Public Policy.* Chicago: University of Chicago Press, 1987.

———. *When Work Disappears: The World of the New Urban Poor.* New York: Knopf, 1995.

Wolch, Jennifer. "Homeless in America: A Review of Recent Books." *Journal of Urban Affairs* 12, 4 (1990): 449-63.

———. "Inside/Outside: The Dialectics of Homelessness." In *Populations at Risk,* edited by G. Demko and M. Jackson. Boulder, CO: Westview Press, 1995.

Wolch, Jennifer, and Michael Dear. *Malign Neglect: Homelessness in an American City.* San Francisco: Jossey-Bass, 1993.

Worth, Mark. "Who Really Runs Seattle? A Who's Who of the City's Backroom Wheeler-Dealers." *Seattle Weekly,* 12 November 1998.

Yoder, Rick. "Hygiene-Center Backers Muddy the Facts." *Seattle Times,* 12 February 1997.

Zinn, Howard. *A People's History of the United States.* New York: HarperPerennial, 1995.

Zukin, Sharon. *Landscapes of Power: From Detroit to Disneyland.* Berkeley, CA: University of California Press, 1991.

———. *The Cultures of Cities.* Cambridge, UK: Basil Blackwell, 1995.

———. "Urban Lifestyles: Diversity and Standardization in Spaces of Consumption." *Urban Studies* 35 (May 1998).

Index

A Contemporary Theater (ACT), 3,
    8, 92, 139, 263, 267
Abbott, Carl, 35, 65-66
ACT block, 72-73, 193-94, 199
Alaska-Yukon-Pacific-Exhibition
    (1909), 35, 36.
Althusser, Louis, 19
American Fordism. *See* Fordism
Amin, Ash, 22
Aramburu, J. Richard, 124, 125, 126
Archdiocesan Housing Authority, 214,
    243
articulation, 135, 236, 238-39, 242,
    243, 253n92, 272-82

Bain, William, 95-96
Baltimore, Maryland, 38, 48, 49, 83-84,
    165
Banerjee, Tridib, 169
Barrett, Michelle, 148n152, 282n9
Bell, Daniel, 19
Benaroya Hall, 3, 7-8, 85, 88, 92, 139,
    197-200, 207, 215, 223, 227, 229,
    246, 249, 252n69, 260, 265, 268,
    270, 279, 290
Benaroya, Jack, 197, 223, 248, 249
Benaroya Music Center (BMC), 229,
    248
Berman, Marshall, 16-17, 134
Bluestone, Barry, 30n32, 31, 39,
    52n12
Boeing Bust, 37-38, 59-60, 66
The Boeing Company, 6, 35-36, 37, 64,
    79n21, 87. *See also* Boeing Bust
Bon Marché (department store), 100,
    119, 215
Boren, Rebecca, 119-120
Boston, Massachusetts, 48, 49, 95, 96
Bourdieu, Pierre, 89-90
Bridge, Herb, 70, 120

broken windows theory, 161-66, 169,
    231-232, 270
Brooks, Bruce, 212, 214, 215, 223, 246
Brower, Jordan, 118

Carey, James W., 289
Carlson, John, 174
Carpenter, Gary, 72-73, 193-4, 199
Center on Budget and Policy Priorities,
    45, 156
Century 21 Exposition (1962), 36-37,
    61, 196
Chicago, Illinois, 39, 40, 95, 96
Chow, Cheryl, 227-29, 242-44
Christians, Clifford, 289
Christopherson, Susan, 170, 272,
    284n29
Citizens to ReStore Our Retail Core
    (CRORC), 124, 125, 127-33, 135,
    136, 137, 138, 146
Cleveland, Ohio, 38, 40
Clotfelter, Dick, 72-73, 193-4, 199
Coles, Catherine, 164, 166, 185n62,
    185n77
Collins, Doug, 115, 117, 118, 144, 146
Colwell, Richard, 192
commodification, urban space and, 85-
    90, 135-36, 139-140, 266-69
Crawford, Margaret, 149n167
crime: urban, 60-61; inflated statistics
    of, 116-17; links to street incivil-
    ity, 162-65; links to homelessness,
    231-33
critical/cultural studies, 289-90
cultural capital, 89-90
Cuomo, Andrew, 118

Daskall, Jennifer, 156, 183n30
Davis, Mike, 49-50, 140, 184n50
Dear, Michael, 156-59, 182n18

Debord, Guy, 135
deindustrialization, 5, 39
Denny Regrade (Seattle neighbohood),
    8, 61, 214-15, 225, 227; neighbor-
    hood representatives of, 206-7.
Denver, Colorado, 83-84
discourse analysis, 289-92
Disneyland, 170
Donaldson, Sue, 92
dot-com boom, Seattle's, 1, 258
downtown establishment, definition of,
    50n1.
Downtown Seattle Association (DSA),
    15, 61, 74, 76, 82n74, 114, 118,
    121, 126, 130-31, 141, 146,
    189n168, 197-8, 202, 204, 206,
    214-15, 224, 225, 227-29, 231,
    239, 242, 246, 257, 262, 264, 271,
    279, 280, 284n42
Detroit, Michigan, 38, 83, 129, 133,
    258, 261
Downtown Task Force (1993-1994),
    92-94, 108-110
Drago, Jan, 92, 128, 214

Eagles Auditorium, 3, 8, 92, 139, 263,
    267
Eat the State! (alternative newspaper),
    239, 243
Economic Development Council of
    Seattle-King County (EDC), 61,
    65
Ellis, James, 37
Entman, Robert, 154
Ericson, Richard, 148n150, 291
Etsekson, Paul, 201-202, 210, 211
Etsekson, Tom, 201

financial district, boom and bust in, 66-
    74
Findlay, John, 36
First United Methodist Church (site for
    hygiene center), 243-244
Fordism, 16-28; crisis of, 37, 42, 59.
Fox, John, 113, 178, 237, 248
Frederick & Nelson (department store),
    59, 74-76, 78, 85, 92-101, 107-8,
    111-12, 115-19, 120, 121, 122,
    123, 124, 126-29, 142, 144, 146,
    149, 153, 180, 181, 263, 264, 265.

Frederick & Nelson site (F&N site).
    See Frederick & Nelson (depart-
    ment store).
Friends of Westlake Park, 124-27, 134,
    136-38, 274

Geertz, Clifford, 292n2
Gellatly, David, 199-205, 207-8,
    219n67
gentrification, urban, 239-41, 254n115,
    269-70, 284n34
Gerbner, George, 154
Glen Hotel, history of, 193-94.
Glen Hotel hygiene center, 7-8, 191-
    256, 264, 270; alternative propos-
    als to, 214-15, 225-27, 243-46.
globalization, 5, 21, 23-5, 28, 39, 280-
    82
"global city" status, competition to
    secure, 46-7, 59
Gotham, Kevin Fox, 283n21
Gramsci, Antonio, 29n17, 30n29
Gratz, Roberta Brandes, 273
Greater Seattle Chamber of Commerce,
    61, 87, 280
Griffin, Matt, 108, 111, 153, 283
Guiliani, Rudolf, 164

Hall, Stuart, 148n160, 253n90, 253n92,
    289
Hannigan, John, 149n163
Harborplace (Baltimore, Maryland), 49
Harrison, Bennett, 30n32, 39, 52n12
Harvey, David, 21-23, 26, 30n17,
    31n37, 48, 54n56, 68, 78, 137
homelessness: association with crime,
    230-31; association with mental
    illness, 230, 251n54; causes of,
    155-59, 187n115; middle-class
    fear of, 165-69, 189n168, 230,
    232-233, 252n68, 252n69; policy
    response to, 159-61, 175-81,
    187n120; in Seattle, 4, 7, 76-77,
    82, 140-41, 173-76, 230-35;
    viewed as threat to revitalization,
    155, 161-65, 173-75, 230-35,
    251n66
housing affordability, crisis of, 156-59,
    171-73, 186n108, 187n112
Houston, Texas, 38

Hudnut, William H., 266
hygiene center. *See* Glen Hotel hygiene
 center.
Hygiene Services Committee (HSC),
 204-8, 209, 210

ideology, definition of, 282n8
income inequality: national, 45-6; in
 Washington State, 79n25
Independent Media Center, 282
interurban competition, 46-50

Jacobs, Jane, 134, 272
Jessop, Bob, 18, 20, 25, 27, 32n62
Jhally, Sut, 186n86
Johnson, Mark, 134, 273
Joncas, Kate, 114, 206, 210, 212-13,
 214, 215, 228, 231, 242, 246
Josephinum Building, 243, 244
Judd, Dennis, 39, 52n21, 102n8
Julie Apartments, 247, 278

Katz, Bruce, 84
Kelling, George, 6, 162-65, 166, 175,
 185n62, 185n77
Keynes, John Maynard, 17-18. *See also*
 Keynesian welfare state
Keynesian welfare state, 25, 27, 41
Kline, Steve, 186n86
Knox, Venerria, 115, 144n51, 210
KOMO-TV (Seattle), 60
Kreielsheimer Foundation, 196-97
Kress Building, 196, 201

Laclau, Ernesto, 148n152
Lakoff, George, 134, 273
Lange, Gentry, 160
Larin, Kathryn, 45
Lash, Scott, 26
Le Corbusier, 133-34
Lee, Sharon, 194-95, 204, 210, 225,
 226, 227, 244, 246
Lees, Lyn Hollen, 275-76
Lefebvre, Henri, 137
Leiss, William, 186n86
Levinson, Anne, 94, 131
Ley, David, 102n5
Lipset, Seymour, 19
Logan, John, 50n1, 254n100
Lonquist, Judith, 181

Los Angeles, California, 49, 69, 141,
 158, 169, 180
Loukaitou-Sideris, Anastasia, 169
Low-income housing. *See* housing
 affordability, crisis in
Low Income Housing Institute (LIHI),
 194-95, 198-99, 200-16, 219n62,
 219n70, 223-28, 230-32, 235-41,
 242-48, 252n68, 255n140,
 256n155, 280
Lowes, Mark, 285n61
Lucas, Eric, 37-38

Mair, Andrew, 140, 166, 167, 170
Manifesto of the Communist Party,
 16-17
Mann Building, 199-201, 203, 205,
 207, 208, 215, 216, 228
Marathon Block, 196, 197, 199, 249
Marcuse, Herbert, 19
Marcuse, Peter, 157, 159, 167-168
Marx, Karl, 16-17, 27
Mayer, Margit, 47, 91
McDermott, Terry, 67, 68
McNichol, Elizabeth, 45
Merkle, Dan, 224
metaphors, urban. *See* organic city
 trope
"Metro Free Ride Zone", 192, 204,
 206, 214
Microsoft, 1, 64, 87
Mills, C. Wright, 132
Mintz, Norman, 273
Mitchell, Don, 167, 168, 169, 170, 267,
 268
mobilization of spectacle, as a response
 to urban decline, 48, 86
mode of regulation, 20, 25, 30n29,
 30n30. *See also* regulation theory
Molotch, Harvey, 50n1, 254n100
Mosco, Vincent, 149n170
Moses, Robert, 134
Mouffe, Chantal, 148n152, 282n9
Moulton, Jennifer, 83
multiaccentuality, as a property of lin-
 guistic signs, 134, 236, 273
Museum of History and Industry, 3, 85

National Law Center on Homelessness
 and Poverty, 159-60, 161

National Low Income Housing Coalition, 159
Nelson, Deborah, 109, 112-13
New York City, New York, 38, 39, 40, 41, 42, 160-1, 164-65, 180
Newark, New Jersey, 41, 46, 282n22
Nielsen, Klaus, 20
Niketown (theme store), 3, 8, 126, 139, 153, 240
Noland, Jane, 112, 191
Nordstrom (department store): 3, 8-9, 15, 64, 88, 93-101, 107-108, 111, 115, 117, 120, 122-31, 135, 136, 146, 147, 149, 153, 259, 264, 267, 268, 279; the Nordstrom family, as controlling owners of, 94, 96, 107-8, 111-12, 116, 119, 123, 125, 130, 263
Nordstrom, Blake, 15, 141
Nordstrom, Bruce, 101
Nordstrom, Jim, 95, 263
Norton, Daniel, 125, 126

Offe, Claus, 26
organic city trope, 131-138, 234-35, 259-62, 263-69, 272-82

Pacific Place (retail-cinema complex): 3, 9, 96, 97, 101, 109, 110, 115, 135, 139, 140, 143, 154, 265, 267; parking garage in, 107-14
Pageler, Margaret, 121, 180
Paramount Theater (Seattle), 119, 139
Peck, Jamie, 31n47, 47
Philadelphia, Pennsylvania, 39
Phoenix, Arizona, 41
Pike Place Market (Seattle), 8, 119, 174, 193, 197, 240, 266
Pine Street Development (LLC), 97, 98, 99, 105n88, 107, 108, 110, 111, 115, 142-43, 263
Pine Street pedestrian mall, 100, 107, 119-26, 129-33, 135-38, 260
Pioneer Square (Seattle neighborhood), 8, 135, 179, 187n112, 192, 201, 207, 226, 233, 262
Piore, Michael, 18, 29nn11-12, 31 n52, 54n56
place entrepreneurs. *See* downtown establishment, definition of

Port of Seattle, 62
Portland, Oregon, 46
Post-Fordism: 22-28, 281; "downsizing" as a corporate strategy in, 24-25; "flexibility" as a corporate strategy in, 23-24, 38, 39; The Post-Fordist city, properties of 35-51
"postindustrial city", conceptual criticism of, 170
poverty rates, urban, 39-40; in Seattle, 79n25
producer services, 42-45, 63-64
project of reassurance, as a part of urban revitalization strategies, 7, 154-55, 259, 270
public-private redevelopment partnerships: 90-92, in Seattle, 92-101, 107-119
Puget Sound Business Journal, editorial positions of, 198, 201, 228
Putnam, Robert, 146n117

Quincy Market (Boston), 49, 120

Radway, Janice, 292n5
Real Change (alternative newspaper), 178, 181, 238, 239, 240, 244
rearticulation. *See* articulation
Reese, John, 178
regime of accumulation, 20. *See also* regulation theory
regulation theory, 19, 30n27, 30n30
Reich, Robert, 23-24, 32n52, 42-43, 53n38, 54n48, 156
revitalization. *See* urban revitalization
Rhodes, Jeff, 94-99, 101, 107-9, 115, 116, 118, 263, 264, 265
The Rhodes Project, 6, 85, 96-101, 107-119, 123-24, 126, 128, 129, 130, 131, 132, 139, 149, 180, 257, 263, 266
Rice, Norm 6, 60, 77, 78, 85, 86, 92, 96, 98, 104, 108, 109, 114, 116, 118, 119, 121, 123, 124, 130, 138, 175, 178, 191, 195, 197, 198, 203, 205, 207, 214, 248, 249, 257, 263
Rice administration (Seattle), 93-94, 99, 113, 118, 119, 138-39, 264, 269, 279. *See also* Rice, Norm

Rojecki, Andrew, 154
Rosen, Gary, 164
Royer, Charles, 120, 121
Ruddick, Susan, 172, 184n52

Sabel, Charles, 18, 29nn11-12, 31n52, 55n56
Safeco Field (Seattle Mariners), 3, 96, 135, 270
Saint Louis, Missouri, 38, 50
San Francisco, California, 162, 165
Sarkowsky, Herman, 69, 70
Sassen, Saskia, 42-43, 44, 53n41, 62-64
Sayer, Andrew, 155
Schell, Paul, 15, 86, 257-58
Schumpeter, Joseph, 17-18, 29n8. *See also* Schumpeterian workfare state
Schumpeterian workfare state, 27
Schwartz, Gerard, 3, 4, 197
Seaboard Building, 96, 97, 98, 108
Seahawks Stadium, 3
Seattle Art Museum, 3, 78, 85, 88, 196, 197, 200, 216, 246, 263, 265, 279
Seattle City Council: 112, 121, 123, 124; in Pine Street debate, 177-78; in hygiene center dispute, 226-28, 242-245
Seattle Displacement Coalition, 113, 117-19, 172, 173, 178, 237, 248
Seattle-King County Convention and Visitors Bureau, 88-89, 139, 153
Seattle Police Department, 116, 117
The Seattle Post-Intelligencer, editorial positions of, 60-61, 112, 124, 211
Seattle Symphony, 3, 36, 78, 196-99, 200-2, 216, 229, 232, 240, 248
The Seattle Times, editorial positions of, 9, 76-77, 112, 113-14, 174-75, 180, 197, 211, 215-216, 228
Seattle Weekly (alternative newspaper), 223
Seattle World's Fair (1962). *See* Century 21 Exposition
Selig, Martin, 67-68, 73, 74
Serrano, Barbara, 109, 112-13
Shearing, Clifford, 148n150, 291
Shields, Rob, 149n164
Sidran, Mark, 77, 175-81, 191, 261, 277

Simmel, Georg, 166-67
single-room occupancy apartments (SROs), 158, 172, 191, 198, 269
skid row, role as housing of last resort, 8, 172
Skogan, Wesley, 166
Smith, Neil, 41, 154, 157, 160, 170, 269
Steinberg, Robert, 194
Steinbrueck, Peter, 137
Steinbrueck, Victor, 120-21, 123, 149
The Stranger (alternative newspaper), 239
Strauss, Elizabeth, 94
Street, Jim, 111, 121
street incivility, debate over, 162-181; ordinances responding to, 77, 261
Swanstrom, Todd, 39, 52n21, 53n24, 102n8
Symphony Hall. *See* Benaroya Hall

Tang, Terry, 9, 139
Thompson, John B., 282n8, 285n60
Tickell, Adam, 31n47, 47
Toffler, Alvin, 1, 101n5
Toffler, Heidi, 101n5
Trade Development Alliance of Greater Seattle, 61, 65, 86-88
trope of the organic city. *See* organic city trope

U.S. Department of Housing and Urban Development (HUD), 99, 107, 114-19, 144, 173, 195, 198, 202, 203, 209, 219n67, 226, 244-46
University of Washington, 62
urban aid, federal cuts to, 40, 90
urban decay, discourses of, 5, 8-9, 128-129, 131-138, 154, 229-30, 234-35, 260-66
urban elite, definition of, 50n1
urban fiscal crisis, 40-41
Urban Investment and Development Company (UIDC), 95
Urban Land Institute (ULI), 84
Urban Reststop. *See* Glen Hotel hygiene center.
Urban Reststop Advisory Committee (URAC), 212, 224

urban revitalization, as an economic
     strategy: nationwide, 5, 46-50, 83-
     84; in Seattle, 2-4, 6, 61-66, 85-
     90, 92-101, 138-40; as a political
     discourse, 133-35, 139-40, 236-
     43, 259-62; social and ethical
     consequences of, 6-9, 140-41,
     262-72
urban spectacle. *See* commodification,
     urban space, and
urban vitality, discourses of, 8-9, 129,
     131-138, 229, 234-35, 238-39,
     260-69, 270-82
Urry, John, 26

Volosinov, V. N., 134, 236, 253n91,
     273

Washington Free Press (alternative
     newspaper), 117-18, 146n103
Washington State Trade and Conven-
     tion Center, 3, 78, 98, 119, 263
Watt, Bob, 76, 92-101, 109-10, 123,
     263
Webb, Wellington, 83

Weiss, Fred, 210
The Weiss Company, 194, 195, 196
Westlake, Inc. proposal, 136
Westlake Park, 8, 107, 119-27, 129,
     131, 133, 134, 136-39, 177, 260,
     263
Wild Ginger Restaurant, 199-200, 205,
     207, 211, 213, 260, 274
Will, George, 171
Williams, Rosalind, 149n164
Wilson, David, 148n149, 282n10
Wilson, James Q., 162-66, 175
Wilson, William Julius, 38, 52n16,
     52n23, 53n30
Wolch, Jennifer, 156-59, 167, 182n18
World Trade Organization (WTO),
     281-282

Yoder, Rick, 199-201, 203, 205, 207-8,
     211-15, 223, 225, 228, 231, 242,
     244, 246, 260
Young, Coleman, 47

Zukin, Sharon, 54n56, 140, 159, 161,
     272

About the Author

Timothy A. Gibson is an Assistant Professor of Communication at George Mason University in Fairfax, Virginia. He has authored a number of articles on media, discourse, and urban politics, including articles published in *Rethinking Marxism*, *Space and Culture*, and the *Journal of Communication Inquiry*. Raised in Ohio, he spent a decade living in the Pacific Northwest prior to moving to the East Coast. He currently lives in Alexandria, Virginia with his wife and two children.

Parts of chapters 5 and 9 were initially published by the author in Timothy Gibson, "The Trope of the Organic City: Discourses of Decay and Rebirth in Downtown Seattle," *Space and Culture* 6 (November 2003). These sections are reproduced here with permission from Sage Publications and the editors of *Space and Culture*.